PERSONALITY, PERSONALITY DISORDER AND VIOLENCE

WILEY SERIES IN
FORENSIC CLINICAL PSYCHOLOGY

Edited by

Clive R. Hollin
Clinical Division of Psychiatry, University of Leicester, UK

and

Mary McMurran
School of Community Health Sciences, Division of Psychiatry,
University of Nottingham, UK

For other titles in this series please visit www.wiley.com/go/fcp

PERSONALITY, PERSONALITY DISORDER AND VIOLENCE

Edited by

Mary McMurran
University of Nottingham, UK

and

Richard C. Howard
University of Nottingham and Rampton Hospital, UK

WILEY-BLACKWELL
A John Wiley & Sons, Ltd, Publication

This edition first published 2009.
© 2009 John Wiley & Sons, Ltd.

Wiley-Blackwell is an imprint of John Wiley & Sons, formed by the merger of Wiley's global
Scientific, Technical, and Medical business with Blackwell Publishing.

Registered office
John Wiley & Sons Ltd, The Atrium, Southern Gate, Chichester, West Sussex, PO19 8SQ, UK

Editorial Offices
The Atrium, Southern Gate, Chichester, West Sussex, PO19 8SQ, UK
9600 Garsington Road, Oxford, OX4 2DQ, UK
350 Main Street, Malden, MA 02148-5020, USA

For details of our global editorial offices, for customer services, and for information about how to
apply for permission to reuse the copyright material in this book please see our website at
www.wiley.com/wiley-blackwell.

Library of Congress Cataloging-in-Publication Data

Personality, personality disorder, and violence / edited by Mary McMurran and Richard C. Howard.
    p. cm.
  Includes index.
  ISBN 978-0-470-05948-7 – ISBN 978-0-470-05949-4
  1. Personality disorders. 2.Violence. I. McMurran, Mary. II. Howard, Richard C.

  RC554.P488 2009
  616.85′82–dc22

                                                  2008052782

A catalogue record for this book is available from the British Library.

Typeset in 10/12pt Palatino by Aptara Inc., New Delhi, India.
Printed in Singapore by Markono Print Media Pte Ltd.

1 2009

CONTENTS

About the Editors   vii

List of Contributors   ix

Series Editors' Preface   xiii

Preface   xvii

    INTRODUCTION   1

1 Personality, Personality Disorder and Violence: An Introduction   3
    Mary McMurran, University of Nottingham, UK

2 The 'Functional Link' Between Personality Disorder and Violence: A
    Critical Appraisal   19
    Conor Duggan and Richard Howard, University of Nottingham, UK

    PART I TRAITS   39

3 A Systematic Review of the Relationship Between Childhood
    Impulsiveness and Later Violence   41
    Darrick Jolliffe, University of Leicester, UK and David P Farrington,
    University of Cambridge, UK

4 The 'Big Five': Neuroticism, Extraversion, Openness, Agreeableness
    and Conscientiousness as an Organisational Scheme for Thinking
    About Aggression and Violence   63
    Vincent Egan, School of Psychology, University of Leicester, UK

5 Narcissism   85
    Caroline Logan, Ashworth Hospital, UK

6 Subtypes of Psychopath   113
    Ronald Blackburn, University of Liverpool, UK

 7 Antisocial Personality Disorder   133
    Stéphane A De Brito and Sheilagh Hodgins, Institute of Psychiatry,
    King's College, London, UK

    PART II AFFECT   155

 8 The Neurobiology of Affective Dyscontrol: Implications for
    Understanding 'Dangerous and Severe Personality Disorder'   157
    Rick Howard, University of Nottingham, UK

 9 The Processing of Emotional Expression Information in Individuals
    with Psychopathy   175
    R. James R. Blair, National Institute of Mental Health, USA

10 Angry Affect, Aggression and Personality Disorder   191
    Kevin Howells, University of Nottingham, UK

11 Attachment Difficulties   213
    Anthony R. Beech and Ian J. Mitchell, University of Birmingham, UK

12 Empathy and Offending Behavior   229
    William L. Marshall, Liam E. Marshall and Geris A. Serran,
    Rockwood Psychological Services, Canada

    PART III COGNITION   245

13 Psychopathic Violence: A Cognitive-Attention Perspective   247
    Jennifer E. Vitale, Hampden-Sydney College, USA and Joseph P.
    Newman, University of Wisconsin-Madison, USA

14 Social Problem Solving, Personality Disorder and Violence   265
    Mary McMurran, University of Nottingham, UK

15 Criminal Thinking   281
    Glenn D. Walters, Federal Correctional Institution-Schuylkill, USA

    CONCLUSION   297

16 Personality, Personality Disorder and Violence: Implications For
    Future Research and Practice   299
    Mary McMurran and Richard Howard, University of Nottingham,
    UK

Index   313

ABOUT THE EDITORS

Mary McMurran, BSc, MSc, PhD, CPsychol, FBPsS, is Professor in the Section of Forensic Mental Health, Division Psychiatry, University of Nottingham, UK. She worked for 10 years as a prison psychologist in HM Young Offenders' Centre Glen Parva. After qualifying as a clinical psychologist, she worked in Rampton Hospital, a maximum secure psychiatric facility, and then at the East Midlands Centre for Forensic Mental Health, which consisted of a medium secure psychiatric facility and a community forensic mental health service. In 1999, she was awarded a 5-year Senior Baxter Research Fellowship by the NHS's National Programme on Forensic Mental Health Research and Development. Her research interests are: (1) Social problem solving theories and therapies for understanding and treating people with personality disorders; (2) The assessment and treatment of alcohol-related aggression and violence; and (3) Understanding and enhancing offenders' motivation to change. She has written over 100 academic articles and book chapters. Her edited text, *Motivating Offenders to Change* (Wiley, 2002), was commended in the British Medical Association's 2003 Book Competition. She is a Fellow of the British Psychological Society and former Chair of the Society's Division of Forensic Psychology. She was founding co-editor of the British Psychological Society journal *Legal & Criminological Psychology* and is currently co-editor of *Criminal Behaviour and Mental Health* and Deputy Editor of the *Journal of Forensic Psychiatry and Psychology*. In 2005, she was recipient of the Division of Forensic Psychology's Award for a Significant Lifetime Contribution to Forensic Psychology.

Richard Howard, PhD, is Reader in Personality Disorders at the University of Nottingham and Senior Research Fellow at the Peaks Academic and Research Unit, Rampton Hospital, UK. He has had an enduring interest in personality disorders since working at Broadmoor Hospital in the 1970's, where he carried out neurophysiological research on affective processing in personality disordered offenders. This work broke new ground in the study of personality disorders and was published by Wiley as a research monograph in 1982. Since then he held academic positions in Northern Ireland, New Zealand and Singapore, before returning to England to take up his current position in 2005. His pioneering work in marrying together cognitive neuroscience and forensic psychology has spawned a sub-discipline - *forensic/cognitive neuroscience* – that has burgeoned over the last 20 years on both sides of the Atlantic. In addition to his work in personality disorders, he has published in the areas of sexual aggression, risk taking, interrogative suggestibility and cross-cultural aspects of personality.

LIST OF CONTRIBUTORS

Anthony Beech

Professor in Criminological Psychology, Centre for Forensic and Family Psychology, School of Psychology, University of Birmingham, Edgbaston, Birmingham, B15 2TT, UK.

Ronald Blackburn

Emeritus Professor, Division of Clinical Psychology, University of Liverpool, Whelan Building, Quadrangle, Brownlow Hill, L69 3GB, UK.

R. James R. Blair

Chief of the Unit of Affective Cognitive Neuroscience, Mood and Anxiety Program, National Institute of Mental Health, 15K North Drive, MSC 2670, Bethesda, Maryland, 20892, USA.

Stephane A de Brito

PhD Student, Department of Forensic Mental Health Science, Institute of Psychiatry, PO Box P023, De Crespigny Park, London, SE5 8AF, UK.

Conor Duggan

Professor of Forensic Psychiatry, University of Nottingham, Division of Psychiatry, Duncan Macmillan House, Porchester Road, Nottingham, NG3 6AA, UK.

Vincent Egan

Senior Lecturer, School of Psychology (Forensic Section), 106 New Walk, Leicester, LE1 7EA, UK.

David P Farrington

Professor of Psychological Criminology, Institute of Criminology, University of Cambridge, Sidgwick Avenue, Cambridge, CB3 9DA, UK.

Sheilagh Hodgins

Professor, Department of Forensic Mental Health Science, Institute of Psychiatry, PO Box P023, De Crespigny Park, London, SE5 8AF, UK.

Richard C. Howard

Associate Professor and Reader in Personality Disorders, University of Nottingham, Institute of Mental Health, The Sir Colin Campbell Building, Triumph Road, Nottingham, NG8 2TU, and Senior Researcher, Peaks Academic Unit, Rampton Hospital, Retford, DN22 0PD, UK.

Kevin Howells

Professor of Forensic Clinical Psychology, University of Nottingham, Institute of Mental Health, The Sir Colin Campbell Building, Triumph Road, Nottingham, NG8 2TU, and Director of Research, Peaks Academic Unit, Rampton Hospital, Retford, DN22 0PD, UK.

Darrick Jolliffe

Senior Lecturer, Department of Criminology, University of Leicester, The Friars, 154 Upper New Walk, Leicester, LE1 7QA, UK.

Caroline Logan

Consultant Specialist Clinical Psychologist in Risk Assessment and Management, Mersey Care NHS Trust, Ashworth Hospital, Magull, Liverpool, L31 1HW, UK.

Liam E. Marshall

Rockwood Psychological Services, 403-303 Bagot Street, Kingston, ON, K7K 5W7, Canada.

William L Marshall

Director, Rockwood Psychological Services, 403-303 Bagot Street, Kingston, ON, K7K 5W7, Canada.

Mary McMurran

Professor, University of Nottingham, Institute of Mental Health, The Sir Colin Campbell Building, Triumph Road, Nottingham, NG8 2TU, UK.

Ian J. Mitchell

Senior Lecturer, School of Psychology, University of Birmingham, Edgbaston, Birmingham, B15 2TT, UK.

Joseph P Newman

Professor, Psychology Department, University of Wisconsin-Madison, Brogden Hall, 1202 West Johnson Street, Madison, WI, 53706-1969, USA.

Geris A. Serran

Rockwood Psychological Services, 403-303 Bagot Street, Kingston, ON, K7K 5W7, Canada.

Jennifer Vitale

Assistant Professor, Department of Psychology, Hampden-Sydney College, Hampden-Sydney, VA, 23943 434-223-6000, USA.

Glenn D Walters

Clinical Psychologist and Co-ordinator of the Drug Abuse Program, Psychology Services, Federal Correctional Institute Schuylkill, PO Box 700, Minersville, PA 17954, USA.

SERIES EDITORS' PREFACE

ABOUT THE SERIES

At the time of writing, it is clear that we live in a time, certainly in the United Kingdom and other parts of Europe, if perhaps less so in areas of the world, when there is renewed enthusiasm for constructive approaches to working with offenders to prevent crime. What do we mean by this statement and what basis do we have for making it?

First, by 'constructive approaches to working with offenders', we mean bringing the use of effective methods and techniques of behaviour change into work with offenders. Indeed, this view might pass as a definition of forensic clinical psychology. Thus, our focus is the application of theory and research in order to develop practice aimed at bringing about a change in the offender's functioning. The word *constructive* is important and can be set against approaches to behaviour change that seek to operate by destructive means. Such destructive approaches are typically based on the principles of deterrence and punishment, seeking to suppress the offender's actions through fear and intimidation. A constructive approach, on the other hand, seeks to bring about changes in an offender's functioning that will produce, say, enhanced possibilities of employment, greater levels of self-control, better family functioning or increased awareness of the pain of victims.

A constructive approach faces the criticism of being a 'soft' response to the damage caused by offenders, neither inflicting pain and punishment nor delivering retribution. This point raises a serious question for those involved in working with offenders. Should advocates of constructive approaches oppose retribution as a goal of the criminal justice system as a process that is incompatible with treatment and rehabilitation? Alternatively, should constructive work with offenders take place within a system given to retribution? We believe that this issue merits serious informed debate.

However, to return to our starting point, history shows that criminal justice systems are littered with many attempts at constructive work with offenders, not all of which have been successful. In raising the spectre of success, the second part of our opening sentence now merits attention, that is, 'constructive approaches to working with offenders *to prevent crime*'. In order to achieve the goal of preventing crime, interventions must focus on the right targets for behaviour change. In addressing this crucial point, Andrews and Bonta (1994) have formulated the *need principle*:

"Many offenders, especially high-risk offenders, have a variety of needs. They need places to live and work and/or they need to stop taking drugs. Some have poor self-esteem, chronic headaches or cavities in their teeth. These are all 'needs'. The need principle draws our attention to the distinction between *criminogenic* and *noncriminogenic* needs. Criminogenic needs are a subset of an offender's risk level. They are dynamic attributes of an offender that, when changed, are associated with changes in the probability of recidivism. Non-criminogenic needs are also dynamic and changeable, but these changes are not necessarily associated with the probability of recidivism" (p. 176).

Thus, successful work with offenders can be judged in terms of bringing about change in noncriminogenic need *or* in terms of bringing about change in criminogenic need. While the former is important and, indeed, may on occasion be a necessary precursor to offence-focused work, it is changing criminogenic need that, we argue, should be the touchstone in working with offenders.

While, as noted above, the history of work with offenders is not replete with success, the research base developed since the early 1990s, particularly the meta-analyses (e.g. Lösel, 1995), now strongly supports the position that effective work with offenders to prevent further offending is possible. The parameters of such evidence-based practice have become well established and widely disseminated under the banner of "*What Works*" (McGuire, 1995, 2002).

It is important to state that we are not advocating that there is only one approach to preventing crime. Clearly, there are many approaches, with different theoretical underpinnings, that can be applied to the task. Nonetheless, a tangible momentum has grown in the wake of the "*What Works*" movement as academics, practitioners and policy makers seek to capitalise on the possibilities that this research raises for preventing crime. The task that many service agencies grapple with lies in turning the research evidence into effective practice.

Our aim in developing this Series in Forensic Clinical Psychology is to produce texts that review research and draw on clinical expertise to advance effective work with offenders. We are both committed to the ideal of evidence-based practice and we encourage contributors to the Series to follow this approach. Thus, the books published in the Series will not be practice manuals or "cook books": they will offer readers authoritative and critical information through which forensic clinical practice can develop. We both continue to be enthusiastic about the contribution to effective practice that this Series can make and look forward to continuing to develop it yet further in the years to come.

ABOUT THIS BOOK

Crimes and the people who commit them come in many guises: crimes range from the relatively trivial to the highly serious; criminals from the naïve to the professional. Crimes of violence are clearly at the serious end of the offence spectrum: violent crimes may injure victims, both physically and psychologically, and they can spread fear through communities, particularly among those individuals who perceive themselves as vulnerable. Similarly, the people who commit violent acts range from those individuals who perpetrate acts of 'low-level aggression'

(Goldstein, 2002) to serious offenders at the extremes of premeditated violence. One particular group of people who commit crimes, including violent crimes, are those people with mental disorders (Hodgins and Müller-Isberner, 2000). The broad category of 'mentally disordered offender' includes people with a personality disorder, a group that has caused some recent concern, exemplified by the advent of the notion of 'Dangerous and Severe Personality Disorder (DSPD)'.

It is abundantly clear that the inter-relationship of personality disorder and anti-social and criminal behaviour stretches our thinking at conceptual, theoretical, legal and clinical levels. In this timely text, Mary McMurran and Richard Howard have drawn together an impressive list of contributors to address these complex issues. The resulting text is a welcome addition to the Series which will be of undoubted interest to those engaged in forensic clinical psychology.

Clive Hollin
Mary McMurran

REFERENCES

Andrews, D.A. and Bonta, J. (1994) *The Psychology of Criminal Conduct*, Anderson, Cincinnati, OH.

Goldstein, A.P. (2002) *The Psychology of Group Aggression*, John Wiley & Sons, Ltd, Chichester.

Hodgins, S. and Müller-Isberner (eds) (2000) *Violence, Crime and Mentally Disordered Offenders: Concepts and Methods for Effective Treatment and Prevention*, John Wiley & Sons, Ltd, Chichester.

Lösel, F. (1995) Increasing consensus in the evaluation of offender rehabilitation? *Psychology, Crime, and Law*, **2**, 19–39.

McGuire, J. (ed.) (1995) *What Works: Reducing Reoffending*, John Wiley & Sons, Ltd, Chichester.

McGuire, J. (ed.) (2002) *Offender Rehabilitation and Treatment: Effective Programmes and Policies to Reduce Re-Offending*, John Wiley & Sons, Ltd, Chichester.

PREFACE

Serious violent behaviour is a matter of grave concern for most members of society. In some cases, the causes of the eruption of violence seem self-evident, for instance, where a mentally ill person in a distressed and deluded state harms someone that is perceived to be a threat. In other cases, the violence may be the consequence of an emotional charge so great that we suspect that we might act in the same way ourselves should we find ourselves in similar circumstances. There are cases, however, where we do not fully understand violence or do not understand it at all. We may understand the effects of influences that impair judgement and disinhibit behaviour, such as drink or drugs, but nonetheless we may wonder what kind of personality it is that is violent under the influence of intoxicating substances. In cases where people appear to be wantonly or uncontrollably violent and there is no obvious, satisfactory explanation, we respond with complete incomprehension.

Personality disorder is often invoked to account for apparently wanton or uncontrolled violence. When this happens, care must be taken to avoid circular reasoning: Q. What is the cause of this person's violence? A. Personality disorder. Q. How do you know this person has a personality disorder? A. Because this person is violent. Circularity is not uncommon when using diagnostic criteria, where adverse behaviours are listed along with traits in the descriptions of disorders. However, when we start to scratch the surface of some of these personality disorders, we begin to see how temperament and basic dispositions can affect an individual's development across the lifespan. In particular, we can see how personality can influence the development of thinking, learning, emotion control and interactions with other people. In some cases, this developmental trajectory, which is a reciprocal interaction between an individual's basic dispositions and influences of the social environment over time, will produce an individual with a propensity for violence.

The purpose of this book is to elucidate the personality factors that are implicated in the development of violent behaviour and the mechanisms whereby these increase the likelihood of violence. To this end, a number of internationally renowned researchers and clinicians present their latest theories and research in a number of domains: *Traits*, including impulsivity, the Big 5, and psychopathic traits; *Disorders*, including anti-social personality disorder and narcissism; *Affect*, including affective dyscontrol, the processing of emotional expression, anger, attachment difficulties and empathy deficits; and *Cognition*, including attention, problem solving and criminal thinking styles. The chapters that follow provide cogent descriptions of each of these specific topics, highlighting the relevance of research to clinical practice.

Services for treating people with personality disorders generally and specifically offenders with personality disorders have developed exponentially in the United Kingdom over the past decade. This surge was prompted first by the joint Department of Health and Home Office development of services for dangerous offenders with severe personality disorders (Department of Health/Home Office 1999, 2000). Subsequently, the National Institute of Mental Health for England (NIMHE; 2003) issued a directive, *Personality Disorder: No Longer a Diagnosis of Exclusion*. In this, general mental health service personnel were instructed not to exclude people with personality disorders from treatment but rather to develop services for this particular group. These services should base their work on current evidence of what is known about personality disorder and its treatment. There is a burning need, therefore, to disseminate up-to-date information.

This book plays a part in the dissemination of information, with particular reference to personality disorder and violence. We hope that this will stimulate thought, influence research and practice, and ultimately improve services. It is our ambition that, by influencing researchers and practitioners, this book will contribute in a modest way to reducing aggression and violence. We offer our thanks to all of the eminent contributors to this book, and we look forward to keeping up with their thinking as their research programmes progress.

Mary McMurran
Richard C Howard

REFERENCES

Department of Health/Home Office (1999) *Managing Dangerous People with Severe Personality Disorder: Proposals for Policy Development*, Department of Health, London.

Department of Health/Home Office (2000) *Reforming the Mental Health Act. Part II: High Risk Patients*, The Stationery Office, Norwich.

National Institute of Mental Health for England (2003) *Personality Disorder: No Longer a Diagnosis of Exclusion*, Department of Health, London.

INTRODUCTION

Chapter 1

PERSONALITY, PERSONALITY DISORDER AND VIOLENCE: AN INTRODUCTION

MARY MCMURRAN
University of Nottingham, UK

INTRODUCTION

Few would argue that interpersonal violence, in its many forms, is a major social problem, causing considerable harm to individuals, families and communities. Indeed, the World Health Organisation (WHO) (2002) has recognised violence as a significant public health issue. The WHO report acknowledges that there are multiple factors that need to be taken into account in explaining violence, including individual, relationship, social, cultural and environmental factors. These are represented in an ecological model (see Figure 1.1). While all levels are clearly important, the focus in this book is on individual-level explanations.

Beginning with the basics, it is useful to define violence. Violence is defined as a range of behaviours intended to harm a living being who is motivated to avoid harm (Baron and Richardson, 1994). This definition is useful in that it excludes harmful acts that are accidental (e.g. a road traffic accident), consensual (e.g. sado-masochism) and ultimately beneficial (e.g. medical procedures). A distinction may be made between violence and aggression: violence is the forceful infliction of physical harm, whereas aggression is behaviour that is less physically harmful (e.g. insults, threats, ignoring), although it is often severely psychologically damaging. Because aggression can be as damaging to the victim as actual physical violence, and sometimes even more so, many mental health and criminal justice practitioners opt to use the term violence to refer to both aggression and physical violence. This avoids appearing to collude with the belief that aggression is not serious or harmful.

There is wide variation between individuals in their proneness to violence, and the agenda in this book is to investigate individual variation in relation to personality and personality disorder. The psychological study of *personality* relates

Personality, Personality Disorder and Violence   Edited by Mary McMurran and Richard C. Howard
© 2009 John Wiley & Sons, Ltd

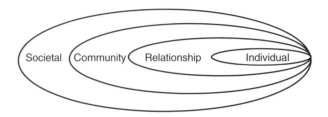

Figure 1.1   An ecological model for understanding violence (World Health Organisation, 2002).

to the understanding of how individual differences (i.e. personality traits) and personality processes (i.e. cognitive, emotional and motivational processes) relate to behaviour (Brody and Ehrlichman, 1998). The study of *personality disorder* relates to a range of clinically important problems with thoughts, feelings and behaviour whose regularities are defined in specific personality pathologies (Livesley, 2001). The term 'personality disorder' references diagnostic categories (see the next section for an elaboration); however, there are mostly no categorical cut-offs for problems in personality traits and personality processes. Hence, in referencing problems in the personality domain, the term 'personality problems' is used here. In this book, both fields of study are represented so that we may best advance our understanding of individual variation in violence.

One of the major reasons for studying personality, personality disorder and violence is to advance psychological and psychiatric treatments. Both criminal justice and mental health professionals play a role in treating and managing people who are violent. Broadly speaking, differing organisational agendas mean that criminal justice personnel see society as the primary client and aim to control crime, whereas mental health professionals view the patient as the client and aim to improve functioning and reduce distress. These days, however, most interventions offered by either group of professionals are designed both to promote individual well-being and reduce risk (Ward, 2002; Ward and Brown, 2004). Nonetheless, the latter aim is still viewed as highly contentious by some mental health professionals (Grounds, 2008).

The contributors to this book, all of whom are internationally renowned researchers and practitioners, will expand on issues related to personality, personality disorder and violence. In this chapter, the aim is to set the scene by addressing some fundamental questions about detention, punishment and treatment of people with personality problems or personality disorders who are violent. Unlike people whose violence is connected with mental illness or developmental disabilities, for whom there is largely agreement on the appropriateness of treatment, the issue of whether or not to treat those with personality disorders or personality problems and an offending history is more controversial. The case for punishment, treatment or a combination of the two requires exploration. If treatment is to be offered, then what should be the treatment goals? Where should treatment be offered: in criminal justice or mental health service locations? However, before embarking on these topics, the scale and nature of the problem needs to be put into perspective.

PERSONALITY DISORDERS AND VIOLENCE

Personality disorders are described in the two major diagnostic classification systems: the Diagnostic and Statistical Manual of Mental Disorders IV (DSM-IV; American Psychiatric Association, 1994, 2000) and the International Classification of Diseases 10 (ICD-10; World Health Organisation, 1992). DSM-IV defines personality disorder as

> An enduring pattern of inner experience and behaviour that deviates markedly from the expectations of the individual's culture, is pervasive and inflexible, has an onset in adolescence or early adulthood, is stable over time, and leads to distress or impairment (p. 629).

ICD-10 defines personality disorder as

> ... deeply ingrained and enduring behaviour patterns, manifesting themselves as inflexible responses to a broad range of personal and social situations. They represent either extreme or significant deviations from the way the average individual in a given culture perceives, thinks, feels, and particularly relates to others. Such behaviour patterns tend to be stable and to encompass multiple domains of behaviour and psychological functioning. They are frequently, but not always, associated with various degrees of subjective distress and problems in social functioning and performance (p. 200).

The personality disorders are listed in Table 1.1, along with their key features. DSM-IV groups the personality disorders in three clusters: Cluster A – odd or eccentric (paranoid, schizoid and schizotypal); Cluster B – dramatic or flamboyant (antisocial, borderline, histrionic and narcissistic); and Cluster C – anxious or fearful (avoidant, dependent and obsessive-compulsive). Psychopathy, a personality disorder that is covered extensively in later chapters, lacks specific status as a personality disorder in DSM-IV and ICD10, although aspects of it are captured in antisocial and dissocial personality disorders. Extensive research on features of psychopathy over recent years has led to it being considered for inclusion in the forthcoming DSM-V.

In a recent study of a representative sample of the UK general population, using a structured clinical interview, the prevalence of personality disorder was identified as 4.4%, with men more likely to have a personality disorder (5.4%) than women (3.4%) (Coid *et al.*, 2006b). Thus, an estimated three and a quarter million people in the United Kingdom have a personality disorder. Most of these are unlikely to be violent. Indeed, in Coid *et al.*'s study, even among those people diagnosable as having an antisocial personality disorder, about half had not been violent in the previous 5 years (Coid *et al.*, 2006a). Nonetheless, Coid *et al.* (2006a) noted that people with Cluster B disorders, compared to those without, were 10 times more likely to have had a criminal conviction and almost 8 times more likely to have spent time in prison. This elevation of criminal risk was not evident for those with Cluster A and C disorders.

Table 1.1   DSM-IV and ICD-10 personality disorders

DSM-IV	ICD-10
Cluster A	
Paranoid – distrust; suspiciousness	Paranoid – sensitivity; suspiciousness
Schizoid – socially and emotionally detached	Schizoid – emotionally cold and detached
Schizotypal – social and interpersonal deficits; cognitive or perceptual distortions	No equivalent
Cluster B	
Antisocial – violation of the rights of others	Dissocial – callous disregard of others; irresponsibility; irritability
Borderline – instability of relationships, self-image, and mood	Emotionally unstable
	(a) Borderline – unclear self-image; intense, unstable relationships
	(b) Impulsive – inability to control anger; quarrelsome; unpredictable
Histrionic – excessive emotionality and attention seeking	Histrionic – dramatic; egocentric; manipulative seeking
Narcissistic – grandiose; lack of empathy; need for admiration	No equivalent
Cluster C	
Avoidant – socially inhibited; feelings of inadequacy; hypersensitivity	Anxious – tense; self-conscious; hypersensitive
Dependent – clinging; submissive	Dependent – subordinates personal needs; needs constant reassurance
Obsessive-compulsive – perfectionist; inflexible	Anankastic – indecisive; pedantic; rigid

Compared with mentally ill offenders, personality disordered offenders are more likely to reoffend after discharge from hospital. In their 12-year follow-up of a cohort of 204 patients discharged from UK high security hospitals in 1984, Jamieson and Taylor (2004) found that 38% were reconvicted, 26% of them for a serious offence. The odds of committing a serious offence were seven times higher for personality disordered offenders compared with the mentally ill offenders. However, although personality disordered offenders were more likely to be reconvicted of a serious offence, note that three-quarters of them were *not* reconvicted of a serious offence and 62% were not reconvicted at all.

In this book, the focus is specifically on those personality dimensions and disorders that are associated with violence. Nestor (2002) suggested that four fundamental personality dimensions operate as clinical risk factors for violence: (1) impulse control, (2) affect regulation, (3) narcissism and (4) paranoid cognitive personality style. These traits, he says, distinguish those who act violently from the majority who do not. Through the identification of the specific personality dimensions that are associated with high risk for violence, we may contribute to the elimination of the stigmatising generalisation that *all* personality disordered people are violent. It is important to remind ourselves that not all people with personality problems or personality disorders are violent. Those we see in forensic psychiatric hospitals and prisons are there because they present a risk and are not representative of all people with personality problems or personality disorders.

The relationship between the type of personality disorder and violence is apparently strongest for antisocial personality disorder (Hiscoke *et al.*, 2003), which is unsurprising since aggressive behaviour is one of the defining criteria of the disorder. There is a clear circularity of reasoning here: if violence is part of the definition of antisocial personality disorder, then the incidence of violence among people diagnosed as having antisocial personality disorder is going to be higher than for those with diagnoses that do not feature violence. Skeem and Cooke (in press) have commented upon this problem of conflating measures and constructs in relation to psychopathy, as measured by Hare's (1991, 2003) Psychopathy Checklist – Revised (PCL-R). Psychopathy is measured by the PCL-R in terms of traits (grandiosity, selfishness and callousness) and behaviours (antisocial, irresponsible and parasitic lifestyle). The PCL-R has been shown to be a good predictor of future violence in convicted offenders (Hare *et al.*, 2000; Hemphill, Hare and Wong, 1998). However, the PCL-R includes items relating to criminality, leading to an unhelpful mix of the behaviours that we are trying to explain (crime, violence) and the explanatory variables (traits). More recent analyses by Cooke and Michie (2001) indicated that seven items relating to criminality and disapproved behaviours could be removed to leave a purer personality model of psychopathy. They found a superordinate construct of psychopathy, with three constituent factors: (1) arrogant and deceitful interpersonal style; (2) deficient affective experience; and (3) impulsive and irresponsible behavioural style. These features may well be the core of psychopathy and the variables that explain crime and violence. Or, as Skeem and Cooke point out, these factors may have no explanatory value at all! Given that research into psychopathy has used a measure that conflates traits and criminal behaviour, it is possible that the observed relationship between psychopathy and violence is the result of the inclusion of the behaviour under study within the measure itself.

What is the likely relationship between personality, personality disorder and violence? Some basic personality characteristics are associated with an increase in the risk of violence whereas others are associated with a decrease in the risk of violence. Studies of the development of antisocial behaviour, for example, find that impulsiveness in children is associated with later antisocial behaviour and aggression, while inhibition is associated with a lower likelihood of later antisocial behaviour and aggression (Farrington, 2005). It is easy to imagine how impulsiveness (acting without thinking) can lead to antisocial behaviour and aggression and how inhibition (fearfulness and shyness) may protect against antisocial behaviour and aggression. However, characteristics such as these are neither necessary nor sufficient to explain the behaviour of interest. Over the person's lifespan, there are continuous reciprocal interactions between the individual and social and environmental variables that account for the development of the complex personality of the adult. That is, biological, psychological, social and contextual variables, singly and through their interaction, all contribute their share to the explanation of a person's propensity for violence. It is unlikely that any one factor alone will contribute sufficiently to warrant designation as the sole causal agent of violence. Of particular interest in this book are the mechanisms whereby basic personality characteristics promote the development of and increase the risk of aggression and violence. These mechanisms include emotional experiences and emotion regulation, perception of and responses to social cues and beliefs about the self and the world. These mechanisms are, at least in theory, open to the possibility of change, with the potential to reduce the likelihood of violent behaviour.

One further question that arises is how can one tell if a violent person has a personality disorder or not? Serious violence contravenes not only the law but also society's moral and ethical codes to such a degree that some people would say that serious violence *must* reflect an underlying personality disorder. One consideration is the degree of choice a person exercises in the use of violence. For some offenders, violence is their chosen means of operating in the world and there is no moral conflict, loss of control or distress. Such people would not normally be described as personality disordered, although our growing knowledge about psychopathy may herald changes to this perspective, with major implications for the legal process (Fine and Kennett, 2004). A second consideration relates to the criteria for diagnosis. As for any other behaviour, serious violence can be explained by reference to an individual's traits, social history, current thoughts and feelings and the context the person is in. Whether these characteristics amount to a personality disorder depends upon the criteria set forth in the classification systems and the cut-offs applied for diagnosis. A person may have problems to some degree but that degree may be insufficient to meet the level for a diagnosis. This situation of having personality problems but not meeting the cut-off for diagnosis is one disadvantage of a categorical model of personality disorders, and it is likely that the next version of the Diagnostic and Statistical Manual of Mental Disorders, DSM-V, will move towards a dimensional model (Widiger and Simonsen, 2005).

PUNISHMENT OR TREATMENT OR BOTH?

Broadly speaking, the aims of punishment are to signal to society what is acceptable and what is not, and to prevent and reduce crime. By applying sanctions for socially proscribed behaviours, members of society in general will be deterred from crime, and the individual offender will be deterred from committing crime again. Additionally, where the crime has been grave, an offender can be incapacitated through long-term detention or even, in some countries, death. Hollin (2002) noted that, if this logic works, we would expect punishment to reduce crime. The truth is that, overall, it does not. Reconviction rates for prisoners in the 2-year period after release run at around 55% to 60% (Cunliffe and Shepherd, 2007). Furthermore, meta-analyses of what is effective in reducing crime by individuals indicate that punitive measures, such as the 'short sharp shock', fines, surveillance and drug monitoring, are not effective in reducing crime, whereas cognitive–behavioural treatments are effective, reducing reoffending by 30% to 40% in adults and as much as 60% in young offenders (McGuire, 2001, 2002). So, as for other types of offenders, there is a utilitarian case for treating offenders with personality problems or personality disorders: treatment works better than punishment.

Personality Problems and Personality Disorder as Mitigation

In mitigating antisocial behaviour and violence, a psychological explanation or psychiatric diagnosis needs to identify specific deficiencies that impair the agency of the person diagnosed. The deficiency may affect the capacity of a person to make rational decisions, impair the control a person has over his or her behaviour and/or impair the degree of awareness of the harm caused by the act.

People with personality problems or personality disorders are usually viewed as being responsible for their behaviour and not warranting excuse or mitigation in the same way as those with mental illness or learning disabilities. The basis of this view lies in the perceived normality of people with personality disorders. They face the same challenges in the same way as the rest of us in relation to controlling their emotions and impulses. We all, at times, have to control anger and aggression under provocation and express our anger appropriately. We all have to practise negotiation, compromise and fair play to achieve what we want without bullying, intimidating or abusing others. The truth is, we all come to these challenges with different personal resources and some are better equipped than others to control their emotions, relate well to other people, and act in non-violent ways. Indeed, a dimensional approach to personality disorders, as mentioned earlier, would likely place people with personality problems and personality disorders at the far end of a continuum that includes the normal range of experiences and behaviours.

A disorder may excuse or mitigate antisocial and violent behaviour because the individual is not fully aware of the legal or moral imperative to refrain from this behaviour or because that person does not fully understand the harmful consequences of that act. Intellectual disability and dementia are examples of such disorders. In any caring society, people who are seriously mentally impaired are unlikely to be punished for violent acts. In relation to people with antisocial personality disorder, there is an assumption of knowing the consequences but nonetheless being unable to exercise control over behaviour. In relation to psychopathy, the case has been made that psychopathic individuals' lack of emotional capacities reduces their responsibility for their actions in that they do not really understand the implications of their antisocial and aggressive acts, either for others or for themselves (Benn, 1999). This has far-reaching implications for the administration of criminal justice.

If we hold people responsible for their actions, then a proportionate punishment is a reasonable option; yet, a final consideration to be taken into account is the effect of punishment on the individual (Benn, 1999). Punishment can lead to behaviour change when it is immediate and inevitable (note that neither of these is typical of punishments in relation to crime) (Hollin, 2002). If the individual can understand the punishment in relation to the deed, and if punishment is likely to lead to a change in attitude or behaviour, then perhaps punishment proportionate to the deed is warranted. An analogy is reprimanding a child for a misdeed. The child may not fully understand why the misdeed transgresses social or moral rules, but through the reprimand he or she begins to learn appropriate behaviour. Concerning people with antisocial personality disorder, violent behaviour may be explicable in terms of biopsychosocial disadvantage; hence there is mitigation of culpability, yet that individual may nevertheless be able to learn from punishment.

Concerning people with psychopathy, biopsychosocial disadvantage may again mitigate culpability, but the nature of the disorder may mean that the individual will not learn from punishment. Hence, to punish is purely for society to signal its disapproval. Some philosophers believe that punishment should be only a just desert and should not be administered to effect behaviour change (Ciocchetti, 2003). Indeed, it was noted earlier that punishment is not the most effective way to reduce recidivism overall (Hollin, 2002); hence, while punishment may be a necessary signal of society's disapproval and a means of exacting retribution for a crime, it is through treatment that behaviour change is most likely to occur.

For offenders with personality problems or personality disorders, treatment takes place within either a criminal justice context or a forensic mental health setting or, most probably, a combination of both of these over time. Thus, there is usually a combination of punishment and treatment. However, not all offenders with personality problems or personality disorders are considered treatable. Issues that need to be considered in making the decision to offer treatment or not are: Can appropriate treatment targets be identified? If they can, do treatments that have a positive effect on these treatment targets exist? An understanding of personality problems, personality disorder and violence is required to identify and address the treatment needs of these offenders.

IDENTIFYING TREATMENT TARGETS

If violence is seen as driven by emotions, primarily anger, and if the person claims an inability to control his or her behaviour in the face of strong emotions, then treatment may be an option, especially if the individual concerned wishes to experience less anger and have greater self-control. In the absence of a major mental illness, people who fit this description may be diagnosed as suffering from an intermittent explosive disorder, defined as aggression disproportionate to the degree of provocation (American Psychiatric Association, 1994), or a personality disorder, particularly antisocial or borderline personality disorders. It is worth noting here that there is no category for disorders of anger or aggression in either of the current psychiatric classification systems, DSM-IV (American Psychiatric Association, 1994) or ICD-10 (World Health Organisation, 1992). Effective treatments for anger problems are available and may be tailored specifically to suit people with personality problems (see Chapter 10).

If violence is driven by what the perpetrator stands to gain from violence, including control over another person and material benefits, this may be seen as less deserving of treatment and more deserving of punishment. This response is even more likely where there is no expressed desire to change or where a desire to change is expressed apparently only for pragmatic reasons, such as avoiding punishment. But what if people with this presentation also have emotional and cognitive deficits that contribute to an explanation of their violent behaviour? Some people do not recognise fear, cannot empathise with another's suffering or cannot use information about another person's feelings to alter their behaviour. This, of course, describes psychopathy, a disorder comprehensively described later in this volume by several eminent researchers in this field.

In both the cases described above, violence may be explained at least partly by behavioural, emotional or cognitive deficits that are evident early on in life and which persist into adulthood. How do these deficits or differences come to express themselves in the form of adult personality disorder? Only an adult can be given a diagnosis of personality disorder, in the belief that personality is still in formation in childhood and adolescence. So, what might be happening over the years that results in adult personality disorder?

Following through the two examples given above, one being violence driven by emotional dysregulation and the other being violence driven by instrumental gain in the absence of empathy or fear, we can trace the genesis of violent behaviour for people with antisocial personality disorder and psychopathy. Individual differences that are present from birth may confer high risk for violence, but the expression of violence additionally depends upon the person's experiences over his or her lifespan. As we shall see, this life-course developmental model helps identify many facets of the person that are likely to be useful to focus upon in treatment. If we accept that the overarching goal of treatment is to reduce violence, for the benefit of the individual, potential victims and society as a whole, then we need an understanding of how people come to be violent.

Antisocial Personality Disorder

Perhaps the best traced developmental sequence is that which identifies early impulsivity, especially where it flourishes into childhood conduct problems, as a direct risk for adult antisocial personality disorder. This developmental pathway traced from early impulsivity and measuring the effects of additional risks accrued along the way has been researched in a number of high-quality longitudinal studies, whose findings are cogently summarised by Farrington (2005). Impulsiveness, particularly in association with low intelligence, may be linked to deficits in the executive functions of the brain, and may indicate an impairment in the abilities necessary for forward planning and goal-directed behaviour, including attention, abstract reasoning and behavioural inhibition. This initial risk for antisocial behaviour and violence is inflated where parental management of the child is harsh and inconsistent, such that the child is seldom rewarded for good behaviour but often punished for bad behaviour. In psychological terms, the child's experience is that being good is unrewarded and that the world is hostile. Furthermore, the child may become desensitised to punishment. Of course, the child's difficult behaviour and the carers' management practices influence each other in a reciprocal relationship, often creating a vicious cycle of adverse effects.

Recent evidence from a longitudinal study has identified a potential genetic and neurobiological mechanism underpinning the differential effects of maltreatment (Caspi et al., 2002). In boys, those who have the variant of a gene that determines low monoamine oxidase A (MAOA) enzyme activity, which leads to low metabolism of neurotransmitters, differ in their response to childhood maltreatment compared with boys who have the variant of that gene that determines high MAOA enzyme activity. Those with low MAOA activity who are maltreated bear threefold greater odds of developing conduct disorder, and nearly 10-fold greater odds of being convicted of a violent crime in adulthood. Hence, certain genetic factors appear to make some people more sensitive to stress, and this may affect the development of the neurotransmitter system, which may translate into antisocial behaviour and violence later in life.

Conflict and antisocial behaviour in families also add to the risk of antisocial personality disorder, possibly because, via parental modelling, the child learns to confront, fight and commit crime. Furthermore, there is an absence of learning the skills of negotiation and prosocial behaviour. Where difficult behaviours occur in the classroom, the child may fail academically, thus decreasing future job prospects and increasing the likelihood of crime as a career. School truancy and mixing with delinquent peers provides opportunities for taking up disapproved behaviours, such as smoking, drinking and drug taking, and antisocial behaviours, such as damaging property, stealing and fighting. The end result of this developmental route is a poorly educated adult, with little or no work experience, who uses violence and aggression as a means of resolving interpersonal problems, may have a criminal record and likely drinks heavily and uses illicit drugs. This person is the product of an interaction between his or her personality, social experiences and current opportunities. All of the violence-exacerbating challenges that he or she has faced in life are more likely when families are economically strained and live in high-crime neighbourhoods.

The pathway of interacting personality traits, personality processes and experiences described above may result in antisocial behaviour and aggression to such a degree that it may be classified as antisocial personality disorder. This is described in detail by DeBrito and Hodgins in Chapter 7. However, understanding the pathway to antisocial personality disorder reveals the specific risk factors, which may also be construed as appropriate targets for prevention or treatment to minimise risk. The pathway described above indicates that antisocial behaviour and violence may be prevented by family support, parent training and school inclusion programmes (Hawkins and Herrenkohl, 2003; Tremblay and Japel, 2003; Utting, 2003). In treating adult antisocial behaviour and violence, the intermediate targets suggested by the pathway include improving people's interpersonal problem solving, conflict resolution and emotion control, and changing the antisocial biases, beliefs and attitudes that support antisocial behaviour, aggression and violence (McGuire, 2006).

Psychopathy

Developmental approaches to understanding psychopathy are gaining currency. In childhood, a significant number of aggressive children show only reactive forms of aggression; yet, there is a subgroup that shows both instrumental and reactive aggression. Callous and unemotional traits in children are associated with especially severe aggression and persistent conduct problems, and there is evidence for high levels of heritability of these traits (Viding et al., 2005). Blair and colleagues (Blair et al., 2006; see also Chapter 9) suggest that this emotional dysfunction is at the heart of psychopathy. While research is as yet inconclusive regarding the genetic and molecular neurobiological factors underpinning low emotional responsiveness, these appear to affect the functioning of the amygdala and the orbital/ventrolateral frontal cortex. Impairment in aversive conditioning circuits manifests as lack of fear and empathy deficits. Indifference to the experience of punishment and to the perception of others' distress (i.e. low empathy, see Chapters 9 and 12) interferes with socialisation, and permits the development of instrumental violence. People with psychopathic traits also show lack of flexibility in altering responses to a stimulus (see Chapter 13), so that when contingencies change (e.g. to signal punishment or non-reward instead of reward), they persevere with previously rewarded behaviour. The lack of reward then causes frustration, which putatively leads to reactive aggression (see Chapter 8).

These neurobiological risk factors pose a risk for violence, but social and environmental influences have an additional role to play over the lifespan. Callous and unemotional traits in children may interfere with early attachment relationships with caregivers, which may exacerbate the absence of concern for others and may also affect the carer's affection for and attention to the child (Saltaris, 2002; see also Chapter 11). Good parenting may have less impact on children with emotional deficits than on those without in terms of teaching the child to be attentive to the feelings of others, but there may be more scope for influence through modelling acceptable means of attaining goals. Thus, prosocial role models have the potential to divert the child from antisocial means of goal attainment.

In terms of prevention and treatment of problems, there has been no real suggestion that the treatment targets should differ for psychopaths. Rather, what has been suggested is that the mode of intervention needs to take psychopathic traits into account, harnessing the need for control, status and success to beneficial effect (Hemphill and Hart, 2002).

TREATMENTS FOR OFFENDERS WITH PERSONALITY DISORDERS

If, in explaining violence, a profile of the individual's biological and psychological functioning may be presented to a legal body in mitigation, then the nature and degree of dysfunction should inform the disposal, whether punishment, treatment or a combination of the two. However, in reality, the decision is made partly in terms of the treatments and services available. People with psychosis have access to mental health professionals willing to take responsibility for their treatment, provide hospital beds and community supervision arrangements, and implement a range of pharmacological, psychosocial and management interventions. Hence, it is relatively easy for a judge to direct a person with psychosis into treatment.

People with personality disorders, until recently, have had fewer mental health professionals willing to take responsibility for their treatment and a dearth of services available to them. The directive encapsulated in the title of the National Institute for Mental Health in England's (2003) document, *Personality disorder: No longer a diagnosis of exclusion*, has prompted a change in service provision. Over the past 5 years, there has been support for the development of specialist community-based treatment services (Crawford and Rutter, 2007). These augment provision in forensic mental health services and the joint Department of Health and Prison Service in England and Wales provision for dangerous people with severe personality disorders (Department of Health/Home Office, 1999, 2000).

To flourish, these services need to have effective treatments available to them. Meta-analyses of outcomes of psychological treatments for people with personality disorders show a strong positive effect of treatment (Cohen's d^1 0.80 to 1.39), with both cognitive–behavioural and psychodynamic approaches showing good effects (Liechsenring, Rabung and Liebing, 2004; Perry, Banon and Ianni,1999). However, good quality research is scarce and this body of treatment research is strongly biased toward borderline personality disorder (Binks et al., 2006; Duggan et al., 2007).

Here, we are particularly interested in treatments for people with antisocial personality disorder and psychopathic individuals. Duggan et al. (2007), in their systematic review of psychological treatments for people with personality disorders, identified only two treatment trials specifically for antisocial personality disorder. These focused on reducing drug use, comparing combinations of contingency management, methadone prescription and cognitive–behavioural therapy. While positive effects were observed for contingency management, this is a very narrow treatment for antisocial personality disorder. Clearly, treatment for antisocial personality disorder is a subject requiring a considerable amount of further research. D'Silva, Duggan and McCarthy (2004) addressed the question of the treatability of psychopaths in a systematic review. They identified 24 studies, most of which were of poor methodological quality. Overall, as many indicated improvement as indicated deterioration; hence, no firm conclusions can yet be drawn about the treatability of those with high psychopathy traits. Again, treatment for psychopathic personality disorder is a subject requiring a considerable amount of further research.

It is imperative to research the effectiveness of treatments so that services can be developed on the basis of empirical evidence, thus giving mental health professionals the confidence to work with people with personality disorder, the judiciary the confidence to direct people with personality disorder into treatment, and the client the confidence to work therapeutically on his or her problem to effect lasting change. With an infrastructure and a knowledge base in place, professionals may begin to have confidence in deciding that, while people with personality disorder need to be held responsible for their behaviour, they may also benefit from treatment.

OFFENDERS WITHOUT PERSONALITY PROBLEMS OR PERSONALITY DISORDERS

Of course, Prison and Probation Services have for years been treating offenders with personality disorders, although they have not been diagnosed as such. In a review of 28 prison surveys worldwide, representing a total of 12 844 prisoners, 65% of men were diagnosable with any personality disorder and 47% with antisocial personality disorder, with the figures for women being 42% and 21% respectively

(Fazel and Danesh, 2002). Treatment programmes for offenders in correctional services are almost certain to be offered to a high proportion of people with personality disorders, although in recent years those scoring high on psychopathic traits have been excluded from treatment.

As mentioned earlier, meta-analyses of treatment outcome studies in correctional services indicate that treatments do reduce recidivism (McGuire, 2001, 2002). Finer-grained meta-analyses of treatment outcome studies have enabled the identification of principles of effective practice (Andrews, 2001). These principles are that treatment should (a) be targeted at high-risk offenders, (b) focus upon major empirically identified risk factors for criminal recidivism and (c) be delivered in ways that are responsive to offenders' learning styles and abilities. Effective treatments focus on changing antisocial cognitions and adverse cognitive–emotional states (e.g. resentment), building self-management, self-regulation and problem-solving skills, decreasing associations with antisocial others and increase anti-criminal networks and reducing substance use.

The fact that treatments work for prison and probation populations raises a number of issues for offenders with personality problems or personality disorders. If treatments that address thinking skills, values, emotion management, self-regulation and substance use work with prisoners and offenders on probation, amongst which groups there is a high proportion of personality disordered offenders, can we extrapolate from this that effective treatments for personality disordered offenders have been developed, albeit incidentally? Or, do personality disordered offenders require additional treatment components that add value to mainstream interventions? If personality disordered offenders can be effectively treated in criminal justice settings, why not treat them in prisons and probation services, rather than in mental health settings, since the cost to the public purse would be much less? There are no simple and straightforward answers to these questions.

CONCLUSION

The purpose of this chapter was to set the scene for the chapters that follow. Some basic definitions have been provided for the topics of the book, namely personality, personality disorder and violence. Apart from these simple clarifications, more questions have been raised than answered with regard to which aspects of personality are relevant to violence, how personality and personality disorder relate to violence and the implications of their relationship for clinical practice. With the spirit of enquiry raised, the subsequent chapters are the rocks that will pave the path to enlightenment.

NOTE

1. Cohen's d is an effect size statistic calculated by subtracting the post-treatment mean from the pre-treatment mean and dividing by the pooled standard deviations. An effect size of 0.20 is considered small, 0.50 medium, and 0.80 large.

REFERENCES

American Psychiatric Association (1994) *Diagnostic and Statistical Manual of Mental Disorders*, 4th edn, APA, Washington DC.

American Psychiatric Association (2000) *Diagnostic and Statistical Manual of Mental Disorders*, 4th edn, text revision, APA, Washington DC.

Andrews, D.A. (2001) Principles of effective correctional programs, in *Compendium 2000 on Effective Correctional Programming* (eds L.L. Motiuk and R.C. Serin), Correctional Services of Canada, Ottawa.

Baron, R.A. and Richardson, D. (1994) Human Aggression, Plenum, New York.

Benn, P. (1999) Freedom, resentment, and the psychopath. *Philosophy, Psychiatry, and Psychology*, **6**, 29–39.

Binks, C.A., Fenton, M., McCarthy, L. *et al.* (2006) Psychological therapies for people with borderline personality disorder. *Cochrane Database of Systematic Reviews*, (1), CD005652. DOI: 10.1002/14651858.CD005652.

Blair, R.J.R., Peschardt, K.S., Budhani, S. *et al.* (2006) The development of psychopathy. *Journal of Child Psychiatry and Psychology*, **47**, 262–75.

Brody, N. and Ehrlichman, H. (1998) *Personality Psychology: The Study of Individuality*, Prentice Hall, Upper Saddle River, NJ.

Caspi, A., McClay, J., Moffitt, T.E. *et al.* (2002) Role of genotype in the cycle of violence in maltreated children. *Science*, **297**, 851–54.

Ciocchetti, C. (2003) The responsibility of the psychopathic offender. *Philosophy, Psychiatry, and Psychology*, **10**, 175–83.

Coid, J., Yang, M., Roberts, A. *et al.* (2006a) Violence and psychiatric morbidity in a national household population: a report from the British Household Survey. *American Journal of Epidemiology*, **164**, 1199–1208.

Coid, J., Yang, M., Tyrer, P. *et al.* (2006b) Prevalence and correlates of personality disorder in Great Britain. *British Journal of Psychiatry*, **188**, 423–31.

Cooke, D.J. and Michie, C. (2001) Refining the construct of psychopathy: Towards a hierarchical model. *Psychological Assessment*, **13**, 171–88.

Crawford, M. and Rutter, D. (2007) Lessons learned from an evaluation of dedicated community-based services for people with personality disorder. *Mental Health Review Journal*, **12**, 55–61.

Cunliffe, J. and Shepherd, A. (2007) *Reoffending of Adults: Results from the 2004 Cohort (Home Office Statistical Bulletin 06/07)*, Home Office, London.

Department of Health/Home Office (1999) *Managing Dangerous People with Severe Personality Disorder: Proposals for Policy Development*, Department of Health, London.

Department of Health/Home Office (2000) *Reforming the Mental Health Act Part II: High Risk Patients*, The Stationery Office, Norwich.

D'Silva, K., Duggan, C. and McCarthy, L. (2004) Does treatment really make psychopaths worse? A review of the evidence. *Journal of Personality Disorders*, **18**, 163–77.

Duggan, C., Huband, N., Smailagic, N. *et al.* (2007) The use of psychological treatments for people with personality disorder: a systematic review of randomized controlled trials. *Personality and Mental Health*, **1**, 95–125.

Farrington, D.P. (2005) Childhood origins of antisocial behaviour. *Clinical Psychology and Psychotherapy*, **12**, 177–90.

Fazel, S. and Danesh, J. (2002) Serious mental disorder in 23 000 prisoners: a systematic review of 62 surveys. *The Lancet*, **359**, 545–50.

Fine, C. and Kennett J. (2004) Mental impairment, moral understanding and criminal responsibility: psychopathy and the purposes of punishment. *International Journal of Law and Psychiatry*, **27**, 425–43.

Grounds, A. (2008) The end of faith in forensic psychiatry. *Criminal Behaviour and Mental Health*, **18**, 1–13.

Hare, R.D. (1991) *The Hare Psychopathy Checklist – Revised*, Multi-Health Systems, North Tonawanda, NY.

Hare, R.D. (2003) *The Hare Psychopathy Checklist – Revised*, 2nd edn, Multi-Health Systems, North Tonawanda, NY.

Hare, R.D., Clark, D., Grann, M. and Thornton, D. (2000) Psychopathy and the predictive validity of the PCL-R: an international perspective. *Behavioral Sciences and the Law*, **18**, 623–45.

Hawkins, J.D. and Herrenkohl, T.I. (2003) Prevention in the school years, in *Early Prevention of Adult Antisocial Behaviour* (eds D.P. Farrington and J.W. Coid), Cambridge University Press, Cambridge.

Hemphill, J.F., Hare, R.D. and Wong, S. (1998) Psychopathy and recidivism: a review. *Legal and Criminological Psychology*, **3**, 139–70.

Hemphill, J.F. and Hart, S.D. (2002) Motivating the unmotivated: Psychopathy, treatment, and change, in *Motivating Offenders to Change: A Guide to Enhancing Engagement in Therapy* (ed. M. McMurran), John Wiley & Sons, Ltd, Chichester.

Hiscoke, U.L., Långström, N., Ottosson, H. and Grann, M. (2003) Self-reported personality traits and disorders (DSM-IV) and risk of criminal recidivism: a prospective study. *Journal of Personality Disorders*, **17**, 293–305.

Hollin, C.R. (2002) Does punishment motivate offenders? in *Motivating Offenders to Change: A Guide to Enhancing Engagement in Therapy* (ed. M. McMurran), John Wiley & Sons, Ltd, Chichester.

Jamieson, L. and Taylor, P.J. (2004) A reconviction study of special (high security) hospital patients. *British Journal of Criminology*, **44**, 783–802.

Liechsenring, F., Rabung, S. and Liebing, E. (2004) The efficacy of short-term psychodynamic psychotherapy in specific psychiatric disorders: a meta-analysis. *Archives of General Psychiatry*, **61**, 1208–16.

Livesley, W.J. (2001) Conceptual and taxonomic issues, in *Handbook of Personality Disorders: Theory, Research, and Treatment* (ed. W.J. Livesley), Guilford, New York.

McGuire, J. (2001) What works in correctional intervention? Evidence and practical implications, in *Offender Rehabilitation in Practice: Implementing and Evaluating Effective Programs* (eds G.A. Bernfeld, D.P. Farrington and A.W. Leschied), John Wiley & Sons, Ltd, Chichester.

McGuire, J. (2002) Integrating findings from research reviews, in *Offender Rehabilitation and Treatment* (ed. J. McGuire), John Wiley & Sons, Ltd, Chichester.

McGuire, J. (2006) General offending behaviour programmes: Concept, theory and practice, in *Offending Behaviour Programmes: Development, Application and Controversies* (eds C.R. Hollin and E.J. Palmer), John Wiley & Sons, Ltd, Chichester.

National Institute for Mental Health in England (2003) *Personality Disorder: No Longer a Diagnosis of Exclusion*, NIMHE, London.

Nestor, P.G. (2002) Mental disorder and violence: Personality dimensions and clinical features. *American Journal of psychiatry*, **159**, 1973–78.

Perry, J.C., Banon, E. and Ianni, F. (1999) Effectiveness of psychotherapy for personality disorders. *American Journal of Psychiatry*, **156**, 1312–21.

Saltaris, C. (2002) Psychopathy in juvenile offenders. Can temperament and attachment be considered as robust developmental precursors? *Clinical Psychology Review*, **22**, 729–52.

Skeem, J. and Cooke, D.J. (in press) Is criminal behaviour a central component of psychopathy? Conceptual directions for resolving the debate. *Psychological Assessment*.

Tremblay, R.E. and Japel, C. (2003) Prevention during pregnancy, infancy and the pre-school years, in *Early Prevention of Adult Antisocial Behaviour* (eds D.P. Farrington and J.W. Coid), Cambridge University Press, Cambridge.

Utting, D. (2003) Prevention through family and parenting programmes, in *Early Prevention of Adult Antisocial Behaviour* (eds D.P. Farrington and J.W. Coid), Cambridge University Press, Cambridge.

Viding, E., Blair, R.J.R., Moffitt, T.E. and Plomin, R. (2005) Evidence for substantial genetic risk for psychopathy in 7 year olds. *Journal of Child Psychology and Psychiatry*, **46**, 592–97.

Ward, T. (2002) Good lives and the rehabilitation of offenders: Promises and problems. *Aggression and Violent Behavior*, **7**, 513–28.

Ward, T. and Brown, M. (2004) The Good Lives Model and conceptual issues in offender rehabilitation. *Psychology, Crime, and Law*, **10**, 243–57.

Widiger, T.A. and Simonsen, E. (2005) Alternative dimensional models of personality disorder: Finding a common ground. *Journal of Personality Disorders*, **19**, 110–30.

World Health Organisation (1992) *10th Revision of the International Classification of Diseases (ICD-10)*, WHO, Geneva.

World Health Organisation (2002) *World Report on Violence and Health*, WHO, Geneva.

Chapter 2

THE 'FUNCTIONAL LINK' BETWEEN PERSONALITY DISORDER AND VIOLENCE: A CRITICAL APPRAISAL

CONOR DUGGAN AND RICHARD HOWARD
University of Nottingham, UK

INTRODUCTION

The development in the last decade of a programme in England and Wales to provide services for those who were deemed to be dangerous because of their severe personality disorder (DSPD) marked a major departure from much of previous thinking in a contentious area of medico-legal practice (Department of Health/Home Office, 1999, 2000). Of special interest for this chapter is that this proposal extended the previously ill-defined criteria such as the legal designation 'psychopathic disorder' and 'treatability' with more precise scientific terms to justify involuntary detention into the service. For within this extended system, in order to be subject to compulsory treatment in a DSPD unit, an individual needed to satisfy, not just these aforementioned conditions, but also criteria from the following triad: (a) have a severe personality disorder (SPD), (b) being more likely than not to behave violently within the next 5 years and (c) there being a 'functional link' between (a) and (b) (DSPD Programme, 2004). Of these, (a) and (b) were operationally defined and anchored to well-defined classifications, namely the Diagnostic and Statistical Manual of Mental Disorders IV (DSM-IV; American Psychiatric Association, 1994, 2000) and the International Classification of Diseases 10 (ICD-10; World Health Organisation, 1992), and empirically-based assessment instruments, including Hare's Psychopathy Checklist-Revised (PCL-R; Hare, 1991; 2003) and various risk assessment protocols. Using these assessments as a basis, an individual's detention might be open to a challenge on scientific grounds in a way that the earlier criteria could never be.

The third criterion (i.e. the 'functional link') was left undefined and this might well be the proposal's Achilles' heel as regards a legal challenge. Use of the term

Personality, Personality Disorder and Violence   Edited by Mary McMurran and Richard C. Howard
© 2009 John Wiley & Sons, Ltd

'functional link' is ambiguous, since it could mean either a functional relationship between personality disorder (PD) and dangerousness, that is, mere covariation between the two, or a causal connection between them. More importantly, this question of a 'functional link' goes beyond the DSPD proposal, extending indeed to the heart of much of what preoccupies forensic mental health practitioners in their quest to 'link' mental disorder to an increased risk of violence.

Although the meaning of a 'functional link' in the DSPD documentation was not made explicit, we believe that it is reasonable to interpret this as implying a 'causal connection' between the severity of the PD and the resultant increased risk of violent behaviour. Put simply, it is the 'severity of the PD' that 'causes' the individual 'to behave violently'. The alternative, weaker interpretation of the 'functional link' is that there is simply covariation between the SPD and dangerousness (D), implying only a significant degree of shared variance. However, such an interpretation would trivialise this relationship and lack clinical importance. Hence, it will be assumed here that the stronger interpretation was intended by the architects of the DSPD programme.

In this chapter, therefore, we will examine the conditions that are deemed necessary to establish a causal claim in behavioural sciences in general and apply these to the DSPD proposal in particular. We will then consider some of the limitations of current approaches to causal modelling in PD and violence and argue that these need to be expanded to models of greater complexity in order to develop a more satisfactory understanding of this relationship. In doing so, we will rely heavily on Stephen Haynes' *Models of Causality in Psychopathology* (Haynes, 1992) to provide us with a sensible approach to several contentious issues.

ESTABLISHING CAUSALITY

For a functional relationship to act as a *causal functional variable*, the following four conditions are generally agreed as being necessary in the behavioural sciences (Haynes, 1992):

(a) *Covariation between the variables*. 'Lack of correlation between variables negates the possibility of a causal relationship because any form of a functional relationship is precluded' (p. 36).

(b) *Temporal precedence of the causal variable*. 'The lack of a reliable temporal precedence of one variable over the other negates a causal relationship between them, since it renders difficult the distinction between causal and non-causal functional relationships' (p. 37).

(c) *Exclusion of an alternative explanation for the relationship*. '. . .to infer that a functional relationship is due to a causal connection between variables, the possibility that the observed covariance is due to causal operation of a third variable (or more than one variable) must be excluded' (p. 39).

(d) *Establishing a logical connection between the variables*. 'For a variable (X) to be considered "causal", it must also have a logical connection with the effect (Y)' (p. 40). Haynes points out that this requires addressing the question 'How does X cause Y?', that is, identification of the causal mechanism.

The critical issue to be examined here is whether, in the light of these criteria, a case can be made for a *causal* functional relationship between SPD and the risk of violence as specified by the DSPD criteria. We argue below that significant difficulties emerge when these criteria are applied to the components of the DSPD proposal.

Covariation between the Variables

This condition would appear fairly straightforward so that indeed one might argue that this association is central to the definition in DSPD. It implies, for instance, that the likelihood of dangerousness is directly related to the severity of the PD. Hence, the more severe the disorder, the more likely is the risk of violent behaviour. Unfortunately, the definition of a SPD within DSPD is ambiguous in that it involves two different constructs, psychopathy and PD, that can be used either individually or combined, thereby giving rise to at least three ways of measuring the 'severity' of the PD. The DSPD criteria specify the following three disjunctive elements:

(i) the presence to a sufficient degree of psychopathic traits (a PCL-R score of 30 or above); or
(ii) a combination of a moderately high psychopathy score (PCL-R 25 – 29) combined with at least one PD other than antisocial personality disorder; or
(iii) two or more PDs, regardless of the PLC-R score.

Using three disjunctive criteria to define the causal variable is problematic, since it 'mixes apples with oranges'. Psychopathy, defined by the PCL-R, is a continuous variable that describes a constellation of core personality traits associated with serious antisocial, including violent behaviour (Hare, 2003). In contrast, DSM-IV and ICD-10 criteria are categorical variables: the disorder is either present or absent. If a score on the PCL-R, for instance, were chosen as the only way of specifying the relationship between the severity of PD and the likelihood of violence, then the relationship between the antecedent and consequent variable would be clear-cut, as both can be specified in a dimensional manner. Here, the implication is that the higher the PCL-R score, the more likely it is that the individual will behave violently; and there is evidence to support this relationship (Hare, 2003; Vitacco, Neumann and Jackson, 2005), including data from at least one longitudinal study (Gretton, Hare and Catchpole, 2004). Moreover, while psychopathy overlaps considerably with antisocial personality disorder (ASPD), the combination of ASPD and psychopathy is more predictive of violence than ASPD alone (Kosson, Lorenz and Newman, 2006).

However, those who drew up the DSPD criteria recognised that there might be some individuals who, while they did not score highly on the PCL-R, might nonetheless be likely to behave violently because of a disturbance in their personality. In part, this was doubtless due to the fact that the relationship between psychopathy, as measured by the PCL-R, and violence is at best a modest one. Using a 4-factor model, Vitacco, Neumann and Jackson (2005) found the affective and antisocial factors of PCL-R to be moderately predictive of violence, while using a

3-factor model showed the affective and lifestyle factors to be only modestly predictive of violence. Moreover, the ability of the PCL-R to predict violence is largely attributable to Factor 2 – an impulsive and antisocial lifestyle (Vitacco, Neumann and Jackson, 2005). The DSPD criteria were therefore widened to include PDs from the DSM-IV and ICD-10 systems, thereby ensuring that these individuals would not inadvertently fall outside of the criteria allowing for their detention.

This extension to include a categorical diagnosis is problematic not just because, as pointed out above, it combines a dimensional with a categorical variable to specify 'severity', but also because it assumes that all of the PDs are equally associated with the likelihood of violence. Consider, for instance, an individual who satisfies criteria only for dependent and avoidant PDs and who thereby can be designated as having a 'SPD' according to the DSPD criteria. While such an individual might, according to DSPD criteria, suffer from a 'SPD', there is no evidence that the presence of dependent and avoidant traits is likely to lead to violent behaviour – in fact the evidence is to the contrary (Coid, 1992). Conversely, an individual who meets all the criteria for paranoid personality disorder might behave violently, yet fail to meet any of the DSPD 'severity' criteria. Unfortunately, there is no guidance in the DSPD literature as to how this dilemma should be resolved. We will return to this issue below when we critically examine the empirical evidence for a relationship between PD and violence.

Temporal Precedence of the Causal Variable

Again, the sense of this criterion is obvious (i.e. if A causes B then A ought to precede B in time). This ought not to create many difficulties for the DSPD proposal in that PD is defined as 'an enduring pattern of inner experience and behaviour ... that is ...stable and of long duration, and its onset traced back at least to adolescence or early adulthood.' (DSM-IV; American Psychiatric Association, 1994). The presence of PD over the lifespan means that the 'antecedent' ought to precede its 'consequence' (i.e. risk of violent behaviour) in time. Unfortunately, establishing this sequence is not so simple for the following reasons. First, when assessing evidence for a functional link between an individual patient's PD and his or her dangerousness, the clinician must essentially construct a narrative of the patient's life history and convince himself or herself that a developing PD not only preceded the emergence of dangerousness but was causally linked to it. In practice, this often means simply asking the question: 'Would this (violent) offence have occurred in the absence of the PD?' In other words: Was the PD a *necessary* condition for the offence to occur? In this case, the clinician would be interpreting the term as implying a *necessary* cause, but as Haynes (1992) points out, some causal variables are neither necessary nor sufficient, particularly when they act in concert with other variables. An answer to the above question is necessarily subjective, resting on the clinician's own interpretation of the 'data', as well as on his or her interpretation of the term 'functional link'. The latter can vary quite widely, from little or no consideration of its meaning to a more reasoned and explicit statement of the process for establishing the link, as in the following note made by a DSPD clinician: 'The link is considered to be present if at least two harmful (sexual or violent) offences are linked to X's PD. Identifying the psychological factors of a patient's PD plus beliefs, thoughts and feelings present in the chain of events leading up to offending can inform this process. A functional link can be inferred from any offence analysis which includes a functional analysis of offending and offence paralleling behaviour.'

While a clinician can of course appeal to epidemiological or group data to support his or her interpretation, precedence, as Haynes (1992) points out, can *never* be established in cross-sectional research, no matter how elegantly designed; rather it can only be established by longitudinal studies.

An example from research in depression illustrates this point. Here, it had long been held that 'learnt helplessness' was an antecedent vulnerability to developing depressive disorder (Peterson and Seligman, 1984). Although plausible, evidence for this position was mainly provided by cross-sectional research that compared the degree of learnt helplessness in those with and without depressive disorder. These studies confirmed that learnt helplessness was more common in the former. When, however, learnt helplessness was measured prospectively as the antecedent variable to subsequent depression, those who subsequently developed depression did not show an increased level of learnt helplessness as would have been predicted by the learnt helplessness hypothesis (Barnett and Gotlib, 1988). Unfortunately, for those who espouse a causal link between the severity of PD and dangerousness, there is a dearth of empirical evidence from longitudinal studies linking PD to violence.

Second, ASPD as defined in DSM-IV presents special problems. While many authors now view PD as emerging developmentally (e.g. Cohen *et al.*, 2005), and this is implicit in the requirement that prior conduct disorder (CD) be present for a diagnosis of ASPD, diagnostically – according to DSM-IV at least – a person cannot be considered to have ASPD before the age of 18. This is problematic insofar as an individual with ASPD can, and often does, exhibit a history of violent behaviour that predates his diagnosis of ASPD at or after the age of 18. Moreover, requiring the presence of childhood CD for an ASPD diagnosis suggests that antisocial (including violent) behaviour (i.e. the 'consequence') is being used as part of the PD definition (i.e. the 'antecedent'). As a consequence, the reasoning whereby PD is linked with violent behaviour becomes circular, that is, 'antisocial behaviour causes antisocial behaviour'. As well as violating the requirement of temporal precedence, this circularity also appears to contravene the requirement of a logical connection between variables, to be considered further below.

Exclusion of an Alternative Explanation for the Relationship

Even if it were possible to demonstrate that the relationship between SPD and violence meets the requirements of covariation and temporal precedence, in order to demonstrate a causal relationship between them it is necessary to exclude a third variable that accounts for the variance common to each (see Figure 2.1). In the case of DSPD, an obvious third variable that might explain the presumed relationship between the 'SPD' and the 'D' is substance misuse (either of drugs or alcohol or both). Here, one could imagine that the misuse of substances at an early age might

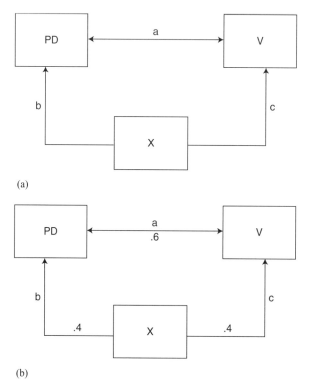

(a)

(b)

Figure 2.1 Causal vector diagrams of a non-causal (correlational) relationship between personality disorder (PD) and violence (V) that results from the common effect of a third variable, X. In **(a)**, the effects of the third variable account for the common variance between PD and V if the path weights of b and c are sufficiently high to render the value of path a approximately zero when they are controlled. In **(b)**, the correlational relationship between PD and V is partially accounted for by the common effects of X. Controlling paths b and c would reduce the value of a, but not to zero. After Haynes, 1992.

have an adverse effect on both the emerging brain and personality, resulting in an increased likelihood of violent behaviour.

If, indeed, such an alternative explanation were established for DSPD, the 'SPD' would then not be causally related to 'D'. This is further complicated by the fact that, as Haynes points out, the covariance between two variables, for example SPD and D, may be *partially* accounted for by the presence of a third variable such as drug/alcohol abuse (see Figure 2.1(b)). In this case, there could be a small direct causal relationship between PD and violence, even after controlling for the effects of a third variable such as drug and/or alcohol abuse.

While the exclusion of alternative explanations is important in drawing any conclusion on causal inference, it is recognised that this can be difficult in practice as it requires the careful measurement of multiple variables in a properly defined temporal sequence (i.e. a longitudinal investigation is required). This condition cannot be met in a DSPD setting where one is faced with offenders whose presentation is the result of multiple disadvantages, the precise temporal sequence of which is difficult to disentangle.

Establishing a Logical Connection between the Variables

While the preceding three criteria are necessary for establishing a causal relationship, they are insufficient (Cliff, 1983); for a variable to be considered 'causal', it must also have a logical connection with its 'effect'. Moreover, as Haynes (1992) points out, a logical connection between cause and consequence requires the identification of the causal mechanism linking the two: 'We must address the question "How (or in what way) does X cause Y?"' (p. 41).

  This is the most challenging (and potentially most interesting) of all of Haynes' criteria since it requires a precise specification and prioritisation of a number of causal variables that might, potentially, lead to an offence. Consider, for example, a woman with borderline personality disorder who commits arson. Specifying which of the many possible intervening variables, for example impulsivity, dysphoria, lack of identity, emotional dysregulation, might have led her to engage in an act of fire setting is clearly a challenging task. Similarly, in the case of DSPD, establishing a causal mechanism is likely to be difficult because, as will be described in the subsequent section, high comorbidity exists, both between the different PDs, and between these disorders and other conditions of mental disturbance. It is recognised, for instance, that for those detained under the DSPD label, comorbidity is likely to be the rule, rather than exception. Indeed, over half of all patients admitted to the Peaks Unit, one of two DSPD units established in the UK health service, have more than one PD diagnosis, and of those who meet the PD severity criterion, three-quarters have more than one disorder.[1] Suppose, for instance, that one finds an individual who meets criteria for both narcissistic and paranoid personality disorders, has multiple Axis I conditions including substance misuse and post-traumatic stress disorder (PTSD), and is prone to violence. Does one give precedence to a blow to the individual's self-esteem (narcissism), or to a suspiciousness of the motives of others (paranoid traits), his or her substance misuse or the activation of his PTSD symptoms in explaining his or her violent behaviour? Hence the question arises: How does one attribute causal primacy to one condition over another in determining its links to violent behaviour?

WHAT IS THE EMPIRICAL EVIDENCE LINKING PERSONALITY DISORDER TO VIOLENT BEHAVIOUR?

While it is now generally accepted by the scientific community that mental disorder is at least associated (if not causally related) to violence, it is important to realise that a diametrically opposite view was held by the same community 25 years ago (Beck and Wencel, 1998). This radical reappraisal ought to make us at least a little cautious in attributing too much weight to the association. Furthermore, a sceptical stance is supported when this association is examined empirically. There are at least three ways in which this can be done.

The first is through epidemiological surveys such as those conducted by Coid and his colleagues (Coid *et al.*, 2006a, b and c).

Coid's early studies of forensic samples, that is, residents of high-secure hospital and prison establishments, aimed to explore the question of how their psychopathology, and their PD in particular, contributed to their violent behaviour (Coid, 1992, 1998). Forty-eight percent of the sample had been convicted of murder, attempted murder or wounding. Most individuals had multiple Axis I (mean of 2.7) and Axis II diagnoses (a mean of 3.6, most commonly borderline, antisocial, narcissistic and paranoid personality disorder). More than a third (36%) had a lifetime diagnosis of alcoholism or alcohol abuse. This confirms previous research that this was a group with complex mental health needs. Notwithstanding this, Coid concluded that PDs 'appear to make a substantial contribution to the motivation of serious criminal behaviour' (Coid, 1998, p. 78). He acknowledged, however, that a number of possible confounding factors had not been measured (see below).

The vignettes presented by Coid make clear that the presentations were complex, often being a combination of several PDs and Axis I conditions acting in concert. A typical example was that of a woman with violent behaviour resulting in a homicide. She presented Axis II disorders of antisocial, borderline, paranoid and histrionic PDs, together with lifetime Axis I diagnoses of depressive disorder, alcohol dependency and drug misuse. It is clear that attributing causality to one or even the multiple disorders on Axis II that might have led to this woman's violent behaviour is problematic, since they may all have made a contribution. Added to this is the possible contribution of the comorbid Axis I conditions. This type of complex presentation will not surprise anyone who works clinically in this area.

One of the major limitations in his study – a limitation that Coid candidly acknowledged – is that the personality and Axis I conditions were not rated blind to the nature of the criminal behaviour; hence, there is the possibility that rater bias influenced the findings. A second limitation is the representativeness of the sample, as this comprised predominantly high-secure hospital residents, who likely have a high level of morbidity, and prisoners who were so disruptive that they required placement in special units to manage them. Despite these limitations, including its correlational nature, this study is one of the very few empirical studies to have examined the relationship of specific PDs to violent offending in forensic samples.

Coid and colleagues (Coid *et al.*, 2006a, b and c) have since pursued their epidemiological enquiries by collecting data regarding PD and offending in more representative community samples. A recent survey of a national household population in the United Kingdom found that the presence of *any* PD was associated with a very small increase in risk of violence which increased markedly when combined with substance dependence (Coid *et al.*, 2006a). Even in the case of ASPD, the PD most clearly associated with risk of violence in the community (Coid *et al.*, 2006b), this was found to be relatively modest – a risk ratio, when adjusted for confounds such as sex, age, social class and comorbid mental disorders, of 6.1. Notably, one-half of the individuals with an ASPD diagnosis reported an absence of violent behaviour over the previous 5 years. From this and other studies, it is clear that it is the comorbidity of PD, and of ASPD in particular, with other disorders (and in particular with alcohol and substance dependence) that is key to understanding the increased risk of violence in personality disordered individuals. In Coid *et al.'s* (2006a) study, 11% of individuals with any PD, compared with 7% of individuals with no disorder, reported violent behaviour in the previous 5 years, yet over half (52%) of the personality disordered individuals reported violence when there was comorbid substance dependence.

Nor is it only the comorbidity between PDs and DSM Axis I disorders such as substance dependence that is important for putting the association between PDs and violence into context. Personality disordered patients typically present with more than one PD (Zimmerman, Rothschild and Chelminski, 2005), and a diagnosis of two or more PDs in the same individual is not uncommon in both clinical and non-clinical samples (Dolan, Evans and Norton, 1995; Nurnberg *et al.*, 1991; Watson and Sinha, 1998). These co-occur both within and across the conventional DSM-IV clusters (see Chapter 1).

A selective co-occurrence between ASPD and borderline personality disorders was suggested by the finding that, among adult admissions to psychiatric hospital, borderline personality disorder co-occurred with antisocial but not with other PDs (Becker *et al.*, 2000). Howard *et al.* (2008) have recently presented evidence that the combination of ASPD and borderline personality disorder in a treatment-seeking community sample is particularly associated with criminality, aggression and emotional dyscontrol. Traits of both ASPD and borderline personality disorder, together with paranoid and narcissistic/histrionic traits, loaded significantly on a higher order 'antisocial' factor associated with a history of violent and non-violent criminal offending. This is consistent with a previous report that the presence of paranoid, narcissistic and passive-aggressive traits in adolescence increased the risk of committing violent acts and criminal behaviour during adolescence or early adulthood (Johnson *et al.*, 2000).

Moreover, the co-occurrence of ASPD and borderline personality disorder varies as a function of level of security. Figure 2.2 shows that the co-occurrence of ASPD and borderline personality disorder follows a gradient from high to low security (and by implication from most to least 'dangerous').

A second approach to empirically examining the relationship between PD and violence is to compare the prevalence of PDs in groups of violent and non-violent offenders. Watzke, Ullrich and Marneros (2006) compared predominantly male German prison inmates with and without a history of violence, using ICD-10. Dissocial personality disorder, the ICD-10 counterpart of ASPD in DSM-IV, was slightly more prevalent in violent (23.6%) than in non-violent offenders (14.6%), but violence was more clearly associated with lifetime mental disorders excluding PDs. The most striking, and significant, difference between groups was in the prevalence of substance use disorder: nearly 70% of violent, compared with 45% of non-violent, offenders evidenced substance use disorder. A related approach is to examine relationships between PD and measures of violence *within* samples of violent offenders. An example is a study by Blackburn (2007) in which he examined the association of PD with criminal history, including total convictions for violent and sexual offences, corrected for time at liberty. Violent convictions correlated significantly, but very modestly ($r = 0.23$), only with ASPD. Sexual offences failed to correlate with any PD. Blackburn pointed out that the correlation between ASPD and violent offending was inflated by criterion contamination, and interpreted the

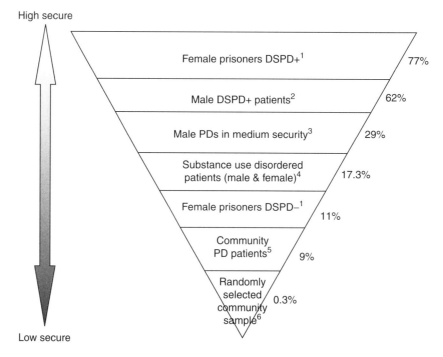

High secure

Female prisoners DSPD+[1]   77%

Male DSPD+ patients[2]   62%

Male PDs in medium security[3]   29%

Substance use disordered
patients (male & female)[4]   17.3%

Female prisoners DSPD–[1]   11%

Community
PD patients[5]   9%

Randomly
selected   0.3%
community
sample[6]

Low secure

Figure 2.2   The co-occurrence of antisocial and borderline PD obtained in samples at different levels of security. **1** Data from the Prison Cohort Study (Coid *et al.*, 2007), courtesy of Laura Bell; **2** Unpublished data from Peaks Unit, Rampton Hospital, UK; **3** Unpublished data from Arnold Lodge medium secure unit, Leicester, UK; **4** Bakken *et al.*, 2004; **5** Howard *et al.*, 2008; **6** Data from the British Household Survey (Coid *et al.*, 2006a), courtesy of J. Coid and S. Ullrich. DSPD+ signifies criteria for DSPD were met. DSPD– signifies criteria for DSPD were not met.

results as suggesting that 'none of the personality disorders is strongly associated with persistent offending' (p. 155).

A third approach, and one that is critical to settling the issue of a causal link between PD and violence, is to follow a cohort of individuals from childhood through adolescence into adulthood. Unfortunately, there is a relative dearth of such studies. The aforementioned study by Johnson *et al.* (2000), a community-based, longitudinal prospective study of 717 youths from upstate New York, investigated whether PDs during adolescence (ASPD had to be excluded) were associated with increased risk of violence during adolescence and early adulthood, after controlling for a number of covariates including co-occurring anxiety, depressive, personality and substance use disorders during mid-adolescence, conduct disorder, age and sex. Cluster A PDs were associated with increased risk of burglary and threatening behaviour, while those with Cluster B PDs (excluding ASPD) during adolescence were more likely than those without these PDs to be involved in arson or vandalism, to start physical fights, commit a mugging or robbery and engage in any violent act. The previously mentioned ability of symptoms of paranoid, narcissistic or passive-aggressive personality disorder to predict violent acts did not interact with substance abuse during mid-adolescence. Relationships between borderline personality disorder and acts of violence were less clear, losing their significance once other variables, including substance abuse, were controlled. It appears from other longitudinal research that adolescent alcohol abuse mediates the relationship between childhood variables and the development of borderline symptoms in adulthood (Thatcher, Cornelius and Clark, 2005). The latter group of researchers are currently examining adolescent antecedents of ASPD, including alcohol use, and it will be interesting to see from their results whether adolescent alcohol and other substance use mediates the relationship between childhood variables and adult ASPD. The importance of early alcohol abuse was indicated in results from another longitudinal study – the Dunedin Multidisciplinary Health and Development Study (Moffitt *et al.*, 2001). Roughly one-half of the males who subsequently showed a pattern of lifecourse persistent offending were diagnosable as alcohol dependent at age 18.[2] This suggests an important causal role for adolescent alcohol abuse in mediating the relationship between PD and adult antisocial (including violent) behaviour.

THE CONSEQUENCES OF LIMITED CAUSAL MODELS

The evidence from this brief review of the empirical data linking PD to violence demonstrates that a clear causal relationship, that is, one that meets the four criteria for causality outlined above, is far from established, and must await results of further longitudinal studies. The evidence, such as it is, suggests that any relationship that exists between PD and violence is weak, and that PD, including ASPD, probably accounts for only a very small proportion of the variance in violent behaviour. However, the DSPD proposal is more significantly flawed in that it falls into the class of limited causal models and consequently suffers from the deficits of such an approach. Here, problems arise when a single cause or a restricted class of causes (as in a limited causal model) are used as the explanatory variable to describe the relationships in complex behavioural disorders.

There are several undesirable effects of this approach (Haynes, 1992), but we shall describe the consequences of only four of these: (a) the incompatibility between different causal models; (b) their tendency to use excessively high-level causal variables; (c) a presumption of unidirectionality; and (d) a presumed stability or finality in the model.

The Incompatibility between Causal Models

When limited causal models with one or a restricted number of causes are used to explain the same behavioural disorder, there is a tendency to view such models as competing with one another (Haynes, 1992). This applies both with regard to an explanation of the occurrence of a disorder, as well as to its treatment. Typical examples include pitting a drug intervention (with its emphasis on a neurochemical disturbance) against a psychological treatment (with its emphasis on social learning or behavioural contingencies). An example provided by Haynes (1992) is that of alprazolam versus behavioural treatment of panic disorder (Klosko *et al.*, 1990). The negative consequences of this approach are clearly spelt out by Haynes (1992): 'In these studies, causal models that lose the "variance race" (i.e. those that fail to account for the largest proportion of the variance in a behaviour disorder or intervention outcome) are often dismissed in deference to the "winning model"' (p. 59). This belief that causal models are incompatible is further propagated by professional organisations that advocate particular conceptual and interventionist strategies to the exclusion of alternative models. Even within the current treatment provision of DSPD, several differing interventions are being tried including the psychological interventions of dialectical behaviour therapy, schema focused therapy, cognitive analytic therapy, violence reduction programme and a psychopathy programme (Chromis). Each of these is based on a set of assumptions that excludes the others. Perhaps, not surprisingly in the light of the complementary, rather than the competitive nature of these models, when these are trialled 'head to head', the usual result is that 'all have won and all should have prizes' (i.e the differing interventions exhibit few if any differences in their therapeutic efficacy). The National Institute of Mental Health treatment trial of major depression is a case in point (Elkin *et al.*, 1989). This pitted cognitive–behavioural therapy (with its emphasis on a cognitive model of depression) against interpersonal therapy (IPT) (emphasising interpersonal deficits as being causal) against antidepressants (emphasising a neurochemical disturbance). The trial found little difference between the three interventions, although medication was more effective when the mood disturbance was more severe. Although these three interventions were set up as being alternative and incompatible models, this may not in fact have been the case. They may have been simply addressing different *levels of explanation* of the same phenomenon.

   The following three distinct levels of explanation are of relevance to the relationship between SPD and violence; although it should be noted that the level may vary from high to low *within* each domain:

1. *Predisposing factors.* A history of alcohol/substance abuse, genetic factors, childhood variables (conduct disorder, child abuse, etc.) may be said to be distal, high-level causes that may be neither necessary nor sufficient for the occurrence of violence in adulthood. Conduct disorder, for example, is thought to predispose to *any* PD (Bernstein *et al.*, 1996), and the Johnson *et al.* (2000) study found significant relationships between PD symptoms and acts of violence that were independent of conduct disorder. It is doubtful whether these predisposing factors determine the precise outcome, in terms of risk of violence, independently of (2) and (3) below. Personality traits should be included under this category of predisposing influences. Nestor (2002), for example, has argued that risk of violence can be understood in terms of four fundamental personality dimensions: impulse control, affect regulation, narcissism and paranoid thinking.
2. *External/internal triggers or precipitants.* These are the events that precipitate an act of violence. For example, in the paranoid case, the trigger may be somebody else's actions or attitudes ('giving me a funny look'). In the case of narcissistic personality disorder, the trigger may be a demeaning comment. Coid's

(1992) example of the latter is where, during a telephone conversation with his ex-girlfriend during which he became increasingly angry and jealous, her mother interrupted with a demeaning comment about his physique. This triggered a rage reaction that resulted in the violent killing of his ex-girlfriend's new partner.

3. *Organismic variables.* These can be said to mediate the effects of predisposing factors and precipitants, and as such specify the causal *mechanisms.* They include neuropsychological variables, affective/cognitive state, and so on. This organismic level of explanation would embrace more than just neurobiological variables; it would include also those generative mechanisms that, within the critical realist tradition, are said to give people the ability to act on the world and to form models of it. Blackburn (2007) points out that these causal powers, residing in consciousness, give us 'the capacity to reason, and to think, and are most likely to be found in cognitive structures and processes' (Blackburn, 2007, p. 147).

The Use of Excessively High-Level Variables

As implied in the previous section, causal models can be expressed at a number of levels and here contributors have been criticised in their use of excessively high-level models. It is of particular relevance to this chapter that Haynes cites the use of personality variables in this respect: 'Personality variables have played a prominent role in the behavioural sciences but are particularly vulnerable to the criticism of being dysfunctionally high level' (Haynes, 1992, p. 63). The problem here is that these high-level personality variables include so many lower level variables that 'they are rendered scientifically and clinically debilitated' (p. 63). The above-mentioned personality dimensions suggested by Nestor (2002) to be risk factors for violence, for example, should be regarded as markers for lower level explanations in terms of brain function, for example neural circuits in prefrontal cortex that mediate affective self-regulation. A similar point is emphasised by Blackburn (2007). He points out that for critical realists, identifying dispositions (personality traits) is but a first step in the identification of generative mechanisms that give people their causal powers.

Another problem identified by Haynes that is relevant to discussions of PD and violence is that excessively high-level causal variables also promote inferential and measurement errors. Hence, the use of a high-level causal variable is prone to the use of the wrong assessment instrument with the wrong population under the wrong conditions and, hence, is likely to lead to error.

A Presumption of Unidirectionality

Here, the criticism is that the relationship posited between the variables in limited causal models is that it occurs only in one direction. In a bi-directional relationship, not only will A affect B but B in turn will affect A. Consider, for instance, a paranoid man who is suspicious and hostile towards his neighbours or the staff that are charged to care for him and is thereby threatening towards them. While it is clear that the man's paranoia has primacy, it is likely that those around him will, in turn, try and avoid having contact with him and that this withdrawal will be interpreted as supporting his paranoid ideation. The problem of unidirectionality in this instance is that it limits the focus and power of the intervention so that one might, in this case, focus more on the individual's social and therapeutic network, rather than on the individual himself. The possibility of a bi-directional relationship between PD and violence has recently been emphasised by Hare and colleagues in relation to psychopathy (Hare and Neumann, 2005). Emphasising that antisocial behaviour (including violence) might as well be a cause as a result of personality deviation, they state: 'It strikes us as too simplistic to assume that antisocial tendencies are merely consequences of other psychopathic features. ... Exposure to, and engagement in, antisocial acts may play a role in the development of callous, manipulative and impulsive psychopathic traits, which may then lead to further antisocial behaviour' (pp. 62–63).

A Presumed Stability or Finality in the Model

The final limitation of such causal models that we will discuss is that they are presented as a 'sufficient' or 'final' explanation for the behaviour in question. As a consequence, it is difficult (if not impossible) (a) to refine the causal pathway and (b) allow for the impact of new causal variables that were non-existent or undiscovered when the model was proposed. Those who espouse a limited causal model are therefore unlikely to be open to refining the causal construct and more likely to react defensively when presented with discomfirmatory data (Haynes, 1992, p. 66).

In addition to the above, a non-limited causal model of the PD–violence relationship should acknowledge (a) its *conditional* nature – the PD–violence relationship is necessarily constrained by boundaries or necessary conditions, such as internal states, developmental stages, temporal factors, and so on; (b) its *probabilistic* nature – a causal model of violent behaviour will always be imperfect in its ability to predict who will and will not show violent behaviour; (c) its *dynamic* nature – it is likely that multiple and cascading causal influences will operate at different critical time periods during development to determine the PD–violence relationship; and finally, (d) that causal variables may be *modifiable or unmodifiable*, so that from a clinical point of view those precipitants and predispositions relevant to the PD–violence nexus that are modifiable are of greatest clinical relevance. Knowing that someone has a genetic vulnerability to borderline personality disorder might not help the clinician in treatment decision making, but knowledge that the patient has a particular remediable brain dysfunction related to poor emotional self-regulation might be very useful.

CLINICAL AND POLITICAL CONSIDERATIONS

It may seem unfair to judge the DSPD proposal in purely scientific terms when it was largely driven by clinical and political considerations. We will briefly review these.

Clinical Considerations

Ethical considerations regarding the detention of individuals for treatment against their will for societal protection has long concerned the mental health community (Appelbaum, 1988). While it has been sanguine about the preventative detention of those with mental illness (largely on the basis that these individuals can be treated with antipsychotic medication, imposed against their will if necessary), it has been more concerned about those with PD who were preventatively detained on the basis that their tacit agreement with their treatment would be required if this is to be effective (Baker and Crichton, 1995). Over time, this 'licence to treat' has been extended to a degree that some believe has become excessive (Duggan, 2007).

For those who show this concern, the DSPD proposals must mark an advance as they place those who are being detained on a more sure scientific footing in as much as the criteria are anchored to well-accepted scientific constructs. Whether or not these expectations are realised in practice remains to be determined. Of greater importance, however, are the clinical implications for those who work in these services, given for example that the *raison d'être* for interventions within the DSPD services is now explicitly a reduction in violent reoffending. If the evidence of a link between the personality disturbance and violence is shown to be weak, one might anticipate that this will affect current service provision and delivery.

Political Considerations

We believe that it would be a fatal mistake to omit consideration of the political dimension in this discussion as, after all, politicians have a major influence in this type of policy development. Here, it is clear that the European Convention on Human Rights (enacted in the United Kingdom in 1998) must have had an influence. This liberal reforming legislation contained several articles to safeguard the rights of individuals (including those with mental disorder). Specifically, articles 3, 5 and 8 (with their caveats) are especially relevant for those detained involuntarily because of their mental disorder. These articles advanced various rights for citizens provided that they did not infringe various societal norms and that they did not suffer from various forms of mental disorder. While politicians have obligations to protect the rights of their citizens, they see themselves as having a greater obligation to safeguard their citizens against harm, with the protection from harm by mentally disordered offenders constantly figuring high on their agenda. It may not be coincidental therefore that the DSPD proposal was introduced at the same time as the European Convention was being enacted, with the politicians believing that this veneer of science might strengthen preventative detention against legal challenge. The argument in this chapter, however, is that in making the criteria explicit and causal, this may have had the reverse effect than that intended resulting in more vigorous and well-considered legal challenges.

SUMMARY AND CONCLUSIONS

In summary, there are clearly major difficulties in applying these criteria of causality to the DSPD concept as it was originally announced. The main difficulties are the following:

1. Defining the severity of PD is problematic. Defining it through sheer aggregation of PDs is not acceptable, since it has become clear from recent research that while some PDs, namely antisocial, paranoid, borderline, narcissistic, histrionic, are associated with criminal, including violent, offending, others, in particular obsessional-compulsive, are inversely related to antisociality (Howard *et al.*, 2008). The definition of 'SPD' therefore needs to be far more nuanced.
2. Suggesting a *causal* link rather than a mere association between PD and risk of violence is problematic, since, as we have attempted to show in this chapter, the conditions for establishing causality have not been met. In particular, while some PDs show covariation with risk of violence, this is not sufficient to infer a causal relationship between them. The required temporal precedence of the supposed cause (personality disorder) over the effect (violence, or risk of such) is not clearly established. Perhaps most importantly, the possibility that a third variable might account for the relationship has not been excluded. Finally, there is a need to establish a logical connection between PD and violence – one that avoids the circularity of statements like 'antisocial people behave violently' – including a specification of possible causal mechanisms to address the question 'How does PD cause violence?'
3. The very high comorbidity, both within Axis II disorders and between Axis I and Axis II disorders, muddies the waters of causation. However, it is precisely what Tyrer *et al.* (2007, p. 54) refer to as the 'morass of comorbidity' that arguably holds the key to developing a comprehensive causal model of the relationship between PD and violence.

We can conclude that while the dispositional nature of personality makes it attractive as a possible causal variable leading to subsequent violent behaviour, it is clear that the current DSPD proposal is too simplistic. Like other types of complex behaviour, violent criminal behaviour is likely to have multiple determinants, with PD accounting for a small proportion of the variance. Moreover, the dependent variable needs to be expanded to include, not only the occurrence of the violent behaviour but also its magnitude and duration as the casual factors involved may vary depending on what is being predicted (Haynes, 1992). All of this suggests that it is dangerous to assume single causes for complex phenomena, however tempting it is to do so, as these are likely to vary across individuals and situations.

All of the foregoing begs the question as to why, if there is so much theoretical evidence against limited causal models, they continue to be used? Here, the answer is clear: limited causal models are heuristically useful in specifying a single (or at most very few variables) that might be targeted within an intervention. Consequently, as more variables are incorporated in any explanation, the more difficult it will be to intervene effectively in a practical manner. Hence, there has to be a trade-off between complexity and parsimony in any causal explanation of the relationship between PD and violence. A complex explanation is likely to be accurate but have little practical utility, while a parsimonious explanation encourages interventions whose efficacy can be tested, but may be seriously misleading when applied to the population as a whole. The trick here is to strike a proper balance between accuracy and utility.

NOTES

1. These figures were ascertained by RH from the research database held by the Peaks Academic and Research Unit.
2. Moffitt, T.E., personal communication to RH, 2003.

REFERENCES

American Psychiatric Association (1994) *Diagnostic and Statistical Manual of Mental Disorders*, 4th edn, APA, Washington DC.

American Psychiatric Association (2000) *Diagnostic and Statistical Manual of Mental Disorders*, 4th edn text revision, APA, Washington DC.

Appelbaum, P.S. (1988) The new preventative detention: Psychiatry's problematic responsibility for the control of violence. *American Journal of Psychiatry*, **145**, 779–85.

Baker, E. and Crichton, J. (1995) *Ex parte* A: Psychopathy, treatability and the law. *Journal of Forensic Psychiatry*, **6**, 101–9.

Bakken, K., Landheim, A.S. and Vaglum, P. (2004). Early and late onset groups of substance misusers: Differences in primary and secondary psychiatric disorders. *Journal of Substance Use*, **9**, 224–34.

Barnett, P.A. and Gotlib, I.H. (1988) Psychosocial functioning and depression: Distinguishing among antecedents, concomitants, and consequences. *Psychological Bulletin*, **104**, 97–126.

Beck, J. and Wencel, H. (1998) Violent crime and Axis 1 psychopathology, in *Psychopathology and Violent Crime* (ed. A.E. Skodol), American Psychiatric Association, Washington DC, pp. 1–13.

Becker, D.F., Grilo, C.M., Edell, W.S. and McGlashan, T.H. (2000) Comorbidity of borderline personality disorder with other personality disorders in hospitalized adolescents and adults. *American Journal of Psychiatry*, **157**, 2011–16.

Bernstein, D.P., Cohen, P., Skodol, A. *et al.* (1996) Childhood antecedents of adolescent personality disorders. *American Journal of Psychiatry*, **153**, 907–13.

Blackburn, R. (2007) Personality disorder and antisocial deviance: comments on the debate on the structure of the Psychopathy Checklist-Revised. *Journal of Personality Disorders*, **21**, 142–59.

Cliff, N. (1983) Some cautions concerning the application of causal modelling. *Multivariate Behavioural Research*, **18**, 115–26.

Cohen, P., Crawford, T.N., Johnson, J.G. and Kasen, S. (2005) The children in the community study of developmental course of personality disorder. *Journal of Personality Disorder*, **19**, 466–86.

Coid, J. (1992) DSM-III diagnosis in criminal psychopaths: a way forward. *Criminal Behaviour and Mental Health*, **2**, 78–94.

Coid, J. (1998) Axis 2 disorders and motivation for serious criminal behaviour, in *Psychopathology and Violent Crime* (ed. A.E. Skodol), American Psychiatric Association, Washington DC, pp. 53–96.

Coid, J., Yang, M., Roberts, A. *et al.* (2006a) Violence and psychiatric morbidity in a national household population – a report from the British Household Survey. *American Journal of Epidemiology*, **164**, 1199–1208.

Coid, J., Yang, M., Roberts, A. *et al.* (2006b) Violence and psychiatric morbidity in a national household population of Britain: public health implications. *British Journal of Psychiatry*, **189**, 12–9.

Coid, J., Yang, M., Tyrer, P. *et al.* (2006c) Prevalence and correlates of personality disorder in Great Britain. *British Journal of Psychiatry*, **188**, 423–31.

Coid, J., Yang, M., Ullrich, S. *et al.* (2007) *Predicting and Understanding Risk of Re-Offending: The Prisoner Cohort Study. Research Summary*, Ministry of Justice, London.

Department of Health/Home Office (1999) *Managing Dangerous People With Severe Personality Disorder: Proposals for Policy Development*, Department of Health, London.

Department of Health/Home Office (2000) *Reforming the Mental Health Act Part II: High Risk patients*, The Stationery Office, Norwich.

Dolan, B., Evans, C. and Norton, K. (1995) Multiple axis-II diagnoses of personality disorder. *British Journal of Psychiatry*, **166**, 107–12.

DSPD Programme (2004) *Dangerous and Severe Personality Disorder (DSPD) High Secure Services. Planning & Delivery Guide*, Department of Health, Home Office, HM Prison Service, May.

Duggan, C. (2007) To treat or not to treat: should the treatability criterion for those with psychopathic disorder be abandoned? in *Treatment Without Consent: An Investigation of the Workings of the Mental Health Act* (eds I. Todd and H. Middleton), Ashgate, Aldershot, UK, pp. 91–104.

Elkin, I., Shea, M.T., Watkins, J.T. *et al.* (1989) National Institute of Mental Health treatment of depression collaborative research program: general effectiveness of treatments. *Archives of General Psychiatry*, **46**, 971–82.

Gretton, H.M., Hare, R.D. and Catchpole, R.E.H. (2004) Psychopathy and offending from adolescence to adulthood: a 10-year follow-up. *Journal of Consulting and Clinical Psychology*, **72**, 636–45.

Hare, R.D. (1991) *The Hare Psychopathy Checklist - Revised*, Multi-Health Systems, North Tonawanda, NY.

Hare, R.D. (2003) *The Hare Psychopathy Checklist – Revised*, 2nd edn, Multi-Health Systems, North Tonawanda, NY.

Hare, R.D. and Neumann, C.S. (2005) Structural models of psychopathy. *Current Psychiatry Reports*, **7**, 57–64.

Haynes, S.N. (1992) *Models of Causality in Psychopathology*. Macmillan, New York.

Howard, R.C., Huband, N., Mannion, A. and Duggan, C. (2008) Exploring the link between personality disorder and criminality in a community sample. *Journal of Personality Disorders*, **22**, 589–603.

Johnson, J.G., Cohen, P., Smailes, E. *et al.* (2000) Adolescent personality disorders associated with violence and criminal behaviour during adolescence and early adulthood. *American Journal of Psychiatry*, **157**, 1406–12.

Klosko, J.S., Barlow, D.H., Tassinari, R. and Cerny, J.A. (1990) A comparison of alpazolam and behavior therapy in treatment of panic disorder. *Journal of Consulting and Clinical Psychology*, **58**, 77–84.

Kosson, D.S., Lorenz, A.R. and Newman, J.P. (2006) Effects of comorbid psychopathy on criminal offending and emotion processing in male offenders with antisocial personality disorder. *Journal of Abnormal Psychology*, **115**, 798–806.

Moffitt, T.E., Caspi, A., Rutter, M. and Silva, P.A. (2001) *Sex Differences in Antisocial Behaviour: Conduct Disorder, Delinquency, and Violence in the Dunedin Longitudinal Study*, Cambridge University Press, Cambridge.

Nestor, P.G. (2002) Mental disorder and violence: personality dimensions and clinical features. *American Journal of Psychiatry*, **159**, 1973–8.

Nurnberg, H.G., Raskin, M., Levine, P.E. *et al.* (1991) The comorbidity of borderline personality disorder and other DSM-III-R axis II personality disorders. *American Journal of Psychiatry*, **148**, 1371–7.

Peterson, C. and Seligman, M.E.P. (1984) Causal explanations as a risk factor for depression: Theory & evidence. *Psychological Review*, **91**, 347–74.

Thatcher, D.L., Cornelius, J.R. and Clark, D.B. (2005) Adolescent alcohol use disorders predict adult personality disorder. *Addictive Behaviors*, **30**, 1709–24.

Tyrer, P., Coombs, N., Ibrahimi, F. *et al.* (2007) Critical developments in the assessment of personality disorder. *British Journal of Psychiatry*, **190** (suppl. 49), s51–59.

Vitacco, M.J., Neumann, C.S. and Jackson, R.L. (2005) Testing a four-factor model of psychopathy and its association with ethnicity, gender, intelligence, and violence. *Journal of Consulting and Clinical Psychology*, **73**, 466–76.

Watson, D.C. and Sinha, B.K. (1998) Comorbidity of DSM-IV personality disorders in a nonclinical sample. *Journal of Clinical Psychology*, **54**, 773–80.

Watzke, S., Ullrich, S. and Marneros, A. (2006) Gender- and violence-related prevalence of mental disorders in prisoners. *European Archives of Psychiatry and Clinical Neuroscience*, **256**, 414–21.

World Health Organisation (1992) *10th Revision of the International Classification of Diseases (ICD-10)*, WHO, Geneva.

Zimmerman, M., Rothschild, L. and Chelminski, I. (2005) The prevalence of DSM-IV personality disorders in psychiatric outpatients. *American Journal of Psychiatry*, **162**, 1911–8.

PART I

TRAITS

Chapter 3

A SYSTEMATIC REVIEW OF THE RELATIONSHIP BETWEEN CHILDHOOD IMPULSIVENESS AND LATER VIOLENCE[1]

DARRICK JOLLIFFE
University of Leicester, UK

DAVID P FARRINGTON
University of Cambridge, UK

Impulsiveness is one of many terms in the literature that refers to a general reduction in the ability to control one's behaviour. Other similar terms include low
self-control, hyperactivity, inattention, a poor ability to delay gratification, risk-
taking, sensation seeking and not considering the consequences before acting.
There are differences in the specific definitions of many of these terms, but it is safe
to say that a relationship has been identified between these variables and poor life
outcomes such as smoking (Burke *et al.*, 2007), gambling (Clarke, 2006), drinking
(Af Klinteberg *et al.*, 1993) and offending (White *et al.*, 1994).

High impulsiveness might contribute to an increased likelihood of offending
either directly or indirectly. By the direct pathway, impulsiveness would have a
fundamental impact on the way in which an individual would act in any given
situation. With less time and cognitive energy available for contemplation of potential responses, an impulsive individual would, on balance, select the option that
provides the most immediate perceived benefit. Numerous researchers and theorists have detailed how criminal offending tends to satisfy immediate urges at the
risk of later, uncertain and occasionally hypothetical consequences (e.g. Farrington
and Welsh, 2007; Gottfredson and Hirschi, 1990).

This direct conceptualisation of impulsiveness comprises the backbone of two
of the most influential theories in criminology. Wilson and Herrnstein (1985) developed a criminological theory that was based on the premise that individuals
differ in their underlying criminal tendencies, and that whether a person chooses

to commit a crime in a situation depends on whether the perceived benefits of offending are considered to outweigh the perceived costs. Wilson and Herrnstein (1985) argued that those with a significant degree of impulsiveness are more likely to commit offences because their calculation of the costs and benefits of offending will be biased by their desire for immediate reinforcement. That is, an impulsive individual gives the most weight to the benefits of offending which offer instant rewards (e.g. material gain, peer approval, etc.) and will be less influenced by the potential costs of offending (e.g. risk of being apprehended, loss of reputation or employment, etc.).

The General Theory of Crime proposed by Gottfredson and Hirschi (1990) is similar to the theory of Wilson and Herrnstein in the importance that it places on impulsiveness as a key explanatory feature. Gottfredson and Hirschi (1990) called this 'low self-control', which referred to the extent to which individuals were vulnerable to the temptations of the moment. People with low self-control were impulsive, took risks, had low cognitive and academic skills, were self-centred, had low empathy and had short time horizons. Hence, they found it hard to defer gratification, and their decisions to offend were insufficiently influenced by the future possible painful consequences of offending.

Other researchers have suggested that high impulsiveness may also contribute to an increased likelihood of offending indirectly through a person-environment interaction (e.g. Moffitt, 1993). For example, an impulsive child may prove a challenge to even the most conscientious parent, over time eliciting poor parenting, in itself an established risk factor for later offending (Farrington and Welsh, 2007). Similarly, impulsivity may lead to offending by reducing the likelihood of school success. Typically, formal education is delivered in a restrictive environment that might prove very difficult for those who are impulsive. Children who have low school achievement are more likely to drop out of school and are more likely to become socio-economically disadvantaged. With reduced opportunity to succeed in conventional ways, these individuals may be more likely to turn to antisocial or criminal methods to obtain rewards.

Therefore, either by directly influencing how individuals make decisions in criminal opportunities or by indirectly influencing their interactions with important individuals or institutions (or perhaps in both ways concurrently), impulsiveness can lead to an increase in the likelihood of offending.

PREVIOUS REVIEWS OF THE RELATIONSHIP BETWEEN IMPULSIVENESS AND OFFENDING

There have been previous reviews of the empirical relationship between measures of impulsiveness and offending. Pratt and Cullen (2000) undertook a review and meta-analysis to empirically test the relationship between low self-control and crime. For their review, low self-control was operationalised using the definition provided by Gottfredson and Hirschi (1990) in their influential General Theory of Crime; that is, someone who is 'impulsive, insensitive, physical as opposed to mental, risk-taking, short-sighted and non-verbal' (Gottfredson and Hirschi, 1990, p. 90). Pratt and Cullen (2000) analysed the results of 21 empirical studies and found that low self-control was a strong predictor of crime (mean effect size (d) in the range of 0.47–0.58).

A number of methods of interpreting the magnitude of effect sizes have been proposed (Lipsey and Wilson, 2001). A widely used convention is that proposed by Cohen (1988). An effect size of about 0.20 is considered small, while an effect size of around 0.50 is considered medium and an effect size greater than 0.80 is considered large. However, this convention seems too conservative. A more meaningful way of interpreting an effect size can be provided by converting the results to the differences in proportions who are impulsive between those who are or are not violent. First, the standardised mean effect size (d) is converted to a phi correlation r.[2] This results in an r value of approximately half that of d, and this value of r or phi is, in turn, equal to the difference in proportions between the two groups (Farrington and Loeber, 1989). Therefore, the d value of 0.47 of Pratt and Cullen (2000) corresponds approximately to 73% of offenders having low self-control compared to 50% of non-offenders (difference in proportions = 0.23).

The most relevant aspect of self-control in this review was termed attitudinal self-control and this was often measured with the Grasmick self-control scale (Grasmick et al., 1993), which provides an operationalisation of self-control from the perspective of Gottfredson and Hirschi (1990). However, limitations of this measure are that it does not allow for the separation of hyperactivity, impulsiveness and inattention, and it is not possible to separate these features of impulsiveness from a number of other concepts which comprise this definition of self-control (e.g. lack of sympathy).

Another review was undertaken by Pratt et al. (2002) who examined the relationship of attention deficit hyperactivity disorder (ADHD) to crime and delinquency. Variables related to ADHD were identified in 20 empirical studies and mean effect sizes were calculated. For the overall measure of ADHD, the mean effect size was found to be $d = 0.31$ (95% CI 0.27–0.36). Usefully, Pratt et al. (2002) disaggregated the ADHD construct into four sub-categories (attention deficit (AD) excluding hyperactivity, AD plus hyperactivity, hyperactivity, and an additional category for ADHD combination or index concepts such as attention problems or emotional or behavioural problems which are often cited as proxies of AD or ADHD) and examined their relationships to crime and delinquency. The mean effect sizes of the different categories can be seen in Table 3.1. The AD excluding hyperactivity category had the strongest relationship with crime and delinquency, and the ADHD combination/index concepts category had the weakest relationship, but none of the categories was significantly different.[3] Pratt et al. (2002) concluded that ADHD in its various forms appeared to have a general effect on crime and delinquency.

A major limitation of these reviews is that, because they included studies where the key construct (self-control/ADHD) was assessed retrospectively, it was not possible to determine causal ordering. That is, self-control or ADHD might contribute to an increased likelihood of offending, but it is also possible that delinquent activity may cause a reduction in people's self-control or make them more impulsive and hyperactive. The precise form of causal ordering can only be established in prospective longitudinal studies where impulsiveness is measured before offending.

Another limitation of these reviews from the perspective of this volume is that they did not allow the relationship between impulsiveness and violence

Table 3.1 Relationship between measures of ADHD and offending

	Mean effect	Lower	Upper
Measures of ADHD	Size (d)	CI	CI
AD (excluding hyperactivity)	0.53	0.24	0.84
AD (including hyperactivity)	0.16	0.06	0.26
Hyperactivity	0.29	0.12	0.46
ADHD combination/index concepts	0.16	−0.06	0.39

Source: Pratt *et al.* (2002)

(specifically) to be investigated. Violence is an important area of enquiry as violent crime is generally considered more serious than other forms of criminal behaviour, because of the harm to the victim of the violence as well as the greater costs incurred by society (Dowden, Blanchette and Serin, 1999). Violent offenders comprise a relatively small proportion of the total number of offenders, but research has found that this group commits a disproportionate amount of both violent and non-violent crime (e.g. Wolfgang, Figlio and Sellin, 1972). In many ways, violent offenders are similar to frequent offenders (Farrington, 1991). A small fraction of the population commits a large fraction of all violent offences. For example, in two large prospective longitudinal studies in the United States, 14–15% of the samples committed 75–82% of all violent offences (Thornberry, Huizinga and Loeber, 1995). Therefore, if impulsivity (measured prospectively) was found to have a relationship with violence, this could suggest methods of intervention that could have the potential to reduce the commission of not only violence but also a large number of other non-violent offences.

Within a larger study examining a wealth of predictors of youth violence, Hawkins *et al.* (1998) reviewed the relationship between measures of impulsiveness and later violence. Importantly, all of the studies included within their review were longitudinal studies. This reduced the number of studies eligible for inclusion to six. In order to aid interpretation of the findings, the authors also separated the impulsivity construct into meaningful categories. These included hyperactivity/low attention, concentration problems, restlessness and risk-taking. This review is the most relevant to this volume.

The results showed that the largest mean effect was for the relationship between risk-taking and violence ($d = 0.50$), followed by restlessness ($d = 0.40$) and concentration problems ($d = 0.34$), with hyperactivity/low attention having the weakest relationship with violence ($d = 0.26$). Hawkins *et al.*, 1998, p. 112) concluded that 'regardless of measurement methods used, there appears to be a consistent relationship between hyperactivity and later violent behavior'.

THE CURRENT INVESTIGATION

The purpose of this review is to update and elaborate upon the findings of Hawkins *et al.* (1998) with the additional restriction of limiting our search to those obtained in prospective longitudinal studies of community samples of individuals.[4] This will provide the best possible assessment of the relationship between early impulsiveness and later violence, and also should be generalisable to the population at large. Also, efforts were made to code factors that might influence the relationship between impulsivity and violence. For example, at what age was impulsivity measured, and was violence measured by self-reports or official records?

Study Objectives

1. To characterise (and as far as possible quantify) the evidence to date on the relationship between early measures of impulsiveness and later violence using only prospective longitudinal studies of large (several hundreds) community samples.
2. To characterise (and as far as possible quantify) the potential mediators and moderators of the relationships identified in 1 above. For example, the results might be influenced by the type of impulsiveness measured (e.g. motor restlessness versus concentration difficulties), the method of measuring impulsiveness (teacher versus self-report) or the length of time between the assessment of impulsiveness and the assessment of violence.

Inclusion Criteria

Our strategy was to identify and analyse the results from only the highest quality studies. Below are the criteria that were used for including a study in the current review:

1. The data must be derived from a prospective longitudinal study of a community sample of at least several hundreds, including at least two personal interviews.
2. In the prospective longitudinal study, there must have been a measure of impulsiveness (broadly defined) that temporally preceded a measure of violence.
3. In order to assess the impact of impulsiveness on later violence, the measure of impulsiveness needed to be made in childhood or early adolescence (i.e. before the age of 14).
4. A quantitative measure of violence (official records or self-reports) was needed, and this measure needed to be presented in a way that allowed the effect size of early impulsiveness on later violence to be calculated.

Measures of impulsiveness included parent, teacher and self-reports of impulsive behaviour (e.g. failing to complete tasks, lacks concentration, fidgets, etc.). Personality scales designed to measure impulsiveness were also eligible for inclusion (e.g. Eysenck Impulsivity Scale; Eysenck and Eysenck, 1977); however, psychomotor tasks such as the Trail Making Test (Ruorke and Finlayson, 1975) and time perception tasks were not included. This decision was made because these measures have not shown a consistent relationship with delinquency, and they also have been demonstrated to overlap somewhat with measures of intelligence (e.g. White *et al.*, 1994).

Search Strategy

Because of the restrictive nature of this review, the strategy of searching for studies was not that of a usual systematic review (Farrington and Petrosino, 2001). The search focused on the 30 prospective community-based longitudinal studies with personal interviews that were known to have a measurement of violence (see Farrington, 2007; Farrington and Welsh, 2007). Articles authored by the main contributor to the study and by researchers who have contributed to the longitudinal studies were searched. Main contributors and associated researchers were also contacted via email and asked for assistance in drawing our attention to appropriate citations in the literature or by making data available.

Of the 30 longitudinal studies identified, 24 were excluded (see Table 3.2). Fifteen of these were excluded because we could not locate a measure of childhood or early adolescent impulsivity. For another six studies, there was some indication of impulsivity having been assessed, but it was not possible to find results relating this to later violence.[5] For three studies, we were informed by the lead contributor or associated researcher that the information we required, while available in principle, was not in a format that was available in practice.

Only six longitudinal studies provided relevant data. These were the Cambridge Study in Delinquent Development (Farrington *et al.*, 2006), the New York State Longitudinal Study (Johnson *et al.*, 2004), the Pittsburgh Youth Study (Loeber *et al.*, 2008), the Seattle Social Development Study (Herrenkohl *et al.*, 2000), the Orebro Project in Sweden (Af Klinteberg *et al.*, 1993) and the Dunedin Multidisciplinary Health and Development Study in New Zealand (Moffitt *et al.*, 2001).

Brief Descriptions of Included Studies

In the Cambridge Study in Delinquent Development, 411 South London boys were followed up from age 8 to 48. In the New York State Longitudinal Study, 976 randomly sampled mothers in two upstate New York counties with a child aged 1–10 were interviewed in 1975, and the children were interviewed at an average age of 30. In the Pittsburgh Youth Studies, three cohorts of boys (each comprising about 500 boys) aged 7, 10 and 13 were followed up to ages 19–25. In the Seattle Social Development Project, 808 children aged 10 were followed up to age 30. In the Orebro Project, 1027 children aged 10 were followed up to age 43–45. In the Dunedin Study, 1037 children were first assessed at age 3 and followed up to age 32.

The key features of the included studies as they relate to the current research are shown in Table 3.3.[6] For example, Farrington (2007) collected information about two measures of impulsiveness which were assessed between the ages of 8 and 10. These impulsivity measures were then compared to self-reported violence between the ages of 15 and 18 and official violence between the ages of 10 and 20 as measures of youth violence. Adult violence was measured by self-reported violence between the ages of 27 and 32 and official violence between the ages of 21 and 40. One measure of impulsiveness (poor concentration) was based on teacher reports of the boy lacking concentration or being restless. The other measure of

Table 3.2 Excluded studies[a]

Major contributors	Study name	Reason for exclusion
Bor, Najman	Mater University Study of Pregnancy	Not possible to identify measures of impulsiveness related to later violence
Denno, Piquero, Buka	National Collaborative Perinatal Project	Not possible to identify measures of impulsiveness
Elliott, Huizinga	National Youth Survey	Not possible to identify measures of impulsiveness
Eron, Huesmann, Dubow	Columbia County Study	Not possible to identify measures of impulsiveness
Fergusson, Horwood	Christchurch Health and Development Study	Not possible to identify measures of impulsiveness related to later violence
Huizinga, Esbensen	Denver Youth Study	Informed by lead contributor that information is not currently available
Janson, Wikstrom	Stockholm Project Metropolitan	Not possible to identify measures of impulsiveness
Kellam, Ensminger, McCord	Woodlawn Project	Not possible to identify measures of impulsiveness
Kolvin, Miller	Newcastle Thousand Island Study	Not possible to identify measures of impulsiveness
Laub, Sampson	Glueck Longitudinal Study	Not possible to identify measures of impulsiveness
LeBlanc	Montreal Two-Samples Longitudinal Study	Informed by lead contributor that information is not currently available
Mednick, Moffitt, Brennan, Hodgins	Danish Birth Cohort Studies	Impulsiveness assessed only among select sample and impulsiveness assessed retrospectively
McCord	Cambridge–Somerville Youth Study	Not possible to identify measures of impulsiveness
Patterson, Dishion, Capaldi	Oregon Youth Study	Not possible to identify measures of impulsiveness related to later violence
Pulkkinen	Jyvaskyla Longitudinal Study of Personality and Social Development	Not possible to identify measures of impulsiveness related to later violence
Raine, Venables Mednick	Mauritius Joint Child Health Project	Not possible to identify measures of impulsiveness
Rasanen	Northern Finland Birth Cohort Study	Not possible to identify measures of impulsiveness
Thornberry, Lizotte, Krohn	Rochester Youth Development Study	Informed by lead contributor that information is not currently available
Tolan, Gorman-Smith, Henry	Chicago Youth Development Study	Not possible to identify measures of impulsiveness
Tremblay	Montreal Longitudinal-Experimental Study	Not possible to identify measures of impulsiveness related to later violence

(*Continued*)

Table 3.2   Excluded studies[a] (*Continued*)

Major contributors	Study name	Reason for exclusion
Wadsworth, Douglas	National Survey of Health and Development	Not possible to identify measures of impulsiveness
Werner, Smith	Kauai Longitudinal Study	Not possible to identify measures of impulsiveness related to later violence
Wolf, Hogh	Copenhagen Project Metropolitan	Not possible to identify measures of impulsiveness
Wolfgang, Figilo, Thornberry, Tracy	Philadelphia Birth Cohort Studies	Not possible to identify measures of impulsiveness

[a] For references to these studies, see Farrington and Welsh (2007).

impulsiveness, high daring, was based on a combination of parent reports of the child's taking many risks and peer ratings of who was the most daring.

Some of the studies included multiple measures of impulsiveness that were compared to later violence. For example, the study by Af Klinteberg *et al.* (1993) included poor concentration and motor restlessness at age 13, and the Herrenkohl *et al.* (2000) project included hyperactivity based on parental and teacher reports, both measured at age 10 as well as a self-report measure of risk-taking at age 14. Other studies that were included had only one measure of impulsivity, and these tended to be more global measures of ADHD. For example, both the Pittsburgh Youth Study and the Dunedin Study used reports by caretakers and youths (Pittsburgh) or by caretakers, teachers and youths (Dunedin) to make an assessment of ADHD. The measure of impulsiveness was taken at eight ages among the seven studies, varying from age 5 to age 13 ($M = 10.8$).

Of the seven studies (Pittsburgh contributes two studies for the oldest and youngest samples), one provided information about the relationship between a measure of impulsiveness and self-reported offending (Herrenkohl *et al.*, 2000), two provided information about the relationship between a measure of impulsiveness and official offending (Cohen, 2008; Af Klinteberg *et al.*, 1993), two provided information about the relationship between a measure of impulsiveness and both self-reported and official offending separately (Farrington, 2007; Moffitt, 2008) and two provided information about the relationship between a measure of impulsiveness and a combined measure of self-reports and official records (Loeber *et al.*, 2008).

The ages when violence was assessed also varied from study to study, and also varied within study depending on whether self-reports or official records were used. For example, in the study by Farrington (2007), youth violence was measured between the ages of 10 and 20 in official records and between 15 and 17 for self-reports. Similarly, in the study by Moffitt (2008), official records of violence were available between the years of 13 and 32 and self-reports of violence were available between the ages of 17 and 18.

An analysis that compared the length of time covered by studies that used official records compared to those that used self-reports demonstrated that those that

Table 3.3 Key features of included studies

Study name, citation	N males / females	Measure of impulsiveness	Measure of violence
Cambridge Study in Delinquent Development, Farrington, 2007	411 M	Two measures were available at ages 8 to 10. 1. High daring – based on parent and peer reports (e.g. boy takes risks: climbing, traffic exploring; peers – who is the most daring). 2. Lacks concentration – based on teacher report (e.g. Does the boy lack concentration or is he restless?)	Self-report Available at 15–18 Available at 27–32 Convictions Available at 10–20 Available at 21–40
Orebro Project, Af Klinteberg et al., 1993	540 M	Two measures were available at age 13. 1. Motor restlessness – based on teacher reports (e.g. boy finds it difficult to sit during lessons, fidgets, talkative, noisy). 2. Concentration difficulties – based on teacher reports (e.g. boy cannot concentrate on work, often daydreams and usually gives up quickly).	Convictions for violence between the ages of 15 and 26
Seattle Social Development Study, Herrenkohl et al., 2000	715 M/F	Two measures were available at age 10. 1. Hyperactive – based on teachers report (e.g. boy/girl fails to finish things, poor concentration/attention, restless/hyperactive, fidgets, difficulty with directions, inattentive/easily distracted, fails to do assignments).	Self-report at ages 17 to 18 'Hit a teacher', 'picked a fight' 3+ times, 'hit someone with intent of hurting him or her' 3+ times, 'threatened someone with a weapon', 'used force or threats of force to get things from others', 'beat someone so badly they required medical attention'

(Continued)

Table 3.3 Key features of included studies (*Continued*)

Study name, citation	N males/females	Measure of impulsiveness	Measure of violence
		2. Hyperactive – based on parents report (e.g. boy/girl can't concentrate, daydreams, demands attention, impulsive). An additional measure was available at age 14. 3. Risk-taking – based on self-report (e.g. it is fun to do things that you are not supposed to do).	Combination of self-reports and convictions available at ages 17–19
Pittsburgh Youth Study, Loeber *et al.*, 2008 – Youngest Sample	503 M	One measure was available at two age ranges (7–9 and 13–15). This was the number of ADHD symptoms based on caretaker and self-report (e.g. fidgets and squirms, difficulty staying seated, easily distracted, difficulty waiting turn, blurts out answers, does not follow instructions, difficulty sustaining attention, shifts activity, difficulty playing quietly, talks excessively, interrupts, does not listen, loses things, dangerous activities). This was dichotomised into the top 25% compared to the remaining 75%.	Self-reports Robbery, attacking to hurt or kill, forced sex Convictions Robbery, aggravated assault, aggravated indecent assault, homicide, forcible rape, involuntary deviate sexual intercourse or spousal assault
Pittsburgh Youth Study, Loeber *et al.*, 2008 – Oldest Sample	507M	One measure was available at 13–15. This was the number of ADHD symptoms based on caretaker report (e.g. fidgets and squirms, difficulty staying seated, easily distracted, difficulty waiting turn, blurts out answers, does not follow instructions, difficulty sustaining attention, shifts activity, difficulty playing quietly, talks excessively, interrupts, does not listen, loses things, dangerous activities). This was dichotomised into the top 25% compared to the remaining 75%.	Combination of self-reports and convictions available at ages 17–19 and 20–25

Study	N (M/F)	Measures	Outcome
New York State Longitudinal Study, Cohen, 2008	760 M/F	Two measures were available at different ages. Maternal report of distractibility of child age about 5. Maternal and youth report of symptoms of AD disorder at age about 13.	Self-reports: Robbery, attacking to hurt or kill, forced sex. Convictions: Robbery, aggravated assault, aggravated indecent assault, homicide, forcible rape, involuntary deviate sexual intercourse or spousal assault. Arrested and charged with a violent offence up to age 28
Dunedin Multidisciplinary Health and Development Study, Moffitt, 2008	1037 M/F	One measure was available and was assessed at age 11, 13 and 15. This was an assessment of ADHD (at any of the three above ages) based on maternal, teacher and self-reported items.	Self-report at ages 17–18: 'Attacked someone you lived with with weapon, hit person you live with this year attacked to seriously hurt or kill, hit someone to hurt them, strongarm robbery this year, involved in gang fights this year, threatened for sex. Convictions up to age 32: Aggravated assault, simple assault, robbery, rape and arson

used official records tended to have average periods of at risk time of 14.2 years (sd = 4.20) compared to that of 2.3 years (sd = 1.7) for those that used self-reports. This difference was significant ($t = 7.9$, $p < 0.0001$).[7] Typically, self-reported offending is available for a more limited time period, because this method is more constrained by the costs of obtaining interviews to get information from participants and by limitations in the accuracy of the recall of self-reported offending over greater time periods (Jolliffe et al., 2003).

Calculation of Effect Sizes

The standardised mean difference (d) was used as the measure of effect size (Lipsey and Wilson, 2001). Given two measures of impulsivity (daring and lacks concentration) and two measures of violence (official and self-reported) at two ages (youth and adult), it was possible to calculate eight effect sizes for the Cambridge Study in Delinquent Development. These along with the effect sizes from other studies, which were calculated or available in the other studies, can be seen in Table 3.4. Overall, a total of 23 effect sizes were available. The greatest effect size was found in the Af Klinteberg et al. (1993) study for the combined measure of concentration difficulties and motor restlessness when compared to convictions for violence between the ages of 15 and 26 ($d = -1.1$). The smallest effect size was found for Farrington (2007) when poor concentration was compared to self-reports of violence between the ages of 27 and 32 ($d = -0.20$). Overall, 17 of the 23 effect sizes were statistically significant, and 10 were greater than 0.50, which corresponds to 50% of non-violent persons versus at least 75% of violent persons being impulsive.

Because many of the effect sizes that were derived were not independent (e.g. eight effect sizes from Farrington, 2007, four from Loeber et al., 2008), strictly speaking it is not appropriate to undertake a meta-analysis including all effect sizes.[8] Instead, meta-analysis was used to address specific questions about the nature of the relationship between early impulsiveness and later violence. Below are the key questions that could be addressed.

What was the Relationship Between Childhood Impulsiveness and Later Official Violence?

Five out of the six studies contributed an effect size to this analysis.[9] Decisions about which effect size to include were made for four out of the five studies. Six effect sizes were selected based on their similarity in the type of measurement of impulsiveness and in order to maximise the separation between the dates of assessment of impulsiveness and later official violence. The effect sizes selected for this analysis can be seen in Table 3.5, along with the overall mean effect size.

The weighted mean effect size in a fixed effects model is obtained by adding each effect size multiplied by its inverse variance, and dividing this sum by the sum of the inverse variance weights (Lipsey and Wilson, 2001). For the six comparisons included in this analysis, the mean effect size using a fixed effect model was

Table 3.4 Effect sizes for the relationship between impulsiveness and violence

Citation	Measure of impulsiveness	Measure of offending Self-report/official record	*d*	95% CI
Farrington, 2007	*Youth violence*			
	Lacks concentration at 8–10	SR (Ages 15–18)	0.25	−0.05–0.59
		OR (Ages 10–20)	0.59*	0.19–0.99
	High daring at 8–10	SR (Ages 15–18)	0.74*	0.46–1.04
		OR (Ages 10–20)	0.81*	0.43–1.21
	Adult violence			
	Lacks concentration at 8–10	SR (Ages 27–32)	−0.20	−0.66–0.22
		OR (Ages 21–40)	0.32	−0.05–0.72
	High daring at 8–10	SR (Ages 27–32)	0.29	−0.05–0.60
		OR (Ages 21–40)	0.41*	0.05–0.76
Af Klinteberg *et al.* (1993)	Motor restlessness at 13	OR (Ages 15–26)	0.93*	0.50–1.36
	Concentration difficulties at 13	OR (Ages 15–26)	0.96*	0.53–1.39
	Combined measure at 13	OR (Ages 15–26)	1.1*	0.57–1.63
Herrenkohl *et al.* (2000)	Hyperactive-teacher rating at 10	SR (Ages 17–18)	0.43*	0.22–0.63
	Hyperactive-parent rating at 10	SR (Ages 17–18)	0.28*	0.10–0.46
	Hyperactive-combined at 10	SR (Ages 17–18)	0.35*	0.11–0.60
	Risk-Taking at 14	SR (Ages 17–18)	0.64*	0.40–0.87
Loeber *et al.* (2008)	*Youngest sample*			
	ADHD symptoms at 7–9	SR+OR (Ages 17–19)	0.14	−0.25–0.52
	ADHD symptoms at 13–15	SR+OR (Ages 17–19)	0.28	−0.15–0.70
Loeber *et al.* (2008)	*Oldest sample*			
	ADHD symptoms at 13–15	SR+OR (Ages 17–19)	0.36*	0.11–0.61
	ADHD symptoms at 13–15	SR+OR (Ages 20–25)	0.14*	−0.15–0.44
Cohen (2008)	Distractibility at 5	OR (Ages 13–28)	0.62*	0.13–1.1
	Mother, youth ADD at 13	OR (Ages 13–28)	0.73*	0.37–1.09
Moffitt (2008)	ADHD at 11, 13 or 15	SR (Ages 17–18)	0.34*	0.05–0.64
		OR (Ages 13–32)	0.90*	0.56–1.24

*$p < 0.05$.

Table 3.5   Relationship between impulsiveness and later official violence (maximum difference between assessment of impulsiveness and later violence)

Citation	d	95% CI
Farrington, 2007	0.32	−0.05–0.72
Af Klinteberg et al., 1993	1.10	0.57–1.63
Cohen, 2008	0.62	0.13–1.1
Loeber et al., 2008 (Youngest sample)	0.14	−0.25–0.52
Loeber et al., 2008 (Oldest sample)	0.14	−0.15–0.44
Moffitt, 2008	0.90	0.56–1.24
Fixed effects (6)	**0.46**	**0.31–0.62**
Random effects (6)	**0.51**	**0.19–0.83**
Q between groups $= 20.2, p < 0.001$		

$d = 0.46$ (95% CI 0.31–0.62). The corresponding z-value of 5.83 calculated for this mean effect size is significant at the $p < 0.0001$ level. The weighted mean effect size in a random effects model is the sum of each effect size multiplied by its inverse variance (modified by an additional random effects variance component to reduce the heterogeneity of the studies), dividing this sum by the sum of the inverse variance weights. For the six comparisons included in this analysis, the mean effect size using a random effects model was $d = 0.51$ (95% CI 0.19–0.83). The corresponding z-value of 3.13 calculated for this mean effect size is significant at the $p < 0.002$ level. Converting these standardised mean effect sizes to the difference in proportions (see earlier), this is approximately equivalent to a 23–26% difference. This means that between 73–76% of violent offenders would be considered impulsive compared to 50% of those without violent offences.

The heterogeneity (Q) of this sample of six studies was calculated to determine if the variability across effect sizes was greater than would be expected from sampling error alone. The resulting Q value of 20.2 (5 df) was significant at the $p < 0.001$ level. Therefore, the variance of these samples of effect size measures was greater than would be expected from sampling error alone. Although some of this variance may have been random, or result from random differences between the studies, a certain amount of the variability might be explained using some of the methodological features of the comparisons.

Because the impact of impulsiveness may change over time, it was considered important to assess the length of time that had elapsed between the assessment of impulsiveness and the assessment of official violence. The average minimum distance between the assessment of impulsivity and the age range of official violence was 5.6 years with a range from 0–12 years. The average maximum distance was 17.8 years with a range of 10.5–31 years.

The next analysis was undertaken to assess the impact of selecting effect sizes based on the maximum time between the assessment of impulsivity and the official record of violence. This was undertaken by conducting another analysis, but instead of selecting effect sizes based on the maximum difference (see Table 3.5), effect sizes were selected that minimised this difference. This resulted in a different effect size from Farrington (2007), Cohen (2008) and two different effect sizes for Loeber et al. (2008) (see Table 3.6).

Table 3.6 Relationship between impulsiveness and later official violence (minimum difference between assessment of impulsiveness and later violence)

Citation	d	95% CI
Farrington, 2007	0.59	0.19–0.99
Af Klinteberg *et al.*, 1993	1.10	0.57–1.63
Cohen, 2008	0.73	0.37–1.09
Loeber *et al.*, 2008 (Youngest sample)	0.28	−0.15–0.70
Loeber *et al.*, 2008 (Oldest sample)	0.36	0.11–0.61
Moffitt, 2008	0.90	0.56–1.24
Fixed effects (6)	**0.59**	**0.45–0.74**
Random effects (6)	**0.63**	**0.39–0.87**
Q Between Groups = 12.6, $p < 0.03$		

When the time between impulsiveness and official violence was minimised, the mean effect size for the fixed effects model was found to be $d = 0.59$ (95% CI 0.45–0.74), and it was $d = 0.63$ (95% CI 0.39–0.87) for the random effects model. Both of these effect sizes were statistically significant. This corresponds to a difference in proportions of about 30%. For this analysis, the average minimum distance between the assessment of impulsivity and the age range of official violence was 1.3 years with a range from 0 to 2.5 years. The average maximum time difference was 11 years with a range of 4.5–19 years. Comparing the results presented in Tables 3.5 and 3.6 suggests that, as might be expected, the relationship between impulsiveness and violence appears stronger when assessed closer together.

What Was the Relationship between Impulsiveness and Later Self-Reported Violence?

Four out of the six studies contributed an effect size to this analysis. Decisions about which effect size to include were made for three out of the four studies. Five effect sizes were selected based on their similarity in the type of measurement of impulsiveness and in order to maximise the separation between the point of assessment of impulsiveness and later self-reported violence. The effect sizes selected for this analysis can be seen in Table 3.7, along with the overall mean effect size.

Table 3.7 Relationship between impulsiveness and later self-reported violence

Citation	d	95% CI
Farrington, 2007	−0.20	−0.66–0.22
Herrenkohl *et al.*, 2000	0.35	0.11–0.60
Loeber *et al.*, 2008 (Youngest sample)	0.14	−0.25–0.52
Loeber *et al.*, 2008 (Oldest sample)	0.14	−0.15–0.44
Moffitt, 2008	0.34	0.05–0.64
Fixed effects (5)	**0.22**	**0.08–0.36**
Random effects (5)	**0.20**	**0.04–0.37**
Q between groups = 5.6, n.s.		

Table 3.8 Summary of results

	d	95% CI
Official violence maximum time difference		
Fixed effects (6)	0.46	0.31–0.62
Random effects (6)	0.51	0.19–0.83
Official violence minimum time difference		
Fixed effects (6)	0.59	0.45–0.74
Random effects (6)	0.63	0.39–0.87
Self-reported violence		
Fixed effects (5)	0.22	0.08–0.36
Random effects (5)	0.20	0.04–0.37

When impulsiveness and self-reports were compared, the mean effect size for the fixed effects model was found to be $d = 0.22$ (95% CI 0.08–0.36). For the random effects model it was $d = 0.20$ (95% CI 0.04–0.37). Both of these effect sizes were statistically significant. This corresponds to a difference in proportions of between 10 and 11% of impulsiveness between violent offenders and those who were not violent. The resulting Q value of 5.6 (df = 5) was not significant, suggesting that all of the effect sizes included in the analysis estimate the same population effect size. For this analysis, the average minimum time between the assessment of impulsivity and the age range of official violence was 8.7 years with a range from 4 to 18 years. The average maximum time difference was 11.5 years with a range of 5–23 years.

It would have been useful to undertake a similar analysis to that conducted with official violence above, where effect sizes were chosen based on proximity between assessment of impulsivity and self-reported violence, but this was not possible. The only change would have been a different effect size for Farrington (2007). Loeber et al. (2008) could also have changed, but these effects include both SR and OR and would be exactly the same as the changes made in the previous analysis of official violence.

The standard mean effect sizes for the results from the comparison of later official violence and self-reports are summarised in Table 3.8. The mean effect sizes show that there might be a stronger relationship between impulsiveness and later official violence compared to later self-reports. However, this comparison was only significant when the relationship between impulsiveness and later self-reports was compared to impulsiveness and later official violence with minimum time difference between the assessment of impulsiveness and the search of official records. This can be seen by the fact that the confidence intervals for official violence minimum time difference do not overlap with those of self-reported violence. This difference might be explained by the greater time periods participants were 'at risk' of an official record compared to being 'at risk' for a self-report, as pointed out earlier.

What is the Relationship Between Daring/Risk-Taking and Later Self-Reported Violence?

In both Farrington (2007) and Herrenkohl et al. (2000) effect sizes comparing a specific type of impulsiveness, daring or risk-taking, to later self-reported violence were available. Table 3.9 shows these effect sizes and the weighted mean effect

Table 3.9 Relationship between daring/risk-taking and later self-reported violence

Citation	d	95% CI
Farrington, 2007	0.74	0.46–1.04
Herrenkohl *et al.*, 2000	0.64	0.40–0.87
Fixed effects (2)	**0.68**	**0.50–0.86**
Random effects (2)	**0.68**	**0.50–0.86**
Q between groups = 0.3, n.s.		

size for the two studies combined. Overall, the mean effect size for both the fixed effects and random effects model was found to be $d = 0.68$ (95% CI 0.50–0.86), and these were both statistically significant at the $p < 0.0001$ level. This corresponds to a difference in proportions of approximately 34%.

From comparing the mean effect sizes in Table 3.7 to those of Table 3.8 it can be seen that the confidence intervals (0.04–0.37 and 0.50–0.86) do not overlap, indicating a statistically significant difference. This suggests that high daring and risk-taking was significantly more likely to be related to later self-reported violence compared to the other measures of impulsiveness.

DISCUSSION

The results of the systematic review and meta-analysis suggest that measures of impulsiveness taken in childhood (as early as age 5) were significantly related to later violence. However, the magnitude of this relationship depended on a number of factors, with one of the most important being how violence was measured. Studies that measured violence using official records tended to show a stronger relationship than those using self-reports. Also, studies in which the assessment of impulsiveness and the assessment of violence were closer together in time yielded greater effect sizes than those with larger gaps between impulsiveness assessment and assessment of violence. It would be interesting to specify the functional relationship between the effect size and the time difference, but we cannot do this on the basis of our small number of studies.

The relationship between early impulsiveness and later violence may also depend on what type of impulsiveness was measured, but because of the limited number of effect sizes available we were less able to explore this possibility. When those studies that compared poor concentration along with more global measures of impulsiveness (e.g. ADHD diagnosis) were compared to later self-reported violence, the mean effect size produced was significantly smaller than the mean effect size of the two studies that compared daring/risk-taking to later self-reported violence. This is not necessarily surprising given the behavioural nature of daring and risk-taking. In fact, many daring and risk-taking behaviours might be closely linked with violence. It might be that this daring and risk-taking type of impulsiveness is an indication of a direct pathway linking early impulsiveness and later violence, whereas poor concentration may have diminished (but still significant) effects because it is operating more through indirect pathways such as disrupting education or influencing the parenting that the child receives.

The results of this systematic review should not be used to suggest that impulsiveness in any of its forms causes violence. It was not possible in this review to consider alternative variables that might explain the observed results. The most relevant of these might be levels of intelligence and socio-economic status. There has been much debate about the nature of the relationship between impulsiveness, intelligence and criminal behaviour (e.g. Block, 1995; Lynam and Moffitt, 1995; Lynam, Moffitt and Stouthamer-Loeber, 1993). Furthermore, research has identified complex interactions between levels of impulsiveness and indicators of neighbourhood disadvantage (e.g. Lynam et al., 2000; Vazsonyi, Cleveland and Weibe, 2006). Future research should attempt to replicate our analyses controlling for measures of intelligence and socio-economic status and other possible third variables.[10]

For the purpose of comparability, the data from the Loeber et al. (2008) study were presented in risk format. That is, the 25% who had scored the highest on the ADHD symptoms versus the remainder were compared on the proportion involved in later violent offending. However, in the original document Loeber et al. (2008) suggested that the relationship between ADHD and offending may be best conceptualised as low ADHD symptoms being a promotive factor as opposed to high ADHD symptoms being a risk factor. Promotive factors are defined as factors that predict a low probability of later delinquency (Loeber et al., 2008).

In their analysis, Loeber et al. (2008) found that individuals who had medium levels of ADHD symptoms (middle 50%) were similar to those with high levels of ADHD symptoms (top 25%) in terms of their risk of later offending. However, those with the lowest levels of ADHD symptoms had a significantly lower probability of future offending. This finding was consistent for each of the five possible independent comparisons for their two data sets (3 for the youngest sample, 2 for the oldest). The implication of this is that prevention targeted at those with high impulsiveness may miss a subset of the population that might also benefit from treatment (i.e. those with moderate levels of ADHD symptoms). Furthermore, any intervention that reduces the impulsiveness of the most impulsive individuals may not appear to have an impact unless impulsiveness is substantially reduced.

Unfortunately, because the results in the primary publications were presented as risk factors, it was not possible to determine whether impulsiveness might be better considered as a promotive factor as opposed to a risk factor. However, in an update of the paper by Herrenkohl et al. (2000) using data from the Seattle Social Development Project, Hawkins, Herrenkohl and Lee (2007) found that attention problems (a combination of parent and teacher reports about hyperactivity, impulsiveness and inattention) measured at ages 10–12 predicted violence at ages 13–14 and 15–18 when considered as a risk factor, but not as a promotive factor.

CONCLUSION

Based on data available from the highest quality studies, we conclude that early impulsiveness predicts later violence. Compared with other relationships in criminology (see e.g. Lipsey and Derzon, 1998) the predictive relationship is quite strong.

This implies that interventions that target impulsiveness (e.g. child skills training, see Lösel and Beelman, 2006; cognitive–behavioural interventions, see Lipsey and Landenberger, 2006; 'Reasoning and Rehabilitation', see Tong and Farrington, 2008) are likely to be effective at reducing later violence.

NOTES

1. The authors would like to thank Mark Lipsey, Sandra J. Wilson, David Wilson, Todd Herrenkohl, Mark LeBlanc, Georgia Zara, Lena Malofeeva, David Huizinga, Britt af Kliteberg, Hakan Stattin, Rebecca Stallings, Magda Stouthamer-Loeber, Terence Thornberry, Helene White, David Olds, Richard Tremblay and Emmy Werner for their help in identifying relevant studies, and Pat Cohen, Terrie Moffitt and Hona Lee Harrington for providing data.
2. $d = 2r/\sqrt{1 - r^2}$ (Lipsey and Wilson, 2001: p.199).
3. This can be seen because all of the confidence intervals overlap.
4. Three studies included in the Hawkins, Herrenkohl and Farrington (1998) review were based on samples of individuals diagnosed as hyperactive compared to a control condition.
5. Both the famous Kauai Longitudinal Study and the famous multi-method study of impulsivity by White *et al.* (1994) were excluded because they related impulsiveness to later serious delinquency and not specifically to violence.
6. The Pittsburgh Youth Study is an accelerated longitudinal study and it was possible to locate the relevant information for two independent samples of boys.
7. The Loeber *et al.* (2008) study was not included in this analysis because it included a combination of self-reports and official records.
8. The mean effect size for the 23 effect sizes was assessed for illustrative purposes. The standardised mean effect size for the fixed-effects model was found to be $d = 0.45$ (95% CI 0.39–0.52) and $d = 0.48$ (95% CI 0.37–0.59). Both were significant at the $p < 0.0001$ level.
9. Herrenkohl *et al.* (2000) was not included because this study only included self-reported violence.
10. The nature of the relationship between impulsiveness and other variables may also vary depending upon the type of impulsiveness under investigation (e.g. risk taking vs poor concentration).

REFERENCES

Af Klinteberg, B., Andersson, T., Magnusson, D. and Stattin, H. (1993) Hyperactive behavior in childhood as related to subsequent alcohol problems and violent offending: a longitudinal study of male subjects. *Personality and Individual Differences*, **15**, 381–88.
Block, J. (1995) On the relation between IQ, impulsivity, and delinquency: Remarks on the Lynam, Moffitt, and Stouthamer-Loeber (1993) interpretation. *Journal of Abnormal Psychology*, **104**, 395–98.
Burke, J.D., Loeber, R., White, H.R. *et al.* (2007) Inattention as a key predictor of tobacco use in adolescence. *Journal of Abnormal Psychology*, **116**, 249–59.

Clarke, D. (2006) Impulsivity as a mediator in the relationship between depression and problem gambling. *Personality and Individual Differences,* **40**, 5–15.

Cohen, J. (1988) *Statistical Power Analysis for the Behavioral Sciences,* 2nd edn, Erlbaum, Hillsdale, NJ.

Cohen, P. (2008) Personal communication, March 28.

Dowden, C., Blanchette, K. and Serin, R. (1999) *Anger Management Programming for Federal Male Inmates: An Effective Intervention,* Correctional Service of Canada, Ottawa. Research Report R-82.

Eysenck, S.B.G. and Eysenck, H.J. (1977) The place of impulsiveness in a dimensional system of personality description. *British Journal of Social and Clinical Psychology,* **2**, 46–55.

Farrington, D.P. (1991) Childhood aggression and adult violence: Early precursors and later life outcomes, in *The Development and Treatment of Childhood Aggression* (eds D.J. Pepler and K.H. Rubin), Lawrence Erlbaum, Hillsdale, NJ, pp. 5–29.

Farrington, D.P. (2007) Origins of violent behavior over the lifespan, in *The Cambridge Handbook of Violent Behavior and Aggression* (eds D.J. Flannery, A.T. Vaszonyi and I. Waldman), Cambridge University Press, Cambridge, pp. 19–48.

Farrington, D.P., Coid, J., Harnett, L. *et al.* (2006) *Criminal Careers and Life Success: New Findings from the Cambridge Study in Delinquent Development,* Research Findings 281, Home Office, London.

Farrington, D.P. and Loeber, R. (1989) RIOC and phi as measures of predictive efficiency and strength of association in 2X2 tables. *Journal of Quantitative Criminology,* **5**, 201–13.

Farrington, D.P. and Petrosino, A. (2001) The Campbell Collaboration Crime and Justice Group. *Annals of the American Academy of Political and Social Science,* **578**, 35–49.

Farrington, D.P. and Welsh, B.C. (2007) *Saving Children from a Life of Crime: Early Risk Factors and Effective Interventions,* Oxford University Press, Oxford.

Gottfredson, M. and Hirschi, T. (1990) *A General Theory of Crime,* Stanford University Press, Stanford.

Grasmick, H.G., Tittle, C.R., Bursik, R.J. and Arneklev, B.K. (1993) Testing the core empirical implication of Gottfredson and Hirschi's General Theory of Crime. *Journal of Research in Crime and Delinquency,* **30**, 5–29.

Hawkins, J.D., Herrenkohl, T., Farrington, D.P. *et al.* (1998) A review of predictors of youth violence, in *Serious and Violent Juvenile Offenders: Risk Factors and Successful Interventions* (eds R. Loeber and D.P. Farrington), Sage, Thousand Oaks, CA, pp. 106–46.

Hawkins, J.D., Herrenkohl, T.I., Lee, J.E. (2007) Risk and Promotive Factors and Youth Violence: Findings from the Seattle Social Development Project. Paper Presented at the American Society of Criminology Meeting, Atlanta.

Herrenkohl, T.I., Maguin, E., Hill, K.G. *et al.* (2000) Developmental risk factors for youth violence. *Journal of Adolescent Health,* **26**, 176–86.

Johnson, J.G., Smailer, E., Cohen, P. *et al.* (2004) Antisocial parental behavior, problematic parenting, and aggressive offspring behavior during adulthood. *British Journal of Criminology,* **44**, 915–30.

Jolliffe, D., Farrington, D.P., Hawkins, J.D. *et al.* (2003) Predictive, concurrent, prospective and retrospective validity of self-reported delinquency. *Criminal Behaviour and Mental Health,* **13**, 179–97.

Lipsey, M.W. and Derzon, J.H. (1998) Predictors of violent or serious delinquency in adolescence and early adulthood: a synthesis of longitudinal research, in *Serious and Violent Juvenile Offenders: Risk Factors and Successful Interventions* (eds R. Loeber and D.P. Farrington), Sage, Thousand Oaks, CA, pp. 86–105.

Lipsey, M.W. and Landenberger, N.A. (2006) Cognitive-behavioral interventions, in *Preventing Crime: What Works for Children, Offenders, Victims and Places* (eds B.C. Welsh and D.P. Farrington), Springer, New York, NY, pp. 33–71.

Lipsey, M.W. and Wilson, D.B. (2001) *Practical Meta-Analysis,* Sage, Thousand Oaks, CA.

Loeber, R., Farrington, D.P., Stouthamer-Loeber, M. and White, H.R. (2008) *Violence and Serious Theft: Development and Prediction from Childhood to Adulthood,* Routledge, New York, NY.

Lösel, F. and Beelman, A. (2006) Child social skills training, in *Preventing Crime: What Works for Children, Offenders, Victims and Places* (eds B.C. Welsh and D.P. Farrington), Springer, New York, NY, pp. 33–71.

Lynam, D.R., Caspi, A., Moffitt, T.E. *et al.* (2000) The interaction between impulsivity and neighbourhood context on offending: The effects of impulsivity are stronger in poorer neighbourhoods. *Journal of Abnormal Psychology*, **109**, 563–74.

Lynam, D.R. and Moffitt, T.E. (1995) Delinquency and impulsivity and IQ: a reply to block. *Journal of Abnormal Psychology*, **104**, 399–401.

Lynam, D., Moffitt, T. and Stouthamer-Loeber, M. (1993) Explaining the relation between IQ and delinquency: Class, race test motivation, school failure, or self-control? *Journal of Abnormal Psychology*, **102**, 187–96.

Moffitt, T. (1993) Adolescent-limited and life-course-persistent antisocial behavior: a developmental taxonomy. *Psychological Review*, **100**, 674–701.

Moffitt, T.E. (2008) Personal communication, April 18.

Moffitt, T.E., Caspi, A., Rutter, M. and Silva, P. (2001) *Sex Differences in Antisocial Behavior: Conduct Disorder, Delinquency, and Violence in the Dunedin Longitudinal Study*, Cambridge University Press, Cambridge.

Pratt, T.C. and Cullen, F.T. (2000) The empirical status of Gottfredson and Hirschi's General Theory of Crime: a meta-analysis. *Criminology*, **38**, 931–60.

Pratt, T.C., Cullen, F.T., Blevins, K.R. *et al.* (2002) The relationship of attention deficit hyperactivity disorder to crime and delinquency: a meta-analysis. *International Journal of Police Science and Management*, **4**, 344–60.

Ruorke, B.P. and Finlayson, M.A.J. (1975) Neuropsychological significance of lateralized deficits on the Grooved Pegboard Test for older children with learning disabilities. *Journal of Abnormal Psychology*, **84**, 412–21.

Thornberry, T.P., Huizinga, D. and Loeber, R. (1995) The prevention of serious delinquency and violence, in *Serious, Violent and Chronic Juvenile Offenders* (eds J.C. Howell, B. Krisberg, J.D. Hawkins and J.J. Wilson), Sage, Thousand Oaks, CA, pp. 213–37.

Tong, L S.J. and Farrington, D.P. (2008) Effectiveness of 'Reasoningand Rehabilitation' in reducing offending. *Psicothema*, **20**, 20–28.

Vazsonyi, A.T., Cleveland, H.H. and Weibe, R.P. (2006) Does the effect of impulsivity and delinquency vary by level of neighborhood disadvantage? *Criminal Justice and Behavior*, **33**, 511–41.

White, J.L., Moffitt, T.E., Caspi, A. *et al.* (1994) Measuring impulsivity and examining its relationship to delinquency. *Journal of Abnormal Psychology*, **103**, 192–205.

Wilson, J.Q. and Herrnstein, R.J. (1985) *Crime and Human Nature*, Simon & Schuster, New York.

Wolfgang, M.E., Figlio, R.M. and Sellin, T. (1972) *Delinquency in a Birth Cohort*, University of Chicago Press, Chicago.

Chapter 4

THE 'BIG FIVE': NEUROTICISM, EXTRAVERSION, OPENNESS, AGREEABLENESS AND CONSCIENTIOUSNESS AS AN ORGANISATIONAL SCHEME FOR THINKING ABOUT AGGRESSION AND VIOLENCE

VINCENT EGAN

School of Psychology, University of Leicester, UK

INTRODUCTION

Costa and MacCrae's five-factor model (FFM) is the dominant personality theory in modern academic psychology, and integrates a variety of models that often seemed to reflect 'jangle fallacies', that is equivalent concepts, measures, and findings with different names (Kelley, 1939). The FFM comprises five trait domains: neuroticism (N), extroversion (E), openness (O), agreeableness (A) and conscientiousness (C). Each dimension has subscales (facet scores) within the overall construct, shown (along with comparable dimensions from other personality measures overlapping with the FFM) in Table 4.1. The FFM is assessed using either the 240-item NEO-Personality Inventory (NEO-PI; Costa and McCrae, 1992), or a shorter, facet-score free 60-item NEO-Five Factor Inventory (NEO-FFI; Costa and McCrae, 1992). The FFM has been widely demonstrated cross-culturally (Schmitt, McCrae and Benet-Martínez, 2007), and has substantial cross-situational and longitudinal consistency (Murray *et al.*, 2003). Dimensions captured by the FFM also predict much of human life: '... happiness, physical and psychological health, spirituality, and identity ... the quality of relationships with peers, family, and romantic others at an interpersonal level .... occupational choice, satisfaction, and performance ... community involvement ... political ideology' (Ozer and Benet-Martínez, 2006, p. 401). The

Personality, Personality Disorder and Violence   Edited by Mary McMurran and Richard C. Howard
© 2009 John Wiley & Sons, Ltd

FFM also predicts antisocial activity, violence and aggression. This chapter reviews evidence for these associations. However, to know why the FFM is an appropriate level of explanation, it is necessary to know how the FFM emerged, how it relates to competing structural models of personality, and why five personality dimensions may be preferable to sixteen, seven, three or even one.

WHY FIVE DIMENSIONS OF PERSONALITY? WHY THE FFM?

The idea of five major dimensions encompassing much of personality is long standing (Fiske, 1949; Norman, 1963). There have been several attempts to reduce or increase the number of purported dimensions. Differences in the number of produced dimensions are an artefact of the methodologies employed, with more dimensions emerging from lexical studies of personality. Lexical methods take personality-descriptive words (e.g. 'aggressive' or 'kind') analysing the higher order concepts these words generate in relation to other personality descriptors (Saucier and Goldberg, 2001). Lexical models can be compared with behaviourally based models of personality, which do not depend on cultural variations in language and can involve self- or observer ratings of behaviour. Behavioural methods readily extend to factor-analytic studies of differing questionnaires that can identify converging concepts across different levels of explanation (Zuckerman, 1992). The lexical approach is descriptive, whereas the factor-analytic approach seeks to move from simple description to scientific explanation (Engler, 2006). Eysenck's 'Gigantic Three' of Psychoticism (P), Extroversion (E) and Neuroticism (N) exemplifies an explanatory, scientifically driven model of personality (Eysenck and Eysenck, 1985).

Lexically derived dimensional systems, for example, Cattell's 16 Personality Factors (16PF; Cattell, 1950) often lack replicability. Only five genuinely robust personality factors have been found in Cattell's 16PF (Noller, Law and Comrey, 1987), although Cattell used to argue that this was due to the failure of other researchers to use his methodology correctly. Tellegen (1982), likewise dissatisfied with the choice of adjectives used to describe personality, sought a different configuration of dimensions and devised a Multidimensional Personality Questionnaire (MPQ; Tellegen and Waller, 1992). The MPQ sought to go beyond the FFM by introducing additional dimensions of positive and negative valence (positive valence being good virtues versus mediocre ones, and negative valence being unkind and cruel qualities versus kind ones). Predictably, Tellegen's three MPQ trait dimensions of positive emotionality, negative emotionality and constraint correlated with Eysenck's E, N and P dimensions at 0.57, 0.60 and -0.52, respectively (all $P < 0.001$; LaRowe et al., 2006). Joint analysis of the NEO-PI and the MPQ found negative emotionality reflected high N and low A, positive emotionality involved E and positive elements of C, and constraint associated with controlled elements of C and low O (Church, 1994).

Cloninger's (1987) tridimensional model of personality is another alternative structural model of personality, and derives from psychiatry rather than psychology. Cloninger's basic dimensions are novelty seeking, harm avoidance, reward dependence and persistence. He later added three environmentally acquired dimensions: self-directedness, cooperation and self-transcendence (Cloninger, Svrakic and Przybeck, 1993). These underlying dimensions allegedly reflect heritable traits, neuroanatomical circuits, and are modulated by neurotransmitter levels (in particular dopamine, serotonin and noradrenaline), which drive behavioural activation, behavioural inhibition and behavioural maintenance. This gives rise to broad individual differences in how persons respond to novelty, punishment and reward (e.g. the anxious individual's tendency for exaggerated harm avoidance). Cloninger suggested that these qualities underlie both normal and abnormal personality, and the model is akin to Gray's behavioural approach and inhibition systems (Gray and McNaughton, 2000), with which his model correlates (Mardaga and Hansenne, 2007).

While Cloninger's theory sounds convincingly scientific, the measures to confirm his theory are problematic. When statistical modelling of the internal structure of his measures was conducted on large normal samples, his model data fitted Eysenckian and FFM models better than the one he proposed himself (Stewart, Ebmeier and Deary, 2004). Moreover, in a large sample of young adults ($n = 897$), Cloninger's dimensions correlated substantially with Eysenck's: N was strongly correlated with harm avoidance, E negatively related to harm avoidance (and positively with novelty seeking and reward dependence), and P related substantially to novelty seeking (and inversely with reward dependence) (Stewart, Ebmeier and Deary, 2005). Cloninger's dimensions also correlated widely across the FFM: harm avoidance was strongly positively correlated with N, and negatively related to E, O and C; novelty seeking was related to E and O, and negatively correlated with C; persistence was highly correlated with C; reward dependence was related to E and O; self-directedness was negatively correlated with N, and positively with C and E; and cooperativeness related to A, E, and O (De Fruyt, Van De Wiele and Van Heeringen, 2000). In relation to more established models, Cloninger's theory lacks reliability and validity. Moreover, it does not seem to capture hostility very well; when his traits were correlated with index measures of aggression, the most replicable positive association was with novelty seeking (e.g. Kim, Lee and Yune, 2006).

How these different structural models, dimensions and elements relate to each using the FFM as an integrative structure is presented in Table 4.1.

The factor-analytic approach has led others to propose even fewer dimensions underlying the FFM. This is partly based on the discovery that the ostensibly independent dimensions of the NEO-PI and NEO-FFI (Costa and McCrae, 1992) have a tendency themselves to correlate (Blackburn et al., 2004; Digman, 1997; Egan, Austin and Deary, 2000). This led the NEO-FFI to be revised into the NEO-FFI-R (McCrae and Costa, 2004). One interpretation of the correlation of subscales in the FFM (or Eysenck's PEN model beforehand) is that they denote super-ordinate, higher order factors. The patterns of correlation (between E and N, or between A, C and low N, depending on whether you consider FFM or PEN models) give rise to higher level abstractions of personality. Digman (1997) called these higher order factors alpha (a mix of E and O) and beta (a combination of A, C and N). Blackburn, Logan and Renwick (2005) also generated these dimensions, viewed them from their negative poles, and labelled them 'anxious-inhibited' or affiliation, and 'acting out' or dominance. It is possible that these highest order factors are a reductionist step too far. Biesanz and West (2004) used a multi-trait, multi-method approach to examine the convergent and divergent validity of the FFM, using self-report data and informant ratings of persons who had rated themselves. Multi-trait, multi-method techniques are a way by which one can disentangle trait

Table 4.1 Trait dimensional models comparing Tellegen, Eysenck, and Costa and McCrae's schemes

Theorist Scale name	Cloninger TPQ	Tellegen MPQ	Eysenck EPQ-R[a] EPP[b]	Costa and McCrae NEO-PI-R[c]	Costa and McCrae NEO-FFI[d]
Neuroticism	Harm avoidance (negatively correlated with self-directedness)	(as *Negative Emotional Temperament*) Stress reaction Alienation Aggression	Inferiority Unhappiness Anxiety Dependence Hypochondria Guilt Obsessiveness	Vulnerability Depression Anxiety Angry hostility Self-consciousness Impulsiveness	Negative affect Self-reproach
Extroversion	Novelty seeking Reward dependence Self-directedness Cooperativeness	(as *Positive Emotional Temperament*) Well-being Social potency Achievement Social closeness	Activity Sociability Assertiveness Expressiveness Ambition Dogmatism Aggressiveness	Activity Gregariousness Assertiveness Warmth Excitement seeking Positive emotions	Activity Positive affect Sociability
Openness	Reward dependence Cooperativeness	(as *Absorption*)		Fantasy Aesthetics Feelings Actions Ideas Values	Aesthetic interests Unconventionality

Agreeableness	Cooperativeness		(Psychoticism) Risk taking Impulsivity Irresponsibility Manipulativeness Sensation seeking Tough-mindedness Practicality	Trust Straightforwardness Altruism Compliance Modesty Tender-mindedness	
Conscientiousness	Persistence Self-directedness (negatively correlated with harm avoidance and novelty seeking)	(as *Constraint*) Harm avoidance		Competence Order	Orderliness Goal striving
		Traditionalism		Dutifulness Achievement Striving Self-discipline Deliberation	Dependability

[a] Bulthelier and Hicker (1997); underlined constructs are facets of test short form.
[b] From Roger and Morris (1991).
[c] From NEO-PI-R test manual (Costa and McCrae, 1992).
[d] Derived from item factor analysis by Saucier (1998).

from method effects, with replication of findings across methods and techniques demonstrating that a given finding is not simply produced by the way it was derived. Biessanz and West found that self-rated FFM dimensions were moderately intercorrelated, whereas no intercorrelations were found for informant ratings of the same individuals on the same trait dimensions. These results suggest that the orthogonality of the FFM depends on the quality and source of the data. It might be that higher order dimensions are a methodological artefact in the same way the profusion of personality dimensions may be if we base ourselves on the vagaries of language.

The foregoing review of the personality literature converges on Costa and McCrae's and Eysenck's models being closer to genuinely explanatory systems for personality than other developments. Rather than be distracted by ambitious but poorly replicable dimensions lacking external validation and incremental value, it is perhaps more productive to build on 'solid grounds in the wetlands of psychology' (Costa and McCrae, 1995, p. 216). In this chapter, I argue that aggression and violence are influenced by the general personality traits of N, A and C. I base my argument on a review of studies involving the 'Big Five'/FFM of personality dimensions as an organising model for considering human behaviour. I will discuss the FFM in relation to populations where aggression and violence are significant problems, namely, adolescents and people with personality disorders. I will also cover the relationships between the FFM and specific antisocial and aggressive behaviours and interests. To describe the importance of the FFM, it is necessary to state why the FFM supersedes what was once seen as equally comprehensive and all-explanatory: Eysenck's 'Gigantic three'.

PERSONALITY TRAITS AND ANTISOCIAL BEHAVIOUR

Personality is an important predictor of offending. Caspi *et al.* (1994) found greater participation in delinquent activities – whether broken down by country, gender and race, and whether delinquency was measured by self-report or official records – was associated with young persons who showed greater negative emotional expression (defined by greater aggression, greater alienation and greater stress reactions) and weaker constraint (i.e. low traditionalism, low harm avoidance and a lack of control). Individual differences in personality interact with social influences; impulsivity is a stronger predictor of antisocial behaviour in poorer communities (Lynam *et al.*, 2000). A meta-analysis by Miller and Lynam (2001) found all four major structural models of personality (Eysenck's PEN, Costa and McCrae's FFM, Tellegen's three-factor model and Cloninger's seven-factor model) had dimensions associated with antisocial acts. A particularly strong relationship was with Eysenck's dimension of P.

EYSENCK'S PEN MODEL

Eysenck's three 'supertraits' of personality – P, E and N – reflect, like other structural models of personality, higher order theoretical constructs emerging out of lower level facets for each dimension. P reflects tough-minded hostility, and involves elements of aggression, coldness, egocentricity, impulsivity and a lack of empathy (Eysenck and Eysenck, 1976). The term 'P' itself derives from Eysenck's observation that criminality and generic antisocial behaviour are more common in the male relatives of families with schizophrenic probands, so is a broad-spectrum indicator of psychopathology (Laurent *et al.*, 2002). Eysenck proposed that P – like E – reflected low cortical arousal, but was driven by abnormalities in neurotransmitter levels rather than physiological mechanisms. This view explains why substance misuse is common in the high-P person, as drugs stimulate pathways perhaps otherwise under-aroused. Persons high in N may also use alcohol and recreational drugs to raise mood, so self-medication may also be a drive to substance misuse, but substance misuse is by no means exclusive to offenders.

Persons high in E are characterised by sociability, liveliness, activity, assertiveness, dominance and venturesomeness. Eysenck theorised that persons high in E had lower levels of spontaneous cortical arousal in the reticular activating centre of the brain stem, and sought excitement to increase their arousal levels to what would be normal for a person with a lower level of E (Eysenck and Eysenck, 1985). The overlap between E and sensation seeking (Zuckerman, 1994) is clear (though there are also overlaps between P and sensation seeking). Eysenck once believed criminals to be higher in E than non-offenders, although he revised this view when impulsivity was found to be intermediate to N and P (Gray, 1981; Gray and McNaughton, 2000).

Eysenck's third omnibus dimension – N – addresses the continuum and control of emotions, with high-N persons being more emotionally unstable and low-N persons less variable in mood. Persons high in N are tense, unstable, guilt-ridden, emotional and negative, while persons low in N are at the opposite poles of these subtraits. Being low-N is not always a virtue; if N operates in conjunction with high P, or low A, or psychopathy, a person may behave antisocially and not care about the implications to themselves, let alone others (Benning *et al.*, 2005). In a meta-analysis of Eysenck's PEN model in relation to antisocial behaviour comprising 52 studies and 97 samples, Cale (2006) found that P was most strongly linked to antisocial behaviour (weighted mean effect size = 0.39, 95% confidence interval (CI) = 0.35 to 0.42); N was also linked, but less so (weighted mean effect size = 0.19, 95% CI = 0.15 to 0.23). The effect of E on antisocial behaviour was minor (weighted mean effect size = 0.09, 95% CI = .06 to 0.12). These results suggest Eysenck's P and N dimensions most contribute to an understanding of antisocial activity.

AGGRESSION AND VIOLENCE AS LEARNED BEHAVIOURS – OR NOT?

Eysenck suggested crime was biosocial, and driven by learning as well as personality. A person associating antisocial behaviour with a penalty and wanting to evade punishment or negative feelings associated with being punished (or even simply being found out in a wrongdoing) encourages the development of internal controls to avoid the unpleasant internal state produced by being chastened (Eysenck and Gudjonsson, 1989). Eysenck said much aggressive behaviour follows from the lack of appropriate pro-social reinforcement contingencies to correct unrestrained behaviour. The parenting of the antisocial child tends to involve neglect, inappropriate permissiveness and excessive physical punishment (Farrington and West, 1990). Antisocial activity may also be actively encouraged. A recently reported child cruelty case in the United Kingdom found four women guilty of taunting two children aged two and three to fight each other on camera (The Independent, 2007). The women on trial refused to accept culpability and insisted the fight was character building, and a way of 'toughening children up'. The positive modelling of antisocial and aggressive behaviour also occurs in the broader social environment. Young persons from criminogenic contexts who are failing at school may see the more socially and materially successful people in their community engaging in violent and criminal activity, and see this behaviour as adaptive and positive. Modelling one's actions on the successful, even if they are following a criminal career path, is, arguably, a rational strategy (Anderson, 1999; Warr, 2002). Such communities often reject state-sanctioned law enforcement, so transgression (or perceived transgression) can only be penalised by the use of defensive violence by the victim or their supporters, and this in turn contributes to reciprocal violence, thus perpetuating the cycle of aggression.

Nevertheless, many persons grow up in poor or socially uncontrolled conditions and do not become aggressive or violent. Such persons may eschew crime despite seeing the material advantages of criminal and antisocial activity, particularly if they have personality traits associated with resilience, namely low N, high E, high A/low P, high C and high O (Davey, Eaker and Walters, 2003). Some of these dimensions may relate to criminal desistance indirectly. For example, trait O divides into facets reflecting intelligence as well as open-mindedness, and intelligence also associates with higher C (Moutafi, Furnham and Crump, 2006). Intelligence is protective against antisocial activity (Lynam, Moffitt and Stouthamer-Loeber, 1993). Personality thus helps the individual to resist environmental influences that may facilitate antisocial and aggressive behaviour in persons without these traits.

PSYCHOTICISM AND VIOLENCE AND AGGRESSION

Eysenck's P is high across many contexts where violence and aggression are manifest. P predicts anger levels in prisoners (Wood and Newton, 2003), premeditated aggression in psychiatric outpatients (Stanford et al., 2003) and the irresponsible use of their weapons by soldiers (Glicksohn, Ben-Shalom and Lazar, 2004). P may be autocatalytic (i.e. provoke a particular reaction), as persons higher in P are more likely to be verbally aggressive, argumentative and inappropriately assertive in interpersonal communication (McCroskey, Heisel and Richmond, 2001). Persons higher in P are more likely to accept the use of violence in conflict resolution (Zillmann and Weaver, 1997), and in a classical interaction effect, males higher in P are more aroused (physiologically and via self-report) by depictions of rape than consensual sexual relations than men lower in P, whilst men lower in P are more aroused by thoughts of consensual sex than committing rape (Barnes, Malamuth and Check, 1984). Violent prisoners lower in IQ and higher in P are more preoccupied with their personal space than non-violent prisoners who are higher in IQ and lower in

P (Eastwood, 1985). Lastly, conduct-disordered children are higher in P than their peers (Raine and Jones, 1987).

PROBLEMS WITH EYSENCK'S THEORY

Eysenck's theories of antisocial behaviour shifted over time, and some facets of his theory have been revised to accommodate replicated empirical findings beyond his purported model. Eysenck initially suggested that criminals would be more extroverted than non-criminals. This was influenced by his view that impulsivity was a facet of E, and led to the inclusion of impulsivity in the E dimension of his earlier personality assessments. When E was revised to accommodate the repositioning of impulsivity as a quality intermediate to his traits of P and N, criminals were found more introverted and high in N (Gudjonsson, 1997). Eysenck's theory of N and conditioning works paradoxically in relation to criminal learning; if high-N persons typically acquire neurotic-type disorders partly through learning, surely the aversive nature of punishment should lead high-N persons to acquire inhibitory associations. The answer is, of course, that punishment only occasionally follows from offending, so there is no consistent association formed between an antisocial or aggressive act and the punitive consequence. When experiments have been conducted examining conditioning processes in offenders, higher autonomic arousal and reactivity ('somatic markers') are greater in persons who resist offending (Raine, 1997).

While there is little major disagreement about the constructs of E or N (Clark and Watson, 1999), P is more controversial. P's association with antisocial, aggressive and violent behaviour is clear, but the dimension is problematic in a way that more prosaic and face-valid dimensions such as A and C are not (McCrae and Costa, 1985). Conceptually, the term 'P' confuses the mentally ill and the sane but behaviourally disordered. The internal reliability of P scales is low, limiting accuracy and replicability of measurement (Caruso et al., 2001). Art students score more highly on P than prisoners or the mentally disordered (Woody and Claridge, 1977). Under pressure to account for P given such shortcomings, Eysenck proposed that P was a higher order construct emerging out of lower apparent facets such as A and C, which are themselves correlated, highly reliable, correlate with P and with P-like phenomena (Eysenck, 1992a, 1992b). While Eysenck's programmatic research has been descriptively accurate, and his identification of hostile personality features as predictors of antisocial and aggressive behaviour correct, the underlying construct of P has to be seen as flawed.

NEUROTICISM

In a field blighted by 'jangle', no dimension of personality has suffered more from synonymous constructs than N (Watson and Clark, 1984). Anxiety, angry hostility, depression and self-consciousness facet scores of N in the FFM model convey the attributes of a person who experiences negative emotions and psychological distress. An example of jangle is shown in Judge et al.'s (2002) meta-analysis of the concepts of 'self-esteem', 'locus of control' and 'generalised self-efficacy', which they found were all strongly predicted by N. These more specific constructs loaded together to form a single factor closer to N than any specific lower order trait, and the lower order trait measures offered limited discriminant validity (or incremental variance) in predicting distress once the higher order construct of N was taken into account. At the behavioural level, constructs correlated with N also correlated with aggression include irritability/anger (Caprara, Barbarnelli and Zimbardo, 1996) and (another 'jangle') 'emotional susceptibility' (Caprara, Babaranelli and Comrey, 1992). Lower order constructs may be relevant as clinical *foci* for intervention, but the force driving them should not be overlooked.

N is a significant facet of aggression and violence, but the route by which it operates is different to disagreeableness or hostility, being primarily attributable to defensive and emotional reactions rather than instrumental and callous hostility. Low self-esteem (one expression of high N) as a predictor of aggressive acts was examined in a series of studies using self-report, teacher and parent ratings using samples from the United States and New Zealand, involving both adolescents and college students, and examining the participants cross-sectionally and longitudinally (Donnellan *et al.*, 2005). Low self-esteem was inversely related to externalising problems such as aggression, antisocial behaviour and delinquency across all samples and methods, and remained influential when confounds such as parenting style and relationships, achievement, socio-economic status and IQ were taken into account. Neurotic aggression is impulsive and emotional, whilst other types of aggression are considered instrumental (Caprara, Perugini and Barbareanelli, 1994). This view is maintained in Costa and McCrae's distinction between hot-blooded and cold-blooded antagonism. Cold-blooded aggression is associated with low N and low A. Some offenders have exaggerated self-esteem, which may be manifest as 'malignant' narcissism (Baumeister, Bushman and Campbell, 2000). Low A and low N further converge descriptively into the classical 'callous and unemotional' presentation of primary psychopathy. Blackburn's work on primary and secondary psychopathy (see Chapter 7), which demonstrates that a distinction can be made between psychopathic individuals, all of whom are high in P or low in A, into primary and secondary forms, requires differentiation by reference to N (Blackburn, 1975).

Aggression does not function in a vacuum; some conditions provoke aggression more than others, and some are better at resisting (or responding to) provocation. Bettencourt *et al.* (2006) meta-analysed 63 studies examining the relationship between personality and behaviour under provocation. The mean personality/aggressive behaviour effect size was 0.5, this being 0.4 under neutral conditions and 0.6 under provocation. Greater aggressive response was seen under provocation for trait anger, type A personality (tense hostility or high N, low A), emotional susceptibility, narcissism and impulsivity.

DEVELOPMENTAL ISSUES

Children are often deemed to show differences in temperament rather than personality; temperament reflecting basic biological differences in activity and emotional reactivity which unfolds with development and experience, eventually coalescing into the higher order traits of the FFM (Shiner and Caspi, 2003). It is questionable just how much discontinuity there is, given temperamental traits measured at the age of 3 significantly correlate with similar traits at the age of 18 (Caspi, 2000). Halverson *et al.* (2003) developed a cross-cultural, cross-age measure of child personality via the use of self-reported parental behavioural descriptors, which they then subjected to factor analysis to generate a cross-validated model. This model produced 15 intermediate traits generating, at a higher level of analysis, a structure similar to the FFM. One exception was that the O factor they produced was closer to general intelligence, consisting of precociousnesss, intelligence and speed of comprehension. This finding is comparable to debates in the adult literature about what O really measures.

Of particular relevance to this chapter is how personality traits such as A and C unfold from child to adulthood, and their relation to aggression and violence (Tackett, 2006). There is overwhelming evidence for a difficult 'externalising' child temperament, involving impulsivity, disinhibition, aggression and transgressive behaviour. This is more common in children subsequently diagnosed with conditions such as child conduct disorder, oppositional defiant disorder and attention-deficit/hyperactive disorder, with these in turn predicting general personality disorders in adulthood. As ever, while simple associations with P or A-type variables and aggression or violence are readily found (e.g. Gleason, Jensen-Campbell and Richardson, 2004), broader trait dimensions modulate findings and reiterate the need to remain mindful of traits beyond those which index antisocial tendencies alone. For example, when adolescent psychopathy was examined in a cohort of detained young offenders using the Antisocial Process Screening Device (Frick and Hare, 2002) and the FFM traits derived from the Big Five version of the Interpersonal Adjective Scales (Trapnell and Wiggins, 1991), greater psychopathy in males was associated with lower A, greater N, lower O and lower C (Salekin *et al.*, 2005). This profile was also found for a different cohort using different assessment instruments to assess childhood psychopathy and the FFM traits (Lynam *et al.*, 2005). Given the caveat of a smaller cohort of females in this study, scores on Lynam's child psychopathy measure (Lynam, 1997) were also associated with lower A and lower C (Salekin *et al.*, 2005).

There is some debate about whether the concept of psychopathy in an adult sense is helpful for considering young offenders and their risk, given the diversity of needs in this population (Marshall, Egan and English, 2006). One plausible hypothesis is that younger offenders tend to be more distressed in their feelings and express this in their higher N and lower E alongside lower A and C (as per Eysenck's theory), but over time adjust to getting into trouble, or worry less about the consequences of their actions. The general lack of consequences after offending may even reduce anxiety to antisocial activity, whilst other, more genuinely psychopathic, offenders are inherently and excessively fearless (Lykken, 1995; Salekin *et al.*, 2004). For emotionally vulnerable offenders, anxiety may provide a window in which intervention is more effective.

THE DIMENSIONAL MODEL OF PERSONALITY DISORDERS

The dimensional model of personality has been repeatedly shown to overlap with the ostensibly categorical nature of personality disorders (Costa and Widiger, 2003), and dramatic 'externalising' personality disorders are disproportionately associated with aggression and violence (Costa and Widiger, 2003). If you are going to be assaulted, you have a one in two chance of the offender being drunk and diagnosed with personality disorder (Coid *et al.*, 2006).

Meta-analysis of the literature examining the FFM in relation to the 10 personality disorders defined by DSM-IV (American Psychiatric Association, 1994) suggests that personality disordered persons are generally characterised by being higher in N, elevated or lower in E depending on whether the personality disorder is withdrawn or dramatic, and routinely lower in A and C. O rarely shows any replicable association with any personality disorder (Saulsman and Page, 2004). This is not to assume that personality disorders are simply extremes of normal personality. N correlates at 0.67 ($P < 0.001$) with self-reported borderline personality disorder (Egan *et al.*, 2003), but borderline personality disorder is qualitatively different from high N. It is misleading to suggest that personality disorders are nothing but extremes of personality trait configurations or that aggression and violence are committed exclusively by persons with either personality disorder or extremes of general personality traits. Nevertheless, the FFM has been described as an effective 'lens' to explore the relationship between personality and violence in psychiatric patients. Skeem *et al.* (2005) assessed a large cohort of hospitalised non-forensic psychiatric patients using the NEO-FFI, the screening version of the PCL-R (the PCL:SV: Hart, Cox and Hare, 1996), and a behavioural history of violence. Low A predicted both violence and scores on the PCL:SV. Shared predictors of violence were captured more specifically by low A than the PCL:SV, as violence is not exclusively committed by the psychopathic.

While personality disorders are spoken of as if they are discrete, this is not the case, and comorbidity is the norm. Personality disorders have been assumed to reflect three clusters: Cluster A (odd-eccentric, comprising schizoid, schizotypal and paranoid disorders), Cluster B (dramatic, comprising borderline, antisocial, narcissistic and histrionic disorders) and Cluster C (anxious, comprising avoidant, dependent and obsessive-compulsive personality disorder). However, some diagnostic symptoms of personality disorder are more cardinal than others, and some symptoms repeat over certain diagnoses. For example, impulsivity, a facet of N, is common across disorders, suggesting that patterns of symptoms cluster together rather than form discrete signs of pathology. Blashfield and Breen (1989) found that clinical practitioners themselves have difficulties differentiating criteria for DSM-IIIR personality disorders, in particular histrionic/narcissistic, avoidant/dependent and schizotypal/paranoid personality disorders. One way out of this diagnostic maze is to work back from basic empirical principles based on what is known about personality, and how it relates to both traits and disorders. Mulder and Joyce (1997) factor analysed the personality disorder symptoms assessed by the Structured Clinical Interview for DSM-IIIR (the SCID) extracting four factors, which they called the 4As. The antisocial factor comprised items measuring impulsivity, instability, self-dramatising and a tendency to get bored easily. The asocial factor captured items indicative of social indifference and stereotyped interests. An aesthenic or anxious factor captured symptoms assessing anxiety, dependency and fearfulness. The final, anankastic factor contained items indicating obsessive-compulsive features, rigidity and excessive perfectionism. Austin and

Deary (2000) examined the 4A model in relation to Eysenck's PEN scheme, and found that the aesthenic dimension corresponded to Eysenck's N, antisociality, was associated with Eysenck's P dimension, and the asocial factor correlated negatively with Eysenckian E. The anankastic dimension did not associate with any major dimension of personality. Egan *et al.* (2003) similarly conducted a joint factor analysis of the NEO-FFI (Costa and McCrae, 1992) and the IPDE self-report screening instrument for DSM-IV personality disorders (Loranger, 1999), and derived a 4A model. The asocial dimension had high positive loadings for high N, and high negative loadings for E and C. The anxious dimension had a high positive loading for N. The antisocial dimension had high negative loadings for A and C. As with Deary *et al.* (1998) (who used a different personality instrument), the anankastic dimension did not share factor space with the NEO-FFI.

Finally, Larstone *et al.* (2002) conducted a study examining the simultaneous influences of the PEN and FFM on traits denoting personality disorder. Their assessment of personality disorder traits derived from the Dimensional Assessment of Personality Pathology (Livesley and Jackson, 2002), which comprises four higher order dimensions: emotional dysregulation (corresponding to anxiety), dissocial behaviour (corresponding to antisociality), inhibition (corresponding to asociality) and compulsivity (i.e. anankastic). Eysenckian and FFM N were associated with emotional dysregulation (with low O and low A being additional loadings). Eysenckian and FFM E were associated with (low) inhibition. Eysenckian P and FFM A loaded on dissocial and aggressive behaviour. FFM C was strongly associated with compulsivity. These findings show that the PEN and FFM essentially demonstrate the same patterns of association in relation to the traits associated with personality disorders. If one wants to understand the elements of personality driving antisocial behaviour and aggression, a focus on trait A has to be central to one's assessment, with other dimensions of personality differentiating how the antisocial activity will be expressed.

A final way in which the FFM maps onto other conceptualisations of personality disorder and integrates them into a simpler structure pertains to what has been called 'the dark triad' of personality (Paulhus and Williams, 2002). The 'dark triad' comprises Machiavellianism, psychopathy and narcissism, and all three constructs converge on a core of self-interest, deception and manipulation, so one would expect (and generally find) their inter-relationship (McHoskey, Worzel and Szyarto, 1998). Low A saturate the dark triad, but the negative correlation between Machiavellianism and anxiety prompts an idea which integrates a number of concepts; this is because anxiety is highly related to N, and N is inversely related to Machiavellianism (Wiggins and Pincus, 1989). Primary and secondary psychopathy differentiate from each other behaviourally in that secondary psychopaths are more neurotic than primary psychopaths, and as a group, secondary psychopaths tend to be more disorganised (Blackburn, 1975). Jakobwitz and Egan (2006) examined the dark triad in relation to the FFM as measured by the NEO-FFI-R in a sample from the general population. It was found that the primary psychopathy factor was determined by very high positive loadings for both facets of psychopathy, Machiavellianism and narcissism. The only dimension of the FFM loading on this dimension was A, which loaded negatively at −0.69. The secondary psychopathy factor also loaded on a second factor, which had a very high loading for

N (0.80), and a high negative loading for C (−0.71). E and O existed as separate dimensions that did not overlap significantly with any aspect of the dark triad. These results show yet again the utility of using the FFM as an integrative model and fulcrum by which to organise what can be disparate concepts into a more coherent scheme, in this case, the cold-blooded aggression and hostility expressed by persons high on the dark triad.

ASSOCIATIONS BETWEEN THE FFM AND MORE SPECIFIC ANTISOCIAL BEHAVIOURS

Miller, Lynam and Leukefeld (2003) examined the relationship between the FFM and a range of antisocial activities. They found that N, A and C predicted the stability, variety and onset of conduct problems, aggression and symptoms of antisocial personality disorder in 481 individuals in the community. At the domain level of these traits, (low) A most consistently related to all five antisocial and aggressive outcomes, with facets from N, A and C all adding significant contributions to predicting outcome, in particular low straightforwardness, low compliance and low deliberation. Other aggressive and antisocial behaviours are also predicted by aspects of the FFM, whether they are self-reported criminal activity and aggression, interests in weapons (and other violent interests), alcohol-violence expectancies or sexual offending.

VIOLENT CRIME AND GENERAL OFFENDING

Heaven (1996) found low A, low C and high N associated with self-reported violence, vandalism and theft in a delinquent cohort. Simple criminal cognitions also relate to the FFM. The eight subscales of the Psychological Inventory of Criminal Thinking Styles (PICTS; Walters, 1995) quickly reduce to two underlying factors: a lack of thoughtfulness (i.e. lack of attention to one's experience) and wilful hostility, with the first factor being most well defined (Egan et al., 2000). This is in some ways an encouraging finding – criminals are more thoughtless than callous, and you can more easily make somebody thoughtful than make a callous person caring. High scores on an adult measure of attention deficit disorder and Disinhibition and Boredom Susceptibility subscales from the Sensation-Seeking Scale (Zuckerman, 1994) correlated with greater endorsement of criminal sentiments; high N, low E and low A were slightly lower correlates of these dimensions.

The most substantial study into the influence of the FFM on actual criminal arrest derives from a longitudinal epidemiological study of psychiatric morbidity in the Baltimore area of the United States (Samuels et al., 2004). In this study, 611 participants assessed in 1981 were reassessed 12 to 18 years later, and were evaluated using DSM-IV criteria for personality disorder along with the full NEO-PI-R. This enabled subfacets of particular trait dimensions to be considered, not just the overall traits themselves. Criminal activity was defined by official state criminal records, rather than self-report. Persons with antisocial, paranoid, borderline and narcissistic personality disorders were significantly more likely to have been arrested. When offending was examined in relation to the dimensions of the FFM, previously arrested persons were more likely to be high in N, this being attributable to the facets of angry hostility, depression and impulsiveness. Although there was no overall difference in E for offenders and non-offenders, non-offenders were higher on the warmth facet of E, whereas offenders were higher on the excitement-seeking facet of E. O was not associated with offending or non-offending. Persons lower in A were more likely to have been arrested, and arrestees were lower on the A facets of trust, straightforwardness, compliance and modesty. Likewise, arrestees and the non-arrested differed in C, with the C facets responsible for this finding being the lower competence, dutifulness and deliberation of persons who had been arrested. The differences between groups were generally equivalent to a difference of about one-half of a standard deviation, and the size of these effects remained when the data were corrected for age, sex, race, substance misuse or personality disorder diagnosis. There were few differences between arrestees when they were divided into primarily violent and non-violent offenders, the only exceptions being that violent arrestees were less gregarious (a facet of E) and less open to their feelings (a facet of O). These findings suggest that the FFM is an effective additional predictor of antisocial behaviour and is not simply a proxy for personality disorder, although overlaps are clearly apparent.

SEXUAL OFFENDING

The FFM has also been employed to examine sexual offenders. Sexual offenders provide quite a good test of the FFM model of offending, as the offence types are very diverse and the offenders likewise. Sex offending encompasses a wide range of behaviours – from hands-off, remote offences such as downloading illicit images from the Internet or stealing clothing from washing lines, to contact offences involving actual sexual assault. Dennison, Stough and Birgden (2001) gave the NEO-PI-R to sexual offenders and found incestuous offenders higher in N than controls, and extra-familial offenders being even higher in N than either controls or intra-familial offenders. These differences were particularly pronounced for the N facet scores of anxiety, depression, self-consciousness and vulnerability. Non-offenders were significantly higher than offenders for E and the facet scores of assertiveness and gregariousness. There was no difference in O between offenders and non-offenders. There was no difference between groups in A, but differences for C were observed, particularly for controls as compared to offenders, controls being higher in competence and deliberation. Discriminant function analysis successfully classified persons as belonging to offender or non-offender categories by reference to lower A, lower C and higher N, but was less good at allocating persons to specific offences.

The FFM can also be used to examine the degree to which generic clinical assessment overlaps with individual differences and other mental disorders. Sexual offenders sometimes collect 'trophies' from victims or have massive collections of downloaded pornographic images from the Internet. Egan, Kavanagh and Blair (2005) examined the degree to which the Sex Offenders Assessment Package (SOAP), routinely used in the United Kingdom to evaluate the social functioning and sexual deviance of sexual offenders, relates to individual differences on the FFM and to obsessive-compulsiveness. Scores on the SOAP, the NEO-FFI and the Maudsley Obsessive-Compulsive Inventory (MOCI; Hodgson and Rachman, 1977) were collected in a sample of 200 sexual offenders against children and produced three reliable factors: emotional distress, cognitions supporting sex with children and concern for others. These factors correlated respectively with higher N and lower E, greater obsessive-compulsiveness on the MOCI and trait A. When partial correlation controlled for the influence of N on the correlation between cognitions supporting sex with children and the MOCI, there was no change in the association between these variables. These results show that negative mood and obsessional tendencies are important underlying influences on the feelings and behaviour of sexual offenders, and that the obsessionality of the group is not simply attributable to N. These findings suggest treating sexual offenders for obsessive thoughts might be helpful therapeutically and behaviourally, and might so help reduce sexual aggression.

WEAPONS CARRYING

Carrying a weapon significantly increases the risk of a person causing significant harm should they get into a fight. Professional criminals may carry weapons, but they tend to use these instrumentally, for example to settle a 'business disagreement'. Young males carry weapons for many other reasons – protection and personal safety, because their friends do, or simply to show off (MORI, 2003). Barlas and Egan (2006) found British adolescents who admitted carrying weapons (primarily knives and firearms) were lower in A and C than age and class-matched controls; they were also higher in delinquency, mating effort (i.e. the amount of time and effort put into acquiring and protecting potential or actual sexual partners) and militaristic sensational interests. Over 90% of adolescents could be correctly classified as being weapons carriers or not by the independent effects of delinquent activity, militaristic interests, and low C; A subsumed into delinquency.

CONCLUSIONS

The FFM is associated with many aspects of antisocial behaviour and aggression, unifies a disparate literature and provides a means of organising a broad range of material so that clinical and academic literatures can be merged, to mutual benefit. Many of the redundancies in the previous century of psychology can be resolved by recognition of the power of the FFM to explain many of the more unpleasant aspects of human behaviour. The task is now to see how the FFM can be used to help ameliorate aggressive and antisocial behaviour, so one can move beyond simply using the model as a better mode of psychological description.

REFERENCES

American Psychiatric Association (1994) *Diagnostic and Statistical Manual of Mental Disorders*, 4th edn, American Psychiatric Press, Washington, DC.

Anderson, E. (1999) *Code of the Street: Decency, Violence and the Moral Life of the Inner City*, Norton, New York.

Austin, E.J. and Deary, I.J. (2000). The 'four As': A common framework for normal and abnormal personality? *Personality and Individual Differences*, **28**, 977–95.

Barlas, J. and Egan, V. (2006) Weapons carrying in British teenagers: the role of personality, delinquency, sensational interests and mating effort. *Journal of Forensic Psychiatry and Psychology*, **17**, 53–72.

Barnes, G.E., Malamuth, N.M. and Check, J.V. (1984) Psychoticism and sexual arousal to rape depictions. *Personality and Individual Differences*, **5**, 273–9.

Baumeister, R.F., Bushman, B.J. and Campbell, W.K. (2000) Self-esteem, narcissism, and aggression: does violence result from low self-esteem or from threatened egotism? *Current Directions in Psychological Science*, **9**, 26–9.

Benning, S.D., Patrick, C., Salekin, R. and Leistico, A.-M. (2005) Convergent and discriminant validity of psychopathy factors assessed via self-report: a comparison of three instruments. *Assessment*, **12**, 270–89.

Bettencourt, B.A., Talley, A., Benjamin, A.J. and Valentine, J. (2006) Personality and aggressive behavior under provoking and neutral conditions: a meta-analytic review. *Psychological Bulletin*, **132**, 751–77.

Biesanz, J.C. and West, S.G. (2004) Towards understanding assessments of the Big Five: Multitrait–multimethod analyses of convergent and divergent validity across measurement occasion and type of observer. *Journal of Personality*, **72**, 845–76.

Blackburn, R. (1975) An empirical classification of psychopathic personality. *British Journal of Psychiatry*, **127**, 456–60.

Blackburn, R., Renwick, S.J.D., Donnelly, J.P. and Logan, C. (2004) Big Five or Big Two? Superordinate factors in the NEO five factor inventory and the antisocial personality questionnaire. *Personality and Individual Differences*, **37**, 957–70.

Blackburn, R., Logan, C. and Renwick, S.J.D. (2005) Higher-order dimensions of personality disorder: hierarchical structure and relationships with the five-factor model, the interpersonal circle, and psychopathy. *Journal of Personality Disorders*, **19**, 597–623.

Blashfield, R.K. and Breen, M.J. (1989) Face validity of the DSM-IIIR personality disorders. *American Journal of Psychiatry*, **46**, 1575–9.

Bulthelier, S. and Hicker, H. (1997) *The Eysenck Personality Profiler – Manual*, SWETS Test Services, Frankfurt/Main.

Cale, E.M. (2006) A quantitative review of the relations between the 'Big 3' higher order personality dimensions and antisocial behaviour. *Journal of Research in Personality*, **40**, 250–84.

Caprara, G.V., Barbaranelli, C. and Comrey, A.L. (1992) A personological approach to the study of aggression. *Personality and Individual Differences*, **13**, 77–84.

Caparara, G.V., Perugini, M. and Barbaranelli, C. (1994) Studies of individual differences in aggression, in *The Dynamics of Aggression: Biological and Social Processes in Dyads and Groups* (eds M. Portegal and J.F. Knutson), Erlbaum, Hillsdale, NJ, pp. 123–53.

Caprara, G.V., Barbaranelli, C. and Zimbardo, P.G. (1996) Understanding the complexity of human aggression: affective, cognitive and social dimensions of individual differences in propensity towards aggression. *European Journal of Personality*, **10**, 133–55.

Caruso, J.C., Witkiewitz, K., Belcourt-Dittloff, A. and Gottlieb, J.D. (2001) Reliability of scores from the Eysenck personality questionnaire: a reliability generalization study. *Educational and Psychological Measurement*, **61**, 675–89.

Caspi, A., Moffitt, T.E., Silva, P.A. *et al.* (1994) Are some people crime-prone? Replications of the personality-crime relationship across countries, genders, races and methods. *Criminology*, **32**, 163–95.

Caspi, A. (2000) The child is the father of the man: personality continuities from childhood to adulthood. *Journal of Personality and Social Psychology*, **78**, 158–72.

Cattell, R.B. (1950) *Personality: A Systematic, Theoretical, and Factual Study*, McGraw Hill, New York.

Church, A.T. (1994) Relating the Tellegen and five-factor models of personality structure. *Journal of Personality and Social Psychology*, **67**, 898–909.

Clark, L.A. and Watson, D. (1999) Temperament: a new paradigm for trait psychology, in *Handbook of Personality: Theory and Research*, 2nd edn (eds L.A. Pervin and O.P. John), Guilford, New York, pp. 399–423.

Cloninger, C.R. (1987) A systematic method for clinical description and classification of personality variants. *Archives of General Psychiatry*, **44**, 573–88.

Cloninger, C.R., Svrakic, D.M. and Przybeck, T.R. (1993) A psychobiological model of temperament and character. *Archives of General Psychiatry*, **50**, 975–90.

Coid, J., Yang, M., Roberts, A. *et al.* (2006) Violence and psychiatric morbidity in the national household population of Britain: public health implications. *British Journal of Psychiatry*, **189**, 12–9.

Costa, P.T. and McCrae, R.R. (1992) *Revised NEO Personality Inventory and NEO Five-Factor Inventory Professional Manual*, Psychological Assessment Resources, Odessa, FL.

Costa, P.T., Jr and McCrae, R.R. (1995) Solid ground on the wetlands of personality – a reply to Block. *Psychological Bulletin*, **117**, 216–20.

Costa, P.T. and Widiger, T.A. (2003) *Personality disorders and the Five-Factor Model of Personality*, American Psychological Association, Washington, DC.

Davey, M., Eaker, D.G. and Walters, L.H. (2003) Resilience processes in adolescents: personality profiles, self-worth, and coping. *Journal of Adolescent Research*, **18**, 347–62.

De Fruyt, F., Van De Wiele, L. and Van Heeringen, C. (2000) Cloninger's psychobiological model of temperament and character and the five-factor model of personality. *Personality and Individual Differences*, **29**, 441–52.

Dennison, S.M., Stough, C. and Birgden, A. (2001) The Big 5 dimensional personality approach to understanding sexual offenders. *Psychology, Crime and Law*, **7**, 243–61.

Digman, J.M. (1997) Higher-order factors of the Big Five. *Journal of Personality and Social Psychology*, **73**, 1246–56.

Donnellan, M.B., Trzesniewski, K.H., Robins, R.W. *et al.* (2005) Low self-esteem is related to aggression, antisocial behavior, and delinquency. *Psychological Science*, **16**, 328–35.

Eastwood, L. (1985) Personality, intelligence and personal space among violent and non-violent delinquents. *Personality and Individual Differences*, **6**, 717–23.

Egan, V., Deary, I.J. and Austin, E. (2000) The NEO–FFI: emerging British norms and an item-analysis suggest N, A, and C are more reliable than O and E. *Personality and Individual Differences*, **29**, 907–20.

Egan, V., McMurran, M., Richardson, C. and Blair, M. (2000) Criminal cognitions and personality: what does the PICTS really measure? *Criminal Behaviour and Mental Health*, **10**, 170–84.

Egan, V., Austin, E., Elliot, D. *et al.* (2003) Personality traits, personality disorders and sensational interests in mentally disordered offenders. *Legal and Criminological Psychology*, **8**, 51–62.

Egan, V., Kavanagh, B. and Blair, M. (2005) Sexual offenders against children: the influence of personality and obsessionality on cognitive distortions. *Sexual Abuse: A Journal of Research and Treatment*, **17**, 223–40.

Engler, B. (2006) *Personality Theories*, 7th edn, Houghton-Mifflin, Boston, MA.

Eysenck, H.J. and Eysenck, S.B.G. (1976) *Psychoticism as a Dimension of Personality*, Hodder & Stoughtonm, London.

Eysenck, H.J. and Eysenck, M.W. (1985) *Personality and Individual Differences: A Natural Science Approach*, Plenum, New York.

Eysenck, H.J. (1992a) Four ways five factors are not basic. *Personality and Individual Differences*, **13**, 667–73.

Eysenck, H.J. (1992b) A reply to Costa and McCrae. P or A and C – the role of theory. *Personality and Individual Differences*, **13**, 867–8.

Eysenck, H.J. and Gudjonsson, G.H. (1989) *The Causes and Cures of Criminality*, Plenum, New York.

Farrington, D.P. and West, D.J. (1990) The Cambridge study in delinquent development: a long-term follow-up of 411 London males, in *Criminality: Personality, Behaviour, Life History* (eds H.J. Kerner and G. Kaiser), Springer Verlag, Berlin, pp. 115–38.

Fiske, D.W. (1949) Consistency of the factorial structures of personality ratings from different sources. *Journal of Abnormal and Social Psychology*, **44**, 329–44.

Frick, P.J. and Hare, R.D. (2002) *The Antisocial Process Screening Device*, Multi-Health Systems, Toronto.

Gleason, K.A., Jensen-Campbell, L.A. and Richardson, D.A. (2004) Agreeableness as a predictor of aggression in adolescence. *Aggressive Behavior*, **30**, 43–61.

Glicksohn, J., Ben-Shalom, U. and Lazar, M. (2004) Elements of unacceptable risk taking in combat units: an exercise in offender profiling. *Journal of Research in Personality*, **38**, 203–15.

Gray, J.A. (1981) A critique of Eysenck's model of personality, in *A Model for Personality* (ed. H.J. Eysenck), Springer, New York, pp. 246–76.

Gray, J.A. and McNaughton, N. (2000) *The Neuropsychology of Anxiety: An Inquiry into the Functions of the Septohippocampal System*, 2nd edn, Oxford University Press, Oxford.

Gudjonsson, G.H. (1997) Crime and personality, in *The Scientific Study of Human Nature* (ed. H. Nyborg), Pergamon, Oxford.

Halverson, C.F., Havill, V.L., Deal, J. *et al.* (2003) Personality structure as derived from parental ratings of free descriptions of children: the inventory of child individual differences. *Journal of Personality*, **71**, 995–1026.

Hart, S.D., Cox, D.N. and Hare, R.D. (1996) *Manual for the Screening Version of Psychopathy Checklist Revised (PCL:SV)*, Multi-Health Systems, Toronto.

Heaven, P.C.L. (1996) Personality and self-reported delinquency: analysis of the 'Big Five' personality dimensions. *Personality and Individual Differences*, **20**, 47–54.

Hodgson, R.J. and Rachman, S. (1977) Obsessional-compulsive complaints. *Behavioural Research and Therapy*, **15**, 389–95.

The Independent (2007) *Women Guilty in 'Toddler-Fighting' Video Trial*. http://news.independent.co.uk/uk/crime/article2369022.ece, retrieved 18 March, 2007.

Jakobwitz, S. and Egan, V. (2006) The dark triad and normal personality traits. *Personality and Individual Differences*, **40**, 331–9.

Judge, T.A., Erez, A., Bono, J.E. and Thoresen, C.J. (2002) Are measures of self-esteem, neuroticism, locus of control, and generalised self-efficacy indicators of a common core construct? *Journal of Personality and Social Psychology*, **83**, 693–710.

Kelley, T.L. (1939) Psychological factors of no importance. *Journal of Educational Psychology*, **30**, 139–43.

Kim, S.J., Lee, S.J. and Yune, S.K. (2006) The relationship between the biogenetic temperament and character and psychopathology in adolescents. *Psychopathology*, **39**, 80–6.

LaRowe, S.D., Patrick, C.J., Curtin, J.J. and Kline, J.P. (2006) Personality correlates of startle habituation. *Biological Psychology*, **72**, 257–64.

Larstone, R.M., Jang, K.L., Livesley, W.J. *et al.* (2002) The relationship between Eysenck's P–E–N model of personality, the five-factor model of personality, and traits denoting personality dysfunction. *Personality and Individual Differences*, **33**, 25–37.

Laurent, A., Gilvarry, C., Russell, A. and Murray, R. (2002) Personality dimensions and neuropsychological performance in first-degree relatives of patients with schizophrenia and affective psychosis. *Schizophrenia Research*, **55**, 239–48.

Livesley, W.J. and Jackson, D.N. (2002) *Manual for the Dimensional Assessment of Personality Pathology – Basic Questionnaire (DAPP)*, Research Psychologist's Press, London.

Loranger, A.W. (1999) *International Personality Disorder Examination*, Psychological Assessment Resources, Odessa, FL.

Lykken, D.T. (1995) *The Antisocial Personalities*, Lawrence Erlbaum Associates, New York.

Lynam, D.R. (1997) Pursuing the psychopath: capturing the fledgling psychopath in a nomological net. *Journal of Abnormal Psychology*, **106**, 425–38.

Lynam, D., Moffitt, T. and Stouthamer-Loeber, M. (1993) Explaining the relation between IQ and delinquency: class, race, test motivation, school failure, or self-control? *Journal of Abnormal Psychology*, **102**, 187–96.

Lynam, D.R., Caspi, A., Moffit, T.E. *et al.* (2000) The interaction between impulsivity and neighbourhood context on offending: the effects of impulsivity are stronger in poorer neighbourhoods. *Journal of Abnormal Psychology*, **109**, 563–74.

Lynam, D.R., Caspi, A., Moffitt, T.E. *et al.* (2005) Adolescent psychopathy and the Big Five: results from two samples. *Journal of Abnormal Child Psychology*, **33**, 431–43.

Mardaga, S. and Hansenne, M. (2007) Relationships between Cloninger's biosocial model of personality and the behavioral inhibition/approach systems (BIS/BAS). *Personality and Individual Differences*, **42**, 715–22.

Marshall, J., Egan, V. and English, M. (2006) The relative validity of psychopathy versus risk/needs-based assessments in the prediction of adolescent offending behaviour. *Legal and Criminological Psychology*, **11**, 197–210.

McCrae, R.R. and Costa, P.T. (1985) Comparison of EPI and psychoticism scales with measures of the five-factor model of personality. *Personality and Individual Differences*, **6**, 587–97.

McCrae, R.R. and Costa, P.T., Jr (2004) A contemplated revision of the NEO Five-Factor Inventory. *Personality and Individual Differences*, **36**, 587–96.

McCroskey, J.C., Heisel, A.D. and Richmond, V.P. (2001) Eysenck's big three and communication traits: three correlational studies. *Communication Monographs*, **68**, 360–6.

McHoskey, J.W., Worzel, W. and Szyarto, C. (1998) Machiavellianism and psychopathy. *Journal of Personality and Social Psychology*, **74**, 192–210.

Miller, J.D. and Lynam, D. (2001) Structural models of personality and their relationship to antisocial behaviour: a meta-analytic review. *Criminology*, **4**, 765–98.

Miller, J.D., Lynam, D. and Leukefeld, C. (2003) Examining antisocial behavior through the lens of the five factor model of personality. *Aggressive Behavior*, **29**, 497–514.

MORI. (2003) *Glasgow Young People's Survey, 2003*. Retrieved 23 July, 2004 (http://www.mori.com/polls/2003/glasgow.shtml).

Moutafi, J., Furnham, A. and Crump, J. (2006) What facets of openness and conscientiousness predict fluid intelligence scores? *Personality and Individual Differences*, **16**, 31–42.

Mulder, R.T. and Joyce, P.R. (1997) Temperament and the structure of personality disorder symptoms. *Psychological Medicine*, **27**, 99–106.

Murray, G., Rawlings, D., Allen, N.B. and Trinder, J. (2003) NEO Five-Factor Inventory scores: psychometric properties in a community sample. *Measurement and Evaluation in Counselling and Development*, **36**, 140–9.

Noller, P., Law, H. and Comrey, A.L. (1987) The Cattell, Comrey, and Eysenck personality factors compared: more evidence for five robust factors? *Journal of Personality and Social Psychology*, **53**, 775–82.

Norman, W.T. (1963) Toward an adequate taxonomy of personality attributes: replicated factor structure in peer nomination personality ratings. *Journal of Abnormal and Social Psychology*, **66**, 574–83.

Ozer, D. and Benet-Martínez, V. (2006) Personality and the prediction of consequential outcomes. *Annual Review of Psychology*, **57**, 401–21.

Paulhus, D.L. and Williams, K. (2002) The dark triad of personality: narcissism, Machiavellianism, and psychopathy. *Journal of Research in Personality*, **36**, 556–68.

Raine, A. and Jones, F. (1987) Attention, autonomic arousal, and personality in behaviorally disordered children. *Journal of Abnormal Child Psychology*, **15**, 583–99.

Raine, A. (1997) Classical conditioning, arousal and crime: a biosocial perspective, in *The Scientific Study of Human Nature* (ed. H. Nyborg), Pergamon, Oxford.

Roger, D. and Morris, J. (1991) The internal structure of the EPQ scales. *Personality and Individual Differences*, **12**, 759–64.

Salekin, R.T., Neumann, C.C., Lestico, A.R. *et al.* (2004) Psychopathy and comorbidity in an offender sample: taking a closer look at the potential importance of psychopathy over disruptive behavioural disorders. *Journal of Abnormal Psychology*, **113**, 416–37.

Salekin, R.T., Leistico, A.-M.R., Trobst, K.K. *et al.* (2005) Adolescent psychopathy and personality theory – the interpersonal circumplex: expanding evidence of a nomological net. *Journal of Abnormal Child Psychology*, **33**, 445–60.

Samuels, J., Bienvenu, J., Cullen, B. *et al.* (2004) Personality dimensions and criminal arrest. *Comprehensive Psychiatry*, **45**, 275–80.

Saucier, G. (1998) Replicable item-cluster subcomponents in the NEO five-factor inventory. *Journal of Personality Assessment*, **70**, 263–76.

Saucier, G. and Goldberg, L.R. (2001) Lexical studies of indigenous personality factors: premises, products, and prospects. *Journal of Personality*, **69**, 847–79.

Saulsman, L.M. and Page, A.C. (2004) The five-factor model and personality disorder empirical literature: a meta-analytic review. *Clinical Psychology Review*, **23**, 1055–85.

Schmitt, D.P., Allik, J., McCrae, R.R. and Benet-Martínez, V. (2007) The geographic distribution of Big Five personality traits: patterns and profiles of human self-description across 56 nations. *Journal of Cross-Cultural Psychology*, **38**, 173–212.

Shiner, R. and Caspi, A. (2003) Personality differences in childhood and adolescence: measurement, development and consequences. *Journal of Child Psychology and Psychiatry*, **44**, 2–32.

Skeem, J.L., Miller, J.D., Mulvey, E. *et al.* (2005) Using a five-factor lens to explore the relation between personality traits and violence in psychiatric patients. *Journal of Consulting and Clinical Psychology*, **73**, 454–65.

Stanford, M.S., Houston, R.J., Villemarette-Pittman, N.R. and Greve, K.W. (2003) Premeditated aggression: clinical assessment and cognitive psychophysiology. *Personality and Individual Differences*, **34**, 773–81.

Stewart, M.E., Ebmeier, K.P. and Deary, I.J. (2004) The structure of Cloninger's tridimensional personality questionnaire in a British sample. *Personality and Individual Differences*, **36**, 1403–18.

Stewart, M.E., Ebmeier, K.P. and Deary, I.J. (2005) Personality correlates of happiness and sadness: EPQ-R and TPQ compared. *Personality and Individual Differences*, **38**, 1085–96.

Tackett, J.L. (2006) Evaluating models of the personality-psychopathology relationship in children and adolescents. *Clinical Psychology Review*, **26**, 584–99.

Tellegen, A. (1982) *A Brief Manual for the Multidimensional Personality Questionnaire.* Unpublished manuscript, University of Minnesota.

Tellegen, A. and Waller, N.G. (1992) *Exploring Personality Through Test Construction: Development of the Multi-Dimensional Personality Questionnaire (MPQ).* Unpublished manuscript. Department of Psychology, University of Minnesota.

Trapnell, P. and Wiggins, J.S. (1991) Extension of the interpersonal adjective scales to the Big Five dimensions of personality. *Journal of Personality and Social Psychology*, **59**, 781–90.

Walters, G.D. (1995) The psychological inventory of criminal thinking styles, Part I: Reliability and preliminary validity. *Criminal Justice and Behaviour*, **22**, 307–25.

Warr, M. (2002) *Companions in Crime*, Cambridge University Press, Cambridge.

Watson, D. and Clark, L.A. (1984) Negative affectivity: the disposition to experience aversive emotional states. *Psychological Bulletin*, **96**, 465–90.

Wiggins, J.S. and Pincus, A.L. (1989) Conceptions of personality disorders and dimensions of personality. *Psychological Assessment*, **1**, 305–16.

Wood, J. and Newton, A.K. (2003) The role of personality and blame attribution in prisoners' experiences of anger. *Personality and Individual Differences*, **34**, 1453–65.

Woody, E. and Claridge, G. (1977) Psychoticism and thinking. *British Journal of Social and Clinical Psychology*, **16**, 241–8.

Zillmann, D. and Weaver, J.B. (1997) Psychoticism in the effect of prolonged exposure to gratuitous media violence on the acceptance of violence as a preferred means of conflict resolution. *Personality and Individual Differences*, **22**, 613–27.

Zuckerman, M. (1992) What is a basic factor and which factors are basic? Turtles all the way down. *Personality and Individual Differences*, **13**, 675–81.

Zuckerman, M. (1994) *Behavioral Expression and Biosocial Bases of Sensation Seeking*, Cambridge University Press, New York.

Chapter 5

NARCISSISM

CAROLINE LOGAN
Ashworth Hospital, UK

WHAT IS NARCISSISM?

Introduction

Narcissism, from its healthy presentation in individuals with no contact with clinical services through to its pathological presentation in narcissistic personality disorder where psychiatric and criminal justice contacts are more likely, has a long and fascinating history. Since the turn of the twentieth century, the mental health field has been both energised and confounded by contradictory opinions about the development and conceptualisation of narcissism, the clinical description of its pathological forms, its distinction from other but related clinical conditions, its treatment, and its impact on the treatment of other conditions (Kernberg, 1998a). In the last 56 years, sequential editions of the *Diagnostic and Statistical Manual of Mental Disorders* (DSM, American Psychiatric Association, 1952, 1968, 1980, 1994) have introduced some welcome consistency in our identification of personality disorder, including narcissistic personality disorder. However, narcissism is a rich, broad and meaningful concept whose relevance and implications for clinical practice extend beyond a set of narrow diagnostic criteria (Cooper and Sacks, 1991). That said, much about the clinical significance of narcissism for interpersonal functioning, self-esteem and affect regulation remains relatively unknown (Ronningstam, 2005). Further, while there is now some broad agreement about the relationship between narcissism and violence, the relevance of pathological narcissism to risk assessment and management is largely unexplored.

The objectives of this chapter are to examine the relationship between narcissism and violence and to explain the potential relevance of narcissism to risk assessment and risk management planning. Therefore, this chapter begins with a description of the concept of narcissism, its history, and current opinion about its normal and

Personality, Personality Disorder and Violence   Edited by Mary McMurran and Richard C. Howard
© 2009 John Wiley & Sons, Ltd

pathological variations and their origins. In addition, consideration is given to the similarities and differences between pathological narcissism and the concept of psychopathy, given that there is considerable overlap between the two conditions. This overview underpins the next part of the chapter, which is a review of what is currently understood about the relationship between narcissism and violence. Practical guidance on the assessment of narcissism for the purpose of an evaluation of risk follows, accompanied by an examination of the practicalities of risk assessment and management with clients with a narcissistic presentation and a history of violence. Options for the psychological treatment of pathological narcissism are then discussed, and the chapter concludes with a statement about the future direction of research and clinical practice, especially with clients in correctional and forensic psychiatric settings.

Origins of the Construct of Narcissism

In the story of Echo and Narcissus, Ovid links the concepts of bodily pleasure, self-love, envy, lack of empathy and death (Holmes, 2001). Narcissus was a child of exceptional beauty born of the rape of the nymph Liriope by the river god Cephisus. Blind Tiresias prophesied that the child would live a long life with such perfect beauty 'unless he learns to know himself' (Hughes, 1997, p. 74). Narcissus grew up a proud and ruthless young man who attracted the interest of many but who kept all at a distance. One day, the nymph Echo saw him hunting in the mountains. She was overcome by desire for Narcissus and let this be known to him but his rejection was outright and brutal: 'No,' he cried 'no, I would sooner be dead than let you touch me' (Hughes, 1997, p. 77). Echo became distraught and faded to nothing but a voice. In revenge, Echo's friends prayed to Nemesis the Corrector and asked that Narcissus be made to love in vain and suffer as Echo did. Nemesis granted their prayer. When Narcissus next went hunting, he came upon a perfect pool of water in which he saw the reflection of his own face and body and he fell in love for the first – and only – time. However, Narcissus' love was tormented – he did not recognise the figure as himself and became distressed when his advances on the beautiful young man were thwarted by the skin of the water. Eventually, Narcissus came to realise that the figure in the pool was himself. Unable to fulfil his love, he let his grief destroy him and Narcissus invited death to take him quickly 'where this pain can never follow' (Hughes, 1997, p. 82).

The story of Narcissus illustrates the dilemma that underpins self-love, the condition that has come to be known as narcissism (Holmes, 2001). On the one hand, the narcissist can dominate a monstrous world of self-love and complete self-interest where the emotional significance of others is minimal; he or she enforces a state of unchallenged and unrivalled perfection but ultimately he or she is lonely and unfulfilled, at ease with no one and nowhere. On the other hand, the narcissist can take the risk of seeking knowledge, closeness and interdependency with others. The cost of doing so, however, is the abandonment of the perfect self because being close to others in this way means being confronted with one's own imperfections and making compromises in order to share and maintain a meaningful and ultimately rewarding attachment. The prophecy of Tiresias encapsulates this dilemma: for Narcissus to survive, he had to transcend his perfect self-love in order to love another. However, Narcissus would not do this – and so he died.

How did the Narcissus myth come to represent an enduringly powerful psychological construct? The myth has been perpetuated, explored, interpreted and reinterpreted across centuries and indeed millennia of art and literature. For example, a first-century AD wall painting of Narcissus captivated by his own reflection has been uncovered in a house in Pompeii. Simple medieval images of Narcissus admiring his image in the spring (e.g. Narcissus at the Source, a book illumination for *Roman de la Rose* by Guillaume de Lorris and Jean de Meun, Paris, 1405) anticipated the dramatic and still popular canvases of Caravaggio (*Narcissus*, 1597–1599), Poussin (*Echo and Narcissus*, 1628–1630), Turner (*Narcissus and Echo*, 1804), and, in the twentieth century, the Pre-Raphaelite John William Waterhouse (*Echo and Narcissus*, 1903) and the surrealist Salvador Dali (*The Metamorphosis of Narcissus*, 1937). In literature, the myth survives in Ovid's still popular *Metamorphoses* (written between the years 2 and 8 AD; see Hughes 1997) and in European texts by, for example, Calderon de la Barca (*Eco y Narciso*, 1661) and Jean-Jacques Rousseau (*Narcissus, or, The Lover of Himself*, 1742). And in allegorical forms, the myth has been explored since by diverse figures such as Mozart (*Don Giovanni*, 1788), Stendhall (*Le Rouge et al Noir*, 1830), Dostoyevsky (*The Double*, 1846), Wilde (*The Picture of Dorian Gray*, 1891), and more recently, Norman Mailer (*The Executioner's Song*, 1979), Elfriede Jelinek (*The Piano Teacher*, 1983), and Bret Easton Ellis (*American Psycho*, 1991). These and many other representations depict some aspect of the dreadful consequences of excessive self- or selfish love. The persistent popularity of the myth that encapsulates these consequences made the eventual progression of Narcissus from cultural icon to clinical entity perhaps inevitable.

The first use of the concept of narcissism in psychiatry was to refer to the 'Narcissus-like' tendency to transform sexual feelings into self-admiration (Ellis, 1898, p. 280; Ronningstam, 2005). Subsequently, Näcke (1899) used the word 'narcissism' to refer to the preoccupation with the sight and pleasures of one's own body in a manner usually reserved for the admiration of others. Thus, Näcke regarded narcissism as a disorder of sexual interest, paving the way for Freud to incorporate the construct into his developing theories of sexuality and personality. In general, Freud regarded narcissism as the choice of the self as the object of libidinal interest, a normal phase or aspect of development. Narcissism becomes problematic when an individual fails to evolve from this phase and it is this restriction in development that generates pathological forms of narcissism in adults (Freud, 1911/1957), where such clinical presentations are associated with problems primarily in attachments and in sexual conduct.

Over the course of the twentieth century, narcissism as a psychological construct has undergone extensive study and application (see Ronningstam, 2005 for a comprehensive review). In brief, the psychoanalytic perspective dominated early thinking on the construct, with its exploration in dreams and psychotherapy (e.g. Freud, 1914/1957; Sadger, 1910; Wälder, 1925). Freud and later Horney (1939) and Reich (1960) explored in detail the relationship between narcissism and the regulation of self-esteem, linking failures in such regulation to depression and hypochondria. Towards the mid-century, attention began to be directed to defining the different 'types' of narcissistic personality and a great many diverse options emerged. For example, Freud (1931/1957) identified the *narcissistic libidinal type* while W. Reich described the *phallic-narcissistic character* (Reich, 1933/1949). And Murray, departing from the popular theme of sexuality, proposed the *Icarus complex* as existing in one who habitually pursued unattainable goals (Murray, 1955). In the late 1960s, however, a more coherent and recognisable understanding of narcissism began to emerge. Still working within a psychoanalytic perspective, Kernberg formulated the narcissistic personality structure (Kernberg, 1967) and, a few years later, Kohut set down the first comprehensive explanation of narcissistic personality disorder in which self-esteem dysregulation featured prominently (Kohut, 1971). Some clarity in the concept of narcissistic injury (Goldberg, 1973) and narcissistic rage (Kohut, 1972) followed as the mechanism by which narcissism may be linked to violence began to be explored. Since the 1970s, discussion has continued into typologies of narcissism (e.g. Bursten, 1973; Millon and Davis, 1996), although in the mainstream, narcissistic personality disorder as defined in the DSM manuals has dominated and informed routine clinical practice. More recently, comorbidity or the clinical or conceptual overlap between narcissistic personality disorder and comparable conditions such as borderline personality disorder (Kernberg, 1975) and psychopathy (Widiger, 2006) has become of increasing interest as are cognitive-based as opposed to psychoanalytic conceptualisations of the condition and its treatment (e.g. Beck *et al.*, 1990; Ronningstam, 1998; Young, 1999).

Normal and Pathological Narcissism

Consistent with contemporary dimensional models of personality, it is proposed that narcissism has normal adaptation-enhancing as well as abnormal maladaptive variations (Ronningstam, 2005; Trull, 2005). Indeed, Kohut (1972) suggests that this 'independent line of development, from the primitive to the most mature, adaptive, and culturally viable' is one of the most essential points to be stressed about the narcissistic sector of the personality (p. 362). The key aspects of narcissism, emphasised in each variation from normal to abnormal, are (a) the quality, cohesiveness and stability of the individual's view of the self, (b) affect regulation, which is linked to the regulation of self-esteem, and (c) psychological and emotional investment in others and the nature and quality of interactions with them (Ronningstam, 2005). The normal functioning of the narcissistic state is now described, followed by its progressively more extreme variations.

Healthy or normal narcissism is essential (Kernberg, 1998a). Stone (1998) suggests that normal narcissism serves a number of important functions. First, individuals must have sufficient regard for their physical safety and security to motivate them to avoid danger and respond appropriately to threat – actions consistent with self-preservation. Second, they must have sufficient regard for themselves as individual entities distinct from others as well as sufficient self-awareness in order to interact equitably with others and avoid being overwhelmed or consumed. Therefore, in an individual whose narcissism is normal or at a healthy level, self-appraisals are on the whole realistic and the disapproval of others is used as an opportunity to extend abilities rather than as a reason to reject them – the individual's self-esteem is regulated (Ronningstam, 2005). Emotions such as pride, envy, shame, inferiority, humiliation and guilt are not excessively prominent, and when they are experienced they are tolerated and responded to adaptively; the management of these emotions is primarily within the control of the individual. Such an achievement represents a regulated affect (Ronningstam, 2005). Finally, interpersonal relationships feature appropriate and fair self-preservation, self-regard and entitlement; those with healthy levels of narcissism are able to experience empathy and compassion towards others, as well as the capacity to belong and commit to others (Ronningstam, 2005). Thus, the individual achieves a realistic balance between attainable ideals and actual capability. In this way, moderate self-regard and entitlement are essential to healthy self-concept and functional interpersonal relationships.

Ronningstam (2005) tracks the breakdown of healthy narcissism into its pathological variants. Between healthy and pathological narcissism is *exaggerated or extraordinary narcissism*. In this personality presentation, heightened self-regard and an exaggerated sense of invulnerability and indestructibility are associated with genuine achievement, arrogance and charisma. Self-confidence is also raised and capacity for risk-taking behaviour is exaggerated. Strong feelings are experienced and used in order to achieve creative or occupational tasks or goals. Heightened entitlement acts in concert with the ability to take on exceptional tasks, leadership and mission. Ideals, standards and achievements are usually high. Therefore, extraordinary narcissism is associated with genuine ability, an understandably – even justifiably – high self-regard, and largely adaptive functioning. Self-esteem and affect are mostly regulated and interpersonal relationships are on the whole acceptable although they may demonstrate more change, conflict and drama than generally features in those whose narcissism is within normal limits. However, the risk of infringing the rights of others in pursuit of the individual's own achievements, interests, desires and rights is elevated in those with extraordinary levels of narcissism.

It is in the realm of *pathological narcissism* that most interest lies among clinicians (Kernberg, 1998a). This is especially the case in forensic settings. The terms disordered narcissism, pathological narcissism, narcissistic personality disorder and even psychopathy are frequently used interchangeably and as if they refer to much the same entity (Ronningstam, 2005). However, some explanation – and differentiation – is required.

On the whole, a pathological level of narcissism is characterised by deficits in each of the key areas. The regulation of self-esteem is poor because actions are oriented towards the protection and sustenance of a grandiose and inflated but ultimately fragile and unstable self. Affect regulation is compromised by difficulties in processing and modulating feelings, specifically anger, shame and envy. Interpersonal relationships are generally dysfunctional because they are used to protect and enhance the individual's self-esteem at the cost of mutual relativeness and intimacy (Ronningstam, 2005). The extent of pathology is determined by the severity of both the disorder and its consequences – the clinical significance of the impairment caused – and the dominance of aggression over shame. Therefore, when the level of pathological narcissism is less severe, when it is temporary or more situationally determined and regular personal, interpersonal, and/or vocational functioning is not markedly disturbed, presentation may be referred to as 'narcissistic disturbance', 'disordered narcissism' or 'narcissistic traits' (Ronningstam, 2005). At this level, there is changeability and fluctuations between extraordinary and pathological narcissistic functioning. Such vicissitudes are constantly present and the coexistence of and intertwined interaction between healthy and pathological aspects can make it challenging to identify and understand (Kohut, 1966; Watson and Biderman, 1993).

When the level of pathological narcissism is more severe, the diagnostic term 'narcissistic personality disorder' (NPD) may be utilised to refer to persistent and pervasive dysfunction that meets DSM criteria for the disorder of the same name. NPD refers to specific deformations in the personality structure. Self-esteem is inconsistent, fragile and maintained by pathologically defensive, expressive and supportive regulatory processes. Affect regulation is influenced by feelings of rage, shame and envy, and the capacity for empathy and interpersonal commitment is impaired. The text-revised fourth edition of DSM (DSM-IV-TR, American Psychiatric Association, 2000) lists the symptoms of NPD as follows:

> A pervasive pattern of grandiosity (in fantasy or behaviour), need for admiration and lack of empathy, beginning by early adulthood and present in a variety of contexts, as indicated by five or more of the following: (1) has a grandiose sense of self-importance (e.g., exaggerates his or her achievements and talents, expects to be recognised as superior without commensurate achievements); (2) is preoccupied with fantasies of unlimited success, power, brilliance, beauty or ideal love; (3) believes that he or she is 'special' and unique and can only be understood by, or should associate with, other special or high-status people (or institutions); (4) requires excessive admiration; (5) has a sense of entitlement, that is, unreasonable expectations of especially favourable treatment or automatic compliance with his or her expectations; (6) is interpersonally exploitative, that is, takes advantage of others to achieve his or her own ends; (7) lacks empathy; is unwilling to recognise or identify with the feelings and needs of others; (8) is often envious of others or believes that others are envious of him or her; and (9) shows arrogant, haughty behaviours or attitudes.

NPD as defined is thought to affect less than 1% of the general population and occur at a rate of between 2% and 16% in clinical populations (American Psychiatric Association, 2000). In offender populations in England, NPD has been diagnosed in 6% of female prisoners, 7% of male sentenced and 8% of male remand prisoners (Singleton, Meltzer and Gatward, 1998), although a higher prevalence – 25% – has been detected in a sample of English male mentally disordered offenders (Blackburn et al., 2003). Prevalence appears to decline with age, although this finding has so far only been reported in non-clinical samples (Foster, Campbell and Twenge, 2003). NPD is marginally more common in men than in women (American Psychiatric Association, 2000), and its frequency is not thought to vary across race, ethnic group or culture (Campbell and Baumeister, 2006).

Beyond DSM-IV-TR, there is some clinical and empirical support for the existence of a number of subtypes of NPD (Ronningstam, 2005): (1) the arrogant, oblivious type; (2) the shy, hypervigilant type; and (3) the psychopathic narcissistic type. Cooper (1998) and others delineate the first two types more closely, also referring to them as overt and covert narcissists, a distinction Wink (1991) has also explored in the form of the grandiosity-exhibitionism and vulnerability–sensitivity types. The psychopathic narcissistic type has also been given much consideration but somewhat separately from the first two types listed.

The *arrogant variant of pathological narcissism* presents with an inflated and vulnerable self-esteem but with an inner sense of superiority and uniqueness; he or she is inherently self-centred, haughty, entitled, boastful and pretentious (Ronningstam and Gunderson, 1990). Criticism is negatively received because it implies imperfection, which threatens feelings of shame or humiliation (Kernberg, 1998a). Grandiose fantasies are used to support, enhance and ultimately protect and stabilise self-esteem (Ronningstam and Gunderson, 1990). Feelings of shame and humiliation, as well as anger and envy, are acutely felt, and reactions to these feelings, to their source and cause, tend to be extreme and may include violence (Morey and Jones, 1998). Variations in mood reflect the instability of self-esteem. Other people are used to protect the vulnerable self-esteem of the arrogant narcissist – others are used to enhance self-esteem through requests if not demands for admiration and favour and also through their denigration, making the narcissist feel powerful, in control and ultimately superior.

In contrast, the *shy variant of pathological narcissism* is an inhibited, ashamed and resentful individual (Ronningstam, 2005). Feelings of shame limit not only the overt expression of grandiosity but also the pursuit of actual opportunities and capabilities. Self-belief is still superior and the individual shares the sense of uniqueness evident in arrogant narcissists. However, while the arrogant narcissist is socially confident, vocationally involved, openly aggressive, and actively in search of narcissistic gratification and self-enhancement, the shy narcissist is constricted in all these areas. The self-esteem of the shy narcissist is maintained primarily by the use of grandiose fantasies that compensate for perceived inadequacies. Criticism is acutely felt and emotions are controlled and concealed suggesting extreme vulnerability. In addition, hypochondria is more evident. Attention from others is welcome or sought compared to the arrogant type and the shy narcissist is inhibited in his or her attempts at intimacy with others for fear of criticism and rejection, such that isolation enhances feelings of incompetence. He or she has an impaired capacity for empathy and genuine commitment to others and the commitments they allow themselves are restricted due to strong feelings of envy. The shy narcissist can feel guilt and remorse, which the arrogant narcissist rarely can, but their shallowness, envy and inability to genuinely and consistently care for others cause other types of interpersonal conflicts and rejections. Mood is usually dysphoric with unhappiness, pessimism, resentment, lack of fulfilment, yearning and waiting predominating (Akhtar, 2003; Wink, 1991). The shy variant of pathological narcissism is easy to overlook and a good deal harder to identify and assess than the arrogant type (Ronningstam, 2005), possibly because this type of pathological narcissism has not been subject to anything like the same level of discussion and empirical scrutiny as the arrogant type. Nonetheless, the shy variant has a great deal of pathology in common with the arrogant type and the consequences of the disorder can be equally disruptive.

The *psychopathic narcissist* shares much with the arrogant narcissist, although a grandiose sense of self-worth, exploitative behaviour, envy, lack of commitment and impaired or lack of empathic capacity predominate in the former. Ronningstam

(2005) lists additional features of the psychopathic narcissist that are common to this type as the following: irritability and raging reactions (Morey and Jones, 1998), callous affect and deceitful interpersonal style (Harpur, Hakstian and Hare, 1988), lack of remorse or guilt (Harpur, Hakstian and Hare, 1988), interpersonal sadism (Kernberg, 1998b), violence (Baumeister, Smart and Boden, 1996) and criminality (Gunderson and Ronningstam, 2001). Kernberg (1998b) uses the expression 'malignant narcissism' to identify the presentation of the individual who is both pathologically narcissistic and antisocial, where self-justifiable violence, sadistic cruelty and self-destructiveness are in service to the very fragile and unstable self-esteem. However, to what extent do these characteristics constitute a difference in type from the arrogant variant of pathological narcissism – or is the difference one of severity?

Recent conceptualisations of the clinical construct of psychopathy distinguish primary and secondary variations (see Poythress and Skeem, 2006 for a comprehensive review). The concept of primary psychopathy emphasises affective deficiency, which is constitutional, an overt conning and deceitful interpersonal style, and aggression, hostility and impulsivity (Blackburn, 1998; Karpman, 1941). Additionally, the primary psychopath is extraverted, confident, dominant and low in anxiety. In contrast, secondary psychopathy emphasises emotional disturbance, which is based on early psychosocial learning, covert social anxiety, withdrawal, submissiveness, shame-proneness, and sensitivity, as well as anger and extreme reactivity (Blackburn, 1998; Karpman, 1941; Wink, 1991). Unlike the primary psychopath, the secondary psychopath can experience empathy and can activate a wish for acceptance by others. The primary and secondary distinction has implications for the formulation of behaviour: 'the primary psychopath often acts purposefully and directly to maximise his gain or excitement, whereas the secondary psychopath typically acts out of such emotions as hatred and revenge, often in reaction to circumstances that exacerbate his or her neurotic conflict' (Skeem et al., 2003, p. 520). The primary psychopath reflects many of the characteristics of the arrogant variant of pathological narcissism – and the secondary psychopath the shy variant – but the difference appears more one of severity than of type. It is possible, therefore, that the psychopathic type of narcissist, rather than being a third variant of pathological narcissism – of NPD – is instead a more extreme or malignant form of the disorder. The most extreme representation of the arrogant variant of pathological narcissism resembles descriptions of primary psychopathy, while the most extreme representation of the shy variant resembles descriptions of secondary psychopathy.

For reasons that are unclear, the literatures on narcissism and psychopathy have evolved quite separately (Hart and Hare, 1998). The narcissism literature largely belongs to the area of psychoanalysis, as well as clinical psychiatry and psychology. In contrast, the psychopathy literature, having matured in the laboratory, now exists primarily in the arena of forensic psychiatry and psychology. How does the clinical concept of pathological narcissism relate to the construct of psychopathy as measured in criminal justice settings by the Psychopathy Checklist-Revised (PCL-R; Hare, 1991, 2003)? The PCL-R measures a constellation of interpersonal, affective and socially deviant characteristics. The inclusion of items measuring social deviance, in particular, criminal conduct, as symptoms of the disorder of psychopathy has been controversial and widely disputed (e.g. Blackburn, 2007;

Widiger, 2006). The consensus of opinion among those who dispute the inclusion of measures of criminal conduct in clinical evaluations of psychopathy is that, conceptually, criminality is a consequence of being psychopathic – a person may be psychopathic but not inherently a criminal (Skeem and Cooke, in press). Based both on theoretical considerations and detailed data analysis, the removal from the PCL-R of items measuring criminality leaves a constellation of items measuring arrogant and deceitful interpersonal style, deficient affective experience, and impulsive and irresponsible behavioural style (Cooke and Michie, 2001; Cooke, Michie and Hart, 2006). The overlap between these 13 items and the characteristics of pathological narcissism is notable and worthy of empirical exploration as a way of uniting the disparate narcissism and psychopathy literatures and improving our overall knowledge of pathological self-love and its consequences for the individual and others. In particular, the literature on narcissism has the potential to explain the origins and process of pathological self-love and its myriad consequences for others in those identified as psychopathic. To date, the PCL-R-dominant literature on psychopathy has largely failed to do this due to its preoccupation with criminality at the expense of understanding the role of self-construct and the quality of attachments to others.

The co-occurrence of pathological forms of narcissism with other mental disorders and disordered personality presentations is an essential subject of study (Ronningstam, 2005), not only to enhance understanding of what is unique about narcissism but also to improve the clinical response to those who present for treatment. Grandiosity and inflated self-esteem are features of both NPD and bipolar spectrum disorders; NPD is one of the most commonly diagnosed personality disorders in clients who have a bipolar condition (Brieger, Ehrt and Merneros, 2003), and bipolar spectrum disorders are common in clients with NPD (5–11%, Ronningstam, 1996). Depression and dysthymia are also detected relatively frequently in those with NPD (42–50%; Ronningstam, 1996) and they are often the reason he or she will access mental health services (Bockian, 2006; Campbell and Baumeister, 2006); acute depression as a reaction to narcissistic injury – humiliation, defeat, failure or loss – can generate a conscious need for help. This type of depression, which has been called 'empty depression', is characterised by 'guiltless despair', self-pity, feelings of emptiness and depletion, hopelessness, meaninglessness and also lethargy (Kohut, 1977). Substance use disorders are also common in clients with NPD (24–50%; Ronningstam, 1996) where intoxication and dependency distracts from – or defends – the client's vulnerability. Addiction has been proposed as an attempt by the narcissist to re-establish lost omnipotence and grandiosity or as a defence against intolerable feelings of rage, shame and depression (Kernberg, 1975; Ronningstam, 2005). Substance use disorders, as with mood disorders, are a common means by which narcissists will access mental health services.

With regards to comorbidity between pathological narcissism and other personality disorders, the most frequent co-occurrence appears to be with the borderline and antisocial disorders (Cooper, 1998; Ronningstam, 2005). With respect to borderline personality disorder (BPD), Holdwick et al. (1998) found that NPD shares with it the symptoms of affect dysregulation and unstable and dysfunctional relationships. Need for attention is also a shared feature (First, Frances and Pincus, 1995) as are sensitivity to criticism and, to some extent, entitlement. However, the narcissist has inflated self-esteem and a more cohesive sense of self, in contrast to the unstable borderline self-image, self-destructiveness, impulsivity and abandonment concerns (First, Frances and Pincus, 1995). Antisocial personality disorder and NPD share deficits in empathy. However, while the antisocial individual modulates a basically functional capacity for empathy in order to facilitate their individual criminal acts, the narcissist appears to have a more pervasive cognitive or emotional inability to identify with and feel for other people (Ronningstam, 2005). Some commonalities can also be found between NPD and histrionic (i.e. need for attention), paranoid (e.g. suspiciousness), obsessive-compulsive (i.e. perfectionism) and schizoid personality disorders (e.g. withdrawal or emotional distancing from others; First, Frances and Pincus, 1995; Ronningstam, 2005). The extent to which these patterns of comorbidity indicate the genuine co-occurrence of disorders or are symptomatic of poorly defined, even arbitrary, diagnostic criteria has yet to be determined (Clark, 2007).

The Development of Pathological Narcissism

The focus of the remainder of this chapter is on pathological forms of narcissism. In this section, attention is given to its origins – where does pathological narcissism come from and what environmental conditions nurture its development? Unfortunately, there is a paucity of good quality research into early parent–child interactions, family communication systems, and family dynamics on the basis of which theories about the aetiology of pathological narcissism have been developed. Interestingly, this is also the case in the study of psychopathy where developmental issues have largely been explored through the study of the heritability of antisocial behaviour (e.g. Farrington, 2006; Waldman and Rhee, 2006), even though this is not a core feature of the disorder. Consequently, the various hypotheses that exist about how healthy narcissism becomes pathological are largely untested.

A number of pathways to the development of pathological narcissism have been suggested (Ronningstam, 2005). First, biological or genetic factors have been examined in a small number of studies looking at personality disorder development in general rather than NPD in particular. For example, Jang et al. (1996) in a study of 483 twins found a median heritability of personality disorder traits of 45%. Livesley et al. (1993), looking at narcissism in particular, estimated heritability at 64% in a study of 175 volunteer twin pairs. Also, in a study of twins, Torgersen et al. (2000) showed that genes could explain nearly 80% of the variation in the traits of NPD. Much more research is required to explain and develop these findings but they suggest that core aspects of narcissism – such as hypersensitivity, strong aggressive drive, low anxiety or frustration tolerance, and problems with the regulation of emotions (Schore, 1994) – are subject to significant genetic influence.

A second strand of research investigating the development of pathological narcissism has examined the relevance of disruption to the neurobiological origins of affect regulation. One of the many roles played by parents (or caregivers) is to help children to develop a realistic level of self-esteem and to modulate and neutralise grandiosity, narcissistic distress and excitement (Ronningstam, 2005). However, if parents are inconsistent in their attunement to their children or the quality of the attachment between them is weak or intermittent, this can lead to deficiencies in the development of self-esteem and affect regulation (Ronningstam, 2005). In addition, specific caregiver–child attachment patterns may lead to the development of NPD. Schore (1994) describes an 'insecure-resistant' attachment between parent and child, which can contribute to a state of hyper-activation and affect under-regulation. This state can result in overt grandiosity, enhanced entitlement and aggressive reactions to others. In contrast, a 'depressed-hypo-arousing' attachment pattern contributes to low energy and affect over-regulation, leading to inhibition, shyness, predominant shame and hidden grandiose strivings. Therefore, Schore proposes if the parent persistently and ineffectively regulates the child out of a low-arousal shame state or fails to offer limit-setting in high-arousal states, the child may not develop autonomic control or the capacity to neutralise grandiosity, regulate excitement, or modulate narcissistic distress. Pathological narcissism in the adult, Schore (1994) hypothesised, is therefore more likely.

The role of parents or caregivers in creating the potential for pathological narcissism to develop is critical in a number of psychosocial models of its aetiology. For example, Fonagy and colleagues have investigated affect mirroring and mental representation by parents (Fonagy et al., 2002). In general, parents mirror the emotions of their children and, in doing so, help their children to label and identify their own emotional states and those of the people around them. However, when this mirroring process is absent or incorrect, as when the parent misinterprets the child's emotions and provides erroneous feedback to the child, this can lead to distortions and mislabeling by the child: 'The self-representation will not have strong ties to the underlying emotional state' (Fonagy et al., 2002, p. 11). Consequently, feelings of emptiness ensue reflecting the disconnection between the secondary representations of emotions and the original self. In addition, the parent who misinterprets and misrepresents their child's emotions in this way is more likely to project their own feelings and ambitions onto their child (Ronningstam, 2005). The child then assumes incredible importance to the parent as he or she becomes the regulator of that parent's self-esteem (Fonagy et al., 2002). The child thus internalises the parent's state of mind as a core part of his or her identity creating an unstable and ultimately false self-esteem, which is increasingly defended by grandiose beliefs originating in this powerful role. The developing child fails to understand others or himself or herself and increasingly relies upon fantasy and interpersonal dominance as a way of maintaining self-esteem.

The quality of the attachment between parent (or caregiver) and child has been studied more generally to understand the origins of the specific difficulties pathological narcissists have in acknowledging the identity and separateness of others. Fonagy (2001) describes a detached-dismissing attachment pattern between parent and child as that most likely to predict the development of pathological narcissism: the dismissing parent creates a child who is dissatisfied, angry or afraid of attachments with others and the child grows up to prefer being alone or at least emotionally independent. Consistent with this view are Rosenfeld's 'thin-skinned' narcissist, who is vulnerable to and confused by others and therefore feels helpless and defective and consequently angry at others, and 'thick-skinned' narcissist, who projects his or her inadequacies onto others thus creating the perfect excuse to devalue them (Fonagy, 2001; Rosenfeld, 1971). There is some empirical support for a dismissing attachment style in adolescents and adults who are narcissistic (e.g. Rosenstein and Horowitz, 1996), although here as with much of this work on the development of pathological narcissism, there is considerable dependence on the extensive interpretation of relatively limited empirical evidence.

How else may parents foster the development of pathological narcissism in their children? P. Kernberg (1989) proposed the following: '[A]s long as the child remains outside of the parent's internal representational world, there is significantly less risk for the development of NPD. Conversely, if the parent's primitive projective mechanisms involve the child excessively in the parent's own narcissistic pathology, the child is also likely to develop a narcissistic disorder' (p. 684). Rinsley (1989) discusses separation failure between parent and child, where the child fails to detach because of the role of the child as the parent's surrogate spouse, sibling, dependent child or accepting parent. This exalted position as the parent's masterpiece of creation (Elkind, 1991) creates a high degree of individuation in the child but also a deep-seated fear of being insignificant and invisible outside of the parent–child relationship, thus enhancing the role of grandiose fantasy in maintaining a position of superiority when challenged. Berkowitz and colleagues also examined separation failure but this time in adolescents (Berkowitz et al., 1974). The adolescent's normal strivings to become independent are perceived by the narcissistic parent as an injury and the parent's reaction is consequently one of competition, devaluation and rage. The child who is repeatedly seduced by their power to influence the parent's self-experiences and self-esteem thus becomes one in whom narcissism is disturbed – entitlement, control and grandiosity are more likely to assume a dominant role in subsequent efforts at attachment with others.

In conclusion, there are a number of hypotheses about the development of pathological narcissism but only patchy evidence to support any one of them. The role of a combination of genetic and environmental – specifically parental – influences seems to be certain here as with all human conditions. However, further evidence is awaited to determine just what the relative influence of these two fundamental forces is and the precise mechanism by which they cultivate pathological narcissism in all its forms.

NARCISSISM AND VIOLENCE

The Link between Narcissism and Violence

Narcissism is more likely to be a major contributor to, if not the origin of actual, attempted or threatened violence when its clinical presentation is pathological. What do we understand about the process by which pathological narcissism creates the potential for violence?

The resting narcissistic state, as it were, is grandiose, exceptional, controlling, exploitative, emotionally shallow, over-dependent on admiration, unjustifiably superior in attitude, excessively self-referential and self-centred, and lacking in capacity for commitment and empathy. Self-esteem is neither statically high nor low but inflated and vulnerable or fragile (Baumeister, Bushman and Campbell, 2000). This vulnerability creates the potential for harm through exposure to situations or people who will highlight imperfections, weaknesses or deficiencies, thus generating feelings of shame, envy, humiliation and guilt, which are perceived as intolerable to one who relies on a superior status to feel whole or complete (Malmquist, 1996). Baumeister, Bushman and Campbell (2000) refer to this phenomenon as 'threatened egotism'. When the potential for such harm is perceived, that is when the narcissistic person has perceived himself or herself to have been injured or to be at risk of injury, the intolerable emotions are evoked followed either immediately or at a later time by a self-righteous defensive response intended to punish the actual or threatened perpetrator and thus repair the damage done to self-esteem (Malmquist, 1996). Self-righteous responses in less serious manifestations of pathological narcissism may occur in fantasy where the individual gains satisfaction and indeed gratification from imagining some form of retribution in which the injuring party is subject to the narcissist's domination and control and made to feel devalued or humiliated. Thus, in some cases, fantasies alone can restore the narcissistic state and re-establish a sense of power (Malmquist, 1996).

However, self-righteous responses in the most serious manifestations of pathological narcissism may involve (a) the breakdown of the ego defences that ordinarily serve to control aggression or violence (Lewis, 1993), followed by (b) a combination of fantasy and actual conduct in which domination, control, humiliation, denigration, damage and even destruction are possible outcomes dependent on the scale of the perceived injury – a phenomenon that Kohut refers to as 'narcissistic rage' (Kohut, 1972). In the view of the narcissist, the scale of the response is proportionate to the injury caused and it is justified given the profound nature of the threat to self (Kohut, 1972); he or she is righting a wrong and, in fighting to restore self-esteem, is fighting for his or her metaphorical life (Malmquist, 1996). In some scenarios, the reaction of the victim may protract the harm being done to them, as in predatory stalking (Meloy, 1998). Regardless, the narcissistic state is restored only on the satisfactory conclusion of the self-righteous response, when the domination of the narcissist has been reasserted and the vulnerability of the self-esteem concealed once again. This hypothesis for the link between narcissism and violence is illustrated in Figure 5.1.

The first of the key elements of this model is the vulnerability of the narcissist to injury. This vulnerability is inherent in the narcissistic state: for an individual to maintain an unjustified favourable self-esteem in a social environment in which evidence of imperfection is likely to be everywhere, he or she must try to control the environment, thus pre-empting and minimising risk of injury (Carroll, 1987). Paradoxically, such efforts at control create the potential for more conflict than might otherwise have been the case, and hostility and aggression may be used as 'weapons' to discourage potential injuries (Kernis, Grannemann and Barclay, 1989). The tendency of narcissists to externalise blame means that they are more likely to react to injury with anger – an externalising emotion – rather than with sadness or anxiety – both internalising emotions (Twenge and Campbell, 2003). Further, the extent to which self-esteem is inflated appears to correlate directly with the scale of the harm used: 'when large groups of people differ in self-esteem, the group with the higher self-esteem is generally the more violent one' (Baumeister, Bushman and Campbell, 2000; p. 26).

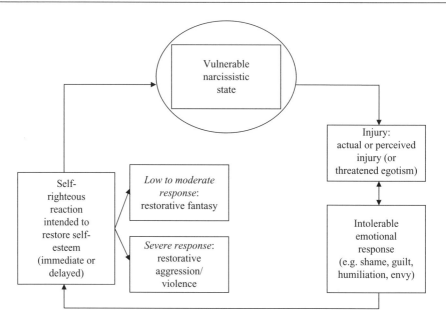

Figure 5.1   Hypothesised link between narcissism and violence.

The second of the key elements of this model is that the objective of the self-righteous response to the perceived injury is restorative through the projection onto the injuring party of the emotions regarded as most intolerable to the narcissist. That is, the narcissist wishes to avoid intolerable feelings such as shame, guilt and humiliation. Therefore, on perceiving themselves as injured or in threat of injury, the narcissist acts to generate in the injuring party the very emotions he or she seeks to avoid (Kohut, 1972), which could explain the socially meaningful, highly personal and vindictive nature of the harm narcissists can cause (Baumeister, Bushman and Campbell, 2000). Injuries to the vulnerable narcissist are excessively threatening – self- or life threatening – and the self-righteous response may restore the narcissist's precarious belief in his or her own superiority and control (Malmquist, 1996). Alternatively, however, extreme reactions may simply discourage others from voicing similar criticisms (Baumeister, Bushman and Campbell, 2000).

The third key element of this model linking narcissism and violence is that there is thought to be a positive association between the severity of the disorder and the scale of the aggression used. A lower level of pathology is generally associated with self-righteous responses by fantasy more so than with actual violence (Meloy, 1997). A more severe level of pathology – its psychopathic variants and those in whom NPD and antisocial personality disorder co-occur – is associated with the use of physical force to restore self-belief. If, however, resolution is incomplete such as when the injuring party is unavailable for the narcissist's version of restorative justice, he or she is condemned to endure the injury and the intolerable emotions it evokes. Therefore, narcissists on the whole do not engage in random aggression because they derive pleasure or relief from aggression itself, which is the critical feature of sadism (Baumeister and Campbell, 1999). Instead, violence is used as the means of defending a highly favourable view of the self against a specific other who seeks (even unwittingly) to challenge it (Baumeister, Bushman and Campbell, 2000).

Narcissism and Sexual Aggression

One of the first clinical uses of the term narcissism was to describe what was at that time referred to as a 'sexual perversion' (Freud, 1914/1957; Näcke, 1899). In psychoanalysis, narcissism retains some very specific definitions and uses, which includes reference to sexuality (Kernberg, 1998a). In mainstream mental health settings, however, the word narcissism has come to represent the normal and pathological regulation of the self-esteem out of which descriptions of NPD have evolved and no specific reference to sexuality is made in its definition. Nonetheless, links between pathological narcissism and sexual aggression have been made (Baumeister and Campbell, 1999; Scully, 1990), and they are highly relevant to a discussion about risk. What is the link between narcissism and sexual aggression? For the majority of individuals, sexual intimacy depends heavily on the mutuality of the partners (Baumeister, Catanese and Wallace, 2002). In contrast, the defining characteristics of disordered narcissism are pathological self-love (i.e. unjustified favourable self-regard), pathological object love (i.e. superficial love for devalued others) and pathological superego (i.e. manipulative, deceptive, corrupt; Kernberg, 1998a; Ronningstam, 2005). Therefore, intimate relationships are an obvious arena in which the deficiencies and vulnerabilities of the narcissist may be exposed; given the vulnerability of pathological narcissists, and their inflated sense of their own sexual attractiveness, their susceptibility to injury in the pursuit of sexual gratification is likely to be enhanced. However, why might a narcissist choose to perpetrate sexual violence against another person rather than non-sexual violence?

Working on the model described in the previous section and illustrated in Figure 5.1, two mechanisms have been put forward to explain why sexualised aggression is the instrument of choice for some injured narcissists. First, a narcissistic person is more likely to perceive the object of his or her desire to be both sexually available and interested in spite of cues to the contrary (Baumeister, Catanese and Wallace, 2002). Sexual contact, therefore, is the enactment of a desire the narcissist believes the recipient wishes him or her to fulfil and aggression is an incidental means by which that end is achieved. The narcissist's engagement in and subsequent recollections of the event are more likely to be of a consenting sexual encounter with all memory of resistance or rejection minimised or dismissed through the vehicle of self-serving cognitive distortions (Scully, 1990).

Second, aggression towards a victim is more likely to be sexualised when the narcissist perceives himself or herself to have been injured as a consequence of rejected sexual advances; by a process of projection, the self-righteous reaction of the injured narcissist is intended to sexually humiliate or shame the victim just as the narcissist perceives himself or herself to have been sexually humiliated or shamed by their rejection. Baumeister and colleagues develop this idea in their narcissistic reactance theory of rape (Baumeister, Catanese and Wallace, 2002), which proposes that the narcissist will desire sex more when it is refused. The risk of sexualised aggression towards the individual denying the narcissist the sex to which he or she feels entitled, therefore, increases. Consequently, the immediate goal of rape is to assert the narcissist's freedom or entitlement to have sex with the person of his or her choice. Intercourse is desired more as a symbolic act of claiming the other person than as a means of gaining sexual satisfaction; while the narcissist's initial desire was sex, the victim's refusal made the narcissist then desire to prove that he could have the sexual access he desired. The primary goal then becomes egotistical rather than physical; the achievement of sexual gratification and orgasm becomes secondary.

Pathological narcissism is not a feature of all sexual offending or even of all rapes. Although the majority of sexual offenders do not suffer from major psychiatric disorder, many do have disorders of personality in the areas of antisocial personality disorder (Craissati, 2004) as well as schizoid, paranoid, narcissistic and psychopathic. All of these conditions involve a relative failure of human attachments and relations with others – a preoccupation with one's own fantasies, wishes and needs, diminished empathy, a desire for control and domination rather than in mutually reciprocal relationships. Thus, the role of personality pathology in sexual offending is an essential consideration in understanding the origins of such violence and its potential to recur and the circumstances in which this might happen.

RISK ASSESSMENT AND MANAGEMENT WITH THE NARCISSISTIC CLIENT

Assessing the Risks of a Narcissistic Client

Narcissism, especially in its pathological forms, should be understood as a potentially relevant risk factor for future violence, sexual or otherwise: 'At best, a highly favourable self-view constitutes a risk factor for turning violent in response to perceptions that one's favourable view of self has been disputed or undermined by others' (Baumeister, Bushman and Campbell, 2000, p. 28). The critical task of the risk assessor is, therefore, to determine the role of personality in general and narcissism in particular, and to identify how this role is influenced by any number of other potentially relevant risk factors (e.g. substance abuse, mental illness, previous violence) and linked to the harmful outcome ultimately to be prevented. An understanding of this nature, encapsulated in a risk formulation, then becomes the basis of a risk management plan whose key components are treatment, supervision, monitoring, and where necessary, victim safety planning (Hart *et al.*, 2003).

The critical first step towards understanding the potential role of pathological narcissism in risk of harm is to assess personality, identify the ways in which narcissism may be regarded as extreme, and explore its past relationship to actual, attempted or threatened violence. Unstructured assessments of narcissism or personality disorder in general are not recommended (Zimmerman, 1994). Such assessments are unreliable and of questionable validity, and they give no basis for the accurate evaluation of change over time such as in response to risk management activity. Using structured processes, however, narcissism may be assessed using any one or all of four approaches: self-report questionnaire, semi-structured clinical interview, structured observations and projective techniques.

Clinically significant personality patterns may be assessed using a self-report personality questionnaire, such as the *Millon Clinical Multiaxial Inventory-III* (MCMI-III, Millon, Davis and Millon, 1997). The MCMI-III has a single scale (scale number 5) dedicated to the measurement of narcissism, consisting of 49 items (such as 'I know I'm a superior person, so I don't care what people think'). The relevance of the narcissism scale is interpreted in the context of performance on modifier indices (e.g. disclosure, desirability), twelve other scales measuring clinical personality patterns and severe personality pathology, and nine scales measuring clinical syndromes. A broader but also detailed overview of personality functioning can be obtained using the self-report *Minnesota Multiphasic Personality Inventory-2* (Butcher *et al.*, 1989). No scale in this 567-item questionnaire addresses narcissism directly but the range of potentially relevant other scales (e.g. the psychopathic deviate, ego inflation and the range of validity sub-scales) ensures that a comprehensive picture of personality functioning – and dysfunction – is nonetheless gained. The *Personality Assessment Inventory* (PAI, Morey, 1991) and the *Dimensional Assessment of Personality Pathology* (DAPP, Livesley and Jackson, in press) also provide good overviews of self-reported personality pathology. While the DAPP directly assesses narcissism as one of its 18 basic dimensions, the focus of the PAI is mainly on antisocial and borderline personality presentations.

Narcissism is assessed directly by only a small number of self-report instruments. Perhaps the best known of these questionnaires is the 40-item *Narcissistic Personality Inventory* (NPI, Raskin and Terry, 1988), which was designed to measure the characteristics of NPD (it is based directly on DSM-III criteria) in the normal population, that is, in non-clinical samples (Twenge and Campbell, 2003). The NPI is used to assess overt or observable narcissism; it is not a sensitive measure of shy or covert narcissism. Sample items from the NPI include 'If I ruled the world it would be a much better place' and 'I am more capable than other people'. Men imprisoned for a violent crime score significantly higher on the NPI than do male college students (Bushman *et al.*, 2001).

There are problems with the use of self-report questionnaires to measure narcissism. Their valid completion is reliant on both a degree of insight into personality functioning and a willingness to portray that self-awareness honestly. Both insight and honesty are likely to be questionable in those whose narcissism is thought to be pathological and in those seeking to create a favourable impression of low risk as a condition of transfer to conditions of lower security or release (Blackburn *et al.*, 2004). In addition, the selective interpretation of the findings of a self-report personality inventory has been criticised due to the risk of confirmatory bias (Rogers, 2003). Consequently, sole reliance on the findings of a self-report personality questionnaire in forensic assessments is widely discouraged (e.g. British Psychological Society, 2006; Hart, 2001).

Semi-structured clinical interviews have been proposed as the 'gold standard' for assessing and diagnosing personality disorder (Clark and Harrison, 2001). Interviews offer the opportunity for evaluators to explore the veracity of evidence in support of the presence of specific symptoms as well as the clinical significance of those detected. Instruments such as the *International Personality Disorder Examination* (Loranger, 1999) and the *Structured Clinical Interview for DSM-IV Axis II Disorders* (First *et al.*, 1997) are popular among practitioners making very detailed assessments of personality disorder and risk, although they are time consuming to administer and require a good level of understanding about personality and personality disorder in order to be administered effectively and usefully. In addition, Axis I clinical conditions need to be evaluated prior to a structured assessment of personality disorder in order to avoid symptoms being ascribed to personality pathology (e.g. grandiosity, suspiciousness of others) when they are better accounted for by a potentially more rapidly treatable condition (e.g. bipolar spectrum disorder, paranoid schizophrenia) (Hart, 2001). The *PCL-R* (Hare, 1991, 2003) is another form of semi-structured personality disorder assessment with some relevance to the evaluation of narcissistic traits, although the depth and breadth of its coverage of pathological narcissism is very limited indeed.

The objective assessment of personality functioning may be undertaken using an instrument like the *Chart of Interpersonal Reactions in Closed Living Environments* (CIRCLE; Blackburn and Renwick, 1996; Blackburn and Glasgow, 2006). Based on research into male mentally disordered offenders, this staff observation scale structures the assessment of interpersonal style as it is exhibited within an institutional context. The measurement of interpersonal style characteristics such as dominance, hostility and coerciveness are particularly relevant to the evaluation of pathological narcissism. Finally, projective tests, such as the *Comprehensive System for the Rorschach* (Exner, 1993) or the *Thematic Apperception Test* (Harder and Greenwald, 2008), offer opportunities to explore personality dimensions in some depth. However, projective measures tend to yield mixed responses from those with NPD (Millon and Davis, 1996), making their use with this client group limited (Campbell and Baumeister, 2006; Garb, Lilienfeld and Fowler, 2008).

In relation to evaluations of risk specifically, clients with pathological narcissism cannot be relied upon to offer accurate estimates of potential for future harm due to their over-confidence or tendency to over-estimate their abilities in addition to a personality-related pattern of risky decision-making (Campbell, Goodie and Foster, 2004); 'Narcissists' grandiose self-views may preclude the realistic appraisal of one's likelihood of success needed for successful decisions, resulting in over-confidence and risk-taking' (p. 298). Also, clients with pathological narcissism should not be relied upon as the sole source of information about any component of a clinical risk assessment because a self-serving bias is likely to influence their interpretation and recall of events (Baumeister, Catanese and Wallace, 2002). As no actuarial instruments for assessing the likelihood of violence or sexual re-offending take into account actual personality disorder diagnosis, none can be relied upon as a means of gauging the risk of harm posed by narcissists. Instead, in order to understand the role of narcissism in the potential to be harmful in the future, and with a view to limiting that potential and preventing harm, the most useful way of assessing, formulating and managing risk is by using a structured professional judgement approach. In respect of actual tools to structure the assessment of risk in men and women in whom narcissism is thought to be a relevant risk factor, the *HCR-20* (Webster *et al.*, 1997; Douglas, Guy and Weir, 2006) and the *Risk for Sexual Violence Protocol* (Hart *et al.*, 2003) are recommended for use to assess and manage the risk of violence and sexual violence, respectively. Risk factors common to both tools include personality disorder and a PCL-R assessment of psychopathy, history of offending behaviour, and attitudes towards violence and sexual violence. Relationship and employment problems, as well as mental health problems and problems with self-awareness, are also common suggesting their role as risk factors potentially core to a number of harmful outcomes. However, the advantage of structured professional judgement approaches to risk assessment over all other approaches designed to assess risk is that they provide a framework for understanding the role of relevant risk factors in relation to risk of future harm and a framework for risk management planning based on the findings of the assessment and a formulation of the risks posed by the individual abuser.

Options for Risk Management

Risk management has at least three components (Hart *et al.*, 2003). The first and most obvious component is *psychopharmacological, psychotherapeutic and psychosocial treatments* for the violence and sexual violence risk factors that are relevant to the individual who is the subject of the assessment and open to modification by such means. For example, in individuals in whom acute symptoms of a psychotic disorder have been linked to potential for violence, the treatment of these symptoms with antipsychotic medication and the psychological management of the consequences of the disorder using cognitive therapy are obvious risk management strategies. The success of these strategies can be measured by monitoring change in the frequency with which symptoms are detected and the patient's satisfaction with care. Treatments for pathological narcissism will be considered in more detail in the next section of this chapter. Comprehensive assessment of a client with NPD should ensure that any additional conditions (e.g. major mood disorder, substance use disorder, bipolar spectrum disorder) are identified and treated so that their role in exacerbating the symptoms of NPD is minimised while treatment for this more protracted condition, if available, is ongoing.

A second important component of risk management is *supervision*. Supervision involves the imposition on violent and sexual offenders of restrictions on activity, movement, association, and communication (such as license conditions following release from prison) designed to limit access to possible victims or scenarios that might initiate an offence influenced by narcissism. Supervision can also include the structures, supports and routines put in place for the client to enhance the power of protective factors to moderate risk (e.g. appropriate employment or other routine activity, secure accommodation, benefits). With a client with NPD, supervision would function in both ways – to limit opportunities to experience narcissistic injury and enhance the ways in which self-esteem can be justifiably stabilised and supported. Supervision should always compliment treatment designed to reduce the clinical significance of NPD symptoms and minimise the negative effect of disorders exacerbating personality pathology. Thus, psychotherapy intended to stabilise self-esteem should be reinforced by a carefully prepared employment or workshop placement in which treatment gains are tried out and consolidated. Unfortunately, such opportunities to join up treatment with supervision are generally only available in highly specialised programmes for individuals with severe personality disorder (Howells and Tennant, 2007).

A third important component of risk management is *monitoring*. Monitoring involves the identification, either in treatment or the course of supervision, of the early warning signs of a relapse to violence or sexual violence. Monitoring also involves deciding upon and notifying those involved with the client about the most appropriate response to make when early warning signs are detected. Ideally, the most appropriate responses to early warning signs should be identified in advance as part of the risk management planning process and, more ideally still, discussed and agreed with the client. Thus, with a client with NPD, early warning signs of a possible relapse to violence may include unresolved problems in an intimate relationship as a result of which the risk of narcissistic injury increases as does the risk of harm to the partner of the client. By involving the client in risk management planning in this way, opportunities are created to agree the steps that will be taken to manage and reduce risk as well as to generate more information that is relevant to managing risk. If clients feel involved in a process that will ultimately keep them in conditions of lower security or even in the community, their motivation to engage could improve to the benefit of the safety of others.

A possible fourth component of risk management is *victim safety planning*. Victim safety planning refers to the steps taken or recommended to improve the safety and security of the possible victims of clients with a history of violence or sexual violence. Steps might include community notification or the location of offenders released from detention to an area far from the home of a former victim. Steps may also include the issue of personal alarms to victims and guidance on maintaining personal safety when feeling at risk. With clients with NPD, victims for whom such plans may need to be made may include former partners and those against whom a self-righteous and restorative response to narcissistic injury has still to be made. By making the targets of offenders harder to victimise, risk to potential future victims may be limited and attempts at violence more detectable and likely to be reported.

TREATMENT

Options and Evidence for the Treatment of Pathological Narcissism

'The complex nature of this disorder – high level of functioning, lack of symptoms or consistent behavioural signifiers, hidden or denied intrapsychic problems (even when severe), and lack of motivation to seek psychiatric treatment out of shame, pride or self-aggrandising denial – have made it difficult to identify people in general psychiatric settings who meet the DSM criteria for NPD' (Ronningstam, 2005; p. 25). Finding clients with NPD in forensic settings – prisons and secure psychiatric facilities – has proven easier. However, the denial of need for help is as endemic there as in general psychiatric settings (Fonagy, 2001), and everywhere, narcissism presents as one of the fiercest forms of resistance to change (Millon and Davis, 1996; Green, 2002). To date, there have been few treatment outcome studies for NPD (Campbell and Baumeister, 2006) and clinical reports suggest individual treatment for NPD is protracted (over a year long), difficult for both therapist and patient, and often not effective. As with the treatment of most other personality disorders, the quality of the alliance between the therapist and client is an essential to maximising any change that is possible, not least because it can act to motivate the client to stay in treatment long enough to give it a chance of having some positive effect. Millon (1999) suggests there are three viable options for the delivery of treatment for NPD, although each has yet to be subject to a good evaluation study: psychodynamic psychotherapy, interpersonal therapy and cognitive–behavioural approaches.

Kernberg (1975) and Kohut (1977) have led in the development of psychoanalytic approaches to the treatment of NPD, the oldest approach to the treatment of this condition. While their views on the presentation or appearance of narcissism are similar, their ideas about its aetiology and therefore its treatment are different. In brief, Kernberg recommends the treatment and management of childhood experiences of abandonment in narcissistic clients. In contrast, Kohut prioritises issues in developing self-awareness and regulation of emotions as a way of compensating for problems with parental mirroring in childhood. However, both place the source of the condition in negative childhood experiences. Therefore, classic psychoanalytic techniques are emphasised, with particular attention being placed on the analysis of transference and counter-transference processes between therapist and patient as a means of facilitating change and overcoming resistance (Gabbard, 1998).

Interpersonal approaches to the treatment of NPD originate with Harry Stack Sullivan and focus on analysing the structure and meaning of social relationships – both past and present – in therapy. Interpersonal approaches appear to show some promise with a disorder that manifests itself in such a profound level of interpersonal dysfunction (Benjamin, 1993). Finally, cognitive–behavioural approaches focus on the current manifestations of disordered narcissism and on the cognitive processes that accompany and perpetuate them. The ultimate goal of cognitive–behavioural approaches to treatment is to moderate the personal beliefs that underpin grandiosity, vulnerable self-esteem and lack of empathy. Thus, schema therapy attends to the development of the early cognitive schemas or mental representations of self and others that give rise to these symptoms (Young, Klosko and Weishaar, 2003), which contrasts with a more strict cognitive approach focusing on current thinking only (e.g. Beck *et al.*, 1990).

On the whole, cognitive approaches to the treatment of NPD are recommended, as is the engagement of a well-trained and supervised therapist (Campbell and Baumeister, 2006). The delivery of therapy to narcissists in a group is not recommended (Millon, 1999), although it is cautiously recommended by some (e.g. Roth, 1998). Certainly, any capacity for interpersonal commitment is an indicator of treatment potential, with those demonstrating some capacity to commit to another likely to show the best treatment effects. Consequently, group or even couple therapies for narcissistic clients should be retained for those with some intact interpersonal skills. Finally, there are no known psychopharmacological treatments for the symptoms of NPD (Campbell and Baumeister, 2006). Psychological treatments, such as they are, are the only known way to make positive change.

FUTURE DIRECTIONS

The presence of narcissism in a user of mental health services is guaranteed to evoke a feeling of concern about the possibility of progress and positive change in practitioners. What needs to be improved in order to make practitioners more hopeful about the prospects of interventions? First, more research needs to be carried out and findings published in the research and clinical literatures on the treatment of narcissism and on its role in the treatment of related conditions. Unfortunately, the majority of people with clinically significant narcissism do not present for treatment for that condition but for conditions that arise as a consequence of its presence (e.g. substance use disorders, bipolar spectrum disorders, major depressive disorder), yet we know comparatively little about how to provide treatment when narcissism is a comorbid complaint.

Second, while there is some very useful work on clinical skills in relation to working with clients who have a personality disorder presentation (e.g. Widiger, 2005), there is a need for more. In particular, there is a need for guidance that will inform practitioners how they may adequately assess the needs of the narcissistic client. Interviewing skills and sustaining engagement in treatment are not routinely taught in training courses for psychiatrists and clinical psychologists, yet they are expected to work with this most demanding of client groups and achieve a modicum of treatment success. Practitioners, researchers and clients themselves need to be more explicit about what they see as the means by which relevant information can be most efficiently gathered and most effectively used to encourage repair and recovery within the therapeutic engagement.

Third, the relationship between NPD and psychopathy requires further research and elucidation. To what extent does the literature on psychopathy apply to those offenders who have a diagnosis of NPD? If antisocial behaviour is no longer to be considered a symptom of psychopathy, is psychopathy anything other than an extreme form of pathological narcissism? While there is scope for much speculation, the findings of empirical research should lead the development of ideas in this area.

In respect of the clinical risk assessment and management of narcissistic clients, emphasis on structured professional judgement approaches is recommended. Such approaches offer practitioners trying to work with narcissistic clients the greatest prospects of managing risk and preventing harm – as long as tools are used to aid thinking and formulation rather than simply as a tick-box checklist. The judgement to be made by practitioners is not what is the level of risk posed by a narcissistic client, but what are the conditions that need to co-occur in order to make risk unacceptable. Simple statements about level of risk – high, medium or low – are meaningless to those charged with its management. Practitioners undertaking assessments of narcissistic clients have a responsibility to be more specific – and therefore more knowledgeable – about what constellation of factors creates an unacceptable risk and what action is required to minimise harm, if not prevent harmful outcomes from occurring altogether. Consequently, more research is required into the mechanism of the relationship between narcissism and violence (and sexual violence). In addition, practitioners and researchers need to make more of an effort to publish their experiences of working with narcissistic clients where formulating the narcissism–violence association was their objective. More work is needed generally into protective factors and into what works to manage risk, with this client group and with clients with other personality disorder and clinical presentations. Correctional and forensic mental health services are excellent at determining retrospectively what has been relevant to an offence occurring; their expertise in determining and justifying prospectively what needs to be done to prevent future offences is still at an early stage of development (Douglas and Kropp, 2002).

CONCLUSIONS

Narcissism is one of the most complex and fascinating, and clinically frustrating, personality presentations yet defined. Rarely the primary reason for presenting for treatment, pathological narcissism is a complicating factor in the violent and sexually violent conduct of a sizeable proportion of offenders in Britain and elsewhere. The peculiar constellation of grandiosity, entitlement, poor empathy and problematic self-awareness lends itself to problems with engaging these clients in supportive and therapeutic relationships, to problems with making lasting changes in the clinical significance of their symptoms of disorder, and to assessing and managing risk of harm. Yet the study of clients with narcissism and the efforts made to engage with them are some of the most interesting and stimulating and ultimately memorable ones in the experience of practitioners. Further research to develop clinical skills, therapies and effective risk management strategies is required; best practice with this client group will not develop without it. In the meantime, practitioners are recommended to use formulation as the basis of their engagement with narcissistic clients and formal evaluation and supervision as the means by which the quality of their practice is monitored and assured.

ACKNOWLEDGEMENT

The author would like to thank Professor David Cooke for comments on an early draft of this chapter.

REFERENCES

Akhtar, S. (2003) *New Clinical Realms: Pushing the Envelope of Theory and Technique*, Jason Aronson, Northvale, NJ.
American Psychiatric Association (1952) *Diagnostic and Statistical Manual of Mental Disorders*, APA, Washington, DC.
American Psychiatric Association (1968) *Diagnostic and Statistical Manual of Mental Disorders*, 2nd edn, APA, Washington, DC.
American Psychiatric Association (1980) *Diagnostic and Statistical Manual of Mental Disorders*, 3rd edn, APA, Washington, DC.

American Psychiatric Association (1994) *Diagnostic and Statistical Manual of Mental Disorders*, 4th edn, APA, Washington, DC.

American Psychiatric Association (2000) *Diagnostic and Statistical Manual of Mental Disorders*, 4th edn, text revised version, APA, Washington, DC.

Baumeister, R.F. and Campbell, W.K. (1999) The intrinsic appeal of evil: sadism, sensational thrills, and threatened egotism. *Personality and Social Psychology Review*, **3**, 210–21.

Baumeister, R.F., Bushman, B.J. and Campbell, W.K. (2000) Self-esteem, narcissism, and aggression: Does violence result from low self-esteem or from threatened egotism? *Current Directions in Psychological Science*, **9**, 26–9.

Baumeister, R.F., Catanese, K.R. and Wallace, H.M. (2002) Conquest by force: a narcissistic reactance theory of rape and sexual coercion. *Review of General Psychology*, **6**, 92–135.

Baumeister, R.F., Smart, L. and Boden, J.M. (1996) Relation of threatened egotism to violence and aggression: the dark side of high self-esteem. *Psychological Review*, **103**, 5–33.

Beck, A.T., Freeman, A. and Associates (1990) *Cognitive Therapy of Personality Disorders*, Guilford, New York.

Benjamin, L.S. (1993) *Interpersonal Diagnosis and Treatment of Personality Disorders*, Guilford, New York.

Berkowitz, D.A., Shapiro, R.L., Zinner, J. and Shapiro, E.R. (1974) Family contributions to narcissistic disturbances in adolescents. *International Review of Psychoanalysis*, **1**, 353–62.

Blackburn, R. (1998) Psychopathy and the contribution of personality to violence, in *Psychopathy: Antisocial, Criminal and Violent Behavior* (eds T. Millon, E. Simonsen, M. Birket-Smith and R.D. Davis), Guilford, New York, pp. 50–67.

Blackburn, R. (2007) Personality disorder and psychopathy: conceptual and empirical integration. *Psychology, Crime and Law*, **13**, 7–18.

Blackburn, R. and Renwick, S.J. (1996) Rating scales for measuring the interpersonal circle in forensic psychiatric patients. *Psychological Assessment*, **8**, 76–84.

Blackburn, R. and Glasgow, D.V. (2006) *Manual for the Chart of Interpersonal Reactions in Closed Living Environments (CIRCLE)*. Unpublished manuscript, University of Liverpool.

Blackburn, R., Logan, C., Donnelly, J. and Renwick, S.J. (2003) Personality disorders, psychopathy, and other mental disorders: comorbidity among patients at English and Scottish high security hospitals. *Journal of Forensic Psychiatry and Psychology*, **14**, 111–37.

Blackburn, R., Donnelly, J.P., Logan, C. and Renwick, S.J. (2004) Convergent and discriminative validity of interview and questionnaire measures of personality disorder in mentally disordered offenders: a multitrait–multimethod analysis using confirmatory factor analysis. *Journal of Personality Disorders*, **18**, 129–50.

Bockian, N.R. (2006) *Personality-Guided Therapy for Depression*, American Psychiatric Association, Washington, DC.

Brieger, P., Ehrt, U. and Merneros, A. (2003) Frequency of comorbid personality disorders in bipolar and unipolar affective disorders. *Comprehensive Psychiatry*, **44**, 28–34.

British Psychological Society. (2006) *Understanding Personality Disorder: A Report by the British Psychological Society*, The British Psychological Society, Leicester.

Bursten, B. (1973) Some narcissistic personality types. *International Journal of Psychoanalysis*, **54**, 287–300.

Bushman, B.J., Baumeister, R.F., Phillips, C.M. and Gilligan, J. (2001) Self-love and self-loathing behind bars: narcissism and self-esteem among violent offenders in a prison sample. Unpublished manuscript.

Butcher, J.N., Dahlstrom, W.G., Graham, J.R. *et al.* (1989) *The Minnesota Multiphasic Personality Inventory-2 (MMPI-2): Manual for Administration and Scoring*, University of Minnesota Press, Minneapolis, MN.

Campbell, W.K. and Baumeister, R.F. (2006) Narcissistic personality disorder, in *Practitioner's Guide to Evidence-based Psychotherapy* (eds J.E. Fisher and W.T. O'Donohue), Springer, New York, pp. 423–31.

Campbell, W.K., Goodie, A.S. and Foster, J.D. (2004) Narcissism, confidence and risk attitude. *Journal of Behavioral Decision Making*, **17**, 297–311.

Carroll, L. (1987) A study of narcissism, affiliation, intimacy, and power motives among students in business administration. *Psychological Reports*, **61**, 355–8.

Clark, L.A. (2007) Assessment and diagnosis of personality disorder: perennial issues and an emerging reconceptualization. *Annual Review of Psychology*, **58**, 227–57.

Clark, L.A. and Harrison, J. (2001) Assessment instruments, in *Handbook of Personality Disorder: Theory, Research, and Treatment* (ed. W. Livesley), Guilford, New York, pp. 277–306.

Cooke, D.J. and Michie, C. (2001) Refining the construct of psychopathy: towards a hierarchical model. *Psychological Assessment*, **13**, 171–88.

Cooke, D.J., Michie, C. and Hart, S.D. (2006) Facets of clinical psychopathy: towards clearer measurement, in *Handbook of Psychopathy* (ed. C.J. Patrick), Guilford, New York, pp. 91–106.

Cooper, A.M. (1998) Further developments in the clinical diagnosis of narcissistic personality disorder, in *Disorders of Narcissism: Diagnostic, Clinical and Empirical Implications* (ed. E.F. Ronningstam), Jason Aronson, Northvale, NJ, pp. 53–74.

Cooper, A.M. and Sacks, M. (1991) Sadism and masochism in character disorders and resistance: panel report. *Journal of the American Psychoanalytic Association*, **39**, 215–26.

Craissati, J. (2004) *Managing High Risk Sex Offenders in the Community: A Psychological Approach*, Brunner-Routledge, Hove, East Sussex.

Douglas, K.S. and Kropp, P.R. (2002) A prediction-based paradigm for violence risk assessment: clinical and research applications. *Criminal Justice and Behavior*, **29**, 617–58.

Douglas, K.S., Guy, L.S. and Weir, J. (2006) *HCR-20 Violence Risk Assessment Scheme: Overview and Annotated Bibliography*, www.violence-risk.com/hcr20annotated.pdf (accessed 10 January 2008).

Elkind, D. (1991) Instrumental narcissism in parents. *Bulletin of the Menninger Clinic*, **19**, 260–99.

Ellis, H. (1898) Auto-eroticism: a psychological study. *Alienist and Neurologist*, **19**, 260–99.

Exner, J.E. (1993) *The Rorschach: A Comprehensive System, Vol. 1, Basic Foundations*, 3rd edn, John Wiley & Sons, Inc., New York.

Farrington, D.P. (2006) Family background and psychopathy, in *Handbook of Psychopathy* (ed. C.J. Patrick), Guilford, New York, pp. 229–50.

First, M.B., Frances, A. and Pincus, H.A. (1995) *DSM-IV Handbook of Differential Diagnosis*, American Psychiatric Press, Washington, DC.

First, M., Gibbon, M., Spitzer, R. *et al.* (1997) *User's Guide for the Structured Clinical Interview for DSM-IV Axis II Personality Disorder*, American Psychiatric Press, Washington, DC.

Fonagy, P. (2001) *Attachment Theory and Psychoanalysis*, Other Press, New York.

Fonagy, P., Gergely, G., Jurist, E.L. and Target, M. (2002) *Affect Regulation, Mentalisation, and the Development of the Self*, Other Press, New York.

Foster, J.D., Campbell, W.K. and Twenge, J.M. (2003) Individual differences in narcissism: inflated self-views across the lifespan and around the world. *Journal of Research in Psychiatry*, **37**, 469–86.

Freud, S. (1911/1957) Psychoanalytic notes on an autobiographical account of a case of paranoia, in *The Standard Edition of the Complete Psychological Works of Sigmund Freud*, Vol. **12** (ed. & Trans. J. Strachey), Hogarth, London, pp. 9–82.

Freud, S. (1914/1957) On narcissism, in *The Standard Edition of the Complete Psychological Works of Sigmund Freud*, Vol. **14** (ed. & Trans. J. Strachey), Hogarth, London, pp. 66–102.

Freud, S. (1931/1957) Libidinal types, in *The Standard Edition of the Complete Psychological Works of Sigmund Freud*, Vol. **21** (ed. & Trans. J. Strachey), Hogarth, London, pp. 217–20.

Gabbard, G.O. (1998) Transference and counter-transference in the treatment of narcissistic patients, in *Disorders of Narcissism: Diagnostic, Clinical and Empirical Implications* (ed. E.F. Ronningstam), Jason Aronson, Northvale, NJ, pp. 125–46.

Garb, H.N., Lilienfeld, S.O. and Fowler, K.A. (2008) Psychological assessment and clinical judgement, in *Psychopathology: Foundations for a Contemporary Understanding*, 2nd edn (eds J.E. Maddux and B.A. Winstead), Routledge/Taylor & Francis Group, New York, pp. 103–24.

Goldberg, A. (1973) Psychotherapy of narcissistic injuries. *Archives of General Psychiatry*, **28**, 722–6.

Green, A. (2002) A dual conception of narcissism: positive and negative organisation. *Psychoanalytic Quarterly*, **71**, 631–49.

Gunderson, J. and Ronningstam, E.F. (2001) Differentiating antisocial and narcissistic personality disorder. *Journal of Personality Disorders*, **15**, 103–9.

Harder, D.W. and Greenwald, D.F. (2008) *A Handbook of Clinical Scoring Systems for Thematic Apperceptive Techniques*, Lawrence Erlbaum Associates, Mahwah, NJ.

Hare, R.D. (1991) *The Hare Psychopathy Checklist-Revised*, Multi-Health Systems, Toronto, OH.

Hare, R.D. (2003) *The Hare Psychopathy Checklist-Revised*, 2nd edn, Multi-Health Systems, Toronto, OH.

Harpur, T.J., Hakstian, A.R. and Hare, R.D. (1988) Factor structure of the psychopathy checklist. *Journal of Consulting and Clinical Psychology*, **56**, 741–7.

Hart, S. (2001) Forensic issues, in *Handbook of Personality Disorder: Theory, Research, and Treatment* (ed. W. Livesley), Guilford, New York, pp. 555–69.

Hart, S.D. and Hare, R.D. (1998) The association between psychopathy and narcissism: theoretical views and empirical evidence, in *Disorders of Narcissism: Diagnostic, Clinical and Empirical Implications* (ed. E.F. Ronningstam), Jason Aronson, Northvale, NJ, pp. 415–36.

Hart, S.D., Kropp, P.K., Laws, D.R. *et al.* (2003) *The Risk for Sexual Violence Protocol: Structured Professional Guidelines for Assessing Risk of Sexual Violence. Mental Health, Law and Policy Institute*, Simon Fraser University, Vancouver.

Holdwick, D.J., Hilsenroth, M.J., Castlebury, F.D. and Blais, M.A. (1998) Identifying the unique and common characteristics among the DSM-IV antisocial, borderline and narcissistic personality disorders. *Comprehensive Psychiatry*, **39**, 277–86.

Holmes, J. (2001) *Narcissism: Ideas in Psychoanalysis*, Icon Books, Cambridge.

Horney, K. (1939) *New Ways in Psychoanalysis*, Norton, New York.

Howells, K. and Tennant, A. (2007) Ready or not, they are coming: dangerous and severe personality disorder and treatment engagement. *Issues in Forensic Psychology*, **7**, 11–20.

Hughes, T. (1997) *Tales from Ovid: Twenty-Four Passages from the Metamorphoses*, Faber and Faber, London.

Jang, K.L., Livesley, W.J., Vernon, P.A. and Jackson, D.N. (1996) Heritability of personality disorder traits: a twin study. *Acta Psychiatrica Scandanavica*, **94**, 438–44.

Karpman, B. (1941) On the need for separating psychopathy into two distinct clinical types: symptomatic and idiopathic. *Journal of Criminology and Psychopathology*, **3**, 112–37.

Kernberg, O. (1967) Borderline personality organization. *Journal of the American Psychoanalytical Association*, **15**, 641–85.

Kernberg, O. (1975) *Borderline Conditions and Pathological Narcissism*, Jason Aronson, New York.

Kernberg, O.F. (1998a) Pathological narcissism and narcissistic personality disorder: theoretical background and diagnostic classifications, in *Disorders of Narcissism: Diagnostic, Clinical and Empirical Implications* (ed. E.F. Ronningstam), Jason Aronson, Northvale, NJ, pp. 29–51.

Kernberg, O.F. (1998b) The psychotherapeutic management of psychopathic, narcissistic and paranoid transference, in *Psychopathy: Antisocial, Violent and Criminal Behavior* (eds T. Millon, E. Simonsen, M. Birket-Smith and R.D. Davis), Guilford, New York, pp. 372–92.

Kernberg, P. (1989) Narcissistic personality disorder in childhood. *Psychiatric Clinics of North America*, **12**, 671–94.

Kernis, M.H., Grannemann, B.D. and Barclay, L.C. (1989). Stability and level of self-esteem as predictors of anger arousal and hostility. *Journal of Personality and Social Psychology*, **56**, 1013–22.

Kohut, H. (1966) Forms and transformations of narcissism. *American Journal of Psychotherapy*, **14**, 243–71.

Kohut, H. (1971) *The Analysis of the Self*, International Universities Press, New York.

Kohut, H. (1972) Thoughts on narcissism and narcissistic rage. *The Psychoanalytic Study of the Child*, **27**, 360–400.

Kohut, H. (1977) *The Restoration of the Self*, International University Press, New York.

Lewis, M. (1993) The development of anger and rage, in *Rage, Power, and Aggression* (eds R.A. Glick and S.P. Roose), Yale University Press, New Haven, CT, pp. 148–68.

Livesley, W.J. and Jackson, D.N. (in press) *Manual for the Dimensional Assessment of Personality Pathology-Basic Questionnaire*, Sigma Press, Port Huron, MI.

Livesley, W.J., Jang, K.L., Jackson, D.N. and Vernon, P.A. (1993) Genetic and environmental contributions to dimensions of personality disorder. *American Journal of Psychiatry*, **150**, 1826–31.

Loranger, A., (1999) *International Personality Disorder Examination Manual: DSM-IV Module*, American Psychiatric Press, Washington, DC.

Malmquist, C.P. (1996) *Homicide: A Psychiatric Perspective*, American Psychiatric Press, Washington, DC.

Meloy, J.R. (1997) *Violent Attachments*, Jason Aronson, New Jersey.

Meloy, J.R. (1998) The psychology of stalking, in *The Psychology of Stalking: Clinical and Forensic Perspectives* (ed. J.R. Meloy), Academic, San Diego, pp. 2–23.

Millon, T. (1999) *Personality-Guided Therapy*, John Wiley & Sons, Inc., New York.

Millon, T. and Davis, R.D. (1996) *Disorders of Personality: DSM-IV and Beyond*, 2nd edn, Wiley-Interscience, New York.

Millon, T., Davis, R. and Millon, C. (1997) *The Millon Clinical Multiaxial Inventory-III Manual*, 2nd edn, National Computer Systems, Minneapolis, MN.

Morey, L.C. (1991) *Personality Assessment Inventory: Professional Manual*, Psychological Assessment Resources, Tampa, FL.

Morey, L.C. and Jones, J.K. (1998) Empirical studies of the construct validity of narcissistic personality disorder, in *Disorders of Narcissism: Diagnostic, Clinical and Empirical Implications* (ed. E.F. Ronningstam), Jason Aronson, Northvale, NJ, pp. 351–74.

Murray, H. (1955) American icarus, in *Clinical Studies in Personality*, Vol. **2** (eds A. Burton and R. Harris), Harper, New York, pp. 615–41.

Näcke, P. (1899) Die sexuellen perversitäten in der irrenanstalt. *Psychiatriche en Neurologische Bladen*, **3**, 67.

Poythress, N.G. and Skeem, J.L. (2006) Disaggregating psychopathy: where and how to look for subtypes, in *Handbook of Psychopathy* (ed. C.J. Patrick), Guilford, New York, pp. 172–92.

Raskin, R.N. and Terry, H. (1988) A principal-components analysis of the narcissistic personality inventory and further evidence of its constructive validity. *Journal of Personality and Social Psychology*, **54**, 890–902.

Reich, A. (1960) Pathological forms of self-esteem regulation. *The Psychoanalytic Study of the Child*, **15**, 215–32.

Reich, W. (1933/1949) *Character Analysis*, 3rd edn (Trans. T.P. Wolfe), Orgone Institute Press, New York.

Rinsley, D.B. (1989) Notes on the developmental pathogenesis of narcissistic personality disorder. *Psychiatric Clinics of North America*, **12**, 695–707.

Rogers, R. (2003) Forensic use and abuse of psychological tests: multiscale inventories. *Journal of Psychiatric Practice*, **9**, 316–20.

Ronningstam, E.F. (1996) Pathological narcissism and narcissistic personality disorder in Axis I disorders. *Harvard Review of Psychiatry*, **3**, 326–40.

Ronningstam, E.F. (ed.) (1998) *Disorders of Narcissism: Diagnostic, Clinical and Empirical Implications*, American Psychiatric Press, Washington, DC.

Ronningstam, E.F. (2005) *Identifying and Understanding the Narcissistic Personality*, Oxford University Press, New York.

Ronningstam, E.F. and Gunderson, J. (1990) Identifying criteria for narcissistic personality disorder. *American Journal of Psychiatry*, **147**, 918–22.

Rosenfeld, H. (1971) A clinical approach to the psychoanalytic theory of the life and death instincts: an investigation into the aggressive aspects of narcissism. *International Journal of Psychoanalysis*, **52**, 169–78.

Rosenstein, D. and Horowitz, H.A. (1996) Adolescent attachment and psychopathology. *Journal of Consulting and Clinical Psychology*, **64**, 244–53.

Roth, B.E. (1998) Narcissistic patients in group psychotherapy: containing affects in the early group, in *Disorders of Narcissism: Diagnostic, Clinical and Empirical Implications* (ed. E.F. Ronningstam), Jason Aronson, Northvale, NJ, pp. 221–68.

Sadger, J. (1910) Ein Fall von multiplier Perversion mit hysterischen Absenzen. *Jahrbuch fur Psychoanalytische und Psychopathologische Forschungen*, **2**, 59–133.

Schore, A. (1994) *Affect Regulation and the Origin of the Self*, Lawrence Erlbaum, Hillsdale, NJ.

Scully, D. (1990) *Understanding Sexual Violence*, HarperCollins Academic, London.

Singleton, N., Meltzer, H. and Gatward, R. (1998) *Psychiatric morbidity among prisoners in England and Wales*, The Stationary Office, London.

Skeem, J.L. and Cooke, D.J. (in press) Is criminal behaviour a central component of psychopathy: conceptual directions for resolving the debate. *Psychological Assessment*.

Skeem, J.L., Poythress, N., Edens, J.F. *et al.* (2003) Psychopathic personality or personalities? Exploring potential variants of psychopathy and their implications for risk assessment. *Aggression and Violent Behavior*, **8**, 513–46.

Stone, M. (1998) Normal narcissism: an etiological and ethological perspective, in *Disorders of Narcissism: Diagnostic, Clinical and Empirical Implications* (ed. E.F. Ronningstam), Jason Aronson, Northvale, NJ, pp. 7–28.

Torgersen, S., Lygren, S., Øien, P.A. *et al.* (2000) A twin study of personality disorders. *Comprehensive Psychiatry*, **41**, 416–25.

Trull, T.J. (2005) Dimensional models of personality disorder: coverage and cutoffs. *Journal of Personality Disorders*, **19**, 262–82.

Twenge, J. and Campbell, W.K. (2003) 'Isn't it fun to get the respect that we're going to deserve?' Narcissism, social rejection, and aggression. *Personality and Social Psychology Bulletin*, **29**, 261–72.

Wälder, R. (1925) The psychoses: their mechanisms and accessibility to influence. *International Journal of Psychoanalysis*, **6**, 259–81.

Waldman, I.D. and Rhee, S.H. (2006) Genetic and environmental influences on psychopathy and antisocial behavior, in *Handbook of Psychopathy* (ed. C.J. Patrick), Guilford, New York, pp. 205–28.

Watson, P.J. and Biderman, M.D. (1993) Narcissistic personality inventory factors, splitting and self-consciousness. *Journal of Personality Assessment*, **61**, 41–57.

Webster, C., Douglas, K., Eaves, D. and Hart, S. (1997) *HCR-20: Assessing Risk for Violence*, 2nd edn, Mental Health, Law and Policy Institute, Simon Fraser University and the British Columbia Forensic Psychiatric Services Commission, Vancouver.

Widiger, T.A. (2005) *Personality disorders, in Clinical and Diagnostic Interviewing*, 2nd edn (ed. R.J. Craig), Jason Aronson, Oxford.

Widiger, T.A. (2006) Psychopathy and DSM-IV psychopathology, in *Handbook of Psychopathy* (ed. C.J. Patrick), Guilford, New York, pp. 156–71.

Wink, P. (1991) Two faces of narcissism. *Journal of Personality and Social Psychology*, **61**, 590–7.

Young, J.E. (1999) *Cognitive Therapy for Personality Disorders: A Schema-Focused Approach*, 3rd edn, Professional Resource Press, Sarasota, FL.

Young, J.E., Klosko, J.S. and Weishaar, M. (2003) *Schema Therapy: A Practitioner's Guide*, Guilford, New York.

Zimmerman, M. (1994) Diagnosing personality disorder: a review of issues and research methods. *Archives of General Psychiatry*, **51**, 225–45.

Chapter 6

SUBTYPES OF PSYCHOPATH

RONALD BLACKBURN

University of Liverpool, UK

INTRODUCTION

Classifying entities on the basis of similarities and differences is fundamental to any science. In the psychology of crime, classification systems that differentiate criminal acts or actors are essential for management and prediction, treatment decisions and theoretical understanding, and most attempts to reduce the heterogeneity of offenders recognise the class of psychopathic personality. Divisions of this group into more homogeneous subgroups have also been proposed, the most widely accepted being the distinction between primary and secondary psychopaths.

This distinction has been overshadowed by the development of the Psychopathy Checklist-Revised (PCL-R: Hare, 2003). Because the PCL-R is assumed to measure Cleckley's construct of the psychopath (Cleckley, 1982), PCL-R-defined psychopaths have been considered homogeneous. However, although it is now accepted that psychopathy represents a continuous dimension (Edens *et al.*, 2006; Hare and Neumann, 2005), the PCL-R is multifactorial, two correlated sub-factors being traditionally identified. The first factor (F1) reflects a selfish and callous use of others, and Cleckley's core traits of psychopathy. The second (F2) reflects socially deviant traits and lifestyle. The two factors are associated with different patterns of personality traits and deviant behaviour (Hare, 2003; Patrick and Zempolich, 1998). Cooke (e.g. Cooke *et al.*, 2004), however, recently proposed that the optimal PCL-R factor structure comprises interpersonal, affective and behavioural sub-factors or facets, while Hare (e.g. Hare and Neumann, 2006) contends that the conventional two-factors or a four-facet model (Cooke's facets plus an antisocial facet) are equally viable alternatives.

Whatever the outcome of this debate, the multifaceted structure of the PCL-R suggests that high scores may encompass distinct subgroups differing in these facets and other attributes rather than representing a homogeneous group. There is, therefore, a renewed interest in the primary–secondary distinction

---

Personality, Personality Disorder and Violence   Edited by Mary McMurran and Richard C. Howard
© 2009 John Wiley & Sons, Ltd

(Brinkley *et al.*, 2004; Poythress and Skeem, 2006; Skeem *et al.*, 2003). As these authors emphasise, if psychopaths are heterogeneous, then generalisations about aetiology, treatability or risk will need to be qualified. This chapter examines the theoretical and empirical basis for considering psychopaths to be heterogeneous. I first examine the distinction between primary and secondary psychopaths and its applications in research. I then review empirical taxonomic studies, including my own research with mentally disordered offenders, and what they indicate about the personality characteristics that identify variants of psychopathy. Finally, I discuss implications of this research for clinical practice with violent offenders.

CONCEPTS OF PRIMARY AND SECONDARY PSYCHOPATHY

Aetiological Conceptions

The primary–secondary distinction originated with Karpman (e.g. Karpman, 1946, 1948). He regarded the label 'psychopath' as a catch-all for various conditions with little in common beyond antisocial behaviour, but differentiated *secondary or symptomatic psychopaths* from *primary or idiopathic psychopaths* in terms of motivation. The antisocial behaviour of the former is secondary to underlying psychotic disturbance or neurotic conflicts arising from parental rejection, and they should be diagnosed as psychotic or neurotic rather than psychopathic. Primary psychopaths, however, display an absence of 'conscience, guilt, and binding and generous emotions. . .while purely egoistic, uninhibited instinctive trends are predominant'. (Karpman, 1948, p. 533). Their aetiology is probably constitutional. He proposed calling these *anethopaths*, and abandoning the label psychopath. He also suggested a division of anethopaths into *aggressive-predatory* and *passive-parasitic* subtypes (Karpman, 1946).

Primary and secondary psychopaths are behaviourally alike. Egoism, callousness, lying, impulsiveness and antisocial behaviour characterise both groups, although primary psychopaths may be less impulsive or hotheaded. Underlying the similarities, however, are motivational differences in strong drives such as hostility or guilt. Uncovering these differences requires psychodynamic exploration, a diagnosis of primary psychopath being justified when nothing of psychogenic significance is elicited. By the same token, secondary psychopaths are treatable, but primary psychopaths are 'incurable'.

An alternative differentiation was made by Mealey (1995). Her evolutionary model distinguishes two types at different points on a continuum of *sociopathy*, a life strategy of predatory social interactions. She proposes a genotype for socially deviant behaviour that makes people less responsive to cues for socialisation and deficient in the social emotions of shame, guilt and love. *Primary sociopaths* are a small but stable number of 'cheaters' selected for in every culture through evolutionary processes. They are the outcome of genetic differences and occur across the social spectrum. *Secondary sociopaths* occupy a less extreme position on the continuum and reflect the outcome of developmental response to environmental conditions in which a cheating strategy is more likely among individuals at a competitive disadvantage. Most upper class sociopaths will be primary sociopaths, but secondary psychopaths are more likely to come from lower class or disadvantaged groups. Primary sociopathy is reflected in PCL-R F1, and secondary sociopathy in F2.

Porter (1996) also distinguished two aetiological pathways, one congenital and the other environmental, both leading to the same phenotypic outcome, the outcome in this case being the affective characteristics of psychopathy. *Fundamental psychopathy*, an inability to form interpersonal bonds and a lack of empathy and conscience, results from genetic predisposition. In *secondary psychopathy*, the same outcome results from early traumatic experiences of physical or sexual abuse or other maltreatment. This produces dissociation of affect in which a capacity for empathy is 'turned off' through disillusionment. The effects may be seen in PTSD (post-traumatic stress disorder) and violence. The two groups will show similar PCL-R patterns on F1 and F2, but as a consequence of different developmental histories.

Primary and Secondary Psychopathy in Personality Theories

Some theories of psychopathy link the primary–secondary distinction to structural models of personality. In Eysenck's theory of criminality (Eysenck, 1977), psychopaths are predicted to be high on neuroticism (N), extraversion (E) and psychoticism (P), but primary psychopaths are higher than secondary psychopaths on P, and lower on N. Gray (e.g. Gray, 1994) modified Eysenck's theory, proposing rotations of N and E to yield dimensions of neurotic introversion (NI) and neurotic extraversion (NE), calling these 'anxiety' and 'impulsivity', respectively. These are dispositional expressions of activity in the Behavioural Inhibition System (BIS), which is sensitive to punishment cues, and Behavioural Activation System (BAS), which responds to reward cues, respectively. Gray relates psychopathy to a weak BIS, implying that primary psychopaths are non-neurotic extraverts. However, the BAS has recently been linked to E and P (see Blackburn, 2006).

In Zuckerman's Alternative Five Factor model (Zuckerman, 1995), primary psychopaths are held to be high on dimensions of impulsivity, E and aggression, low on N and high on both F1 and F2 of the PCL-R. Secondary psychopaths differ in being low on E, high on N and high mainly on PCL-R F2. Zuckerman, therefore, differs from Eysenck and Lykken (below) in seeing primary psychopaths as low in N and secondary psychopaths as introverted.

In a more comprehensive theory, Lykken (1995) divides antisocial personalities into genera of those with abnormal temperaments that make them difficult to socialise (*psychopaths*), those who are badly socialised (*sociopaths*) and those who are normally socialised but show intermittent antisocial behaviour related to neurotic impulses (*character neuroses*). The latter resemble Karpman's secondary psychopaths, but Lykken differentiates them from psychopaths. He also suggests that Mealey's secondary sociopaths correspond to his sociopaths rather than a subtype of psychopath.

Personality and biological characteristics are held to distinguish primary and secondary species of psychopath. Personality is described in terms of Tellegen's higher order dimensions of negative emotionality (NEM), positive emotionality

(PEM) and Constraint (CON), which correspond to Eysenck's N, E and low P, respectively. Lykken does not believe that psychopaths are deficient in emotional experience generally, but that *primary psychopaths* are specifically deficient in *fear* or harm avoidance. Although *secondary psychopaths* will show greater NEM, PEM and harm avoidance than primary psychopaths, harm avoidance is the critical distinguishing trait. This is a primary trait contributing to Tellegen's CON factor.

Lykken combines his theory with the Fowles–Gray theory of psychopathy (Fowles and Dindo, 2006). Primary psychopaths have a weak BIS associated with low fear, risk proneness and sensation seeking. Secondary psychopaths have a normal BIS but an overactive BAS, which also produces risk-taking and impulsivity, but additionally, vulnerability to stress. Primary psychopaths are likely to score higher on PCL-R F1, while secondary psychopaths will score higher on F2.

Problems with the Distinction

These conceptions of primary and secondary psychopathy have only superficial similarities, and differ on the variables distinguishing the two groups. They vary particularly on the aetiological contributions of genetics and development, and on phenotypic differences in N, E and PCL-R F2. Karpman's distinction has had the most influence on research, but there are problems with the distinction.

First, Karpman identified primary psychopaths largely by default as those for whom an active psychogenic cause of deviant behaviour was lacking. Most investigators follow Lykken (1957) in identifying primary psychopaths with Cleckley's 'true' psychopaths, but this creates terminological and taxonomic confusion. Karpman's primary and secondary psychopaths are species of the same antisocial genus. Cleckley, however, does not mention primary or secondary psychopaths, and regarded psychopaths and neurotics as different genera. Psychopaths are characterised by a lack of anxiety 'and less than the average person, show what is widely regarded as basic in the neurotic' (1982, p. 146). His criteria of psychopathy contain the exclusionary criteria 'absence of delusions and other signs of irrational thinking' and 'absence of nervousness or psychoneurotic manifestations'. For Cleckley, then, psychopathy excludes a secondary or neurotic variant *by definition*. This is not merely a semantic issue because secondary psychopaths should not be 'psychopathic' on the PCL-R if it is a valid measure of Cleckley's construct (see below).

Second, there is no 'true' concept of primary or secondary psychopath. Theoretically derived categories are provisional hypotheses, to be judged by their utility for prediction and explanation. As with psychological tests, attempts to identify them empirically must be subject to construct validation (Hogan and Nicholson, 1988). This is a dialectical process requiring investigators to work back and forth between questions of whether the hypothesised categories exist and whether they are reliably distinguished by the variables used to identify them. Most investigators treat Karpman's 'neurotic motivation' and Cleckley's lack of anxiety as the phenotypic basis for the distinction, interpreting absence of neurotic problems in terms of low anxiety, as assessed by measures such as the Welsh Anxiety Scale (WAS: Welsh, 1956). These scales are integral to the personality dimension of N or negative affectivity (Watson and Clark, 1984). However, identifying subtypes operationally in this way is a necessary but only a preliminary step in validating the primary–secondary distinction.

Aetiological typologies pose a problem in this respect. Porter (1996) suggests that aetiological theories specifying different pathways to the same phenotypic outcome are untestable except by longitudinal research. The genetic versus environmental origin that some theories propose is an unlikely basis for the primary–secondary distinction, because genetic variation contributes to most personality variables. Differences in genetic-environmental mix are hence more probable (Baldwin, 1995; Zuckerman, 1995). This implies a role for behaviour genetics and developmental research in differentiating variants of psychopathy (Poythress and Skeem, 2006; Skeem et al., 2003), but phenotypic discrimination of subtypes is necessary for research and intervention, as Mealey (1995) acknowledged.

The following discussion focuses first on the utility of anxiety or negative affectivity in distinguishing primary from secondary psychopaths, and second, on empirical taxonomic approaches to identifying psychopathic subtypes. Although the PCL-R has become the 'gold standard' for assessing psychopathy, much of the relevant research preceded the development of the PCL-R, and used ratings of Cleckley's criteria or questionnaire measures to assess psychopathy. The discussion includes reference to some of this research.

PSYCHOPATHY, ANXIETY AND PERSONALITY

Much research has made the primary–secondary distinction using scales of anxiety or negative affectivity mainly to identify 'purer' representatives of Cleckley's psychopaths. Lykken (1957), for example, defined neurotic sociopaths as patients diagnosed clinically as psychopathic who did not meet Cleckley's criteria 'in important respects'. Neurotic sociopaths were found to score higher than primary sociopaths and controls on the Taylor Manifest Anxiety Scale, but primary sociopaths scored lower than controls on a measure of real-life anxiety (fear). Lykken construed the latter as an index of a specific affective deficit, and as noted earlier, he does not believe that primary psychopaths have any generalised affective deficit (Lykken, 1995).

Subsequent investigators, however, assume that low scores on anxiety scales reflect the interpersonal-affective deficits emphasised by Cleckley, and have identified primary and secondary psychopaths as those who are *equated* on a measure of psychopathy, but differ in anxiety (e.g. Fagan and Lira, 1980; Newman et al., 2005; Schmauk, 1970; Widom, 1976). These studies define psychopathy in different ways, but have established differences between primary and secondary groups on variables such as learning under laboratory conditions, personal construct systems or institutional misconduct. Newman et al. (2005), for example, found that despite Lykken's objections to the use of anxiety scales to make the primary–secondary distinction, PCL-R psychopaths identified as primary or secondary by the WAS differed on BIS and BAS scales as predicted by Lykken's theory. Other studies also show that differences between psychopaths and non-psychopaths on theoretically relevant measures are moderated by the level of anxiety (Brinkley et al., 2004).

Although this research supports the utility of anxiety in making the primary–secondary distinction, it raises questions about the relation of the PCL-R to Cleckley's construct. As noted earlier, because of Cleckley's use of the exclusionary criterion 'absence of nervousness', secondary or anxious psychopaths should score lower on the PCL-R if it is a valid measure of Cleckley's construct, and the PCL-R should be inversely related to anxiety. However, Cleckley's exclusionary criterion is not included in the PCL-R, and high anxiety is clearly compatible with high PCL-R scores.

Schmitt and Newman (1999) found that total PCL-R and F1 and F2 scores were uncorrelated with measures of anxiety, N or fear, and concluded that the PCL-R is independent of anxiety. They suggest that the PCL-R does not faithfully represent Cleckley's construct. Hare (2003) argues that absence of nervousness is not critical to Cleckley's construct, and that lack of anxiety is in any case covered by PCL-R items relating to more general emotional experiences and processes, such as lack of remorse or guilt, shallow affect or callousness/lack of empathy. The equally high PCL-R scores of primary and secondary psychopaths argue against this.

However, although correlations of anxiety with total PCL-R are generally weak (Hare, 2003), other studies have found differential relationships between negative affectivity and the two factors of the PCL-R. Patrick and his colleagues (e.g. Hicks and Patrick, 2006; Patrick, 1994; Patrick and Zempolich, 1998) have shown that differential relationships become more apparent when the common variance in F1 and F2 is partialled out and specific facets of emotionality are examined. Using Tellegen's Multidimensional Personality Questionnaire (MPQ), they have found with some consistency that F1 correlates negatively with the stress reactivity (anxiety) scale of NEM and positively with the social potency (dominance) and achievement scales of PEM. F2, however, correlates positively with all primary scales of NEM, negatively with the well-being and achievement scales of PEM and negatively with CON. Total PCL-R correlates only with the aggression scale of NEM scale, the relationship being positive.

Hicks and Patrick (2006) suggest that the unique variance of F1 may capture the lack of anxiety emphasised by Cleckley. The weak relationship of total PCL-R to anxiety conceals the opposing relationships of NEM to the two PCL-R factors. However, they note that the PCL-R is clearly multidimensional and goes beyond Cleckley's construct.

Tellegen's NEM and PEM dimensions contain elements of the agreeableness dimension of the Five Factor Model (FFM: see Lynam and Derefinko, 2006), and the above findings are consistent with other work indicating that the PCL-R represents a complex constellation of personality traits. In their 'translation' of the PCL-R into the domains and facets of the FFM, Lynam and Widiger (2007) argue that most PCL-R criteria are related to low agreeableness (antagonism) or low conscientiousness, while facets of N and E make both positive and negative contributions. This analysis places more emphasis on the contribution of antagonism than of N to the PCL-R, but it nevertheless underscores the complexity of the PCL-R.

The multidimensional nature of the PCL-R accounts for findings that some high PCL-R scorers are also highly anxious. Because the PCL-R is only partially aligned with Cleckley's construct, only some high scorers will be 'pure' Cleckley psychopaths. Dividing high PCL-R scorers into high- and low-anxious subgroups compensates for the opposing relationships of anxiety to the PCL-R factors, and serves to identify groups of PCL-R psychopaths overlapping in deviant traits, one of which approximates to Cleckley's psychopath. The traditional use of anxiety scales to distinguish primary and secondary psychopaths is, therefore, justified by the multidimensional structure of the PCL-R. At the same time, this structure suggests that high scores may encompass homogeneous subgroups differentiated by more complex patterns of personality traits than anxiety alone.

EMPIRICAL CLASSIFICATIONS

Empirical classifications seek objective identification of naturally occurring multidimensional patterns, and the cluster analytic methods of numerical taxonomy provide the most powerful means of achieving this (Sokal, 1974). Cluster analysis aims to identify relatively homogeneous and mutually exclusive groups according to similar profiles of attributes. However, cluster analysis always places entities into groups, and different clustering methods may generate different solutions to the same data. Like exploratory factor analysis, traditional clustering methods are also subject to procedural indeterminacies, such as deciding the optimal number of clusters, and some authors are sceptical of their ability to resolve typological issues in abnormal psychology.

Methodological developments that employ a statistical, goodness-of-fit criterion for deciding among alternative solutions (model-based clustering: Fraley and Raftery, 2002) may resolve some of these issues, and have been applied in recent studies of psychopathy (see below). Nevertheless, the robustness of empirical clusters determined through traditional methods can be established through replication and external validation. To date, efforts to identify psychopathic subtypes have employed self-report questionnaires, the PCL-R or a combination of the two. The main findings are summarised here (for comprehensive reviews, see Poythress and Skeem, 2006 and Skeem *et al.*, 2003).

Variants Within the PCL-R

Some have identified psychopathic subtypes through cluster analyses that include PCL-R scores. Two analysed PCL-R variables alone. Haapasalo and Pulkinnen (1992) clustered PCL items in non-violent offenders, identifying one group scoring higher on F1 items, a second scoring higher on F2 items and a third low on most items. The second had the most convictions, and were more extraverted and impulsive, while the first scored higher on Gough's Socialisation (*So*) scale, but the groups were similar on N. The first group approximates Cleckley's psychopath, but the primary–secondary distinction was not considered.

In an unpublished study, Hervé and Hare (2004: reported by Poythress and Skeem, 2006) limited clustering variables to Cooke's PCL-R facets and the antisocial component in high-scoring PCL-R offenders. Four psychopathic groups identified were described as *prototypical* (higher on all facets), *macho* (lower interpersonal facet), *manipulative* (lower lifestyle facet) and *pseudo-psychopathic* (low affective facet). Offence differences were found, but Poythress and Skeem criticise this study for criterion contamination (offences influence PCL-R scoring) and lack of external validation.

Using a wider range of variables, Alterman *et al.* (1998) identified antisocial variants of opiate dependent men, clustering adult and conduct disorder components of antisocial personality disorder (PD), total PCL-R and Gough's *So* scale, and compared groups on clinical and personality measures. Of six groups, three had relatively high PCL-R scores. The first, *early onset highly antisocial men*, had serious substance abuse problems, high anxiety, depression, hostility, insecure attachment and marked paranoid and borderline PD. The second, *late onset antisocial men*, were similar, but had the highest levels of histrionic and narcissistic PD. The third, *psychopathic criminal but more socialised men*, had lower levels of anxiety, hostility, guilt, depression and PD. Again, the primary–secondary distinction was not addressed, but the psychopathology of the first two groups suggests secondary psychopathy.

Vassileva *et al.* (2005) derived clusters among prison inmates using PCL-R F1 and F2, the Interpersonal Measure of Psychopathy (*IM-P*), ratings of alcohol and drug abuse and dependence, and an anxiety scale. Four clusters were validated from demographics and criminality data. *Secondary psychopaths* scored highest on F2 and anxiety, had more severe substance abuse problems and were average on F1 and *IM-P*. They were older, more criminally versatile, and had more charges for non-violent offences. *Non-psychopathic criminals with alcohol and drug problems* had lower scores on F1, F2, anxiety and *IM-P*, and were less criminal. *Primary psychopaths* were higher on F1 and *IM-P*, average on F2, less anxious, and had less severe substance abuse problems. They were the most violent and criminally versatile. *Criminals with psychopathic features* were lower on F1, *IM-P*, anxiety, had fewer substance abuse problems, and were less criminal. Two clusters supported the primary–secondary distinction.

In contrast to these analyses, Blackburn and Coid (1999) used the PCL-R, criminal career and psychopathology as external criteria to validate clusters of DSM-III PDs among violent male offenders. Three of six groups scored very highly on the PCL-R and equally on F1 and F2, had the highest levels of criminality and had more frequent histories of lifetime substance abuse. These groups were the most antisocial and narcissistic. One was also histrionic and reported the lowest levels of lifetime Axis I anxiety and mood disorders. A second group was also histrionic, but displayed borderline, avoidant and other PDs, and high levels of anxiety and mood disorders. A third was paranoid, schizotypal and borderline, and the majority had a lifetime history of psychosis. We identified the first group as primary psychopaths, and the other two as variants of secondary psychopath.

Poythress and Skeem (2006) criticise these studies for being atheoretical, and for using traditional methods of cluster analysis. They also argue that psychopathic subtypes should be determined within those who are psychopathic on PCL-R criteria rather than among heterogeneous samples. However, they note that limiting analysis to those scoring above the conventional PCL-R cut-off of 30 assumes a categorical rather than dimensional concept of psychopathy, and risks missing significant psychopathic variants. For example, not only is the conventional cut-off relatively arbitrary, it may exclude individuals displaying the core characteristics of F1 who may score low on F2.

Two recent studies avoid some of these limitations. Hicks *et al.* (2004) used model-based clustering of the 11 primary trait scales of Tellegen's MPQ with prisoners having PCL-R scores of 30 or more, hypothesising a low anxiety, primary sub-type and a high anxiety, impulsive, aggressive secondary subtype. The best-fitting model indicated two clusters. *Emotionally stable psychopaths* (ES) scored low on stress reaction and high on social potency. *Aggressive psychopaths* (AP) were high in aggression, alienation and stress reaction. AP were younger, scored slightly higher on PCL-R F2, and higher on the NEM factor, but lower on CON and Agentic PEM. On external criteria, AP had a more prominent history of fighting and were slightly younger at first criminal charge. ES had a higher IQ and scored higher on Gough's *So* scale, but lower on the WAS. The authors conclude that ES resembles the pri-mary psychopath and Cleckley's psychopath while AP resembles the life-course persistent offender (Moffitt, 1993).

Skeem *et al.* (2007) also used model-based clustering to identify subgroups of violent psychopathic inmates, but analysed trait anxiety and PCL-R facets. Two clusters identified as *primary* (P) and *secondary* (S) *psychopaths* best fit the data. P scored lower on trait anxiety and higher on Cooke's three PCL-R facets, but not the antisocial factor. On external criteria, S showed, as predicted, more self-report borderline PD, more irritability, social withdrawal, lack of as-sertiveness, poorer clinical functioning and more mental illness. They were not, however, more impulsive or narcissistic, and were judged only marginally more responsive to treatment. The groups were considered similar to those of Hicks *et al.* (2004).

Variations in these studies preclude firm conclusions. Nevertheless, where anx-iety is included as a clustering variable, more and less anxious subtypes of psy-chopath typically emerge, supporting the primary–secondary distinction. The anx-ious subtype is also likely to display borderline PD traits, but narcissistic PD seems common to both groups. Less consistent, but suggestive, is a tendency for the non-anxious group to be more intelligent, better socialised, less impulsive and to score lower on PCL-R F2.

A Questionnaire Typology of Mentally Disordered Offenders

In tests of the hypothesis that violent offenders can be divided into overcontrolled, inhibited and undercontrolled psychopathic types (Megargee, 1966), cluster anal-yses of MMPI (Minnesota Multiphasic Personality Inventory) profiles of mentally disordered offenders identified two undercontrolled and two overcontrolled pat-terns (e.g. Blackburn, 1975). The same patterns emerged using a questionnaire, the Special Hospitals Assessment of Personality and Socialisation (SHAPS: Blackburn, 1987), based on MMPI scales measuring N (the WAS) and E, and other instruments, and a later revision, the Antisocial Personality Questionnaire APQ: Blackburn and Fawcett, 1999). The APQ measures eight primary factors and two higher order fac-tors of impulsivity (I: hostility, aggression and non-compliance versus self-control and conformity) and withdrawal (W: social withdrawal, anxiety and submissive-ness versus sociability, self-confidence and assertiveness). The research is reviewed in more detail elsewhere (Blackburn, 1999).

The four profile classes are described as: (1) *primary psychopaths* (P: impulsive, aggressive, hostile, extraverted, self-confident, low to average anxiety); (2) *secondary psychopaths* (S: hostile, impulsive, aggressive, socially anxious, introverted, moody, low self-esteem); (3) *controlled* (C: defensive, controlled, sociable, very low anxiety and high self-esteem); (4) *inhibited* (I: shy, withdrawn, controlled, moderately anxious, low self-esteem). Primary psychopaths are distinguished by traits held to define the psychopath, particularly as described by McCord and McCord (1964: 'an asocial, aggressive, highly impulsive person, who feels little or no guilt and is unable to form lasting bonds of affection with other human beings', p. 3). Secondary psychopaths share most of these traits, but their anxiety and psychopathology suggests correspondence to Karpman's secondary psychopaths. The personality profiles of the two groups are also close to those of primary and secondary psychopaths suggested by Zuckerman (1995): both are unsocialised, impulsive and aggressive, but are differentiated by E–I as well as by N.

These four patterns reflect extremes on the APQ higher order I and W factors. P and S fall towards the impulsive-aggressive extreme of the I dimension, but at opposite extremes on the W dimension. The C and I groups fall towards the controlled extreme of the I factor but are also differentiated by the W dimension. The I and W dimensions were originally construed as 45° rotations of the N and E dimensions, and hence equivalent to Gray's impulsivity and anxiety dimensions. However, we recently found that although W clearly represents NI, I represents N and antagonism of the FFM (Blackburn *et al.*, 2004). I and W were also good markers for the two higher order factors of the FFM.

The robustness of the typology is indicated by its replication across clustering methods and also different samples of mentally disordered offenders, offenders in English prisons and American female prisoners (see Blackburn, 1999). The four groups were also recovered from cluster analysis of the PD scales of the Millon Clinical Multiaxial Inventory (MCMI-1: Blackburn, 1996). Differences between groups on behavioural, affective and social cognitive variables support the validity of the typology. For example, consistent with self-reported differences in control and conformity, P and S have more convictions than C and I, and earlier onset of criminal careers (Blackburn, 1975, 1999; Pollock, 1999).

P and S also describe more intense anger to provocation or threat (Blackburn and Lee-Evans, 1985; Morrison and Gilbert, 2001), and group differences in patterns of violence and emotional reaction to the offence were found among murderers by Pollock (1999). A cognitive-interpersonal model proposes differences between P and S in interpersonal style and self-presentation (Blackburn, 1998). Supporting this, Morrison and Gilbert (2001) found that P perceived themselves to have significantly higher social rank than did S, and reported less shame, angriness, self-blame and anger towards others. Groups also differ in patterns of PD (Blackburn, 1996, 1998). For example, on an interview measure of DSM-III PDs, S met criteria for more PDs than other groups, and a majority met criteria for borderline PD (Blackburn, 1998). Compared with S, more P patients met criteria for narcissistic and antisocial PD, and fewer were schizoid or schizotypal.

The APQ Typology and the PCL-R

The APQ typology provides a valid classification of variants of *offender*, but two small studies suggested that P and S groups are not variants of PCL-R *psychopath* (Blackburn, 1999). Although more of P met conventional PCL-R criteria of psychopathy, most members of other groups did not. However, this means that some members of APQ groups will show psychopathic attributes according to the PCL-R, and that combining the APQ with the PCL-R may identify meaningful variants of psychopath. We recently examined this possibility in 165 mentally disordered offenders on whom extensive data on personality, psychopathology and psychopathy were available (Blackburn *et al.*, 2008).

Given that the PCL-R represents a continuous dimension (Edens *et al.*, 2006), any cut-off score for distinguishing 'psychopaths' is arbitrary, but for purposes of the study, we divided the sample at the median PCL-R score of 20, the 79 patients with a score of 21 or more being considered psychopathic. Of the P, S, C and I groups, 28 (57%), 16 (55%), 23 (47%) and 12 (37%), respectively, were psychopathic on this PCL-R criterion. We examined the utility of the APQ classification applied to psychopaths by comparing these psychopathic members of the four groups on variables suggested as discriminating by theoretical conceptions of the primary–secondary distinction or by previous research. Specifically, we looked at PCL-R factors and facets, criminal history, Axis I psychopathology, history of childhood abuse, personality, PDs, observer ratings of interpersonal behaviour and clinical ratings of risk and treatability.

Groups were similar on total PCL-R, but were differentiated by PCL-R factors and facets, P being higher than C on F2 and lower than C on F1 and Cooke's interpersonal and affective facets. Although P had more convictions for violence and the most convictions overall, differences in criminal history were not significant. However, P were rated more at risk of future violence than C. C also had a higher IQ than P.

We compared the groups on lifetime history of Axis I anxiety disorders, depression, psychosis and PTSD. S showed more Axis I disorder than P or C, but were similar to I. There were no differences in lifetime depression or psychosis, but a majority of both S and I had lifetime diagnoses of anxiety, compared to a third of P and a quarter of C. On NEO Five Factor Inventory (NEO-FFI) N, both S and I were also higher than P and C. P and S, therefore, resemble Karpman's primary and secondary psychopath, respectively, but I represents a further 'neurotic' variant, while C appears to represent a further variant of primary psychopath. However, clinical ratings of treatability provided no support for Karpman's proposal that secondary psychopaths are more treatable.

A majority of S and I also reported symptoms of PTSD, and history of childhood abuse provided further evidence for traumatic experiences. Most of S reported some form of childhood abuse, and a half of S and I reported sex abuse. These findings are consistent with Porter's differentiation of secondary from fundamental psychopaths in terms of traumatising history (Porter, 1996). However, again, I seems a variant of secondary psychopath.

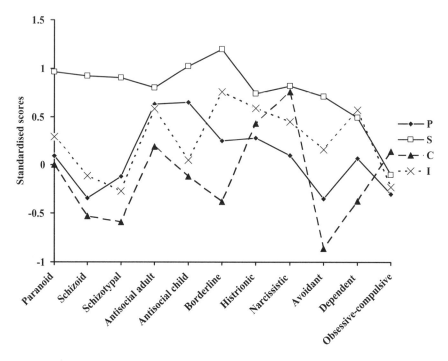

Figure 6.1 Standardised (z) scores on personality disorder dimensions of the International Personality Disorder Examination of APQ groups with higher PCL-R scores: P = primary psychopaths (N = 28); S = secondary psychopaths (N = 16); C = controlled (N = 23); I = inhibited (N = 12).

On the NEO-FFI, P and S were more antagonistic than C, but S were more introverted than P and C, and C had the highest levels of agreeableness and conscientiousness. On nurse ratings of interpersonal style (Blackburn and Renwick, 1996), P showed a predominantly hostile-dominant style, S being more submissive as suggested by Blackburn (1998), but differences fell short of significance. These personality differences indicate that 'high interpersonal antagonism, pan-impulsivity, the absence of negative self-directed affect, the presence of angry hostility and interpersonal assertiveness', considered the broad components of psychopathy by Lynam and Widiger (2007, p. 171), exemplify only one variant of psychopath.

The groups also differed on DSM-IV PDs assessed by the International Personality Disorder Examination (IPDE). Figure 6.1 shows group mean dimensional scores (sum of criteria in each category), standardised against the total sample of 165. Antisocial PD is divided into adult and child conduct disorder components. The groups did not differ on adult antisocial, histrionic, dependent or obsessive-compulsive PDs, but five points can be noted. First, all groups show pronounced histrionic and adult antisocial traits. Second, S has the most severe personality pathology, C the least. Third, P are similar to S in histrionic, narcissistic and adult and child antisocial traits, but P show significantly fewer traits of schizoid, schizotypal, borderline and avoidant PD. Fourth, P differ from C mainly in showing more child conduct disorder, suggesting earlier onset of antisocial disorder. Fifth,

I differ from S in showing fewer traits of paranoid, schizoid, schizotypal and child conduct disorder, again suggesting later onset of antisocial disorder, but also more circumscribed PD.

When combined with higher PCL-R scores, then, the APQ typology reflects distinct variants of psychopath, and confirms the heterogeneity of psychopaths. However, our results suggest that greater discrimination will be achieved by multidimensional distinctions than by a simple primary–secondary dichotomy. For example, the differing patterns of PD would be less apparent from a high-versus low-anxiety distinction. The results for C and I are surprising, given that these more controlled and conforming groups have not hitherto been considered 'psychopathic'. However, the results are consistent with other findings of relatively well-socialised variants of PCL-R psychopath (Alterman *et al.*, 1998; Haapasalo and Pulkinnen, 1992; Hicks *et al.*, 2004).

A likely reason for finding two variants of primary psychopath is that the PCL-R subsumes the overlapping constructs of psychopathy proposed by Cleckley and the McCords (Blackburn, 2005, 2007). PCL-R items relating to impulsivity and criminality are not among Cleckley's criteria, suggesting construct drift (Blackburn, 2005; Cooke, Michie and Skeem, 2007). These criteria, however, form part of the McCords' definition. These two constructs are reflected in the PCL-R variants indicated by our findings. Whereas the impulsive, aggressive, interpersonally hostile traits of the P group are those of the McCords' psychopath, the lack of anxiety and high self-esteem, higher intelligence, agreeableness and histrionic and narcissistic traits of the C group are closer to Cleckley's concept.

CLINICAL IMPLICATIONS

Assessment

Beliefs about the treatability and risk of psychopaths rest on assumptions of homogeneity. Emerging evidence of heterogeneity requires reappraisal of these beliefs, and indicates that personality assessment should routinely accompany PCL-R assessment. The utility of the primary–secondary distinction is now firmly established, and anxiety or N is reliably assessed by several standard questionnaires. However, anxiety is unlikely to be sufficient to identify other traits that research suggests discriminate subtypes. Impulsivity and aggression, for example, are also facets of the agreeableness-antagonism dimension, and submissiveness and lack of self-assertion that may characterise secondary psychopaths are facets of introversion. In our own research, it is 'NI' that distinguishes APQ primary and secondary psychopaths. Multidimensional personality assessment is therefore indicated.

Because 'pathological lying' is a trait of the PCL-R, it is sometimes argued that psychopaths cannot be trusted to complete self-report measures. Yet lying is commonplace human behaviour that serves functions of self-presentation (DePaulo *et al.*, 1996). Personality assessment through self-report is concerned less with eliciting verifiable facts than with beliefs about the sort of person one is, and self-presentation is present in any assessment (Hogan and Nicholson, 1988). Self-reports should, therefore, be considered a guide to a person's identity.

Aggression and Violence

Differentiating psychopathic subtypes may facilitate understanding of the relation between psychopathy and violence (Skeem *et al.*, 2003). First, subtypes may differ in proneness to different forms of assaultive behaviour. The primary psychopaths of Vassileva *et al.* (2005) had more convictions for violence than secondary psychopaths, and in our own studies, the APQ P group tend to have more violent convictions. Among APQ groups higher on the PCL-R, P were also rated by clinicians as at greater risk of further violence. There have been no follow-ups of psychopathic subgroups, but the possibility that primary psychopaths pose a greater risk of violent recidivism than other subtypes seems worth pursuing.

Second, subtypes may differ in risk of aggressive behaviour within institutions. Relevant evidence is limited, but using MMPI criteria, Fagan and Lira (1980) found in two studies that primary psychopaths more frequently engaged in serious incidents in a correctional institution and spent more time in segregation than secondary psychopaths or non-psychopaths. The more hostile-dominant, confrontational style of our APQ P group also suggests that they are likely to present more management problems than other groups. Heilbrun and Heilbrun (1985), however, found that secondary psychopaths with low IQ exhibited the most aggressive behaviour within a prison. IQ may, therefore, be a significant moderator of the aggression of subtypes.

Third, there may be qualitative differences in the aggression of psychopathic subtypes. Some studies suggest that compared with the crimes of non-psychopaths, the violence of psychopaths is more commonly *instrumental* (premeditated, goal-directed, non-affective) rather than *reactive* (unplanned, non-goal-directed, angry: Patrick and Zempolich, 1998). Skeem *et al.* (2003) suggest that instrumental violence may be more characteristic of primary psychopaths, reactive violence of secondary psychopaths. Evidence for this among PCL-R psychopaths is indirect, but Pollock (1999) found some support using the APQ typology with homicides. The offences of primary psychopaths were more likely to be instrumental or goal-directed and their victims were more commonly strangers. Secondary psychopaths showed more mixed forms of violence, while the offences of C and I were primarily reactive violence directed against acquaintances.

It might be expected that secondary psychopaths would be more prone to reactive, angry aggression, but findings with the APQ typology do not support this. Blackburn and Lee-Evans (1985) found that both P and S groups reported more intense anger and aggression to hypothetical scenarios of interpersonal attack situations, and this was replicated by Morrison and Gilbert (2001) using the Novaco Anger Scale. However, in the former study, relative to primary psychopaths, secondary psychopaths reported more autonomic arousal to attack situations, suggesting that provocation arouses anxiety as well as anger. Differences between the aggression of primary and secondary psychopaths may, therefore, lie less in propensity to anger than in their perceived self-efficacy in coping with conflict situations.

Bushman and Anderson (2001) argued that the reactive-instrumental dichotomy oversimplifies because many acts of aggression have both anger and planning components. For example, aggression for revenge is rooted in anger but may be expressed immediately or following planning. They suggest that the dichotomy should be replaced by an information processing perspective emphasising knowledge structures in the form of schemas and scripts. Self-schemas are likely to be a significant source of variation in the aggression of psychopathic subtypes. Self-esteem is a major component of negative affectivity (Watson and Clark, 1984), and in the APQ typology, secondary psychopaths are characterised by very low levels of self-esteem. The C group, in contrast, have very high levels of self-esteem.

Baumeister and Campbell (1999) proposed that narcissism is the most relevant self-concept for understanding aggression, and that violence results from threatened egotism when negative evaluation challenges an individual with inflated, unrealistic self-esteem. Except for P, our APQ groups with higher PCL-R scores had marked narcissistic traits, but the C group most clearly shows the combination of narcissism and inflated self-esteem. In fact, the main indications of PD in this group were narcissistic and histrionic traits.

The difference between this group and secondary psychopaths, who were equally narcissistic, may lie in perceived self-efficacy. Skeem *et al.* (2003), for example, note the distinction made in the literature between *overt narcissism*, characterised by grandiosity and self-assurance, and *covert narcissism* characterised by grandiosity but emotional vulnerability, and suggest that this may parallel the primary–secondary distinction. Our C group show overt narcissism in these terms. They may, therefore, be more vigilant for threats to their status. Differences in self-concept and in coping with interpersonal challenges may hence be a more fruitful way of understanding variations in aggression between psychopathic subgroups.

Treatment

Despite widespread pessimism about the treatability of psychopaths, treatment outcome research has been inconclusive (Lösel , 1998). Treatment studies typically assume that psychopaths are homogeneous, but interest in the primary–secondary distinction stems partly from Karpman's view that the two groups differ in treatability. Apart from a few suggestive reports from substance abuse programmes that depression moderates the treatment responsiveness of antisocial patients (Blackburn, 2000), empirical support for this view is lacking, and clinical ratings of treatability failed to distinguish the primary and secondary psychopaths of Skeem *et al.* (2007) and Blackburn *et al.* (2008). However, it remains plausible that psychopathic subtypes differing in personality and clinical status differ not only in amenability to treatment but also in responsiveness to available treatment methods.

Skeem *et al.* (2007) suggest that secondary psychopaths may more easily form a therapeutic alliance, and have problems that may be more amenable to traditional psychotherapy than those of primary psychopaths. The latter require structured approaches that focus on cognitions and behaviours precipitating violence and on providing constructive outlets for meeting their goals rather than attempting personality change. However, the data suggest that variants of psychopathy differ in both intrapersonal and interpersonal characteristics. Moreover, change in personality traits is a significant component in the outcome of treatment for PDs

(Warner *et al.*, 2004). A broader range of treatment targets therefore needs to be considered.

Secondary psychopaths are likely to have multiple problems for which a range of cognitive and behavioural treatments have been established. These include symptoms of Axis I anxiety and trauma-related disorders, and problems of hostility and anger control. Similarly, they are more prone to the emotional dysregulation of borderline PD, for which interventions such as dialectical behaviour therapy have been developed with at least moderate success. They are also likely to display problems of coping and self-efficacy for which problem-solving approaches may be appropriate. Some, however, may also have neuropsychological deficits (Hicks *et al.*, 2004) that require behavioural regimes or pharmacological intervention.

Karpman defined primary psychopaths as individuals whose antisocial behaviour could not be traced to psychogenic factors other than lack of conscience, but in more contemporary terms, primary psychopaths are identified by dysfunctional personality traits. Our recent findings on APQ types with higher PCL-R scores suggest that it may be useful to recognise two variants of primary psychopath represented by our P and C groups. The P group share with secondary psychopaths problems of hostility, anger and over-rehearsed aggressive scripts, and may similarly benefit from anger management and related techniques. However, they seem particularly concerned with maintaining interpersonal status. Interpersonal therapy may be appropriate for this group (Blackburn, 1998; Kiesler, 1996).

The controlled group, however, have the lowest level of anxiety and do not experience generalised problems of hostility or anger that might be amenable to intervention. On conventional indices of adjustment and social functioning, they will appear problem free. Their dysfunction appears to centre on narcissistic egocentricity and grandiosity, which is apparent to observers but not to themselves. They are, therefore, likely to resist therapeutic engagement and acceptance of a patient role. But without change in their unrealistic self-concept, they are liable to further acts of violence in response to threats to their self-esteem. Cognitive or dynamic therapies that focus on their self-appraisals seem needed for this group, but they present the greatest challenge for intervention.

SUMMARY AND CONCLUSIONS

The PCL-R has become one of the most widely used instruments in research and practice with offenders, and high scores have considerable implications for how the criminal justice and mental health systems deal with offenders. Not only are psychopaths seen as the most dangerous offenders, clinicians continue to be wary of attempting psychological interventions with this group on the assumption that psychopathy is not a treatable disorder. Yet, despite a large volume of accumulated research, theoretical understanding of psychopaths continues to be limited, and the answer to the question 'What is psychopathy?' remains elusive.

Attempts to understand psychopaths may have been hindered by the assumption that they represent a homogeneous group. Although psychopathic offenders share antisocial traits and typically have long histories of harmful behaviour, the work reviewed in this chapter indicates that the PCL-R is complex and that high scores encompass distinct subtypes of abnormal personality. The 'classical' distinction between primary and secondary psychopaths now has empirical support, but as research described here suggests, there may also be other significant subtypes.

Research on the differentiation of PCL-R subtypes is at an early stage, and the clinical implications of recognising the heterogeneity of psychopaths remain speculative. As yet, there is little firm empirical justification for supposing that different subtypes differ in risk of further violence or responsiveness to available interventions, or that differing aetiological mechanisms will be detected for different subgroups. Nevertheless, evidence for significant variations between subtypes in psychopathology and personality is growing. Research and practice can no longer afford to ignore these variations.

REFERENCES

Alterman, A.I., McDermott, P.A., Cacciola, J.S. *et al.* (1998) A typology of antisociality in methadone patients. *Journal of Abnormal Psychology*, **107**, 412–22.

Baldwin, J.D. (1995) Continua outperform dichotomies. *Behavioral and Brain Sciences*, **18**, 543–44.

Baumeister, R.F. and Campbell, W.K. (1999) The intrinsic appeal of evil: Sadism, sensational thrills, and threatened egotism. *Personality and Social Psychology Review*, **3**, 210–21.

Blackburn, R. (1975) An empirical classification of psychopathic personality. *British Journal of Psychiatry*, **127**, 456–60.

Blackburn, R. (1987) Two scales for the assessment of personality disorder in antisocial populations. *Personality and Individual Differences*, **8**, 81–93.

Blackburn, R. (1996) Replicated personality disorder clusters among mentally disordered offenders and their relation to dimensions of personality. *Journal of Personality Disorders*, **10**, 68–81.

Blackburn, R. (1998) Psychopathy and personality disorder: Implications of interpersonal theory, in *Psychopathy: Theory, Research and Implications for Society* (eds D.J. Cooke, S.J. Hart and A.E. Forth), Kluwer, Amsterdam, pp. 269–301.

Blackburn, R. (1999) Personality assessment in violent offenders: the development of the Antisocial Personality Questionnaire. *Psychologica Belgica*, **39**, 87–111.

Blackburn, R. (2000) Treatment or incapacitation? Implications of research on personality disorders for the management of dangerous offenders. *Legal and Criminological Psychology*, **5**, 1–21.

Blackburn, R. (2005) Psychopathy as a personality construct, in *Handbook of Personology and Psychopathology* (ed. S. Strack), John Wiley & Sons, Inc., New York, pp. 271–91.

Blackburn, R. (2006) Other theoretical models of psychopathy, in *Handbook of Psychopathy* (ed. C.J. Patrick),Guildford Press, New York, pp. 35–57.

Blackburn, R. (2007) Personality disorder and antisocial deviance: Comments on the debate on the structure of the Psychopathy Checklist-Revised. *Journal of Personality Disorders*, **21**, 142–59.

Blackburn, R. and Coid, J.W. (1999) Empirical clusters of DSM-III personality disorders in violent offenders. *Journal of Personality Disorders*, **13**, 18–34.

Blackburn, R. and Fawcett, D.J. (1999) The Antisocial Personality Questionnaire: an inventory for assessing deviant traits in offender populations. *European Journal of Psychological Assessment*, **15**, 14–24.

Blackburn, R. and Renwick, S.J.D. (1996) Rating scales for measuring the interpersonal circle in forensic psychiatric patients. *Psychological Assessment*, **8**, 76–84.

Blackburn, R. and Lee-Evans, J.M. (1985) Reactions of primary and secondary psychopaths to anger-evoking situations. *British Journal of Clinical Psychology*, **24**, 254–69.

Blackburn, R., Logan, C., Donnelly, J. and Renwick, S.J.D. (2008) Identifying psychopathic subtypes: Combining an empirical personality classification of offenders with the Psychopathy Checklist-Revised. *Journal of Personality Disorders*, **22**, 604–22.

Blackburn, R., Renwick, S.J.D., Donnelly, J.P. and Logan, C. (2004) Big Five or Big Two? Superordinate factors in the NEO Five Factor Inventory and the Antisocial Personality Questionnaire. *Personality and Individual Differences*, **37**, 957–90.

Brinkley, C.A., Newman, J.P., Widiger, T.A. and Lynam, D.R. (2004) Two approaches to parsing the heterogeneity of psychopathy. *Clinical Psychology: Science and Practice*, **11**, 69–94.

Bushman, B.J. and Anderson, C.A. (2001) Is it time to pull the plug on the hostile versus instrumental aggression dichotomy? *Psychological Review*, **108**, 273–79.

Cleckley, H. (1982) *The Mask of Sanity*, 6th edn., Mosby, St. Louis (Original work 1941).

Cooke, D.J., Michie, C., Hart, S.D. and Clark, D. (2004) Reconstructing psychopathy: Clarifying the significance of antisocial and socially deviant behaviour in the diagnosis of psychopathic personality disorder. *Journal of Personality Disorders*, **18**, 337–57.

Cooke, D.J., Michie, C. and Skeem, J. (2007) Understanding the structure of the Psychopathy Checklist-Revised. *British Journal of Psychiatry*, **190** (suppl 49), s39–50.

DePaulo, B.M., Kashy, D.A., Kirkendol, S.E. *et al.* (1996) Lying in everyday life. *Journal of Personality and Social Psychology*, **70**, 979–95.

Edens, J.F., Marcus, D.K., Lilienfeld, S.O. and Poythress, N.G. (2006) Psychopathic, not psychopath: Taxometric evidence for the dimensional structure of psychopathy. *Journal of Abnormal Psycholology*, **115**, 131–44.

Eysenck, H.J. (1977) *Crime and Personality*, 3rd edn, Paladin, London.

Fagan, T.J. and Lira, F.T. (1980) The primary and secondary sociopathic personality: Difference in frequency and intensity of antisocial behavior. *Journal of Abnormal Psychology*, **89**, 493–96.

Fowles, D.C. and Dindo, L. (2006) A dual-deficit model of psychopathy, in *Handbook of Psychopathy* (ed. C.J. Patrick), Guildford Press, New York, pp. 14–34.

Fraley, C. and Raftery, A.E. (2002) Model-based clustering, discriminant analysis, and density estimation. *Journal of the American Statistical Association*, **97**, 611–31.

Gray, J.A. (1994) Framework for a taxonomy of psychiatric disorder, in *Essays on Emotion Theory* (eds S.H.M. van Gootzen, N.E. van de Poll and J.A. Sergeant), Erlbaum, Hillsdale, NJ, pp. 29–57.

Haapasalo, J. and Pulkinnen, L. (1992) The Psychopathy Checklist and non-violent offender groups. *Criminal Behaviour and Mental Health*, **2**, 315–28.

Hare, R.D. (2003) *The Hare Psychopathy Checklist-Revised*, 2nd edn, Multi-Health Systems, Toronto.

Hare, R.D. and Neumann, C. (2005) Structural models of psychopathy. *Current Psychiatry Reports*, **7**, 57–64

Hare, R.D. and Neumann, C.S. (2006) The PCL-R assessment of psychopathy, in *Handbook of Psychopathy* (ed. C.J. Patrick), Guildford, New York, pp. 58–88.

Heilbrun, A.B. and Heilbrun, M.R. (1985) Psychopathy and dangerousness: Comparison, integration, and extension of two psychopathic typologies. *British Journal of Clinical Psychology*, **24**, 181–95.

Hervé, H.F. and Hare, R.D. (2004) Psychopathic subtypes and their crimes: a validation study. *Paper presented at the annual conference of the American Psychology-Law Society, Scottsdale, AZ*.

Hicks, B.M. and Patrick, C.J. (2006) Psychopathy and negative emotionality: Analyses of suppressor effects reveal distinct relations with emotional distress, fearfulness, and anger-hostility. *Journal of Abnormal Psychology*, **115**, 276–87.

Hicks, B.M., Markon, K.E., Patrick, C.J. *et al.* (2004) Identifying psychopathy subtypes on the basis of personality structure. *Psychological Assessment*, **16**, 276–88.

Hogan, R. and Nicholson, R.A. (1988) The meaning of personality test scores. *American Psychologist*, **43**, 621–26.

Karpman, B. (1946) Psychopathy in the scheme of human typology. *Journal of Nervous and Mental Disease*, **103**, 276–88.

Karpman, B. (1948) The myth of the psychopathic personality. *American Journal of Psychiatry*, **104**, 523–34.

Kiesler, D.J. (1996) *Contemporary Interpersonal Theory and Research: Personality, Psychopathology, and Psychotherapy*, John Wiley & Sons, Inc., New York.

Lösel, F. (1998) Treatment and management of psychopaths, in *Psychopathy: Theory, Research, and Implications for Society* (eds D.J. Cooke, A.E. Forth and R.D. Hare), Kluwer, Amsterdam, pp. 303–54.

Lykken, D.T. (1957) A study of anxiety in the sociopathic personality. *Journal of Abnormal and Social Psychology*, **55**, 6–10.

Lykken, D.T. (1995) *The Antisocial Personalities*, Erlbaum, Hillsdale, NJ.

Lynam, D.R. and Derefinko, K.J. (2006) Psychopathy and personality, in *Handbook of Psychopathy* (ed. C.J. Patrick), Guildford Press, New York, pp. 133–55.

Lynam, D.R. and Widiger, T.A. (2007) Using a general model of personality to identify the basic elements of psychopathy. *Journal of Personality Disorders*, **21**, 160–78.

McCord, W.M. and McCord, J. (1964) *The Psychopath: An Essay on the Criminal Mind*, Van Nostrand, New York.

Mealey, L. (1995) The sociobiology of sociopathy: an integrated evolutionary model. *Behavioral and Brain Sciences*, **18**, 523–99.

Megargee, E.I. (1966) Undercontrolled and overcontrolled personality types in extreme antisocial aggression. *Psychological Monographs*, **80**, Whole No. 611.

Moffitt, T.E. (1993) Adolescence-limited and life-course persistent antisocial behaviour: a developmental taxonomy. *Psychological Review*, **100**, 674–701.

Morrison, D. and Gilbert, P. (2001) Social rank, shame and anger in primary and secondary psychopaths. *Journal of Forensic Psychiatry*, **12**, 330–56.

Newman, J.P., MacCoon, D.G., Vaughn, L.J. and Sadeh, N. (2005) Validating a distinction between primary and secondary psychopathy with measures of Gray's BIS and BAS constructs. *Journal of Abnormal Psychology*, **114**, 319–23.

Patrick, C.J. (1994) Emotion and psychopathy: Startling new insights. *Psychophysiology*, **31**, 319–30.

Patrick, C.J. and Zempolich, K.A. (1998) Emotion and aggression in the psychopathic personality. *Aggression and Violent Behavior*, **3**, 303–38.

Pollock, P.H. (1999) When the killer suffers: Post-traumatic stress reactions following homicide. *Legal and Criminological Psychology*, **4**, 185–201.

Porter, S. (1996) Without conscience or without active conscience? The etiology of psychopathy revisited. *Aggression and Violent Behavior*, **1**, 179–89.

Poythress, N.G. and Skeem, J.L. (2006) Disaggregating psychopathy: Where and how to look for subtypes, in *Handbook of Psychopathy* (ed. C.J. Patrick), Guildford Press, New York, pp. 172–92.

Schmauk, F.J. (1970) Punishment, arousal, and avoidance learning in sociopaths. *Journal of Abnormal Psychology*, **76**, 325–35.

Schmitt, W.A. and Newman, J.P. (1999) Are all psychopathic individuals low anxious? *Journal of Abnormal Psychology*, **108**, 353–58.

Skeem, J., Johansson, P., Andershed, H. *et al.* (2007) Two subtypes of psychopathic violent offenders that parallel primary and secondary variants. *Journal of Abnormal Psychology*, **116**, 395–409.

Skeem, J.L., Poythress, N., Edens, J.F. *et al.* (2003) Psychopathic personality or personalities? Exploring potential variants of psychopathy and their implications for risk assessment. *Aggression and Violent Behavior*, **8**, 513–46.

Sokal, R.R. (1974) Classification: Purposes, principles, progress, prospects. *Science*, **185**, 1115–23.

Vassileva, J., Kosson, D.S., Abramowitz, C. and Conrod, P. (2005) Psychopathy versus psychopathies in classifying criminal offenders. *Legal and Criminological Psychology*, **10**, 27–43.

Warner, M.B., Morey, L.C., Finch, J.F. *et al.* (2004) The longitudinal relationship of personality traits and disorders. *Journal of Abnormal Psychology*, **113**, 217–27.

Watson, D. and Clark, L.A. (1984) Negative affectivity: the disposition to experience aversive emotional states. *Psychological Bulletin*, **96**, 465–90.

Welsh, G. (1956) Factor dimensions A and R, in *Basic readings on the MMPI in Psychology and Medicine* (eds G.S. Welsh and W.G. Dahlstrom), University of Minnesota Press, Minneapolis, pp. 264–81.

Widom, C.S. (1976) Interpersonal and personal construct systems in psychopaths. *Journal of Consulting and Clinical Psychology*, **44**, 614–23.

Zuckerman, M. (1995) Is the distinction between primary and secondary sociopaths a matter of degree, secondary traits, or nature vs nurture? *Behavioral and Brain Sciences*, **18**, 578–79.

Chapter 7

ANTISOCIAL PERSONALITY DISORDER

Stéphane A de Brito and Sheilagh Hodgins

Institute of Psychiatry, King's College, London, UK

INTRODUCTION

Antisocial personality disorder (ASPD) is one of the 10 personality disorders included in the Diagnostic and Statistical Manual of Mental Disorders (DSM-IV-TR; American Psychiatric Association, 2000). The criteria for the disorder consist of a series of items indexing a lifelong pattern of overt antisocial acts plus traits of impulsivity, irritability and remorselessness. ASPD is considered to be one of the most reliable of all diagnostic categories (Coid, 2003), while its validity is often questioned (Hare, 1996). We will show, however, that the diagnosis of ASPD is based on robust scientific evidence identifying a group of individuals who display antisocial behaviour from a very young age that remains stable across the lifespan. This population of persons with ASPD is heterogeneous, composed of distinct sub-types defined by co-morbid disorders. This fact has implications for understanding the association of ASPD with violence, for effective treatment and for research on the aetiology of the disorder.

Little is known about ASPD. This is primarily due to the fact that almost no research has been published that examines persons with ASPD while excluding those who meet diagnostic criteria for psychopathy. Additionally, few studies of children distinguish those on a pathway towards ASPD from those who present traits similar to adults with psychopathy. Evidence indicates that ASPD and psychopathy, as defined by the Psychopathy Checklist Revised (PCL-R; Hare, 2003), are very different disorders (Hare, 1996; Hodgins, 2007). Many articles and chapters purporting to focus on ASPD review findings about offenders with psychopathy (e.g. see Fitzgerald and Demakis, 2007; Widiger and Trull, 1994). The lack of research on ASPD is surprising given that most incarcerated offenders present this disorder (Fazel and Danesh, 2002). Individuals with ASPD pose a significant burden to society. They fail to contribute by their absence from the workforce, and cause significant levels of harm and distress to their intimate partners and children, and to others as a result of the crimes that they commit. They are an essential part of the illicit drug trade as they almost all present from early adolescence onwards, serious patterns of abuse and dependence (Kessler *et al.*, 1996; Robins and McEvoy, 1990). Finally, both men and women with ASPD contribute to creating another generation of individuals with ASPD through inadequate parenting (Jaffee *et al.*, 2004).

The chapter begins by defining ASPD, showing that the disorder indexes a syndrome that is well documented in prospective, longitudinal investigations of population cohorts and that is distinct from both psychopathy, as defined by the PCL-R, and from Dissocial Personality Disorder, as defined by the International Classification of Diseases (ICD-10; World Health Organisation, 1992). Studies of the prevalence of ASPD are reviewed, highlighting the difficulties inherent in designing and conducting investigations of community samples that derive accurate estimates. Next, the few studies of the socio-demographic correlates of ASPD are presented followed by a review of the evidence on disorders that are co-morbid with ASPD. This evidence, we suggest, is essential for understanding the repeated finding that only half of persons with ASPD are convicted of criminal offences. The chapter then moves on to a presentation of the limited and contradictory findings concerning violence by persons with ASPD. Finally, a hypothesis is presented for orienting future research on the aetiology of ASPD and the development of effective programmes for reducing violence among persons with ASPD.

THE DIAGNOSIS OF ASPD

As with all diagnoses of personality disorders, the diagnosis of ASPD is given only to persons 18 years old or older. Unlike the other personality disorders, however, ASPD requires evidence that a similar disorder existed in childhood. To make the diagnosis of ASPD, a diagnosis of Conduct Disorder (CD) prior to age 15 is required. CD indexes a 'repetitive and persistent pattern of behavior in which the basic rights of others or major age appropriate social norms or rules are violated . . .' (p. 98, American Psychiatric Association, 2000). The criteria include a series of behaviours – various types of aggressive behaviours towards other people and animals, destruction of property, deceitfulness or theft and serious violations of rules. The diagnosis of CD is made when the disturbance in behaviour causes clinically significant impairment in social, academic or occupational functioning. Evidence supports the existence of two sub-types, Childhood Onset indicating presence prior to age 10 and Adolescent Onset when criteria are met only between the ages of 10 and 15 years. Approximately one-half of adults diagnosed with ASPD meet criteria for CD before age 10 and 95% by the age of 12 (Swanson, Bland, and Newman, 1994).

Among adults, if CD was present prior to age 15, the diagnosis of ASPD is made if there is evidence of a 'pervasive pattern of disregard for and violation of the rights of others occurring since age 15' (p. 706, American Psychiatric Association, 2000). Criteria refer to a series of behaviours – a failure to conform to social norms, including laws, repeated fights or assaults, reckless disregard for the safety of self and others, and traits of impulsivity or failure to plan ahead, irritability, irresponsibility and lack of remorse.

Prospective, longitudinal investigations of population cohorts, studies of children with CD and juvenile delinquents, as well as cross-sectional studies of large population cohorts concur in showing that the syndrome indexed by ASPD onsets in childhood and persists across the lifespan. (Goldstein *et al.*, 2006b; Lahey *et al.*, 2005; Moffitt *et al.*, 2001; Robins, Tipp and Przybeck, 1991; Washburn *et al.*, 2007). Thus, the DSM requirement that the diagnosis of ASPD is only given if CD was present prior to age 15 is supported by a substantial body of research. The younger the age of onset and the higher the number of symptoms, the greater is the likelihood that CD develops into ASPD in adulthood (Lahey *et al.*, 2005; Robins, 1966). While, by definition, all adults with a diagnosis of ASPD have a childhood history of CD, only about one-half of children with CD develop ASPD (Simonoff *et al.*, 2004).

This conceptualization of ASPD first appeared in version three of the DSM that was published in 1980. It was based on evidence from longitudinal studies that had followed delinquent youth into adulthood and that has subsequently been replicated many times in similar samples of delinquents, and importantly, in large, representative samples of the general population. This evidence supports the notion of a behavioural syndrome of persistent violation of social norms that onsets in childhood and continues through adult life (Loeber, Green and Lahey, 2003; Washburn *et al.*, 2007). The DSM-III-R added the criterion of lack of remorse primarily because it characterized the subgroup with psychopathy, thereby increasing the heterogeneity of the population who meet diagnostic criteria for the diagnosis of ASPD.

Although the conceptualization of ASPD reflected by the DSM-III is based on robust scientific evidence for the syndrome, many consider the diagnosis to be flawed and/or useless. The primary reason given is that it does not refer to personality traits but rather to a behavioural syndrome. It has been claimed that the diagnosis identifies a heterogeneous population of individuals who present different personalities, attitudes and motivations (Lykken, 1995). Widiger and Trull (1994) have pointed out that there are 848 ways an individual can meet criteria for ASPD. Herein lies the problem that obstructs understanding of this disorder.

DIFFERENTIAL DIAGNOSIS

The criteria for Dissocial Personality Disorder as defined in the ICD-10 (World Health Organisation, 1992) include irresponsibility, incapacity to maintain enduring relationships, low tolerance to frustration, proneness to blame others – and the core traits of psychopathy – callousness, lack of empathy and lack of guilt. Similar to the diagnosis of ASPD, the criteria for Dissocial Personality Disorder include irritability and aggressiveness, lack of remorse and irresponsibility and disregard for social norms, but do not include criteria such as deceitfulness, impulsivity and recklessness. There is almost no research specifically on Dissocial Personality Disorder.

As mentioned above, little is known about ASPD. By contrast, a great deal of research has been conducted on psychopathy as defined by a score of 30 or higher in North America and 25 or higher in Europe on the PCL-R (Patrick, 2006). While both diagnoses require evidence of a stable pattern of conduct problems beginning in childhood, according to the three-factor model conceptualization of psychopathy, the diagnosis of psychopathy requires, in addition, the presence of traits of personality labelled Deficient Affective Experience and Arrogant and Deceitful Interpersonal Behaviour. More recently, it has been suggested that a model consisting of four factors – arrogant and deceitful, Deficient Affective Experience, impulsive and irresponsible lifestyle and antisocial behaviour – may refine the construct of psychopathy (Hare and Neumann, 2006). The trait of deficient affective experience has been shown to be the core deficit of psychopathy (Cooke *et al.*, 2005). Importantly, while almost all individuals with a diagnosis of psychopathy would meet criteria for a diagnosis of ASPD, only one-third of individuals with a diagnosis of ASPD meet criteria for psychopathy (Coid, 1998).

A large body of robust evidence has accumulated describing the features that distinguish offenders who meet criteria for a PCL-R diagnosis of psychopathy from other offenders (Patrick, 2006). The distinguishing features are marked and include differences in behaviour and offending patterns, and cognitive and emotional processing (see for example, Blair, Mitchell and Blair, 2005). Not excluding psychopaths from studies of ASPD may not be particularly important when examining, for example, the prevalence of ASPD in the general population of men where the prevalence of psychopathy is thought to be less than 1% of males. Including those with psychopathy when estimating the prevalence of ASPD would inflate the estimates, but given that such individuals may be less likely than others without this disorder to volunteer to participate in a tedious diagnostic interview, there is no way of estimating the real effect on prevalence estimates of ASPD. The failure to exclude individuals with psychopathy from studies of the correlates of ASPD may be more serious and lead to an inaccurate understanding of ASPD. For example, studies of offenders suggest that those with psychopathy have more convictions and charges for violent crimes than other offenders (Hare and McPherson, 1984; Kosson, Lorenz and Newman, 2006). A recent study that compared offenders with ASPD with and without psychopathy to offenders with neither disorder illustrates the problem (Kosson, Lorenz and Newman, 2006). Among the offenders with ASPD, those with psychopathy had more convictions for violent and nonviolent offences and were more criminally versatile than the offenders with ASPD without psychopathy and than the offenders with neither diagnosis. Consistent with the large body of evidence on psychopathic offenders (Patrick, 2006), on a task requiring them to indicate if a string of letters constituted a word in English, the performance of the offenders with psychopathy was less affected by emotional words than the performance of the two other groups of offenders. Finally, among the offenders who met diagnostic criteria for both psychopathy and ASPD, the less their performance was affected by emotional words, the more severe was their criminal history. By contrast, among the offenders with ASPD and not psychopathy, the effect of emotional words on task performance was not associated with criminal activity (Kosson, Lorenz and Newman, 2006). This adds to the body of evidence suggesting that the diagnosis of psychopathy identifies individuals characterized by a distinctive form of emotion-processing abnormalities who differ from those with ASPD.

Studies examining violence among persons with ASPD that do not exclude individuals with psychopathy are misleading. There is little research on ASPD and the few existing studies fail to exclude persons with psychopathy from their study samples. Readers who are easily frustrated by incomplete, and perhaps misleading findings, may be well advised to move on to the next chapter. Despite a careful search of the published literature in many fields, both on children and adults, the information that we have drawn together is seriously limited by the lack of research focusing on persons with ASPD who do not have psychopathy.

PREVALENCE OF CD

Recent findings from large community samples in the United States and Great Britain have reported prevalence rates of CD of 9.5% and 5.8%, respectively (Green et al., 2004; Nock et al., 2006). In line with previous research, these studies show that CD is twice as common among boys than girls (for a review, see Maughan et al., 2004a). For example, in a British sample of 7977 children aged 5–16 years of age, 7.5% of boys and 3.9% of girls met ICD-10 criteria for CD (Green et al., 2004). In a US sample of 3199 children, a retrospective assessment of CD based on a structured interview using DSM-IV criteria identified lifetime prevalence rates for CD of 12.0% among males and 7.1% among females (Nock et al., 2006).

PREVALENCE OF ASPD

Similarly, estimates of the lifetime prevalence of ASPD vary considerably from one study to another and across countries. Despite the varying prevalence rates across countries and studies, all published reports find that ASPD is much more prevalent among men than women consistent with the well-replicated findings on children with CD. In the Epidemiological Catchment Area (ECA) study, the Diagnostic Interview Schedule was used to examine 18 571 persons representative of the US population. The lifetime prevalence of ASPD among men (4.5%) was found to be almost six times higher than among women (0.8%) (Robins, Tipp and Przybeck, 1991). Similarly, in a study of a community sample of 3258 individuals in Canada using the same diagnostic interview protocol, the lifetime prevalence among men (6.5%) was eight times higher than among women (0.8%) (Swanson, Bland and Newman, 1994). More recently, in a US study of 43 093 individuals, the lifetime prevalence of ASPD was 5.5% among men and 1.9% among women (Compton et al., 2005). In a study conducted in Baltimore using the International Personality Disorder Examination, the prevalence of ASPD was estimated at 6.5% among men and 2.5% among women (J. Samuels, personal communication). By contrast, a recent study of a representative sample of Norwegians aged between 18 and 65 years, used the Structured Interview for DSM-III-R personality disorder (Pfohl et al., 1989), and identified no case of ASPD among the 1142 women, and a lifetime prevalence of 1.3% among the 911 men (Torgensen, Kringlen and Cramer,

2001). In a recent study of a general population sample in Britain, the prevalence of ASPD was estimated at 1.0% among men and 0.2% among women (Coid *et al.*, 2006b).

The reported differences in the prevalence of ASPD across countries may reflect real national differences in the true prevalence of the disorder or they may simply result from distinctive methodological features of the studies. While all the prevalence rates reported above derive from studies that used DSM-III, III-R and IV criteria, it is possible that differences in rates resulted from differences in sampling procedures, sample biases and diagnostic interview protocols (Coid *et al.*, 2006b; Samuels *et al.*, 2002, for a review, see Moran, 1999). The results of the recent study of a representative community sample of Britons illustrate the variation in rates arising from different sampling and diagnostic procedures. In the first stage of this investigation, 8397 persons completed the self-report screening questionnaire of the Structured Clinical Interview for DSM-IV Axis II disorders (SCID-II; First *et al.*, 1997). This provided a prevalence estimate of 4.0% (Coid *et al.*, 2006a). When a subset of 626 individuals from this sample completed face-to-face interviews using the interview protocol of the SCID-II, the estimated prevalence dropped to 0.6% (Coid *et al.*, 2006b). It is likely that the reported prevalence rates for community samples are underestimates of the real prevalence of ASPD. The studies reviewed above required individual informed consent to participate and, except for the first phase of the British study (Coid *et al.*, 2006a), made diagnoses using face-to-face interviews. Recently, after conducting two studies of ASPD in general population samples, Samuels *et al.* (2002) noted: 'we were unable to interview subjects in the target sample who were deceased, unable or unwilling to participate, or could not be traced' (p. 540). Individuals with ASPD are more likely than others of similar age and sex to be deceased (Black *et al.*, 1996), to be unwilling to participate in a research project (Hodgins *et al.*, 2007), and less likely to have a stable address and telephone number to allow identification for a sample and tracing (Robins, 1978).

CORRELATES OF ASPD

Individuals, and most specifically males, with ASPD evidence elevated rates of premature death that result largely from repeated engagement in reckless behaviours (Repo-Tiihonen, Virkkunen and Tiihonen, 2001). In addition, these reckless behaviours may lead to incapacitation. For example, in a study of a large Danish birth cohort followed into their 40s, approximately one-half of the hospitalized cases of organic brain syndrome had previously presented a syndrome of antisocial behaviour (Grekin *et al.*, 2001).

ASPD and CD are also associated with low socio-economic status. The prevalence of CD increases as the level of social deprivation of the child's family decreases (Green *et al.*, 2004). In adulthood, individuals with ASPD are poor and live in socially deprived inner-city neighbourhoods (Grant *et al.*, 2004; Moran, 1999). Poverty in adulthood is consistent with high rates of unemployment. Indeed, one of the diagnostic criteria for ASPD is difficulty in maintaining stable employment. Unemployment, in turn, is associated with poor academic achievement evidenced by children with CD (Lösel and Bender, 2003).

DISORDERS CO-MORBID WITH CD

Children with CD are exposed earlier than other children to alcohol and illicit drugs and they go on to more quickly develop substance misuse disorders that remain throughout adulthood (Cottler *et al.*, 1995; Myers, Stewart and Brown, 1998; Robins and McEvoy, 1990). While almost all children and adolescents with CD will abuse alcohol and/or drugs, between 8.7% and 45.4% of boys and between 1.2% and 61.4% of girls with CD also present ADHD (Disney *et al.*, 1999; McCabe *et al.*, 2004). The combination of CD and ADHD, as compared to CD alone, is associated with an earlier age of onset of conduct problems, aggressive behaviour, persistent antisocial behaviour through adolescence and adulthood, lower verbal and social-cognitive abilities and more problems with peers (Lahey *et al.*, 2005; Lynam, 1996; Waschbusch, 2002).

Among children with CD identified in community samples, the prevalence of co-morbid anxiety disorders ranges from 22% to 33%, while among children with CD who have sought treatment 60–75% present anxiety disorders (Russo and Beidel, 1994). This association varies by age and gender with higher rates among males than females and in middle childhood (Marmorstein, 2007). In a study of 24-month-old boys with conduct problems, a subgroup with co-morbid anxiety problems was identified suggesting that this combination of problems emerges early in life (Gilliom and Shaw, 2004). As we will show in a subsequent section, there is now evidence suggesting that this combination of disorders may remain stable across the lifespan. Some studies of children with CD support the commonly held view that anxiety limits antisocial and aggressive behaviour (Kerr *et al.*, 1997; Walker *et al.*, 1991). The association between CD and anxiety may be epiphenomenal since both are associated with depression as shown by a cross-sectional study of a nationally representative sample of 10 438 children aged 5–15 years old (Maughan *et al.*, 2004a).

The prevalence of depression is much higher among children with than without CD and the combination is associated with more severe symptoms and higher levels of social impairment (Angold, Costello and Erkanli, 1999; Wolff and Ollendick, 2006). Among boys with CD, depression is most likely to occur prior to adolescence, whereas among girls with CD, depression develops later in mid-adolescence and is more serious (Loeber and Keenan, 1994).

In summary, children with CD constitute a very heterogeneous population. Most present substance misuse problems once into adolescence, but before that large proportions present ADHD, anxiety and depressive disorders. There are almost no data available on the associations between these various co-morbid disorders and the likelihood that children with CD will transition to ASPD in adulthood. As the next section shows, however, all three disorders characterize adults with ASPD.

DISORDERS CO-MORBID WITH ASPD

Results of the ECA study conducted at the beginning of the 1980s showed that fewer than 10% of individuals who attracted a diagnosis of ASPD had no additional Axis I diagnoses (Robins, Tipp and Przybeck, 1991). Subsequent studies have confirmed these high rates of co-occurring disorders among those with ASPD. Consistent with the evidence reviewed above on children and adolescents with CD, the prevalence of substance misuse disorders (e.g. Compton *et al.*, 2005), anxiety disorders (J.W. Coid, personal communication; Grant *et al.*, 2005) and depression (Robins, Tipp and Przybeck, 1991) are higher among persons with than without ASPD. To the best of our knowledge, there is no study that has examined the prevalence of ADHD among adults with ASPD, either in the community or in prison, as was previously noted (Young *et al.*, 2003).

Epidemiological investigations have consistently shown that substance misuse is the most common disorder associated with ASPD (Compton *et al.*, 2005; Kessler *et al.*, 1996; Robins, Tipp and Przybeck, 1991). For example, in the US National Co-morbidity Survey, nearly 80% of all respondents with ASPD also had a lifetime substance misuse disorder (Kessler *et al.*, 1996). In the ECA study, men with ASPD, as compared to those without ASPD, were three times and five times more likely to abuse alcohol and illicit drugs, respectively (Robins, Tipp and Przybeck, 1991). Among women, those with as compared to those without ASPD were 13 times more likely to attract diagnoses of alcohol abuse and 12 times more likely to attract diagnoses of drug abuse. ASPD has been reported to be the personality disorder with the strongest association with substance abuse; with stronger associations among women than among men (Compton *et al.*, 2005; Robins, Tipp and Przybeck, 1991).

Two recent epidemiological investigations of large population cohorts have revealed that almost half of those with ASPD met criteria for at least one anxiety disorder. The National Co-morbidity Survey studied a representative sample composed of 5877 adults from 48 of the US states (Goodwin and Hamilton, 2003). More than half, 53.3%, of those with ASPD received a lifetime diagnosis of an anxiety disorder. Further, the individuals with both ASPD and an anxiety disorder were at increased risk for major depression, substance use disorders and suicidal ideation as compared to those without both disorders. These findings were replicated by Sareen *et al.* (2004) in two large epidemiological samples, one from the United States and one from Canada. The researchers found that 47% of adults with ASPD, or with a history of CD, or who presented only the adult criteria for ASPD presented at least one lifetime anxiety disorder. The association between the disorders remained significant after controlling for socio-demographic characteristics, depression and alcohol and drug use disorders. More recently, in a large US community sample, the prevalence of any anxiety disorder among individuals with ASPD reached 47.5% (Lenzenweger *et al.*, 2007).

In the ECA study, depression was found to occur among individuals with ASPD at more than three times the general population rate (prevalence ratio of 3.2 and 3.5 for males and females, respectively) (Robins, Tipp and Przybeck, 1991). More recently, in a study of a US community sample composed 5692 persons, 9.1% of the individuals with ASPD had a major depressive disorder and 27.7% met criteria for any mood disorders (Lenzenweger *et al.*, 2007).

In summary, the available evidence suggests that individuals with ASPD do not constitute a homogeneous population. Not only are persons with psychopathy not excluded from studies of ASPD, but very distinct sub-types that are easily identified by co-morbid disorders are lumped together in the same diagnostic category. This, we propose, seriously limits understanding of the syndrome characterized by an early onset of antisocial behaviour that remains stable across the lifespan. As we have shown, co-morbid anxiety and depression among individuals with ASPD emerge early in life and continue to re-occur through adulthood.

CRIMINALITY

Results of epidemiological investigations are consistent in showing that approximately one-half of individuals with a diagnosis of ASPD have a record of criminal offending (Robins, Tipp and Przybeck, 1991; J. Samuels, personal communication). These studies of community samples, all required informed consent and voluntary participation, and in one information on criminality was provided by self-report (Robins, Tipp and Przybeck, 1991), while in the other it was based on criminal records (Samuels et al., 2004). In a Danish birth cohort composed of 324 401 individuals followed up to age of 43 years, the official criminal records of persons with ASPD who had been admitted to a psychiatric ward were compared to cohort members with no psychiatric admissions. The relative risk to be convicted of a violent crime given a diagnosis of ASPD was 7.2 (95% CI 6.5–8.0) for men and 12.1 (95% CI 8.8–16.9) for women (Hodgins et al., 1996). While this investigation used de-identified criminal register information thereby avoiding the problems resulting from participation bias and subjective reports of crime, the results may be misleading because persons with ASPD who are admitted to hospital probably differ from the great majority of persons with this disorder.

By contrast, among incarcerated offenders, ASPD is very common. For instance, a systematic review of 62 studies, conducted over several decades in 12 countries assessed the prevalence of mental disorders among representative samples of convicted offenders. Among 13 844 prisoners, 47% of males and 21% of females were diagnosed with ASPD using standardized assessment methods (Fazel and Danesh, 2002). Consistent with the findings from the systematic review, among prisoners in England and Wales, 49% of men and 31% of women received a diagnosis of ASPD based on face-to-face interviews (Singleton et al., 1998).

Studies among prisoners have not consistently found ASPD to be associated with violent criminality. For example, in a random sample of 461 prisoners from Québec with a sentence of 2 years or longer, those with, as compared to those without ASPD, had more convictions, more convictions for non-violent offences, but equal numbers of convictions for violent offences (Hodgins and Cote, 1993). Importantly, this study, like the others, did not exclude inmates who would meet criteria for psychopathy. More recently, in a validation study of the Liverpool Violence Assessment, an investigator-based standardized interview for measuring patterns of violence, the violence scores of 61 British prisoners with a past history of violence with and without a diagnosis of ASPD were compared. (The ratings of ASPD omitted the contribution of violent behaviours.) The inmates with ASPD obtained significantly higher scores for violence than those without ASPD. There was, however, substantial variability in the levels of violence within the ASPD group with one-third presenting only occasional incidents of low levels of violence and another third presenting repeated acts of violence (Nathan et al., 2003).

It has been suggested that individuals with ASPD engage in reactive violence and not in instrumental violence (Blair, Mitchell and Blair, 2005). We recently examined a representative sample of male offenders incarcerated in Scotland. We excluded those with psychopathy from among those with ASPD. Among those with ASPD, 70.6% had engaged in instrumental aggression (De Brito *et al.*, under review). These results are important: this was a random sample of incarcerated offenders and the distinction between reactive and instrumental violence was based on lifetime assessments. These results challenge the commonly held view that only psychopaths engage in instrumental aggression.

VIOLENCE TOWARDS OTHERS

Despite consistent findings that less than half of individuals with ASPD have histories of convictions for crime, and even fewer for violent crimes, the study that examined 18 571 persons representative of the US population in the early 1980s found that 85% of individuals with a diagnosis of ASPD engaged in violence towards others (Robins, Tipp and Przybeck, 1991). By contrast, a recent study that examined a British community sample of 8397 persons aged 16–74 years old reported very different results. In this study, diagnoses were derived from the self-report screening questionnaire of the SCID II. One-half of those with ASPD reported not having engaged in violence towards others during the past 5 years, while 29% reported violence towards others when intoxicated, 26% reported injuring a victim and 23% reported five or more violent incidents (Coid *et al.*, 2006a). The discrepancy in the results of these two studies may result from differences in diagnostic criteria (DSM-III vs. DSM-IV), diagnostic procedure (lay interviewer using the Diagnostic Interview Schedule vs. self-report on SCID II screening questionnaire) and/or differences across countries and time periods (1980 and 2000).

Among children with conduct problems, those most at risk to develop ASPD present with antisocial behaviour that is more persistent and more severe, and that includes physical aggression and violence (Moffitt *et al.*, 1996). The earlier the onset of the physically aggressive behaviour, the more likely it is to persist into adulthood (Goldstein *et al.*, 2006b; Loeber and Stouthamer-Loeber, 1987; Maughan *et al.*, 2000; Robins, 1966). Taken together, the extant literature suggests that people with ASPD, as compared to those without ASPD, are at increased risk to engage in violence, and equally important that a substantial proportion of persons with ASPD do not engage in violence towards others. While little work has been done to identify the characteristics that distinguish those within this population who do engage in violence, the available evidence strongly indicates that violence in adulthood is a continuation of aggressive behaviour in childhood.

ASPD AND VIOLENCE: A NEW HYPOTHESIS

As noted throughout, our understanding of ASPD is very limited, and knowledge about violence by persons with ASPD is presently based on a very small number of studies that have obtained contradictory results. We propose that findings from prospective longitudinal studies of birth cohorts and samples of at-risk children concur in identifying a syndrome characterized by an early onset of antisocial behaviour that remains stable over the lifespan. While the DSM refers to this syndrome as ASPD, others have labelled it the externalizing syndrome (Krueger *et al.*, 2002). Men with this syndrome are responsible for most of the violent offences that are committed, while women with this syndrome are responsible for approximately one-third of violent offences committed by women (Farrington and West, 1993; Kratzer and Hodgins, 1999). Robust evidence shows that among individuals with an early onset and stable pattern of antisocial behaviour, the subgroup with psychopathy is responsible for a disproportionate amount of violence, both incidents that do and that do not lead to criminal prosecution (Hare and McPherson, 1984).

Behavioural-genetic studies suggest that the syndrome of early onset antisocial behaviour that remains stable over the lifespan includes substance misuse and that it is heritable (Krueger *et al.*, 2002). A large body of evidence shows that the genetic vulnerability to the syndrome is enhanced by factors operative during pregnancy such as maternal smoking (Maughan *et al.*, 2004b) and malnutrition (Neugebauer, Hoek and Susser, 1999), but most importantly by parenting practices (Hodgins *et al.*, 2001), including physical abuse (Caspi *et al.*, 2002).

The syndrome of early onset antisocial behaviour that remains stable over the lifespan includes sub-types identified by co-morbid disorders that differ as to personality traits, levels of anxiety, cognitive style and abilities, emotion processing and behaviour patterns. A schematic view is presented in Figure 7.1. Based on studies of children and adults, we propose that one-half of this population is characterized from childhood onwards by anxiety as well as persistent antisocial

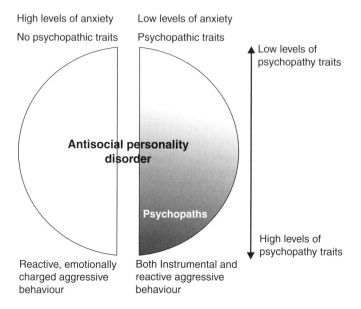

Figure 7.1   The population of persons with early onset antisocial behaviour that remains stable across the lifespan.

behaviour. The other half, by contrast, presents normal to low levels of anxiety, varying levels of psychopathic traits and includes a distinct subgroup who meet criteria for a diagnosis of psychopathy. Among this non-anxious half of the ASPD population, those who do not meet criteria for the diagnosis of psychopathy, we propose, present levels of psychopathic traits higher than those with ASPD plus anxiety and than the general population. We speculate that the criminal and violent behaviours of these three sub-types – anxious, low levels of psychopathic traits and psychopathy – differ as to frequency and form, but also as to aetiological mechanisms. To conclude the chapter, we draw together what is known about ASPD into hypotheses that can be tested in future research. In our view, this is the only way to move the field forward. Investigations that either support or refute our hypotheses would contribute to advancing understanding of this syndrome that places such a heavy burden on society.

Consider first, the sub-type with anxiety and persistent antisocial behaviour. As children, they are distinguished from others with CD, by showing low levels of callous-unemotional traits. Boys with conduct problems who do not present callous-unemotional traits display aggressive behaviour that is emotionally charged in response to provocations that may be real or result from their tendency to attribute hostility towards others, even to neutral faces (Dadds et al., 2006; Frick and Marsee, 2006). These children report emotional distress, are more reactive to distress and especially to negative emotional stimuli. They are, however, responsive to good parenting practices and benefit when their parents complete parent-training programmes (Hawes and Dadds, 2005). These boys present high levels of impulsivity, a tendency towards anger, and like children with anxiety disorders lower than average verbal abilities (Frick and Marsee, 2006). These children with CD differ from those with CD plus callous-unemotional traits in many ways: they display less severe conduct problems, are less likely to engage in violence towards others, are able to recognize fear and sadness, present lower verbal abilities and general neurocognitive deficits (Frick and Marsee, 2006; Raine et al., 2005). Yet, they respond to punishment in the form of time-out when it is used appropriately by their parents (Hawes and Dadds, 2005).

As noted by others (Sareen et al., 2004), a positive association between ASPD and anxiety might seem counter-intuitive in light of evidence of a small number of studies showing that anxiety is protective against criminality (Pfeffer and Plutchik, 1989; Walker et al., 1991) and many studies showing that low levels of anxiety are associated with persistent criminality (Ortiz and Raine, 2004). Recent evidence, however, points towards a more complicated picture. Secondary analyses of data from the National Household Survey of Great Britain suggest that the presence of any neurotic disorder (defined as panic disorder, generalized anxiety, mixed anxiety/depressive disorder, obsessive compulsive disorder, any phobia and depressive episode, the condition being present in the past 2 weeks) was significantly more common among respondents with ASPD (32.2%) than the rest of the population (16.0%). Among those with ASPD, similar proportions of those with and without a co-morbid neurotic disorder reported engaging in violence towards others. Those with co-morbid neurotic disorders were more likely, however, to report assaulting other family members, people known to them, and their children (J.W. Coid, personal communication, 13 February 2007). Similarly, in a study of a random sample of 650 male penitentiary inmates in Québec, those who had been convicted of a homicide presented higher rates of depression in combination with ASPD, alcohol or drug abuse and/or dependence than those convicted of other types of offences (Cote and Hodgins, 1992).

Many years ago describing individuals with ASPD, Robins (1978) noted that 'If one considers that in response to their early antisocial behaviour, parents beat them, schools expel them, and police chase them, their subjective experience of the world as unfriendly and dangerous may not be wholly irrational' (p. 269). It is known that physical abuse is associated with an increased risk of developing conduct problems (Kunitz et al., 1999). Several studies have shown that children's responses to physical abuse differ depending on their characteristics, both biological and psychological. For example, it has been shown that among males, physical maltreatment in childhood of those who carry the low activity allele of the MAOA gene confers a vulnerability for CD in childhood and violent offending in adulthood (for a review, see Kim-Cohen et al., 2006). Other studies have indicated that the effects of this genetic polymorphism and childhood maltreatment are independent (Reif et al., 2007). A recent study of healthy adults showed that among men, the low activity allele of the MAOA gene is associated with differences in brain structure and function. Importantly, in a task requiring the men to match angry and fearful faces to a target face, those who carried the low activity allele, as compared to those with the high activity allele, displayed excess activity in limbic and paralimbic areas (amygdala and insula) and diminished activity of regions in the cortex (orbitofrontal and anterior cingulate) that are known to regulate emotional responses. Further, the men with the low activity allele showed greater activation of the amygdala when retrieving aversive memories and less activity in the dorsal cingulate, a region involved in the inhibition of previously learned responses (Meyer-Lindenberg et al., 2006). Another study, also of healthy adults, found that those with the low activity allele of the MAOA gene, as compared to those who carried the high activity allele, reported higher levels of trait aggression and of interpersonal sensitivity. In addition, they showed greater activation of the dorsal anterior cingulate cortex when distressed by being excluded from a simulated ball game. Statistical analyses revealed that the association between the low activity MAOA allele and the trait of aggressiveness was mediated by the greater activity in the cingulate cortex in response to exclusion (Eisenberger et al., 2007).

Low activity of the MAOA genetic polymorphism leads to low levels of serotonin in the brain that have long been known to be associated with impulsive and reactive violence (Virkkunen et al., 1995). The 5HTT gene serotonin transporter also regulates expression and uptake of serotonin in the brain. The low activity allele results in decreased uptake of serotonin. A recent study compared violent and non-violent offenders and non-criminal men and found that the presence of this low activity allele, 5HTTLPR, in men who experienced physical maltreatment as children was associated with persistent violent offending (Reif et al., 2007). Investigations of both humans and primates strongly implicate the serotonergic system in reactive–impulsive violence (Lesch and Merschdorf, 2000), and most particularly in the anterior cingulate cortex (Frankle et al., 2005).

We hypothesize that the anxious sub-type males with early onset antisocial behaviour that remains stable over the lifespan carry the low activity variants of the MAOA gene and/or the serotonin transporter (5HTTLPR). This would confer a vulnerability to being highly reactive to stressful environments. Maltreatment during a critical period in development would alter their biological stress reactivity systems making them chronically hyper-reactive to their environments and reinforce or even initiate their tendency to view others as hostile. In adulthood, this would result in an individual who perceives others as threatening and who is emotionally labile. Violence towards others would be reactive and impulsive, in response to a feeling of being threatened.[1]

As suggested by others, (see for example, Blair, Mitchell and Blair, 2005), a very different mechanism likely underlies the violence of those with a diagnosis of psychopathy and those without the diagnosis but who present lower levels of the traits of psychopathy. As depicted in Figure 7.1, we hypothesize that individuals with ASPD with neither co-morbid anxiety or depressive disorders nor psychopathy are characterized by low levels of the personality traits of psychopathy and as children would present no anxiety and low levels of callous-unemotional traits. As compared to the anxious sub-type, these individuals more persistently engage in violence towards others from an early age onwards. Further, it is in this sub-type that callousness releases the usual constraints on aggressive behaviour and leads to purposeful injuries to others (see Blair, Mitchell and Blair, 2005 for a review). This hypothesis is in line with the findings from a study of a community sample of 43 093 persons and from a study of drug abusers. In both studies, among the participants with ASPD those with lower levels of remorse presented violent behaviour from childhood through adulthood (Goldstein et al., 1996; Goldstein et al., 2006a).[2]

Behavioural-genetic studies have shown that the combination of callous-unemotional traits and conduct problems is highly heritable as is psychopathy in adolescence (Larsson, Andershed and Lichstenstein, 2006; Viding, Frick and Plomin, 2007) and the psychopathic trait of Deficient Affective Experience (Larsson, Andershed and Lichtenstein, 2006). No studies have identified specific genetic polymorphisms associated with psychopathic traits. We hypothesize that the genes will be associated with the deficit in the recognition of fear and sadness that distinguishes children with conduct problems and callous-unemotional traits (Blair et al., 2001) and adults with psychopathy[3] (Blair et al., 2004) and that this deficit will be found to be the origin of callousness. Children with CD and callous-unemotional traits have been shown to be relatively unaffected by poor parenting (Wootton et al., 1997), to fail to respond to time-out (Hawes and Dadds, 2005), and insist, despite evidence to the contrary, that aggressive behaviour leads to rewards (Frick and Marsee, 2006). Such children would be expected to show less distress than others if physically abused, but may learn from chronic maltreatment how to humiliate, bully and hurt others.

The proposed hypotheses are based on evidence from studies of men. As noted, the prevalence rates of CD and ASPD, and violence are much higher among males than females, and much more is known about these disorders and behaviour patterns among males than females. Emerging evidence suggests, however, that the developmental mechanisms may differ. For example, a recent study suggests that CD among girls may be strongly influenced by genetic factors, while among boys it is more strongly influenced by parents' antisocial behaviour (D'Onofrio *et al.*, 2007). Other studies show that while the MAOA genetic polymorphism confers a vulnerability for CD and persistent violence in adulthood among men, this gene operates differently in women who, unlike men, carry two copies.

Prospective, longitudinal studies beginning when children are very young are needed to sort out antecedents and consequences so as to inform the development of effective prevention programmes that appropriately target aetiological processes. Given, the evidence on sex differences in aetiological mechanisms that has recently been reported, these studies need to examine boys and girls separately. Further, such investigations need to focus on sub-types who, we hypothesize, develop patterns of aggressive behaviour via different mechanisms. The failure to distinguish sub-types of persons with ASPD hampers progress in research aimed at furthering understanding of the aetiology of persistent antisocial behaviour (Hodgins, 2007). For example, a recent fMRI study comparing boys with CD to non-disordered boys illustrates the problem. Contrary to the hypothesis, no differences in activity in the amygdala were observed between the two groups when viewing negatively valenced pictures. This absence of difference, however, was due to high anxiety scores among some of the boys with CD. Post-hoc analyses showed that anxiety scores, as would be expected, were related to amygdala activation and aggressive behaviour scores were related to amygdala inactivity (Sterzer *et al.*, 2005). The available evidence clearly suggests that a more accurate description of the subgroups that comprise the population of ASPD is needed to unravel the aetiology.

A recent systematic review identified only two treatment studies of persons with ASPD (Duggan *et al.*, 2007). While most men in the trials of the offender rehabilitation programmes would likely have met criteria for ASPD, they were not diagnosed (McGuire, 1995). Based on our hypothesis of sub-types, we propose that different treatments are required from childhood onwards to reduce violence among the distinctive sub-types of individuals, all of whom present an early onset and stable pattern of antisocial behaviour. Children and adults who present anxiety disorders co-morbid with persistent antisocial behaviour are often distressed and may be more accepting of psychological interventions than others with ASPD. These individuals require interventions designed to reduce their hyper-reactivity to environmental stimuli and their persistent feelings of being threatened, and to alter their perception that the world is a frightening place. Such interventions may involve helping these individuals change their environments – removing children from abusive families, helping adults move to neighbourhoods with lower rates of crime, substance misuse and antisocial associates – as well as cognitive re-structuring (Mortberg *et al.*, 2007) and learning prosocial skills. By contrast, interventions for those with psychopathic traits would initially need to focus on convincing these individuals that it is in their interest to change and to become less callous. Increasing sensitivity to the distress of others would be essential.

Given the robust evidence that ASPD emerges in childhood, prevention should be the priority. Parent-training programmes have been shown to lead to change in the children's behaviour (Scott, 2005). Modifying these programmes to target distinct sub-types of children with conduct problems is a priority (Frick and Morris, 2004). In addition, prospective studies that identify when and in what quantity further interventions are needed to prevent the development of ASPD and violence in adulthood are critical.

NOTES

1. It is essential to be clear about the role of heredity and genes associated with CD, APSD and violence. There is good evidence for three findings. One, a pattern of antisocial behaviour that onsets in childhood and that remains stable over the life course is heritable (Patrick *et al.*, in press; Rhee and Waldman, 2002). These findings mean that genes are one among many factors contributing to the development of the syndrome. Two, to date, findings identify two genetic polymorphisms (the low activity alleles of the MAOA gene and the serotonin transporter gene 5HTTLPR) related to persistent violence. Neither are deterministic as they are carried by more than 30% of male Caucasians (Reif *et al.*, 2007) Rather, each confers an increase in the likelihood that the carriers as adults will present a pattern of persistently violent behaviour.
2. Recent studies have shown that among PCL-R diagnosed psychopaths some display high levels of anxiety as measured by the Karolinska Scales of Personality (see Skeem *et al.*, 2007) and the Welsh Anxiety Scale (see Newman and Schmitt, 1998). As shown by Derefinko and Lynam (2007), however, different measures of anxiety lead to different associations with psychopathy. It will be necessary in future studies to distinguish lifelong traits of anxiety severe enough to warrant diagnoses of anxiety disorders, that we posit characterize one-half of persons with ASPD, from state anxiety that could result, for example, from incarceration or drug use.
3. We are aware that not all studies have found that psychopaths show a deficit in the recognition of fear and sadness in faces (e.g. Glass and Newman, 2006). The inconsistent results may be due to methodological differences between studies.

REFERENCES

American Psychiatric Association (2000) *Diagnostic and Statistical Manual of Mental Disorders*, 4th edn, text revision, American Psychiatric Association, Washington, D.C.

Angold, A., Costello, E.J. and Erkanli, A. (1999) Comorbidity. *Journal of Child Psychology and Psychiatry and Allied Disciplines*, **40** (1), 57–87.

Blair, J., Mitchell, D. and Blair, K. (2005) *The Psychopath: Emotion and the Brain*, Blackwell Publishing, Malden, MA.

Blair, R., Colledge, E., Murray, L. and Mitchell, D. (2001) A selective impairment in the processing of sad and fearful expressions in children with psychopathic tendencies. *Journal of Abnormal Child Psychology*, **29** (6), 491–8.

Blair, R., Mitchell, D., Peschardt, K. *et al.* (2004) Reduced sensitivity to others' fearful expressions in psychopathic individuals. *Personality and Individual Differences*, **37** (6), 1111–22.

Black, D.W., Baumgard, C.H., Bell, S.E. and Kao, C. (1996) Death rates in 71 men with antisocial personality disorder. A comparison with general population mortality. *Psychosomatics*, **37** (2), 131–6.

Caspi, A., McClay, J., Moffitt, T. *et al.* (2002) Role of genotype in the cycle of violence in maltreated children. *Science*, **297** (5582), 851–4.

Coid, J. (1998) The management of dangerous psychopaths in prison, in *Psychopathy: Antisocial, Criminal, and Violent Behavior* (eds T. Millon, E. Simonson, M. Birket-Smith and R. Davis), Guilford, New York, pp. 431–57.

Coid, J.W. (2003) Formulating strategies for the primary prevention of adult antisocial behaviour: "High risk" or "population" strategies? in *Early Prevention of Adult Antisocial*

Behaviour (eds D.P. Farrington and J.W. Coid), Cambridge University Press, Cambridge, pp. 32–78.

Coid, J., Yang, M., Roberts, A. *et al.* (2006a) Violence and psychiatric morbidity in the national household population of Britain: public health implications. *British Journal of Psychiatry*, **189**, 12–9.

Coid, J., Yang, M., Tyrer, P. *et al.* (2006b) Prevalence and correlates of personality disorder in Great Britain. *British Journal of Psychiatry*, **188**, 423–31.

Compton, W.M., Conway, K.P., Stinson, F.S. *et al.* (2005) Prevalence, correlates, and comorbidity of DSM-IV antisocial personality syndromes and alcohol and specific drug use disorders in the United States: results from the national epidemiologic survey on alcohol and related conditions. *Journal of Clinical Psychiatry*, **66** (6), 677–85.

Cooke, D.J., Michie, C., Hart, S.D. and Clark, D. (2005) Searching for the pan-cultural core of psychopathic personality disorder. *Personality and Individual Differences*, **39**, 283–95.

Cote, G. and Hodgins, S. (1992) The prevalence of major mental disorders among homicide offenders. *International Journal of Law and Psychiatry*, **15** (1), 89–99.

Cottler, L.B., Price, R.K., Compton, W.M. and Mager, D.E. (1995) Subtypes of adult antisocial behavior among drug abusers. *Journal of Nervous and Mental Disease*, **183** (3), 154–61.

Dadds, M.R., Perry, Y., Hawes, D.J. *et al.* (2006) Attention to the eyes reverses fear-recognition deficits in child psychopathy. *British Journal of Psychiatry*, **189** (3), 280–1.

De Brito, S.A., Hodgins, S., Cooke, D.J. *et al.* (under review) Life-long patterns of aggressive behavior among offenders: is instrumental aggression unique to psychopathy?

Derefinko, K.J. and Lynam, D.R. (2007) *The Misconception of Psychopathic Low Anxiety: Meta-analytic Evidence for the Absence of Inhibition, not Affect.* Poster session presented at the biennial meeting of the Society for the Scientific Study of Psychopathy, Tampa, Florida.

Disney, E.R., Elkins, I.J., McGue, M. and Iacono, W.G. (1999) Effects of ADHD, conduct disorder, and gender on substance use and abuse in adolescence. *American Journal of Psychiatry*, **156** (10), 1515–21.

D'Onofrio, B.M., Slutske, W.S., Turkheimer, E. *et al.* (2007) Intergenerational transmission of childhood conduct problems: a children of twins study. *Archives of General Psychiatry*, **64** (7), 820–9.

Duggan, C., Adams, C., Ferriter, M. *et al.* (2007) The use of psychological treatments for people with personality disorder: a systematic review of randomized controlled trials. *Personality and Mental Health*, **1**, 95–125.

Eisenberger, N.I., Way, B.M., Taylor, S.E. *et al.* (2007) Understanding genetic risk for aggression: clues from the brain's response to social exclusion. *Biological Psychiatry*, **61** (9), 1100–8.

Farrington, D.P. and West, D. (1993) Criminal, penal and life histories of chronic offenders: risk and protective factors and early identification. *Criminal Behaviour and Mental Health*, **3**, 492–523.

Fazel, S. and Danesh, J. (2002) Serious mental disorder in 23000 prisoners: a systematic review of 62 surveys. *Lancet*, **359** (9306), 545–50.

First, M.B., Spitzer, R.L., Gibbon, M. and Williams, J.B.W. (1997) *Structured Clinical Interview for DSM-IV Axis I Disorders*, Biometrics Research Department, New York.

Fitzgerald, K.L. and Demakis, G.J. (2007) The neuropsychology of antisocial personality disorder. *Disease-a-Month*, **53** (3), 177–83.

Frankle, W.G., Lombardo, I., New, A.S. *et al.* (2005) Brain serotonin transporter distribution in subjects with impulsive aggressivity: a positron emission study with [11C]McN 5652. *American Journal of Psychiatry*, **162** (5), 915–23.

Frick, P.J. and Marsee, M.A. (2006) Psychopathy and developmental pathways to antisocial behavior in youth, in *Handbook of the Psychopathy*, Guilford, New York, pp. 353–74.

Frick, P.J. and Morris, A.S. (2004) Temperament and developmental pathways to conduct problems. *Journal of Clinical Child Adolescent Psychology*, **33** (1), 54–68.

Gilliom, M. and Shaw, D.S. (2004) Codevelopment of externalizing and internalizing problems in early childhood. *Development and Psychopathology*, **16** (2), 313–33.

Goldstein, R.B., Grant, B.F., Huang, B. *et al.* (2006a) Lack of remorse in antisocial personality disorder: sociodemographic correlates, symptomatic presentation, and comorbidity with

Axis I and Axis II disorders in the National Epidemiologic Survey on Alcohol and Related Conditions. *Comprehensive Psychiatry*, **47** (4), 289–97.

Goldstein, R.B., Grant, B.F., Ruan, W. *et al.* (2006b) Antisocial personality disorder with childhood- vs. adolescence-onset conduct disorder: results from the National Epidemiologic Survey on Alcohol and Related Conditions. *Journal of Nervous and Mental Disease*, **194** (9), 667–75.

Goldstein, R.B., Powers, S.I., McCusker, J. *et al.* (1996) Lack of remorse in antisocial personality disorder among drug abusers in residential treatment. *Journal of Personality Disorders*, **10** (4), 321–34.

Goodwin, R.D. and Hamilton, S.P. (2003) Lifetime comorbidity of antisocial personality disorder and anxiety disorders among adults in the community. *Psychiatry Research*, **117** (2), 159–66.

Grant, B.F., Hasin, D.S., Stinson, F.S. *et al.* (2004) Prevalence, correlates, and disability of personality disorders in the United States: results from the national epidemiologic survey on alcohol and related conditions. *Journal of Clinical Psychiatry*, **65** (7), 948–58.

Grant, B.F., Stinson, F.S., Dawson, D.A. *et al.* (2005) Co-occurrence of DSM-IV personality disorders in the United States: results from the National Epidemiologic Survey on Alcohol and Related Conditions. *Comprehensive Psychiatry*, **46** (1), 1–5.

Green, H., McGinnity, A., Meltzer, H. *et al.* (2004) *Mental Health of Children and Young People in Great Britain 2004*, Office for National Statistics.

Grekin, E.R., Brennan, P.A., Hodgins, S. and Mednick, S.A. (2001) Male criminals with organic brain syndrome: two distinct types based on age at first arrest. *American Journal of Psychiatry*, **158** (7), 1099–104.

Hare, R.D. (1996) Psychopathy and antisocial personality disorder: a case of diagnostic confusion. *Psychiatric Times*, **13**, 39–40.

Hare, R.D. (2003) *Manual for the Revised Psychopathy Checklist*, 2nd edn, Multi-Health Systems, Toronto, ON, Canada.

Hare, R.D. and Neumann, C.N. (2006) The PCL-R assessment of psychopathy: development, structural properties, and new directions, in *Handbook of Psychopathy* (ed. C.J. Patrick), Guilford, New York, pp. 58–88.

Hare, R.D. and McPherson, L.M. (1984) Violent and aggressive behavior by criminal psychopaths. *International Journal of Law and Psychiatry*, **7** (1), 35–50.

Hawes, D.J. and Dadds, M.R. (2005) The treatment of conduct problems in children with callous-unemotional traits. *Journal of Consulting and Clinical Psychology*, **73** (4), 737–41.

Hodgins, S. (2007) Persistent violent offending: what do we know? *British Journal of Psychiatry, Supplement*, **49**, s12–4.

Hodgins, S. and Cote, G. (1993) The criminality of mentally disordered offenders. *Criminal Justice and Behavior*, **20** (2), 115–29.

Hodgins, S., Kratzer, L. and McNeil, T.F. (2001) Obstetric complications, parenting, and risk of criminal behavior. *Archives of General Psychiatry*, **58** (8), 746–52.

Hodgins, S., Mednick, S.A., Brennan, P.A. *et al.* (1996) Mental disorder and crime: evidence from a Danish birth cohort. *Archives of General Psychiatry*, **53** (6), 489–96.

Hodgins, S., Tengstrom, A., Eriksson, A. *et al.* (2007) A multisite study of community treatment programs for mentally ill offenders with major mental disorders: design, measures, and the forensic sample. *Criminal Justice and Behavior*, **34** (2), 211–28.

Jaffee, S.R., Caspi, A., Moffitt, T.E. and Taylor, A. (2004) Physical maltreatment victim to antisocial child: evidence of an environmentally mediated process. *Journal of Abnormal Psychology*, **113** (1), 44–55.

Kerr, M., Tremblay, R.E., Pagani, L. and Vitaro, F. (1997) Boys' behavioral inhibition and the risk of later delinquency. *Archives of General Psychiatry*, **54** (9), 809–16.

Kessler, R.C., Nelson, C.B., McGonagle, K.A. *et al.* (1996). The epidemiology of co-occurring addictive and mental disorders: implications for prevention and service utilization. *American Journal of Orthopsychiatry*, **66** (1), 17–31.

Kim-Cohen, J., Caspi, A., Taylor, A. *et al.* (2006) MAOA, maltreatment, and gene-environment interaction predicting children's mental health: new evidence and a meta-analysis. *Molecular Psychiatry*, **11** (10), 903–13.

Kosson, D.S., Lorenz, A.R. and Newman, J.P. (2006) Effects of comorbid psychopathy on criminal offending and emotion processing in male offenders with antisocial personality disorder. *Journal of Abnormal Psychology*, **115** (4), 798–806.

Kratzer, L. and Hodgins, S. (1999) A typology of offenders: a test of Moffitt's theory among males and females from childhood to age 30. *Criminal Behaviour and Mental Health*, **9** (1), 57–73.

Krueger, R.F., Hicks, B.M., Patrick, C.J. *et al.* (2002) Etiologic connections among substance dependence, antisocial behavior, and personality: modeling the externalizing spectrum. *Journal of Abnormal Psychology*, **111** (3), 411–24.

Kunitz, S.J., Gabriel, K.R., Levy, J.E. *et al.* (1999) Risk factors for conduct disorder among Navajo Indian men and women. *Social Psychiatry and Psychiatric Epidemiology*, **34** (4), 180–89.

Lahey, B.B., Loeber, R., Burke, J.D. and Applegate, B. (2005) Predicting future antisocial personality disorder in males from a clinical assessment in childhood. *Journal of Consulting and Clinical Psychology*, **73** (3), 389–99.

Larsson, H., Andershed, H. and Lichtenstein, P. (2006) A genetic factor explains most of the variation in the psychopathic personality. *Journal of Abnormal Psychology*, **115** (2), 221–30.

Lesch, K.P. and Merschdorf, U. (2000) Impulsivity, aggression, and serotonin: a molecular psychobiological perspective. *Behavioral Sciences and the Law*, **18** (5), 581–604.

Lenzenweger, M.F., Lane, M.C., Loranger, A.W. and Kessler, R.C. (2007) DSM-IV personality disorders in the National Comorbidity Survey Replication. *Biological Psychiatry*, **62** (6), 553–64.

Loeber, R., Green, S.M. and Lahey, B.B. (2003) Risk factors for antisocial personality, in *Early Prevention of Adult Antisocial Behaviour* (eds J. Coid and D.P. Farrington), Cambridge University Press, Cambridge, pp. 79–108.

Loeber, R. and Keenan, K. (1994) Interaction between conduct disorder and its comorbid conditions: effects of age and gender. *Clinical Psychology Review*, **14** (6), 497–523.

Loeber, R. and Stouthamer-Loeber, M. (1987) Prediction, in *Handbook of Juvenile Delinquency* (ed. H.C. Quay), John Wiley & Sons, Ltd, New York.

Lösel, F. and Bender, D. (2003) Protective factors and resilience, in *Early Prevention of Adult Antisocial Behaviour* (eds D.P. Farrington and J.W. Coid), Cambridge University Press, Cambridge, pp. 130–204.

Lykken, D.T. (1995) *The Antisocial Personalities*, Erlbaum, Hillsdale, NJ.

Lynam, D.R. (1996) Early identification of chronic offenders: who is the fledgling psychopath? *Psychological Bulletin*, **120** (2), 209–34.

Marmorstein, N.R. (2007) Relationships between anxiety and externalizing disorders in youth: the influences of age and gender. *Journal of Anxiety Disorders*, **21** (3), 420–32.

Maughan, B., Pickles, A., Rowe, R. *et al.* (2000) Developmental trajectories of aggressive and non-aggressive conduct problems. *Journal of Quantitative Criminology*, **16**, 199–221.

Maughan, B., Rowe, R., Messer, J. *et al.* (2004a) Conduct disorder and oppositional defiant disorder in a national sample: developmental epidemiology. *Journal of Child Psychology and Psychiatry*, **45** (3), 609–21.

Maughan, B., Taylor, A., Caspi, A. and Moffitt, T.E. (2004b) Prenatal smoking and early childhood conduct problems: testing genetic and environmental explanations of the association. *Archives of General Psychiatry*, **61** (8), 836–43.

McCabe, K.M., Rodgers, C., Yeh, M. and Hough, R. (2004) Gender differences in childhood onset conduct disorder. *Development and Psychopathology*, **16** (1), 179–92.

McGuire, J. (1995) *What Works: Reducing Re-offending: Guidelines from Research and Practice*, John Wiley & Sons, Ltd, Chichester.

Meyer-Lindenberg, A., Buckholtz, J.W., Kolachana, B. *et al.* (2006) Neural mechanisms of genetic risk for impulsivity and violence in humans. *Proceedings of the National Academy of Sciences of the United States of America*, **103** (16), 6269–74.

Moffitt, T.E., Caspi, A., Dickson, N. *et al.* (1996) Childhood-onset versus adolescent-onset antisocial conduct problems in males: natural history from ages 3 to 18 years. *Development and Psychopathology*, **8**, 399–424.

Moffitt, T.E., Caspi, A., Rutter, M. and Silva, P.A. (2001) *Sex Differences in Antisocial Behaviour: Conduct Disorder, Delinquency, and Violence in the Dunedin Longitudinal Study*, Cambridge University Press, New York.

Moran, P. (1999) *Antisocial Personality Disorder: An Epidemiological Perspective*, Gaskell, London.

Mortberg, E., Clark, D.M., Sundin, O. and Wistedt, A. (2007) Intensive group cognitive treatment and individual cognitive therapy vs. treatment as usual in social phobia: a randomized controlled trial. *Acta Psychiatrica Scandinavica*, **115**, 142–54.

Myers, M.G., Stewart, D.G. and Brown, S.A. (1998) Progression from conduct disorder to antisocial personality disorder following treatment for adolescent substance abuse. *American Journal of Psychiatry*, **155** (4), 479–85.

Nathan, R., Rollinson, L., Harvey, K. and Hill, J. (2003) The Liverpool Violence Assessment: an investigator-based measure of serious violence. *Criminal Behaviour and Mental Health*, **13** (2), 106–20.

Neugebauer, R., Hoek, H.W. and Susser, E. (1999) Prenatal exposure to wartime famine and development of antisocial personality disorder in early adulthood. *JAMA*, **282** (5), 455–62.

Newman, J.P. and Schmitt, W.A. (1998) Passive avoidance in psychopathic offenders: a replication and extension. *Journal of Abnormal Psychology*, **107** (3), 527–32.

Nock, M.K., Kazdin, A.E., Hiripi, E. and Kessler, R.C. (2006) Prevalence, subtypes, and correlates of DSM-IV conduct disorder in the National Comorbidity Survey Replication. *Psychological Medicine*, **36** (5), 699–710.

Ortiz, J. and Raine, A. (2004) Heart rate level and antisocial behavior in children and adolescents: a meta-analysis. *Journal of the American Academy of Child and Adolescent Psychiatry*, **43** (2), 154–62.

Patrick, C.J. (2006) *Handbook of the Psychopathy*, Guilford Press, New York.

Pfeffer, C.R. and Plutchik, R. (1989) Co-occurrence of psychiatric disorders in child psychiatric patients and nonpatients: a circumplex model. *Comprehensive Psychiatry*, **30** (4), 275–82.

Pfohl, B., Blum, N., Zimmerman, M. and Stangl, D. (1989) Structured Interview for DSM-III-R Personality (SIDP-R), University of Iowa.

Raine, A., Moffitt, T.E., Caspi, A. *et al.* (2005) Neurocognitive impairments in boys on the life-course persistent antisocial path. *Journal of Abnormal Psychology*, **114** (1), 38–49.

Reif, A., Rosler, M., Freitag, C.M. *et al.* (2007) Nature and nurture predispose to violent behavior: serotonergic genes and adverse childhood environment. *Neuropsychopharmacology*, **32** (11), 2375–83.

Repo-Tiihonen, E., Virkkunen, M. and Tiihonen, J. (2001) Mortality of antisocial male criminals. *Journal of Forensic Psychiatry*, **12**, 677–83.

Rhee, S.H. and Waldman, I.D. (2002) Genetic and environmental influences on antisocial behavior: a meta-analysis of twin and adoption studies. *Psychological Bulletin*, **128** (3), 490–529.

Robins, L.N. (1966) *Deviant Children Grown Up: A Sociological and Psychiatric Study of Sociopathic Personality*, Williams & Wilkins, Baltimore, MD.

Robins, L.N. (1978) Sturdy childhood predictors of adult antisocial behavior: replication from longitudinal studies. *Psychological Medicine*, **8** (4), 611–22.

Robins, L.N. and McEvoy, L. (1990) Conduct problems as predictors of substance abuse, in *Straight and Devious Pathways from Childhood to Adulthood* (eds L.N. Robins and M. Rutter), Cambridge University Press, Cambridge, pp. 182–204.

Robins, L.N., Tipp, J. and Przybeck, T. (1991) Antisocial personality, in *Psychiatric Disorders in America: The Epidemiological Catchment Area Study* (eds L.N. Robins and D.A. Regier), The Free Press, New York, pp. 258–90.

Russo, M.F. and Beidel, D.C. (1994) Comorbidity of childhood anxiety and externalizing disorders: prevalence, associated characteristics, and validation issues. *Clinical Psychology Review*, **14** (3), 199–221.

Samuels, J., Bienvenu, O.J., Cullen, B. *et al.* (2004) Personality dimensions and criminal arrest. *Comprehensive Psychiatry*, **45** (4), 275–80.

Samuels, J., Eaton, W.W., Bienvenu, O.J., III *et al.* (2002) Prevalence and correlates of person-ality disorders in a community sample. *British Journal of Psychiatry*, **180** (6), 536–42.

Sareen, J., Stein, M.B., Cox, B.J. and Hassard, S.T. (2004) Understanding comorbidity of anxiety disorders with antisocial behaviour: findings from two large community surveys. *The Journal of Nervous and Mental Disease*, **192**, 178–86.

Scott, S. (2005) Do parenting programmes for severe child antisocial behaviour work over the long term, and for whom? One year follow-up of a multi-centre controlled trial. *Behavioural and Cognitive Psychotherapy*, **33**, 1–19.

Simonoff, E., Elander, J., Holmshaw, J. *et al.* (2004) Predictors of antisocial personality. Continuities from childhood to adult life. *British Journal of Psychiatry*, **184**, 118–27.

Singleton, N., Meltzer, H., Gatward, R. *et al.* (1998) *Psychiatric Morbidity among Prisoners in England and Wales*, HMSO, London.

Skeem, J., Johansson, P., Andershed, H. *et al.* (2007) Two subtypes of psychopathic violent offenders that parallel primary and secondary variants. *Journal of Abnormal Psychology*, **116** (2), 395–409.

Sterzer, P., Stadler, C., Krebs, A. *et al.* (2005) Abnormal neural responses to emotional visual stimuli in adolescents with conduct disorder. *Biological Psychiatry*, **57** (1), 7–15.

Swanson, M.C., Bland, R.C. and Newman, S.C. (1994) Epidemiology of psychiatric disorders in Edmonton. Antisocial personality disorders. *Acta Psychiatrica Scandinavica. Supplementum*, **376**, 63–70.

Torgensen, S., Kringlen, E. and Cramer, V. (2001) The prevalence of personality disorders in a community sample. *Archives of General Psychiatry*, **58**, 590–6.

Viding, E., Frick, P.J. and Plomin, R. (2007) Aetiology of the relationship between callous-unemotional traits and conduct problems in childhood. *British Journal of Psychiatry. Supplement*, **49**, s33–8.

Virkkunen, M., Goldman, D., Nielsen, D.A. and Linnoila, M. (1995) Low brain serotonin turnover rate (low CSF 5-HIAA) and impulsive violence. *Journal of Psychiatry and Neuroscience*, **20** (4), 271–5.

Walker, J.L., Lahey, B.B., Russo, M.F. *et al.* (1991) Anxiety, inhibition, and conduct disorder in children: I. Relations to social impairment. *Journal of the American Academy of Child and Adolescent Psychiatry*, **30** (2), 187–91.

Waschbusch, D.A. (2002) A meta-analytic examination of comorbid hyperactive-impulsive-attention problems and conduct problems. *Psychological Bulletin*, **128** (1), 118–50.

Washburn, J.J., Romero, E.G., Welty, L.J. *et al.* (2007) Development of antisocial personality disorder in detained youths: the predictive value of mental disorders. *Journal of Consulting and Clinical Psychology*, **75** (2), 221–31.

Widiger, T.A. and Trull, T.J. (1994) Personality disorders and violence, in *Violence and Mental Disorder: Developments in Risk Assessment* (eds J. Monahan and H.J. Steadman), University of Chicago Press, Chicago, pp. 203–26.

Wolff, J.C. and Ollendick, T.H. (2006) The comorbidity of conduct problems and depression in childhood and adolescence. *Clinical Child and Family Psychology Review*, **9** (3–4), 201–20.

Wootton, J.M., Frick, P.J., Shelton, K.K. and Silverthorn, P. (1997) Ineffective parenting and childhood conduct problems: the moderating role of callous-unemotional traits. *Journal of Consulting and Clinical Psychology*, **65** (2), 301–8.

World Health Organisation (1992) *The ICD-10 Classification of Mental and Behavioural Disorders: Clinical Descriptions and Diagnostic Guidelines*, WHO, Geneva.

Young, S.J., Gudjonsson, G.H., Ball, S. and Lam, J. (2003) Attention Deficit Hyperactivity Disorder (ADHD) in personality disordered offenders and the association with disruptive behavioural problems. *Journal of Forensic Psychiatry and Psychology*, **14** (3), 491–505.

PART II

AFFECT

Chapter 8

THE NEUROBIOLOGY OF AFFECTIVE DYSCONTROL: IMPLICATIONS FOR UNDERSTANDING 'DANGEROUS AND SEVERE PERSONALITY DISORDER'

Rick Howard

University of Nottingham, UK

INTRODUCTION

The purpose of this chapter is to explore links between personality disorder (PD), emotional self-regulation and violence. From the perspective of general systems theory (Von Bertalanffy,1968), personality and its disorders can be expressed at (at least) three different levels: interpersonal, personal and intrapersonal. At an interpersonal level, PDs commonly manifest in behaviours that are difficult, unpleasant and troublesome to others. These characteristic styles of interpersonal behaviour can be described in terms of a two-dimensional interpersonal space, such as the warmth–hostility and dominance–submission dimensions measured by the Chart of Interpersonal Reactions in Closed Living Environments (CIRCLE: Blackburn and Renwick, 1996). At a personal level, PDs are expressed by characteristic ways of thinking, feeling and behaving in relation to the world and the self that are in some sense maladaptive, self-defeating or, in relation to prevailing social norms, objectionable. This corresponds to standard psychiatric definitions of PDs in terms of 'inflexible and maladaptive traits' (DSM) or 'more or less well-defined abnormalities or deviations of personality' (ICD). Intrapersonally, PDs can be described either from the point of view of structural phenomenology, the general approach adopted in reversal theory, which involves identifying the structures of experience (Apter, 2005) or, at the level of the brain, by aberrant processing of information within discrete neural processing streams: cognitive, motoric and affective (Howard, 2001).

The focus of this chapter will be on affective self-control. It has been argued that 'the major feature of personality disorders is a failure of affect regulation' (Sarkar

Personality, Personality Disorder and Violence   Edited by Mary McMurran and Richard C. Howard
© 2009 John Wiley & Sons, Ltd

and Adshead, 2006, p. 297), and violence can be said to represent the extreme interpersonal manifestation of dysregulated affect. Some critical questions will be addressed here. Firstly, what is the relationship between PDs and violence? Secondly, what is the relationship of between dysregulation of affect and PDs? Finally, and most importantly, how are PDs linked to both affective dyscontrol and violence – that is, what are the mechanisms that mediate any relationship that may exist between PDs on the one hand, and affective dyscontrol and violence on the other hand?

The central thesis of this chapter is that the link between PD, affect regulation and violence has to be understood within a developmental context, and particularly within the context of a history of alcohol (and other substance) abuse occurring during adolescence, the period of life during which most young people initiate and escalate alcohol use. Evidence to be reviewed below suggests that neural circuitry involving orbital and lateral prefrontal cortex underlies affective impulsivity or affective dyscontrol (these terms are used here interchangeably). Affective dyscontrol, common to a number of PDs but antisocial and borderline in particular, is said to reflect impairment of this circuitry. While this impairment may, to some degree, be present in pre-adolescent children prior to exposure to alcohol and other drugs in the teenage years, it is argued that exposure to significant amounts of alcohol and other substances during adolescence, for a sufficiently long period of time, results in a progressive and incremental impairment of the neural circuitry underlying affective impulsivity, and hence in impaired emotional self-regulation in adulthood (see Howard, 2006, for a detailed exegesis). This is consistent with a recent suggestion by Sisk and Zehr (2005) that, in addition to the perinatal period of brain reorganisation under the influence of gonadal sex hormones, there is a further period of steroid-dependent refinement of neural circuits occurring in adolescence. This is said to result in relatively long-lasting effects on adult behaviour, including effects on risk for alcoholism (and, one might add, risk for antisocial, and particularly violent, behaviour). Findings from animal studies of the effects of alcohol on the developing brain suggest that adolescence is a period of heightened susceptibility to the adverse effects of alcohol: the adolescent brain is more susceptible to overt damage and disruption of cellular, physiological, neurochemical and behavioural processes as a result of both acute and chronic exposure to alcohol (Crews *et al.*, 2000, 2006; Sircar and Sircar, 2006; Slawecki *et al.*, 2001; White and Swartzwelder, 2005).

WHAT IS THE RELATIONSHIP BETWEEN PERSONALITY DISORDER AND VIOLENT OFFENDING?

Epidemiological evidence suggests a relationship between some types of PDs and offending in general, and violent offending in particular. For example, in the general population, Cluster B PDs (the 'dramatic, emotional and erratic' cluster) have been found to be associated with criminality and offending (Coid *et al.*, 2006). In forensic samples, in whom Cluster B PDs are disproportionately represented, both antisocial personality disorder (APD) and borderline personality disorder (BPD) were significantly associated with previous criminal convictions, and, in the case of APD, particularly with violent convictions (Coid *et al.*, 1999). Notwithstanding the very high co-occurrence of PDs both within and across clusters, the forensic history correlates of particular combinations of PD have not been systematically described. However, Coid (1992) noted that a proportion of his forensic sample had both APD and BPD 'in devastating combination' (p. 89), and this combination was said by Mullen (1992, p. 238) to represent 'a very particular constellation of abnormalities of mental state with a wide range of disorderly conduct', abnormalities said to be developmental in origin. Emphasising the importance of patterns of covarying traits, rather than single PD categories, Blackburn and Coid (1999) identified a 'borderline-antisocial-passive aggressive' cluster among a forensic sample. More recently, more than two-thirds of patients detained under conditions of very high security who met criteria for 'dangerous and severe personality disorder' (DSPD), that is, had a history of violent offending and a high severity of PD, were found to meet the criteria for *both* APD and BPD. This combination has been found to occur far less frequently (around 30%) in forensic PD patients detained under conditions of medium security, and far less frequently (less than 10%) in treatment-seeking personality disordered patients living in the community (Howard *et al.*, 2008). Compared with the rest of the community sample, those having the APD+BPD combination had significantly more violent convictions and a significantly greater history of drug and alcohol problems. They also showed significantly higher levels of anger and impulsivity, indicating that they were affectively impulsive, an issue that will be discussed later. Interestingly, the presence of obsessional-compulsive traits was inversely related to measures of criminality in this community sample, suggesting a complex relationship between PD and criminality.

If the central thesis being proposed here regarding the connection between early alcohol abuse and later PD and violence is to be supported, then APD+BPD combination should be particularly associated with a history of early-onset alcohol and substance abuse. Results of a study by Bakken, Landheim and Vaglum (2004) are pertinent to this. These authors divided a large sample of substance abusers into early (before age 24) and late (after age 24) onset groups, and compared the prevalence of PDs, defined in terms of the Millon Multiaxial Clinical Inventory II (MCMI-II: Millon, 1987), between groups. Avoidant, antisocial, passive-aggressive and borderline PDs occurred with significantly greater frequencies in the early-onset group. In contrast, dependent and compulsive PDs occurred more frequently in the late-onset group. Bakken *et al.* did not report data for those who showed combinations of PDs. However, in a personal communication (23 February 2007), Bakken identified 29 of 114 polysubstance-dependent patients with the APD+BPD combination, and of these 29, 24 were reported as early onset. These results support the idea that those PDs that are particularly associated with violence, and the combination of APD+BPD in particular, are also associated with early-onset substance abuse.

AFFECTIVE IMPULSIVITY AND PERSONALITY DISORDERS

Affective impulsivity may be defined as the *response to a stimulus or event on the basis of an immediate emotional reaction such as desire or anger, with little if any checking of long-term consequences* (Wingrove and Bond, 1997). The affective dimension of impulsivity has been largely neglected, both in theoretical accounts of impulsivity and in the development of instruments to measure it. In contrast, Shapiro's (1965) early theoretical account regarded impulsivity as the failure to control internal emotional impulses, its expression involving affective, as well as cognitive and behavioural, manifestations. With few exceptions, for example Blackburn's (1971) MMPI-derived impulsivity measure and the Urgency scale from Whiteside and Lynam's (2001) 'Urgency, Perseverance, Premeditation and Sensation-Seeking >' (UPPS) scale, self-report measures of impulsivity have generally not captured the affective dimension of impulsivity, despite its overarching relevance in forensic contexts. Moreover, behavioural tasks used to measure impulsivity typically lack an emotional component, and fail to capture the essence of affectively impulsive behaviour. UPPS Urgency, measuring 'a tendency to experience strong impulses, frequently under conditions of negative affect' (Whiteside and Lynam, 2001, p. 685), has been reported to predict aggression and appears to capture a dimension of affective dyscontrol shared by several psychological disorders, including BPD, eating disorders and depression (Miller *et al.*, 2003). It correlates with alcohol abuse in pathological samples (particularly in those with antisocial traits: Whiteside and Lynam, 2003), and with alcohol use in community samples (e.g. Miller *et al.*, 2003).

Some have argued that it is the failure to emotionally self-regulate that is the defining feature of PDs (e.g. Sarkar and Adshead, 2006). However, as these authors note, affective dysregulation is most prominent in Cluster B, and is particularly salient in APD and BPD, which share many features in common. For example, in terms of the 'Big 5' personality traits described by Zuckerman and colleagues (Zuckerman *et al.*, 1993), APDs and BPDs share high scores on impulsive sensation seeking and aggression-hostility, while BPDs are additionally characterised by high scores on neuroticism-anxiety (Aluja *et al.*, 2007). In terms of the two higher-order PD factors, 'anxious-inhibited' and 'acting out', identified by Blackburn *et al.* (2005), patients who meet criteria for both APD and BPD should score high on both factors. Indeed, this has been shown to be the case in forensic patients detained under conditions of very high security. Arguably, what is common to APD and BPD is affective impulsivity as defined above. It is the tendency to act out when in a state of heightened affect (positive or negative) that, arguably, is the hallmark of the dangerous and severely personality disordered offender. This tendency will be most saliently seen in those who have the APD+BPD combination, who score highly on a higher-order psychopathy factor identified using International Personality Disorder Examination (IPDE) data in both forensic (Ullrich and Marneros, 2004, 2007) and community (Howard *et al.*, 2008) samples.

The foregoing assumes a relationship between violence and affective impulsivity, but this bears closer scrutiny. Traditionally, violence has been dichotomised as impulsive/affective versus instrumental, that is, violence with and without an accompanying negative emotional state. There is some evidence, reviewed in Porter and Woodworth, 2006, to suggest that instrumental violence is more clearly associated with psychopathy than is affective violence. Another dichotomy in the violence literature, grounded in animal research on aggression, is between two types of goal-directed aggression, defensive and offensive (Blanchard and Blanchard, 2003). A third type, instinctual or predatory aggression, is not associated with affect, positive or negative. According to the schema shown in Table 8.1, both

Table 8.1 A typology of violence

		Offensive/appetitive	Defensive
Impulsive	Goal	Enhancement of positive affect by infliction of harm and suffering	Reduction of negative affect through removal of interpersonal threat
	Affect	Positive	Negative
	Emotion	Exhilaration/excitement; desire to maximise excitement	Fear, distress, desire to eradicate threat
	Anger type	'Thrill-seeking anger'	'Explosive/reactive anger'
Controlled	Goal	Achievement of positive outcome/reinforcement	Removal of interpersonal threat/grievance by considered, premeditated action
	Affect	Positive	Negative
	Emotion	Pleasant anticipation; desire for positive outcome	Vengefulness; desire to 'get even' with source of grievance
	Anger type	'Coercive anger'	'Vengeful/ruminative anger'

offensive and defensive aggression can occur either in an affectively impulsive state, or in a state of self-control. Offensive aggression[1] and violence are associated with positive affect, while defensive aggression and violence are associated with negative affect. This gives rise to four types of violence: offensive/controlled, offensive/impulsive, defensive/controlled and defensive/impulsive, each with its specific goals, affects and emotions.

According to this typology, impulsive violence could occur in either a positive or a negative affective state (top half of Table 8.1). When in the form of offensive violence (top left of table), it arises in a state of positive affect, there is an irresistible desire to maximise a state of excitement by inflicting harm and suffering on another, accompanied by thrill-seeking anger that is experienced as affectively positive-pleasant anger, or in the language of reversal theory, parapathic anger (Apter, 2005).[2] The goal of inflicting harm and suffering on some other is not so much driving the violent behaviour as acting as an excuse for the behaviour. This is primarily motivated by a desire to maximise the powerfully reinforcing emotional state of excitement and exhilaration. Evidence for a thrill-seeking motivation in the violence of psychopaths, and for their derivation of pleasure from the suffering of others (Porter and Woodworth, 2006), suggests that psychopaths' violence falls disproportionately within this impulsive/offensive category.

If in the form of defensive violence (top right of Table 8.1), the violent impulse arises in a state of negative affect, there is an irresistible desire to eradicate the source of some perceived threat, resulting in a violent act accompanied by anger and with minimal appraisal of negative consequences. The anger, characterised as explosive/reactive, is experienced as affectively negative (unpleasant anger). The trigger here would typically be some behaviour on the part of another that is interpreted (often wrongly) as indicating malevolent intent. The goal of the violent act is to reduce the negative affect by eradicating the source of the (perceived) threat. It seems plausible, though it is yet to be verified, that defensive violence, accompanied by unpleasant anger, is more commonly elicited in borderline patients and those scoring high on Blackburn et al.'s (2005) 'anxious-inhibited' PD factor; while offensive violence, accompanied by pleasant anger, may be more common in those with APD and those scoring high on 'acting out'. Those showing the APD+BPD combination would, by virtue of their affective impulsivity, be prone to both defensive and offensive violence. The type of violence manifested would depend both on the context, specifically whether this was conducive to a state of negative or positive affect (e.g. presence of an interpersonal threat or a stimulus that provoked excitement and thrill-seeking), and more importantly, the state of the individual concerned. If this were characterised by an orientation that was hedonistic and focused on the here-and-now, impulsive/offensive violence (accompanied by thrill-seeking anger) would more likely occur. If, on the other hand, it were characterised by an orientation that was focused on the goal of eliminating the perceived threat, impulsive/defensive violence (accompanied by explosive/reactive anger) would more likely ensue.

Two other forms of violence are indicated in the lower half of Table 8.1: offensive/controlled and defensive/controlled. The former corresponds closely to what traditionally has been referred to as instrumental violence, where the goal is achievement of some positive outcome, and the violence is purely instrumental in achieving that outcome. A classic example of this is armed robbery where the goal, for example robbing a mail train of money, is thwarted by the presence of someone for example the train driver, whose elimination proves necessary to achieve the goal. Defensive/controlled violence is motivated by the removal of some interpersonal threat or grievance and is accompanied by the emotion of vengefulness. The scorned lover's desire to get even with a rival for the beloved's affections is a classic example of this.[3]

BRAIN MEASURES OF AFFECTIVE IMPULSIVITY IN PERSONALITY DISORDERED INDIVIDUALS

The first studies to investigate neuroaffective processing in personality disordered individuals were carried out in the 1970s and 1980s by the author and colleagues at Broadmoor high-secure hospital in England (Howard, Fenton and Fenwick, 1982). Patients, all males, were admitted under UK Mental Health legislation as mentally ill or psychopathically disordered, the latter being given the clinical diagnosis of PD. This work predated the advent of Hare's Psychopathy Checklist (PCL: Hare, 2003), so it was not possible to rigorously assess psychopathy in these patients. Later work with this population (Coid, 1992) indicated that roughly one-quarter meet the PCL criterion for psychopathy, but that almost all (including those classified as mentally ill) meet criteria for at least one, and usually several, DSM-III PDs. The most commonly diagnosed are BPD and APD, and in terms of Blackburn's primary versus secondary distinction (see Blackburn, this volume), most personality disordered patients are secondary psychopaths. Rather than focusing on clinical diagnosis, this work focused on brain correlates of personality dimensions, particularly impulsivity/belligerence and anxiety/social withdrawal, that previous work (Blackburn, 1974) had indicated were key to describing a ty- pology of mentally disordered offenders. Impulsivity/belligerence, which opera- tionalises what is here referred to as affective impulsivity, was a particular focus, in view of Blackburn's (1974) suggestion that impulsivity may be a defining attribute of the psychopath.

Among various behavioural paradigms used to evoke event-related brain ac- tivity was a Go/No Go paradigm that elicited slow brain potentials ('Go/No Go CNV') found to be related to psychometric measures of affective impulsivity (Howard, Fenton and Fenwick, 1982; Brown, Fenwick and Howard, 1989). The CNV is a slow negative-going shift in brain potential, recorded from scalp elec- trodes, that develops over several seconds as someone prepares to respond to a cue. A warning stimulus (S1 in Figure 8.1) precedes an imperative stimulus (S2 in Figure 8.1) that requires a motor response (manual button-press). In the Go/No Go avoidance paradigm illustrated in Figure 8.1, a warning cue signalled either Go (button-press) or No Go (no button-press) to the imperative stimulus. Omission of the aversive noise stimulus (non-punishment) was contingent on a correct and timely response to the imperative stimulus. As shown in Figure 8.1, the relative amplitude of the slow negative shift in brain potential elicited between S1 and S2 on Go and No Go trials was found to be related to affective impulsivity. Affectively impulsive, compared with non-impulsive, personality disordered patients showed a lack of brain potential difference comparing Go and No Go conditions: inspec- tion of Figure 8.1 (bottom set of traces) reveals a lack of 'daylight' between the Go and No Go waveforms in the impulsive group compared with non-impulsive and control groups (upper sets of traces). Impulsive mentally ill patients showed the same difference relative to non-impulsive mentally ill patients.

When patients were categorised as a priori high or low risk on the basis of their CNV results and followed up post-discharge, CNV was found to successfully predict both general and violent reoffending with reasonable accuracy (Howard and Lumsden, 1996, 1997). A later study found that among personality disordered prison inmates, of whom 80% met DSM criteria for APD, those with a history of predominantly early-onset alcohol abuse, compared with those without such a history, showed the 'impulsive' brain-wave pattern, that is, a lack of difference be- tween Go and No Go conditions (Neo, McCullagh and Howard, 2001). This raised the possibility that the high-risk patients in the Howard and Lumsden studies were at increased risk of violence by virtue of their history of early-onset alcohol abuse, giving rise to the hypothesis suggesting that the link between PD and vio- lence was early-onset alcohol abuse (Howard, 2006). By impairing the function of prefrontal cortex during adolescence, a period that is critical for its development, early-onset alcohol abuse was hypothesised to lead to deficits in the neuropsy- chological substrates of goal-directed behaviour and emotional self-regulation, placing the individual at high risk for becoming a life-course persistent offender in adulthood. Those individuals who show disinhibitory psychopathology (e.g. conduct disorder, attention deficit hyperactivity disorder, childhood psychopathic traits) during childhood would be at increased risk of engaging in alcohol abuse during adolescence, which in turn would disrupt the frontal cortical substrates of emotional self-regulation, leading to increased use of alcohol and yet further

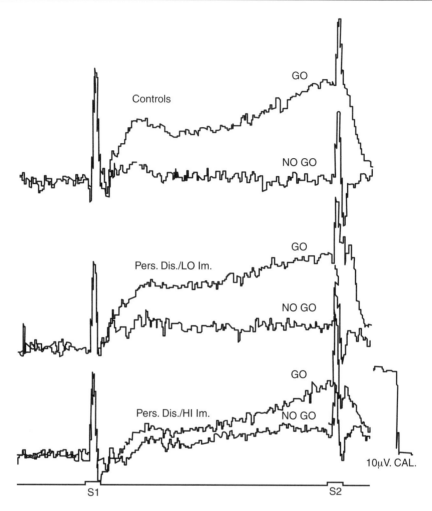

Figure 8.1 Go/No Go CNV in healthy controls (top traces), non-impulsive PD patients (middle traces), and impulsive PD patients (bottom trcaes). Impulsivity was measured using Blackburn's (1971) impulsivity scale. On Go trials, an auditory cue (S1) signals the delivery, some 3 s later, of a second cue (S2), to which the subject responds with a button-press in order to avoid a noxious white noise stimulus. On No Go trials, a different S1 signals that he should refrain from responding to S2, again to avoid the noise. A negative (up-going) potential develops in the Go condition between S1 and S2, but is of lower amplitude in the No Go condition (Howard, Fenton and Fenwick, 1982).

impairment of emotional self-regulation, so that they would emerge into adulthood with a high risk of general and violent offending. This scenario would apply particularly to those PDs that have been shown, in the epidemiological literature, to be associated with a history of adolescent alcohol abuse. Cluster B disorders, in particular, have been found to be significantly associated with alcohol dependence in the general community (Coid *et al.*, 2006). In forensic samples, APD and BPD are each significantly associated with alcoholism and alcohol misuse (Coid *et al.*, 1999). Those bearing the double jeopardy of the APD+BPD combination, who qualify as dangerous and severe in terms of their PD, would be expected to show a history of particularly severe and long-lasting alcohol (and other substance) abuse during adolescence.

Brain event-related potentials other than the CNV have also been linked to affective impulsivity and, hypothetically, to early alcohol abuse. One such is the error-related negativity (ERN), a small negative voltage change evoked on error trials, relative to error-free trials, when subjects are required to behaviourally distinguish target from non-target letters on a visual display. For example, the target letters S and H displayed on a computer screen might require a key-press, and are flanked by distractors (same or different letters). Non-target letters (e.g. X, Y) are also flanked by distractors to encourage errors of commission. There have to date been no studies of the ERN in forensic samples, but a recent study of ERN in students found that ERN was diminished in 'externalisers', that is, those scoring at the high end of the externalising spectrum that captures variance common to different forms of disinhibitory psychopathology (Hall, Bernat and Patrick, 2007). Impulsivity in general, and affective impulsivity in particular (e.g. 'impatient urgency' from the Externalising Inventory), contributes importantly to the externalising dimension (Krueger *et al.*, 2007). De Bruijn *et al.* (2005) reported that ERN recorded in a choice reaction time task was reduced in patients with BPD, who showed an impulsive response style, relative to controls. In a previous study, Dikman and Allen (2000) reported that ERN was reduced in those scoring low on Gough's Socialisation measure, which is known to correlate highly with measures of affective impulsivity such as Blackburn's (1971) impulsivity measure, and reflects high levels of rebelliousness, aggression and impulsivity.

Another brain-wave measure that has been linked to 'externalising' is the P300, a late positive shift in brain potential occurring when a rare target must be detected among common non-targets (the so-called 'oddball' task, for example in the auditory modality, common 'beeps' interspersed with rare 'boops' that must be detected and responded to). While amplitude of P300 is diminished in those who show early alcohol abuse (Justus, Finn and Steinmetz, 2001), its diminution has been suggested as a neurobiological marker for alcoholism, being found both in alcoholics and their non-alcoholic offspring (Kamarajan *et al.*, 2005). However, findings by Patrick *et al.* (2006) suggest that it is more closely related to the externalising supertrait that accounts for variance common to various forms of disinhibitory psychopathology, including alcohol abuse.

A critical, and as yet incompletely answered, question that arises in regard to all these brain correlates of affective impulsivity is: To what extent do they reflect childhood traits, such as those associated with externalising that predispose to alcohol abuse, and to what extent do they reflect the neuropsychological sequelae of early-onset alcohol abuse? With regard to P300, findings from a recent study by Carlson, McLarnon and Iacono (2007) support the former alternative. These authors reported a P300 amplitude reduction in males aged 17 years who, at the time of their P300 recording, were free of substance (including alcohol) use disorder, and who subsequently, by age 24, developed an externalising disorder, be it early-onset (prior to age 20) substance use or some other externalising disorder, in particular adult antisocial behaviour. However, these two alternatives are by no means mutually exclusive; possibly both are true, and this possibility is implicit in the hypothesis proposed by Howard (2006). According to this, early-onset alcohol and other substance abuse in those already predisposed to disinhibitory psychopathology is a necessary but not sufficient antecedent of adult violent offending in personality disordered individuals. Those in whom childhood externalising tendencies give rise to significant early alcohol (and other substance) abuse will, as a result of that abuse, manifest PDs characterised by antisocial and borderline features which, particularly in combination, give rise to a propensity to engage in violent behaviour. This can only be confirmed when longitudinal studies are carried out to verify the hypothesis.

Another important question concerns the specific nature of the neuropsychological deficits underlying APD and BPD, given that both are associated with affective dyscontrol. It was suggested above (p. 162) that defensive/impulsive violence, accompanied by explosive/reactive anger, might be relatively specific to borderline patients, while offensive/impulsive violence, and thrill-seeking anger, might be more typical of those with APD. With regard to the underlying brain dysfunction, a speculative suggestion would be that borderline patients may, as indicated by results of several structural imaging studies (reviewed in Johnson et al., 2003), show reduced orbito-frontal inhibition of limbic/amygdala activation to emotional stimuli. Antisocial PDs, on the other hand, may show dysfunction of dorsolateral prefrontal cortex. Those showing the APD+BPD combination would then show both types of dysfunction, perhaps as a result of particularly severe or long-lasting exposure to alcohol and other drugs during adolescence, in conjunction with specific predisposing influences unique to each disorder.

ASSESSING RISK OF VIOLENCE: NEW APPROACHES

As indicated above, the Go/No Go CNV, a brain correlate of affective impulsivity, shows promise as a measure of risk of violence. Predicting general and violent reoffending on the basis of the CNV showed a relative improvement over chance (a measure that adjusts for base rate of reoffending) of 0.73 and 0.68 respectively (Howard and Lumsden, 1996, 1997). In this respect, the Go/No Go CNV compares favourably with other predictors of reoffending, for example Hare's PCL which has been reported as showing a relative improvement over chance of 0.62 (Harris, Rice and Cormier, 1991).

However, as static risk measures, brain-wave measures probably add very little to existing actuarial risk measures such as the PCL and other measures that rely on the PCL as part of the risk assessment. Rather, it is as potential measures of risk *state* that they offer the greatest promise. The recent forensic literature highlights the limitations of existing measures of violence risk, most of which do nothing to track the ebb and flow of risk within individuals over time (Douglas and Skeem 2005). The practical utility of static risk measures when applied to the task of monitoring and intervening with high-risk individuals, is therefore compromised.

Douglas and Skeem (2005) point out that, to be maximally effective in the key task of reducing violence potential, clinicians must go beyond evaluating baseline risk status, which focuses on inter-individual variability in risk, to assessing risk state, which focuses on intra-individual variability in violence potential. In this respect, brain-wave measures like the CNV and ERN offer potential value as trait markers that are also state dependent. For example, abnormality of the ERN in psychotic patients is reported to partially normalise during treatment (Bates *et al.*, 2004), and like the ERN, the Go/No Go CNV can reflect temporary changes in brain state brought about by mind-altering drugs or sleep deprivation. A state of cannabis intoxication, associated in personality disordered individuals with violent crime (Niveau and Dang, 2003), is accompanied by severe disruption of the Go/No Go CNV (Howard and Menkes, 2007). This, it is argued, reflects a neurobiological state in which there is an increased tendency for the individual to act out in an emo-tionally disinhibited way. This acting out could take the form of either offensive (in a positive affective state) or defensive (in a negative affective state) violence (Table 8.1), depending both on the context the individual finds him- or herself in, as well as on internal variables such as blood sugar level, blood alcohol level and the frame of mind of the individual. The threshold at which some precipitant will trigger acting out behaviour will depend both on the 'resting state' at which the individual normally operates (trait) as well as on the contextual and internal factors operating at any given moment (state). Future studies need to validate the use of brain-wave measures as risk state measures. Changes in these measures could be tracked in individual high-risk cases over time and correlated with ac-tual episodes of aggression and violence, self-report state measures of affective impulsivity, and observer-rated measures of impulsive behaviour known to pre-dict dynamic changes in violence risk, such as the dynamic appraisal of inpatient aggression (Ogloff and Daffern, 2006). If, as predicted, changes in affective impul-sivity and Go/No Go CNV/ERN proved to be precursors of aggressive episodes, these measures, either alone or in combination with an observer-rated measure, might provide a clinically useful risk state measure.

Slow brain potentials such as the CNV are modifiable through biofeed-back both in healthy adults (Birbaumer, 1999) and in children with attention-deficit/hyperactivity disorder (Strehl *et al.*, 2006). It should, therefore, in principle be possible to modify the Go/No Go CNV of impulsive individuals in a non-impulsive direction through biofeedback training. Whether this would result in modification of their behaviour such that affective self-regulation is improved is an open question but one that merits investigation. Results of the Strehl *et al.* (2006) study augur well in this regard; after biofeedback training, ADHD children showed significant improvements in behaviour, attention and IQ that were sus-tained at 6-month follow-up. Another avenue worth exploring would be to track changes in Go/No Go CNV with therapeutic change following treatment. Some forms of therapy, for instance social problem solving (Howard *et al.*, 2008), have been reported to decrease impulsivity in personality disordered individuals. As-pects of dialectical behaviour therapy (DBT) are aimed at improving emotional self-regulation. It would clearly be of interest to explore use of Go/No Go CNV and ERN as measures of therapeutic change.

NEUROBIOLOGICAL SUBSTRATES OF AFFECTIVE SELF-REGULATION

It is beyond the scope of this chapter to review in detail the neuroanatomical and neurophysiological substrates of affective processing and self-regulation (the interested reader is referred to recent reviews by Johnson *et al.*, 2003 and Sarkar and Adshead, 2006). A neuropsychological model involving reciprocal Go and No Go neural systems, analogous to Gray's (1981) Behavioural Activation and Inhibition Systems, was developed by the present author and colleagues (Howard, Fenton and Fenwick, 1982) to explain CNV findings in personality disordered offenders, particularly the relative loss of Go/No Go CNV differentiation observed in affectively impulsive individuals. This model proposed a frontal cortical 'action acceptor' mechanism, through which expectancies for positive (reward/non-punishment) and negative (punishment/non-reward) outcomes are neurally encoded. Discrepancy between expected and obtained outcomes is said to generate a mismatch signal which modulates activity in Go and No Go centres and biases behaviour towards approach or withdrawal. When reward/non-punishment is anticipated (as in the foreperiod of the Go/No Go avoidance paradigm), a mismatch signal of moderate strength is generated which activates the Go centre, resulting in a negative voltage shift (CNV) and an approach tendency. If, however, this mismatch signal is strong and persistent, for example with continued omission of reward or receipt of punishment, the No Go centre is activated, generating a positive potential shift (contingent positive variation) and biasing behaviour towards withdrawal. The physiological reality of the proposed mismatch signal is attested to by findings of a recent study by Oya *et al.* (2005). Recordings of intracerebral electrical activity using depth electrodes were carried out in an epileptic man while performing the Iowa Gambling Task. When confronted with a choice between high- and low-risk card decks, he gradually, as a result of experiencing monetary loss from high-risk choices, switched from a high-risk strategy to a low-risk behavioural strategy, as is found in normal subjects. The mismatch between expected and obtained outcomes was reflected in an alpha-band component of the event-related potential recorded from medial prefrontal cortex. This mismatch signal correlated closely with the individual's behaviour in the task, being associated with reward-related error obtained from a reinforcement learning model of the subject's choice behaviour. Although, as the findings of Oya *et al.* (2005) suggest, the mismatch signal originates in medial prefrontal cortex (the presumed site of the action acceptor), the model suggests that it is transmitted to more lateral aspects of prefrontal cortex where it directly modulates sub-cortical Go and No Go centres. Consistent with this, lesions of dorsolateral prefrontal cortex disrupt the Go/No Go CNV in a manner similar to the disruption seen in impulsive patients (Rosahl and Knight, 1995).

The results obtained by Howard, Fenton and Fenwick (1982) in affectively impulsive personality disordered individuals in the Go/No Go task suggested that the mismatch signal generated in their reward/non-punishment action acceptor is relatively weak. A strong mismatch signal from the reward/non-punishment action acceptor is, according to the model, necessary both for generating an expectancy for reward/non-punishment (reflected in the Go CNV), and for transforming a Go signal into a No Go signal (reflected in the lack of negative voltage, or a positive voltage, in the No Go condition). Therefore, affectively impulsive individuals show both a low Go CNV and a high No Go CNV – that is, a lack of difference between Go and No Go – both during acquisition of the Go/No Go task and when the discrimination is reversed – when the Go signal comes to signal No Go, and vice versa.

SEX DIFFERENCES IN PERSONALITY DISORDERS: DO THEY PROVIDE CLUES ABOUT AETIOLOGY?

While impaired emotional self-regulation is common to both APD and BPD, it is, of course, the case that many patients show one disorder but not the other, either APD alone or BPD alone. What accounts for their co-occurrence in some patients? This appears particularly anomalous in females, given the sex bias in favour of males for both APD and BPD in the general (UK) community (Coid et al., 2006). Recent evidence from the UK Prisoner Cohort Study (Bell, Rogers and Coid, 2006) suggests that both male and female sexual and violent offenders who meet criteria for 'DSPD' show very similar characteristics. A co-occurrence of APD and BPD was far more common in both male and female offenders who met DSPD criteria compared with their non-DSPD counterparts. The latter showed approximately the same frequency, 10–11%, as was found by Howard et al. (2008) in treatment-seeking community PD patients. In contrast, nearly half of male DSPD prisoners, and a remarkably high 77% of female DSPD prisoners, showed the APD+BPD combination.[4] This suggests that among those offenders deemed, by current criteria, to be 'dangerous and severely personality disordered', women are not only well represented but show a particularly severe deficit in affective self-control and hence are particularly prone to impulsive violence.[5]

Despite the overall higher prevalence, in the general UK community, of BPD in males than females, it is well established that in treatment-seeking and forensic samples, prevalence of BPD is higher in females than males (e.g. Bell, Rogers and Coid, 2006; Watzke, Ullrich and Marneros, 2006). A possible explanation of this might be that women with a BPD diagnosis in forensic, particularly high-secure, samples would score high on the broad psychopathy factor identified from IPDE data in forensic and community PD samples (Ullrich and Marneros, 2004, 2007; Howard et al., 2008). This factor embraces histrionic/narcissistic, borderline and paranoid traits in addition to antisocial traits in childhood and adulthood, and is associated with criminality, including violent offending. Women with a BPD diagnosis in the general community, in contrast, might be expected to score low on this psychopathy factor. The former, but not the latter, would be expected to show a history of significant alcohol and other drug abuse during their teenage years.

The marked sex difference, favouring males, in the prevalence of APD in the general community (Coid et al., 2006; see also De Brito and Hodgins, this volume) may reflect sex differences both in the drinking trajectories of males and females across adolescence, and in the rate of development of specific brain regions. By

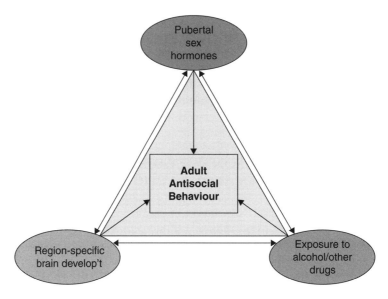

Figure 8.2   Pubertal sex hormones, regionally specific brain development during adolescence, and exposure to alcohol and other substances interact to produce long-term effects on adult antisocial versus prosocial behaviour.

late puberty, sex specific drinking patterns emerge, with females showing fewer episodes of heavy drinking and lower prevalence of alcohol abuse and dependence than males. At the same time, increases of grey matter volume in limbic structures associated with emotional regulation and the alcohol reward system proceed in a sex-dependent manner (Giedd *et al.*, 1999).

There is likely a complex, three-way interaction, whose details remain to be worked out, between pubertal sex hormones, adolescent brain development and alcohol/substance use (see Figure 8.2). Suffice it to say that this interaction will operate differently in males and females, and its results, in terms of effects on adult behaviour, may explain, at least in part, sex differences in the prevalence of APD and BPD. It remains for future research to address the question of how these three factors interact to produce adult antisocial behaviour. An answer to this question will require a longitudinal study to track hormonal outputs, drinking patterns and regional brain development in a cohort of at-risk and low-risk children from pre-puberty through adolescence into early adulthood.

SUMMARY AND CONCLUSION

Evidence reviewed here suggests that the combination of antisocial and borderline traits confers a high risk for violence, and that this relationship is mediated by affective impulsivity. Neurophysiological evidence supports the idea that affective impulsivity reflects a functional impairment of prefrontal cortex. Recent evidence from developmental neurobiology suggests the possibility that the development of neural circuitry involving medial and lateral prefrontal cortex, which are critically involved in affective self-regulation, is adversely affected by exposure of the adolescent brain to alcohol and possibly other substances. Impairment of this neural circuitry during adolescence is hypothesised to result in a predisposition to impulsive violence in adult life, carried out in states of both positive and negative affect. Longitudinal studies will be required to verify this.

NOTES

1. Perhaps a better term to describe this form of aggression/violence is 'appetitive', to emphasise its positive reinforcement aspect and the positive affect that is associated with it.
2. According to reversal theory, emotions that are supposedly unpleasant are termed 'parapathic' when they are experienced as pleasant in a present-oriented, hedonistic state. Parapathic anger occurs when, for example, we enjoy being angry at the villain when watching a film. In watching a soccer game, we may enjoy being angry at the referee.
3. Perhaps the most notorious recent case is that of Lisa Nowak, the NASA astronaut, who raced 900 miles in her car from Houston to Orlando on 5 February 2007 to confront a woman she viewed as a rival for a space shuttle pilot's affections.
4. The author is grateful to Ms Laura Bell for providing this information (personal communication, 31 March 2007).
5. This is supported by recent results of a review of daily (mostly violent) incident reports at Rampton Hospital, United Kingdom, which is organised by directorates (mental illness, personality disorder, learning disability and women's service). The review found that daily incidents were most common among women patients.

REFERENCES

Aluja, A., Cuevas, L., Garcia, L.F. and Garcia, O. (2007) Zuckerman's personality model predicts MCMI-III personality disorders. *Personality and Individual Differences*, **42**, 1311–21. doi: 10.1016/j.paid.2006.10.009.

Apter, M.J. (2005) *Personality Dynamics: Key Concepts in Reversal Theory*, Apter International, Loughborough, U.K.

Bakken, K., Landheim, A.S. and Vaglum, P. (2004) Early and late onset groups of substance misusers: Differences in primary and secondary psychiatric disorders. *Journal of Substance Use*, **9**, 224–34.

Bates, A.T., Liddle, P.F., Kiehl, K.A. and Ngan, E.T.C. (2004) State dependent changes in error monitoring in schizophrenia. *Journal of Psychiatric Research*, **38**, 347–56.

Bell, L., Rogers, R.D. and Coid, J. (2006) *Gender Differences in DSPD Offenders*. Paper presented at Research Conference, Dangerous and Severe Personality Disorder, November 2006, Leeds.

Birbaumer, N. (1999) Slow cortical potentials: plasticity, operant control, and behavioural effects. *Neuroscientist*, **5**, 74–78.

Blackburn, R. (1971) MMPI dimensions of sociability and impulse control. *Journal of Consulting and Clinical Psychology*, **37**, 166.

Blackburn, R. (1974) *Personality and the Classification of Psychopathic Disorders. Special Hospitals Research Report, 10*. Special Hospitals Research Unit, London.

Blackburn, R. and Coid, J. (1999) Empirical clusters of DSM-III personality disorders in violent offenders. *Journal of Personality Disorders*, **13**, 18–34.

Blackburn, R., Logan, C., Renwick, S.J.D. and Donnelly, J.P. (2005) Higher-order dimensions of personality disorder: hierarchical structure and relationships with the five-factor model, the interpersonal circle, and psychopathy. *Journal of Personality Disorders*, **19**, 597–623.

Blackburn, R. and Renwick, S.J. (1996) Rating scales for measuring the interpersonal circle in forensic psychiatric patients. *Psychological Assessment*, **8**, 76–84.

Blanchard, D.C. and Blanchard, R.J. (2003) What can animal aggression tell us about human aggression? *Hormones and Behavior*, **44**, 171–77.

Brown, D., Fenwick, P.B.C. and Howard, R.C. (1989) The contingent negative variation (CNV) in a Go/No Go avoidance situation: relationships with personality and subjective state. *International Journal of Psychophysiology*, **7**, 5–45.

Carlson, S.R., McLarnon, M.E. and Iacono, W.L. (2007) P300 amplitude, externalizing psychopathology, and earlier-versus later-onset substance-use disorder. *Journal of Abnormal Psychology*, **116**, 565–77.

Coid, J. (1992) DSM-III diagnosis in criminal psychopaths: a way forward. *Criminal Behaviour and Mental Health*, **2**, 78–94.

Coid, J., Kahtan, N., Gault, S. and Jarman, B. (1999) Patients with personality disorder admitted to secure forensic psychiatry services. *British Journal of Psychiatry*, **175**, 528–36.

Coid, J., Yang, M., Tyrer, P. *et al.* (2006) Prevalence and correlates of personality disorder in Great Britain. *British Journal of Psychiatry*, **188**, 423–31.

Crews, F.T., Braun, C.J., Hoplight, B. *et al.* (2000) Binge ethanol consumption causes differential brain damage in young adolescent rats compared with adult rats. *Alcohol: Clinical and Experimental Research*, **24**, 1712–23.

Crews, F.T., Mdzinarishvili, A., Kim, D. *et al.* (2006) Neurogenesis in adolescent brain is potently inhibited by ethanol. *Neuroscience*, **137**, 437–45.

De Bruijn, E.R.A., Grootens, K.P., Verkes, R.J., Buchholz, V., Hummelen, J.W. and Hulstijn, W. (2005) Neural correlates of impulsive responding in borderline personality disorder: ERP evidence for reduced action monitoring. *Journal of Psychiatric Research*, **40**, 428–37.

Dikman, Z.V. and Allen, J.J.B. (2000) Error monitoring during reward and avoidance learning in high- and low-socialized individuals. *Psychophysiology*, **37**, 43–54.

Douglas, K. S. and Skeem, J.L. (2005) Violence risk assessment. Getting specific about being dynamic. *Psychology, Public Policy and Law*, **11**, 347–83.

Giedd, J.N., Blumenthal, J., Jeffries, N.O. *et al.* (1999) Brain development during childhood and adolescence: a longitudinal MRI study. *Nature Neuroscience*, **2**, 861–63.

Gray, J.A. (1981) A critique of Eysenck's theory of personality, in *A Model of Personality* (ed. H.J. Eysenck), Springer Verlag, New York, pp. 246–76.

Hall, J.R., Bernat, E.M. and Patrick, C.J. (2007) Externalizing psychopathology and the error-related negativity. *Journal of Abnormal Psychology*, **18**, 326–33.

Hare, R.D. (2003) *The Hare Psychopathy Checklist – Revised*, 2nd edn, Multi-Health Systems Inc., Toronto.

Harris, G.T., Rice, M.E. and Cormier, C.A. (1991) Psychopathy and violent recidivism. *Law and Human Behavior*, **20**, 625–37.

Howard, R.C. (2001) Bringing brain events to mind: functional systems and brain event-related potentials. *Journal of Psychophysiology*, **15**, 69–79.

Howard, R.C. (2006) How is personality disorder linked to dangerousness? A putative role for early-onset alcohol abuse. *Medical Hypotheses*, **67**, 702–8.

Howard, R.C., Fenton, G.W.F. and Fenwick, P.B.C. (1982) *Event-Related Brain Potentials in Personality and Psychopathology: A Pavlovian Approach*, John Wiley & Sons, Ltd, Research Studies Press, Letchworth.

Howard, R.C., Huband, N., Duggan, C. and Mannion, A. (2008) Exploring the link between personality disorder and criminality in a community sample. *Journal of Personality Disorders*, **22**, 589–603.

Howard, R.C. and Lumsden, J. (1996) A neurophysiological predictor of re-offending in Special Hospital patients. *Criminal Behaviour and Mental Health*, **6**, 147–56.

Howard, R.C. and Lumsden, J. (1997) CNV predicts violent outcomes in patients released from special hospital. *Criminal Behaviour and Mental Health*, **7**, 237–40.

Howard, R.C. and Menkes, D.B. (2007) Changes in brain function during acute cannabis intoxication: preliminary findings suggest a mechanism for cannabis-induced violence. *Criminal Behaviour and Mental Health*, **17**, 113–17.

Huband, N., McMurran, M. , Evans, C. and Duggan, C. (2007) Social problem solving plus psychoeducation for adults with personality disorder: a pragmatic randomised controlled trial. *British Journal of Psychiatry*, **190**, 307–13.

Johnson, P.A., Hurley, R.A., Benkelfat, C. *et al.* (2003) Understanding emotion regulation in borderline personality disorder: contributions of neuroimaging. *Journal of Neuropsychiatry and Clinical Neuroscience*, **15**, 397–402.

Justus, A.N., Finn, P.R. and Steinmetz, J.E. (2001) P300, disinhibited personality, and early-onset alcohol abuse. *Alcoholism: Clinical and Experimental Research*, **25**, 1457–66.

Kamarajan, C., Porjesz, B., Jones, K.A. *et al.* (2005) Spatial-anatomical mapping of NoGo-P3 in the offspring of alcoholics: evidence of cognitive and neural disinhibition as a risk for alcoholism. *Clinical Neurophysiology*, **116**, 1049–61.

Krueger, R.F., Markon, K.E., Patrick, C.J. *et al.* (2007) Linking antisocial behavior, substance use, and personality: an integrative quantitative model of the adult externalizing spectrum. *Journal of Abnormal Psychology*, **116**, 645–66.

Millon, T. (1987) *Millon Clinical Multiaxial Inventory – II*, National Computer Systems, Inc.

Miller, J., Flory, K., Lynam, D. and Leukefeld, C. (2003) A test of the four-factor model of impulsivity-related traits. *Personality and Individual Differences*, **34**, 1403–18.

Mullen, P.E. (1992) Psychopathy: a developmental disorder of ethical action. *Criminal Behaviour and Mental Health*, **2**, 234–44.

Neo, L.H., McCullagh, P. and Howard, R.C. (2001) An electrocortical correlate of a history of alcohol abuse in criminal offenders. *Psychology, Crime and Law*, **7**, 105–17.

Niveau, G. and Dang, C. (2003) Cannabis and violent crime. *Medicine, Science and the Law*, **43**, 115–21.

Ogloff, J.R.P. and Daffern, M. (2006) The dynamic appraisal of situational aggression: an instrument to assess risk of imminent aggression in psychiatric inpatients. *Behavioral Sciences and the Law*, **24**, 799–813.

Oya, H., Adolphs, R., Kawasaki, H. *et al.* (2005) Electrophysiological correlates of reward prediction error recorded in the human prefrontal cortex. *Proceedings of the National Academy of Sciences*, **102**, 8351–6.

Patrick, C.J., Bernat, E.M., Malone, S.M. *et al.* (2006). P300 amplitude as an indicator of externalizing in adolescent males. *Psychophysiology*, **43**, 84–92.

Porter, S. and Woodworth, M. (2006) Psychopathy and aggression, in *Handbook of Psychopathy* (ed. C.J. Patrick), Guilford, New York, pp. 481–94.

Rosahl, S.K. and Knight, R.T. (1995) Role of prefrontal cortex in generation of the contingent negative variation. *Cerebral Cortex*, **2**, 123–34.

Sarkar, J. and Adshead, G. (2006) Personality disorders as disorganisation of attachment and affect regulation. *Advances in Psychiatric Treatment*, **12**, 297–305.

Shapiro, D. (1965) *Neurotic Styles*, Basic Books, New York.

Sircar, R. and Sircar, D. (2006) Repeated alcohol treatment in adolescent rats alters cortical NMDA receptor. *Alcohol*, **39**, 51–58.

Sisk, C.L. and Zehr, J.L. (2005) Pubertal hormones organize the adolescent brain and behavior. *Frontiers in Neuroendocrinology*, **26**, 163–74.

Slawecki, C.J., Betancourt, M., Cole, M. and Ehlers, C.L. (2001) Periadolescent alcohol exposure has lasting effects on adult neurophysiological function in rats. *Developmental Brain Research*, **128**, 63–72.

Strehl, U., Leins, U., Goth, G. *et al.* (2006) Self-regulation of slow cortical potentials: a new treatment for children with attention-deficit/hyperactivity disorder. *Pediatrics*, **118**, e1530–40.

Ullrich, S. and Marneros, A. (2004) Dimensions of personality disorders in offenders. *Criminal Behaviour and Mental Health*, **14**, 202–13.

Ullrich, S. and Marneros, A. (2007) Underlying dimensions of ICD-10 personality disorders: risk factors, childhood antecedents, and adverse outcomes in adulthood. *Journal of Forensic Psychiatry and Psychology*, **18** (1), 44–58.

Von Bertalanffy, O. (1968) *General System Theory: Foundations, Development, Applications*, George Braziller, New York.

Watzke, S., Ullrich, S. and Marneros, A. (2006) Gender- and violence-related prevalence of mental disorders in prisoners. *European Archives of Psychiatry and Clinical Neuroscience*, **256**, 414–21.

White, A.M. and Swartzwelder, S. (2005) Age-related effects of alcohol on memory and memory-related brain function in adolescents and adults. *Recent Developments in Alcohol*, **17**, 161–76.

Whiteside, S.P. and Lynam, D.R. (2001) The five factor model and impulsivity: using a structural model of personality to understand impulsivity. *Personality and Individual Differences*, **30**, 669–89.

Whiteside, S.P. and Lynam, D.R. (2003) Understanding the role of impulsivity and externalizing psychopathology in alcohol abuse: application of the UPPS impulsive behaviour scale. *Experimental and Clinical Psychopharmacology*, **11**, 210–17.

Wingrove, J. and Bond, A.J. (1997) Impulsivity: a state as well as trait variable. Does mood awareness explain low correlations between trait and behavioural measures of impulsivity? *Personality and Individual Differences*, **22**, 333–39.

Zuckerman, M., Kuhlman, D.M., Teta, P. *et al.* (1993) A comparison of three structural models of personality: the big three, the big five, and the alternative five. *Journal of Personality and Social Psychology*, **65**, 757–68.

Chapter 9

THE PROCESSING OF EMOTIONAL EXPRESSION INFORMATION IN INDIVIDUALS WITH PSYCHOPATHY

R. James R. Blair

National Institute of Mental Health, USA

INTRODUCTION

The goal of the current chapter is to consider the ability of individuals with psychopathy to process the emotional expressions of others. This ability is important because responding to the emotional expressions of others is critical for those aspects of empathy that are central to socialization. It appears likely that the selective impairment in the processing of expression information, seen in individuals with psychopathy, leads to their difficulties in socialization and thus to the development of their disorder.

The goals of this paper are threefold. First, I will consider the basic response to emotional expressions at the super-ordinate level; that is, what the empathic process might be. Second, I will consider the nature of the impairment in responding to the emotional expressions of others seen in individuals with psychopathy; that is, what the nature of the impairment is in psychopathy. Third, I will consider the developmental implications of the impairment in responding to the emotional expressions of others seen in individuals with psychopathy; that is, why the impairment in moral reasoning arises.

EMPATHY

The term empathy has been broadly applied to processes where an observer uses information about the internal state of another individual. However, there are a wide variety of definitions of empathy. Some include cognitive perspective taking (also known as Theory of Mind) as a form of empathy (Decety and Moriguchi,

Personality, Personality Disorder and Violence   Edited by Mary McMurran and Richard C. Howard
© 2009 John Wiley & Sons, Ltd

2007), while others stipulate that an emotional reaction, isomorphic to that other individual's affective state, must occur (de Vignemont and Singer, 2006). I will follow here a previous argument (Blair, 2005) that 'empathy' should be considered to subsume a variety of dissociable neuro-cognitive processes and that three main divisions, each reliant on at least partially dissociable neural systems, can be identified: motor, cognitive and emotional empathy. Motor empathy occurs when the individual mirrors the motor responses of an observed actor. The term cognitive empathy has been used where the individual represents the internal mental state (their beliefs, thoughts and intentions) of another individual. Cognitive empathy can be considered to be synonymous with Theory of Mind (see Frith and Frith, 2006). Neither motor nor cognitive empathy is relevant here and thus will not be considered further.

Understanding emotional empathy, the emotional response to another individual's emotional state, is of most relevance to psychopathy. However, there are a variety of positions regarding the neuro-cognitive architecture that mediates emotional empathy. Three will be considered below: the mirror neuron position, the mirror neuron analogy position and the emotional response position.

Emotional Empathy: The Mirror Neuron Position

The term *mirror neurons* comes from research on non-human primates, and refers to neurons seen to respond both when a monkey performs a particular goal-directed action and when it observes another individual performing the same or very similar action (e.g. Rizzolatti, Fogassi and Gallese 2001). On the basis of an overlap in regions recruited in movements and when watching these movements, identified through fMRI work, the suggestion has been made that there is a human mirror neuron system that involves parts of the inferior frontal cortex and posterior parietal cortex (Iacoboni and Mazziotta, 2007). The core importance of this proposal is that the observation of an action leads to the activation of parts of the same cortical neural network that is active during its execution (Gallese, Keysers and Rizzolatti, 2004).

Mirror neurons and the human mirror neuron system have been proposed to be the basis of emotional empathy within perception-action mechanism accounts (Decety and Jackson, 2004; Decety and Moriguchi, 2007; Iacoboni and Mazziotta, 2007; Preston and de Waal, 2002). These accounts suggest that perception of emotion activates in the observer the neural mechanisms that are responsible for the generation of similar emotion. For example, 'while watching someone smile, the observer activates the same facial muscles involved in producing a smile at a sub-threshold level and this would create the corresponding feeling of happiness in the observer' (Decety and Moriguchi, 2007). Potentially, direct evidence was provided by Carr *et al.* (2003). In this study, participants either viewed facial stimuli or viewed facial stimuli while they were asked to 'internally generate the target emotion' (Carr *et al.*, 2003). Carr *et al.* reported that imitation and viewing of emotion 'activated a largely similar network of brain areas'.

There are several difficulties for perception-action accounts of emotional empathy, however (cf. Blair, 2005). In particular, the study held up as providing the most direct evidence (Carr *et al.*, 2003) has notable limitations, including (a) the extent of similarity of the networks is difficult to quantify as conjunction analysis was not used; (b) both conditions involved the viewing of face stimuli and, as such, a degree of overlap of neural response is unsurprising; and (c) a second neuro-imaging study of the same issue reported a *dissociation* between the neural systems involved in face imitation and those involved in the response to a viewed expression (Leslie, Johnson-Frey and Grafton, 2004).

There are additional, more general, difficulties for perception-action accounts of emotional empathy. For example, the majority of studies examining blood oxygen level dependent (BOLD; an indirect measure of neural activity) responses to expression stimuli do not identify activity in regions considered to make up the human mirror neuron system (see Murphy, Nimmo-Smith and Lawrence, 2003). In addition, a perception-action-based account of emotional empathy would seem to necessarily predict that the emotional reaction to the observed emotion is congruent with the emotional reaction shown by the observer. Indeed, the suggestion is that the 'perception of a given behavior in another individual automatically activates one's own representations of that behavior' (p. 75; Decety and Jackson, 2004). In other words, a pained grimace shown by another individual should activate similar responses as pain experienced by the self. While this may frequently be the case (see below), it is not always the case. In one recent study, pain-like neural responses were only seen to observed individuals in pain who had previously interacted with the subjects fairly in a Prisoner's Dilemma game (Singer *et al.*, 2006). If the individuals observed to be in pain had previously acted unfairly to male subjects, no pain-like empathic responses to the observed individuals were observed. Instead, there was recruitment of regions which respond to rewarding stimuli. These last data in particular pose serious difficulties for a perception-action account of empathy. Such an account cannot explain how the context (whether the observed individual is fair or unfair) determines whether the emotion experienced is congruent (pain in the observed and the observer) or incongruent (pain in the observed and pleasure in the observer).

In short, a mirror neuron based account of emotional empathy appears to be inadequate.

Emotional Empathy: The Mirror Neuron Analogy Position

There is a second account of emotional empathy that makes reference to mirror neurons. This account uses the concept of mirror neurons analogously (de Vignemont and Singer, 2006; Gallese, Keysers and Rizzolatti, 2004). Rather than relating to the perception of action, the account stresses the overlap in regions activated when the individual is in a particular emotional state and when observing another individual in that emotional state. The proposal is that a similar mirroring mechanism, bridging first- and third-person experiences, also exists for emotions (Gallese, Keysers and Rizzolatti, 2004). For example, 'when we witness the disgusted facial expressions of someone else, we activate that part of our insula that is also active when we experience disgust' (p. 400; Gallese, Keysers and Rizzolatti, 2004). The idea is that 'the human brain is endowed with structures that are active both during the first- and third-person experience of actions and emotions' (p. 400; Gallese, Keysers and Rizzolatti, 2004).

This second mirror neuron based account of empathy has led to an interesting body of work relating to the response to another individual in pain. Individuals exposed to painful stimulation demonstrate activity in the dorsal anterior cingulate cortex (dACC), insula and primary somatosensory cortex (Peyron, Laurent and Garcia-Larrea, 2000; Rainville, 2002). Exposure to another in pain, whether viewing another's hand being pricked by a needle (Jackson *et al.*, 2006; Jackson, Meltzoff and Decety, 2005; Morrison *et al.*, 2004; Singer *et al.*, 2004) or a pained facial expression (Botvinick *et al.*, 2005), is also associated with activity in dACC and the insula though not primary somatosensory cortex. Interestingly, in a study involving microelectrode exploration of the ACC of 11 patients undergoing bilateral cingulotomy for chronic depression or obsessive-compulsive disorder, a cell in one of these patients was recorded showing responses to pinpricks to the self as well as when observing pinpricks to others (Hutchison *et al.*, 1999). Similarly, a study examining responses to disgusting odors and other individuals smelling the content of a glass and displaying disgust revealed the same region within the anterior insula activated by both (Wicker *et al.*, 2003). Importantly for the argument, conjunction analyses have suggested that the region of dACC responding to pain of the self also responds to the pain of others (Morrison *et al.*, 2004; Singer *et al.*, 2004). However, it should be noted that later work has indicated that this was a function of the spatial smoothing that occurs in fMRI analysis, and that regions of dACC responding to pain of the self also respond to the pain of others may be at least partially dissociable (Morrison and Downing, 2007).

Singer and colleagues' (2006) data showing that a pain response was only shown to observed individuals in pain if they had been fair partners in the Prisoner's Dilemma game is problematic for the mirror neuron analogy position as well; the empathic response is clearly not an automatic mirroring of the observed individuals emotional state. Indeed, to reflect this, Singer and colleagues expanded the position to emphasize an important role for appraisal processes on empathy (de Vignemont and Singer, 2006). They considered two models: one where these appraisal processes modulated the automatic empathic response and one where the emotional cue and emotional context are evaluated by appraisal processes, which then generated the emotional response.

In short, the mirror neuron analogy position of emotional empathy is of interest. The main difficulty facing this position is its explanatory power. In particular, while it may provide an account of emotional empathy for situations where there is an individual to be observed, what about situations where the individual is only verbally described? People appear able to generate emotional empathic reactions to such stimuli (cf. Batson, Fultz and Schoenrade, 1987).

Emotional Empathy: The Emotional Response Position

Rather than make reference to an analogy with mirror neurons, the emotion-based view of empathy considers that the empathic reaction is simply a form of emotional response (Blair, 2003, 2005); that is, the emotional expression is a conditioned or unconditioned stimulus that activates emotion-relevant regions either because this has been innately specified or due to prior learning. Importantly, according to this position, there is nothing intrinsically different in the basic response to a tiger or an electric shock. Indeed, an individual can experience fear because they have been exposed to a tiger, a blue square previously associated with electric shock, or another individual's fearful expression at the sight of the tiger/blue square. The suggestion is that the neuro-cognitive architecture initiating the emotional response in all three cases is identical. There would be differences in the observer's emotional *experience* to each of these events. However, it is argued here that such differences would be a product of the causal reasoning that is part of conscious experience and, in the absence of an adequate model of consciousness, will not be considered further here.

Emotions have been defined as 'states elicited by rewards and punishers, including changes in rewards and punishments' (p. 60; Rolls, 1999). Within this view, emotional expressions are 'reinforcers that modulate the probability that a particular behavior will be performed in the future' (p. 564; Blair, 2003). Emotional expressions are considered to be primary reinforcers; it is thought, for example, that fearful faces, if processed, are innately specified to initiate aversive conditioning and happy faces to initiate appetitive conditioning (Blair, 2003, 2005). Given claims regarding the coarse grained processing capacity of subcortical systems likely to provide this genetically specified information (see Vuilleumier *et al.*, 2003), it is likely that richer representations of facial expressions, mediated through temporal cortical processing, have also become secondary reinforcers (acquiring their reward/punishment status due to pairing with the coarsely processed primary information) (see Blair, 2003, 2005).

The suggestion is that individuals show emotional reactions to stimuli, represented in temporal cortex, which are either primary reinforcers themselves or have been previously associated with reinforcement. Such stimuli can be non-social (e.g. the large teeth of the tiger or the blue square) or social (e.g. the fearful expression of another or the description of a frightening event suffered by another). If they are social, the activation of the consequent emotional response can be considered to be empathic. Importantly, the response to 'emotional stimuli' is not automatic but under considerable top-down attentional control (thought to be mediated by lateral regions of frontal and parietal cortex). This was seen clearly in Singer's elegant study showing that a pain response was only shown to be observed in individuals in pain if they had been fair partners in the Prisoner's Dilemma game (if they were unfair partners, their apparent pain activated regions were implicated in reward processing in male participants) (de Vignemont and Singer, 2006). It has also been seen with respect to the response to fearful expressions. Attentional manipulations that reduce the processing of fearful expressions reduce the response of the amygdala to these expressions (Mitchell *et al.*, 2007; Pessoa, 2005).

Emotional Empathy as Emotional Responding: A Unitary System or Multiple Systems?

A variety of researchers have ascribed, either explicitly or implicitly, to unitary models of emotion. This tradition is exemplified in MacLean's limbic system theory of emotion (MacLean, 1949) and can also be seen in more recent work (Damasio,

1994; Kiehl, 2006). Alternative positions have argued for dual system models; that is, at least partially separable systems for processing positive and negative emotions (e.g. Davidson, 2004). A third tradition has argued for multiple emotion systems (Blair, 2003; Ekman, 1992; Izard, 1977). This divergence of opinion has been present in the expression processing literature with arguments as to whether different neural systems process different emotional expressions. There have been suggestions, for example, that the amygdala responds to all emotional expressions (Fitzgerald *et al.*, 2006; Winston, O'Doherty and Dolan, 2003), while other work has not supported this view (Blair *et al.*, 1999; LaBar *et al.*, 2003; Morris *et al.*, 1996). However, a recent meta-analytic review has partially settled this debate by reporting that the BOLD responses associated with fear, disgust and anger differed significantly from one another and from the BOLD response to happy expressions (Murphy, Nimmo-Smith and Lawrence, 2003).

Assuming that there are at least partially separable neural responses to different emotional expressions, the function of these separable systems must be considered. For example, one influential view suggests that the 'amygdala monitors the environment for stimuli that signal an increased probability of threat' and that the 'magnitude of amygdala activation may be inversely related to the amount of information concerning the nature of the threat' (p. 180; Whalen, 1998). According to this view, fearful faces 'engage the amygdala to a greater degree than angry faces because they require more information concerning the nature of a probable threat' (p. 180; Whalen, 1998). Further, fearful expressions are considered more ambiguous threats than angry expressions because they provide less information regarding the source of the threat and thus lead to increased amygdala activity.

A second view suggests that fearful faces should be viewed as 'reinforcers that modulate the probability that a particular behavior will be performed in the future' and this function of reinforcement leads to amygdala activity (p. 564; Blair, 2003). In contrast, angry expressions are considered to 'serve to inform the observer to stop the current behavioral action' and 'can be seen as triggers for response reversal' (p. 564; Blair, 2003). In line with this position, angry faces have been shown to activate regions of inferior frontal cortex (Murphy, Nimmo-Smith and Lawrence, 2003). This region is consistently implicated in reversal learning (Budhani *et al.*, 2007; Cools *et al.*, 2002).

A recent study by Hooker and colleagues (2006) allowed a direct contrast of these views. In this study, healthy participants were presented with images of individuals displaying fearful and happy expressions either toward novel objects (i.e. probable threats) or empty space (i.e. no information was provided regarding the nature of the threat). If amygdala activation was inversely related to the amount of information regarding the nature of the threat (i.e. related to increased ambiguity), then there should be greater activation to the fearful expression when presented alone, relative to when it was presented as a response to an object. Alternatively, if the amygdala treats particular expressions as reinforcers (i.e. cues to stimulus-reinforcement learning), then the amygdala should show greater activity when there were object stimuli to associate with the expression reinforcement. The data clearly supported the latter suggestion; there was significantly greater amygdala activity when there were object stimuli to associate with the expression reinforcement (Hooker *et al.*, 2006). In short, and as noted by Hooker and colleagues, the data indicated that the 'amygdala uses social signals to rapidly and flexibly learn threatening and rewarding associations' (p. 8915).

The argument thus suggested here is that emotional expressions are reinforcers that have specific communicatory functions, imparting specific information to the observer (Blair, 2003, 2005). From this view, emotional empathy is defined as the translation of the communication by the observer. Data suggest that different brain regions respond to different types of reinforcer. For example, the amygdala is critical for fear-based conditioning (Davis, 2000; LeDoux, 2000). It is thus unsurprising that fearful expressions preferentially activate the amygdala (Blair, 2003). This is because one role of fearful expressions may be to rapidly convey information to others that a novel stimulus is aversive and should be avoided (Mineka and Cook, 1993). The insula, similarly, is critical for taste aversion learning (e.g. Cubero, Thiele and Bernstein, 1999). It is thus unsurprising that disgusted expressions preferentially activate the insula (Phillips *et al.*, 1998; Sprengelmeyer *et al.*, 1998). Disgusted expressions are reinforcers that most frequently provide valence information about foods (Rozin, Haidt and McCauley, 1993); for an extended version of this argument, see Blair (2003, 2005).

Angry expressions are used to curtail the behavior of others when social rules/expectations have been violated (Averill, 1982). They appear to serve to inform the observer to stop the current behavioral action rather than necessarily conveying any information as to whether that action should be initiated in the future. In other words, angry expressions can be seen as triggers for response reversal (Blair, 2003; Blair *et al.*, 1999). Inferior frontal cortex is important for response reversal (Budhani *et al.*, 2007; Cools *et al.*, 2002; O'Doherty *et al.*, 2001). Interestingly, similar areas of inferior frontal cortex are activated by angry expressions and by response reversal as a function of contingency change (Blair *et al.*, 1999; Sprengelmeyer *et al.*, 1998).

RESPONDING TO EMOTIONAL EXPRESSIONS IN PSYCHOPATHY

In the second section of this chapter, three questions will be considered. First, are there any indications of impairment in expression processing in individuals with psychopathy? Second, are there indications of *generalized* impairment in the processing of expressions in individuals with psychopathy? Third, what is the nature of the impairment in expression processing seen in individuals with psychopathy? These questions will be considered in turn.

Are There Any Indications of Impairment in Expression Processing in Individuals with Psychopathy?

As noted above, an impairment in empathy is one of the defining features of psychopathy (Hare, 2003). As such, a degree of impairment in processing the emotional expressions of others in individuals with the disorder might be expected. Three main methodologies have been used to examine expression processing in psychopathy. Most studies have indexed the ability to process emotional expressions through emotion recognition scores (Blair *et al.*, 2001; Dolan and Fullam, 2006; Glass and Newman, 2006; Kosson *et al.*, 2002). However, some studies have indexed skin conductance responses to expression stimuli (Aniskiewicz, 1979; Blair *et al.*, 1997) or BOLD responses (Deeley *et al.*, 2006; Gordon, Baird and End, 2004; Marsh *et al.*, 2008).

With respect to the expression recognition literature, there have been isolated reports of no impairment in expression recognition or even superior recognition of fearful expressions in individuals with psychopathy in some conditions (Glass and Newman, 2006). However, rather more consistently studies have reported evidence of impaired expression recognition in individuals with psychopathy and individuals with subclinical psychopathic tendencies (e.g. Blair *et al.*, 2001, 2004; Dolan and Fullam, 2006; Kosson *et al.*, 2002; Montagne *et al.*, 2005). Moreover, a meta-analysis of this literature which included findings from other predominantly instrumentally aggressive populations reported clear evidence of expression recognition impairment in individuals with psychopathy (Marsh and Blair, 2007). In addition, the skin conductance response studies have relatively consistently reported reduced autonomic responses in individuals with psychopathy to the distress of others (Aniskiewicz, 1979; Blair, 1999; Blair *et al.*, 1997; House and Milligan, 1976). Similarly, the few studies that have examined neural responses via BOLD responses have reported anomalous responding to expression stimuli (see below) in individuals with psychopathic tendencies (Deeley *et al.*, 2006; Gordon, Baird and End, 2004; Marsh *et al.*, 2008).

In short, there are strong indications that individuals with psychopathy do show impairment in expression recognition.

Are There Indications of Generalized Impairment in the Processing of Expressions in Psychopathy?

Unitary models of empathy such as the perception-action account (Decety and Jackson, 2004; Decety and Moriguchi, 2007; Iacoboni and Mazziotta, 2007; Preston and de Waal, 2002) require that a disorder of emotional empathy, such as psychopathy, should show generalized impairment in expression processing. The mirror neurons necessary for responding to the emotional expressions of others should be disrupted. Such accounts have difficulty explaining selective impairments in emotional processing and consider that a single system processes all expressions (cf. Carr *et al.*, 2003). Could there be generalized impairment in the processing of the emotional expression of others in psychopathy?

Across the studies examining expression recognition, there have been reports of impairment in the processing of a variety of expressions in individuals with psychopathy. Thus, there have been reports of impaired recognition of sad, fearful (Blair *et al.*, 2001; Dolan and Fullam, 2006) and disgusted expressions (Kosson *et al.*, 2002). This might indicate that there is generalized expression recognition in individuals with psychopathy. However, it should be noted that findings of recognition deficits for fearful expressions are more common than those for sad expressions (e.g. Blair *et al.*, 2001, 2004; Dadds *et al.*, 2006; Dolan and Fullam,

2006; Montagne *et al.*, 2005). Moreover, the impairment for disgusted expressions was only seen in one study and then only when the participants responded with their left hands and not when they responded with their right hands (Kosson *et al.*, 2002). In addition, the results of the recent meta-analysis found no evidence of impairment for the recognition of angry, disgusted, happy or surprised expressions. This analysis found only that individuals with psychopathy showed significant impairment for the recognition of fearful and, to a lesser extent, sad expressions (Marsh and Blair, 2007).

The studies examining skin conductance and BOLD responses have been generally less informative regarding whether the impairment in expression processing in psychopathy is generalized or selective. The skin conductance literature only properly investigated the response of individuals with psychopathy to distress cues, rather than other expression stimuli additionally (Aniskiewicz, 1979; Blair, 1999; Blair *et al.*, 1997; House and Milligan, 1976). Two of the studies did include an angry expression in the set of comparison 'threat' stimuli and found no evidence of reduced skin conductance responses to these stimuli in individuals with psychopathy (Blair, 1999; Blair *et al.*, 1997), a result similar to findings by Patrick and colleagues (Levenston *et al.*, 2000; Patrick, Bradley and Lang, 1993). However, the response to angry expressions in isolation was not examined. Similarly, the studies examining BOLD responses have typically collapsed across expression categories (Deeley *et al.*, 2006; Gordon, Baird and End, 2004) and thus cannot inform this issue. However, Marsh and colleagues (2008) did observe that their children with psychopathic tendencies only showed anomalous responding in response to fearful and not angry or neutral expressions. These data are clearly in line with the expression recognition data and support the suggestion of a selective impairment.

One set of findings, or lack of findings, is worth noting from the fMRI studies. If psychopathy was related to impairment in the mirror neuron system, then individuals with psychopathy should show impairment in the mirror neuron system when responding to emotional expressions. However, there are no data to indicate that this is the case. Individuals with psychopathic tendencies showed no indications of reduced activity in the human mirror neuron system in any of the three studies that have examined response to emotional expression stimuli (Deeley *et al.*, 2006; Gordon, Baird and End, 2004; Marsh *et al.*, 2008).

In short, currently there are no reasons to believe that there is impairment in the mirror neuron system in individuals with psychopathy. Moreover, the impairment in expression processing appears to be selective rather than generalized.

What Is the Nature of the Impairment in Expression Processing Seen in Individuals with Psychopathy?

As noted above, the recent meta-analysis of the expression recognition data in individuals with psychopathy and other instrumentally aggressive populations demonstrated that the deficit was selective (Marsh and Blair, 2007). The recognition of fearful, and to a lesser extent sad, emotional expressions, was significantly impaired. In contrast, there was no significant impairment for happy, surprised, angry or disgusted expressions.

The selective nature of the expression recognition impairment suggests a degree of specificity in the neural regions that may be dysfunctional in individuals with this disorder. An impairment in the processing of fearful expressions has been particularly associated with damage to the amygdala (Adolphs, 2002). Moreover, meta-analytic work has shown that the amygdala is significantly more responsive to fearful relative to other expressions (Murphy, Nimmo-Smith and Lawrence, 2003). Amygdala dysfunction was first related to the development of psychopathy by Patrick (Patrick, 1994) and an amygdala-centric account of this disorder has received considerable development and refinement (see below; Blair, 2007; 2001, 2003, 2005). More recently, others have also implicated amygdala dysfunction in psychopathy (Dadds et al., 2006; Kiehl, 2006; Viding, 2004).

Consistent with these suggestions of amygdala dysfunction in psychopathy, two of the three fMRI studies examining BOLD responses in individuals with psychopathic tendencies to expression stimuli have reported reduced amygdala activity to facial expressions (Gordon, Baird and End, 2004; Marsh et al., 2008). The third reported a reduced differential response within fusiform cortex to fearful expressions relative to neutral expressions in the individuals with psychopathy (Deeley et al., 2006). This reduced differential response within fusiform cortex was also seen in the study by Marsh et al. (2008). These data would be expected if this disorder was associated with amygdala dysfunction – there should be a consequent reduction in priming of emotion-relevant representations in temporal cortex by reciprocal amygdala activation (though only Marsh et al. (2008) observed reduced amygdala activity).

In short, the impairment in expression processing seen in psychopathy is selective – specifically responding to fearful and sad expressions is affected. This impairment appears to be related to the amygdala dysfunction that is seen in individuals with this disorder.

DEVELOPMENTAL IMPLICATIONS OF THIS SELECTIVE IMPAIRMENT IN EXPRESSION PROCESSING: THE DIFFICULTIES IN SOCIALIZATION

It has been argued that the impairment in expression processing seen in individuals with psychopathy is important with respect to the emergence of the disorder because an adequate response to the fear and sadness of others is critical for appropriate moral socialization (Blair, 1995). Considerable recent work has suggested the importance of emotional responses for moral development (Blair, 1995; Greene et al., 2001; Moll et al., 2002; Nichols, 2004; Prinz, 2007). A specific version of this view suggests that healthy individuals are predisposed to find the distress of others aversive and that we learn to avoid actions associated with this distress (i.e. acts that harm others; Blair, 1995).

The suggestion stresses the roles of the amygdala and ventromedial prefrontal cortex (vmPFC) (see Blair, 2007). In addition to its role in responding to expressions, the amygdala is crucial for stimulus-reinforcement learning (Davis and Whalen, 2001; Everitt et al., 2003). This learning allows representations of conditioned stimuli within temporal cortex to be linked to emotional responses mediated by the amygdala and other structures. In other words, the amygdala allows the individual to learn the goodness and badness of objects and actions. The suggestion is that fearful and sad expressions serve as aversive reinforcers and thus the individual learns to avoid stimuli associated with these expressions (Blair, 1995, 2007). In short, the basis of care-based morality, learning that some actions harm others and because of this are to be avoided, relies on the critical roles of the amygdala in stimulus-reinforcement learning and responding to distress cues. In psychopathy, aversive conditioning (Birbaumer *et al.*, 2005) and the response to other's fear (Blair *et al.*, 2001) are profoundly impaired. These impairments mean that the individual with psychopathy is significantly more difficult to socialize (Oxford, Cavell and Hughes, 2003).

The amygdala sends outputs forward to vmPFC. The basic suggestion is that the amygdala provides reinforcement expectancy information to orbitofrontal cortex (OFC)/vmPFC which then represents this information (Schoenbaum and Roesch, 2005). Human neuro-imaging work has confirmed the role of the OFC/vmPFC in outcome representation (Knutson and Cooper, 2005).

The suggestion is that the individual's 'automatic moral attitude' to a care-based moral transgression thus involves the activation of the amygdala by the conditioned stimulus that is the individual's representation of the moral transgression (Blair, 2007). The amygdala then provides expected reinforcement (both positively and negatively valenced) information which is represented as a valenced outcome within vmPFC. Other systems then use this information to select appropriate responses (Blair, 2007). Indeed, considerable fMRI work indicates that vmPFC and, to a lesser extent, the amygdala has a major role in moral reasoning (Greene *et al.*, 2004; Harenski and Hamann, 2006; Heekeren *et al.*, 2005; Luo *et al.*, 2006; Moll *et al.*, 2002). Dysfunction in the amygdala and vmPFC should thus lead to problems in moral reasoning. Problems with moral reasoning are seen in individuals with psychopathy (Blair, 1995, 1997).

In short, the selective impairment in expression processing seen in psychopathy interferes with socialization. Moreover, due to the neural systems that are dysfunctional, care-based moral reasoning is disturbed. The individual is thus less likely to learn to avoid actions that harm others and is impaired when reasoning about whether such actions should be undertaken.

CONCLUSIONS

There are four main conclusions that can be drawn from the work reviewed above:

- First, it appears that mirror neuron based accounts of emotional empathy are unsatisfactory. A central tenet of such accounts – that the neurons responding to the action by the self also respond when the action is committed by another – is violated by the data from Singer *et al.* (2006). In this study, males only showed an empathic response to individuals in pain that had been previously fair to them and not to those who had not. In addition, such accounts cannot explain how we can experience empathic emotional reactions simply to descriptions of another individual's distressing situation.

- Second, mirror neuron analogy based accounts of empathy suffer with respect to predictive power. While they do predict an overlap in regions responding to another's pain (or fear or disgust) as well as pain to the self, they do not predict that other stimuli, such as non-social associated with the pain, should also activate these very same regions. In contrast, such results are directly predicted by emotion-based accounts of emotional empathy.
- Third, if emotional empathy is a form of emotional response then it is to be expected that different regions will respond to different emotional expressions because of the type of emotional learning that these emotional expressions engage. This is seen and it can be predicted that there will be psychiatric or neurological conditions that may be found with selective empathy impairments for disgust or anger in other individuals.
- Fourth, the empathy impairment seen in individuals with psychopathy is not generalized but is, in contrast, relatively selective. Their difficulty is in processing the fearfulness and sadness of others. This impairment relates to dysfunction within the amygdala and vmPFC. Developmentally, this impairment leads to atypical moral development, interference with socialization and impaired moral reasoning.

The importance of this work is in its future clinical implications. While there is a relative consensus implicating the amygdala and vmPFC in psychopathy (Blair, 2001, 2007; Dadds *et al.*, 2006; Kiehl, 2006; Patrick, 1994), we currently are unable to treat this disorder. However, even if we obtained a pharmacological compound that allowed increased amygdala and vmPFC responding in individuals with psychopathy, this is only going to be fully useful with a full consideration of the functional impact of their impairment. In other words, our knowledge of the expression processing deficit and the impairment in socialization means that we should know that any pharmacological treatment needs to be combined with explicit socialization such that the individual learns the actions to avoid those actions which induce sadness and fear in others.

REFERENCES

Adolphs, R. (2002) Neural systems for recognizing emotion. *Current Opinion in Neurobiology*, **12**, 169–77.

Aniskiewicz, A.S. (1979) Autonomic components of vicarious conditioning and psychopathy. *Journal of Clinical Psychology*, **35**, 60–7.

Averill, J.R. (1982) *Anger and Aggression: An Essay on Emotion*, Springer, New York.

Batson, C.D., Fultz, J. and Schoenrade, P.A. (1987) Adults' emotional reactions to the distress of others, in *Empathy and its Development* (eds N. Eisenberg and J. Strayer), Cambridge University Press, Cambridge, pp. 163–85.

Birbaumer, N., Veit, R., Lotze, M. *et al.* (2005) Deficient fear conditioning in psychopathy: a functional magnetic resonance imaging study. *Archives of General Psychiatry*, **62**, 799–805.

Blair, R.J. (2007) The amygdala and ventromedial prefrontal cortex in morality and psychopathy. *Trends in Cognitive Sciences*, **11**, 387–92.

Blair, R.J.R. (1995) A cognitive developmental approach to morality: investigating the psychopath. *Cognition*, **57**, 1–29.

Blair, R.J.R. (1997) Moral reasoning in the child with psychopathic tendencies. *Personality and Individual Differences*, **22**, 731–9.

Blair, R.J.R. (1999) Responsiveness to distress cues in the child with psychopathic tendencies. *Personality and Individual Differences*, **27**, 135–45.

Blair, R.J.R. (2001) Neuro-cognitive models of aggression, the antisocial personality disorders and psychopathy. *Journal of Neurology, Neurosurgery and Psychiatry*, **71**, 727–31.

Blair, R.J.R. (2003) Facial expressions, their communicatory functions and neuro-cognitive substrates. *Philosophical Transactions of the Royal Society of London. Series B, Biological Sciences*, **358**, 561–72.

Blair, R.J.R. (2005) Responding to the emotions of others: dissociating forms of empathy through the study of typical and psychiatric populations. *Consciousness and Cognition*, **14**, 698–718.

Blair, R.J.R., Colledge, E., Murray, L. and Mitchell, D.G. (2001) A selective impairment in the processing of sad and fearful expressions in children with psychopathic tendencies. *Journal of Abnormal Child Psychology*, **29**, 491–8.

Blair, R.J.R., Jones, L., Clark, F. and Smith, M. (1997) The psychopathic individual: a lack of responsiveness to distress cues? *Psychophysiology*, **34**, 192–8.

Blair, R.J.R., Mitchell, D.G.V., Colledge, E. *et al.* (2004) Reduced sensitivity to other's fearful expressions in psychopathic individuals. *Personality and Individual Differences*, **37**, 1111–21.

Blair, R.J.R., Morris, J.S., Frith, C.D. *et al.* (1999) Dissociable neural responses to facial expressions of sadness and anger. *Brain*, **122**, 883–93.

Botvinick, M., Jha, A.P., Bylsma, L.M. *et al.* (2005) Viewing facial expressions of pain engages cortical areas involved in the direct experience of pain. *Neuroimage*, **25**, 312–9.

Budhani, S., Marsh, A.A., Pine, D.S. and Blair, R.J. (2007) Neural correlates of response reversal: considering acquisition. *Neuroimage*, **34**, 1754–65.

Carr, L., Iacoboni, M., Dubeau, M.C. *et al.* (2003) Neural mechanisms of empathy in humans: a relay from neural systems for imitation to limbic areas. *Proceedings of the National Academy of Sciences of the United States of America*, **100**, 5497–502.

Cools, R., Clark, L., Owen, A.M. and Robbins, T.W. (2002) Defining the neural mechanisms of probabilistic reversal learning using event-related functional magnetic resonance imaging. *Journal of Neuroscience*, **22**, 4563–7.

Cubero, I., Thiele, T.E. and Bernstein, I.L. (1999) Insular cortex lesions and taste aversion learning: effects of conditioning method and timing of lesion. *Brain Research*, **839**, 323–30.

Dadds, M.R., Perry, Y., Hawes, D.J. *et al.* (2006) Attention to the eyes and fear-recognition deficits in child psychopathy. *British Journal of Psychiatry*, **189**, 280–1.

Damasio, A.R. (1994) *Descartes' Error: Emotion, Rationality and the Human Brain*, Putnam (Grosset Books), New York.

Davidson, R.J. (2004) What does the prefrontal cortex 'do' in affect: perspectives on frontal EEG asymmetry research. *Biological Psychology*, **67**, 219–33.

Davis, M. (2000) The role of the amygdala in conditioned and unconditioned fear and anxiety, in *The Amygdala: A Functional Analysis* (ed. J.P. Aggleton), Oxford University Press, Oxford, pp. 289–310.

Davis, M. and Whalen, P.J. (2001) The amygdala: vigilance and emotion. *Molecular Psychiatry*, **6**, 13–34.

de Vignemont, F. and Singer, T. (2006) The empathic brain: how, when and why? *Trends in Cognitive Sciences*, **10**, 435–41.

Decety, J. and Jackson, P.L. (2004) The functional architecture of human empathy. *Behavioral and Cognitive Neuroscience Reviews*, **3**, 71–100.

Decety, J. and Moriguchi, Y. (2007) The empathic brain and its dysfunction in psychiatric populations: implications for intervention across different clinical conditions. *Biopsychosocial Medicine*, doi: 10.1186/1751-0759-1-22.

Deeley, Q., Daly, E., Surguladze, S. *et al.* (2006) Facial emotion processing in criminal psychopathy. Preliminary functional magnetic resonance imaging study. *British Journal of Psychiatry*, **189**, 533–9.

Dolan, M. and Fullam, R. (2006) Face affect recognition deficits in personality-disordered offenders: association with psychopathy. *Psychological Medicine*, **36**, 1563–9.

Ekman, P. (1992) Are there basic emotions? *Psychological Review*, **99**, 550–3.

Everitt, B.J., Cardinal, R.N., Parkinson, J.A. and Robbins, T.W. (2003) Appetitive behavior: impact of amygdala-dependent mechanisms of emotional learning. *Annual New York Academy of Sciences*, **985**, 233–50.

Fitzgerald, D.A., Angstadt, M., Jelsone, L.M. *et al.* (2006) Beyond threat: amygdala reactivity across multiple expressions of facial affect. *Neuroimage*, **30**, 1441–8.

Frith, C.D. and Frith, U. (2006) The neural basis of mentalizing. *Neuron*, **50**, 531–4.

Gallese, V., Keysers, C. and Rizzolatti, G. (2004) A unifying view of the basis of social cognition. *Trends in Cognitive Science*, **8**, 396–403.

Glass, S.J. and Newman, J.P. (2006) Recognition of facial affect in psychopathic offenders. *Journal of Abnormal Psychology*, **115**, 815–20.

Gordon, H.L., Baird, A.A. and End, A. (2004) Functional differences among those high and low on a trait measure of psychopathy. *Biological Psychiatry*, **56**, 516–21.

Greene, J.D., Nystrom, L.E., Engell, A.D. *et al.* (2004) The neural bases of cognitive conflict and control in moral judgment. *Neuron*, **44**, 389–400.

Greene, J.D., Sommerville, R.B., Nystrom, L.E. *et al.* (2001) An fMRI investigation of emotional engagement in moral judgment. *Science*, **293**, 1971–2.

Hare, R.D. (2003) *Hare Psychopathy Checklist-Revised (PCL-R; 2nd edn)*, Multi Health Systems, Toronto.

Harenski, C.L. and Hamann, S. (2006) Neural correlates of regulating negative emotions related to moral violations. *Neuroimage*, **30**, 313–24.

Heekeren, H.R., Wartenburger, I., Schmidt, H. *et al.* (2005) Influence of bodily harm on neural correlates of semantic and moral decision-making. *Neuroimage*, **24**, 887–97.

Hooker, C.I., Germine, L.T., Knight, R.T. and D'Esposito, M. (2006) Amygdala response to facial expressions reflects emotional learning. *Journal of Neuroscience*, **26**, 8915–22.

House, T.H. and Milligan, W.L. (1976) Autonomic responses to modeled distress in prison psychopaths. *Journal of Personality and Social Psychology*, **34**, 556–60.

Hutchison, W.D., Davis, K.D., Lozano, A.M. *et al.* (1999) Pain-related neurons in the human cingulate cortex. *Nature Neuroscience*, **2**, 403–5.

Iacoboni, M. and Mazziotta, J.C. (2007) Mirror neuron system: basic findings and clinical applications. *Annals of Neurology*, **62**, 213–8.

Izard, C.E. (1977) *Human Emotions*, Plenum, New York.

Jackson, P.L., Brunet, E., Meltzoff, A.N. and Decety, J. (2006) Empathy examined through the neural mechanisms involved in imagining how I feel versus how you feel pain. *Neuropsychologia*, **44**, 752–61.

Jackson, P.L., Meltzoff, A.N. and Decety, J. (2005) How do we perceive the pain of others? A window into the neural processes involved in empathy. *Neuroimage*, **24**, 771–9.

Kiehl, K.A. (2006) A cognitive neuroscience perspective on psychopathy: Evidence for paralimbic system dysfunction. *Psychiatry Research*.

Knutson, B. and Cooper, J.C. (2005) Functional magnetic resonance imaging of reward prediction. *Current Opinion in Neurology*, **18**, 411–7.

Kosson, D.S., Suchy, Y., Mayer, A.R. and Libby, J. (2002) Facial affect recognition in criminal psychopaths. *Emotion*, **2**, 398–411.

LaBar, K.S., Crupain, M.J., Voyvodic, J.T. and McCarthy, G. (2003) Dynamic perception of facial affect and identity in the human brain. *Cerebral Cortex*, **13**, 1023–33.

LeDoux, J.E. (2000) The amygdala and emotion: a view through fear, in *The Amygdala: A Functional Analysis* (ed. J.P. Aggleton), Oxford University Press, Oxford, pp. 289–310.

Leslie, K.R., Johnson-Frey, S.H. and Grafton, S.T. (2004) Functional imaging of face and hand imitation: towards a motor theory of empathy. *Neuroimage*, **21**, 601–7.

Levenston, G.K., Patrick, C.J., Bradley, M.M. and Lang, P.J. (2000) The psychopath as observer: emotion and attention in picture processing. *Journal of Abnormal Psychology*, **109**, 373–86.

Luo, Q., Nakic, M., Wheatley, T. *et al.* (2006) The neural basis of implicit moral attitude – an IAT study using event-related fMRI. *Neuroimage*, **30**, 1449–57.

MacLean, P.D. (1949) Psychosomatic disease and the 'visceral brain': recent developments bearing on the Papez theory of emotion. *Psychosomatic Medicine*, **11**, 338–53.

Marsh, A.A. and Blair, R.J. (2007) Deficits in facial affect recognition among antisocial populations: a meta-analysis. *Neuroscience and Biobehavioral Reviews*.

Marsh, A.A., Finger, E.C., Mitchell, D.G.V. *et al.* (2008) Reduced amygdala response to fearful expressions in adolescents with callous-unemotional traits and disruptive behavior disorders. *American Journal of Psychiatry*, **165**, 712–20.

Mineka, S. and Cook, M. (1993) Mechanisms involved in the observational conditioning of fear. *Journal of Experimental Psychology: General*, **122**, 23–38.

Mitchell, D.G., Nakic, M., Fridberg, D. *et al.* (2007) The impact of processing load on emotion. *Neuroimage*, **34**, 1299–309.

Moll, J., de Oliveira-Souza, R., Eslinger, P.J. *et al.* (2002) The neural correlates of moral sensitivity: a functional magnetic resonance imaging investigation of basic and moral emotions. *Journal of Neuroscience*, **22**, 2730–6.

Montagne, B., van Honk, J., Kessels, R.P.C. *et al.* (2005) Reduced efficiency in recognising fear in subjects scoring high on psychopathic personality characteristics. *Personality and Individual Differences*, **38**, 5–11.

Morris, J.S., Frith, C.D., Perrett, D.I. *et al.* (1996) A differential response in the human amygdala to fearful and happy facial expressions. *Nature*, **383**, 812–5.

Morrison, I. and Downing, P.E. (2007) Organization of felt and seen pain responses in anterior cingulate cortex. *Neuroimage*, **37**, 642–51.

Morrison, I., Lloyd, D., di Pellegrino, G. and Roberts, N. (2004) Vicarious responses to pain in anterior cingulate cortex: is empathy a multisensory issue? *Cognitive, Affective and Behavioral Neuroscience*, **4**, 270–8.

Murphy, F.C., Nimmo-Smith, I. and Lawrence, A.D. (2003) Functional neuroanatomy of emotions: a meta-analysis. *Cognitive, Affective and Behavioral Neuroscience*, **3**, 207–33.

Nichols, S. (2004) *Sentimental Rules: On the Natural Foundations of Moral Judgment*, Oxford University Press, New York.

O'Doherty, J., Kringelbach, M.L., Rolls, E.T. *et al.* (2001) Abstract reward and punishment representations in the human orbitofrontal cortex. *Nature Neuroscience*, **4**, 95–102.

Oxford, M., Cavell, T.A. and Hughes, J.N. (2003) Callous-unemotional traits moderate the relation between ineffective parenting and child externalizing problems: a partial replication and extension. *Journal of Clinical Child and Adolescent Psychology*, **32**, 577–85.

Patrick, C.J. (1994) Emotion and psychopathy: startling new insights. *Psychophysiology*, **31**, 319–30.

Patrick, C.J., Bradley, M.M. and Lang, P.J. (1993) Emotion in the criminal psychopath: startle reflex modulation. *Journal of Abnormal Psychology*, **102**, 82–92.

Pessoa, L. (2005) To what extent are emotional visual stimuli processed without attention and awareness? *Current Opinion in Neurobiology*, **15**, 188–96.

Peyron, R., Laurent, B. and Garcia-Larrea, L. (2000) Functional imaging of brain responses to pain: a review and meta-analysis. *Clinical Neurophysiology*, **30**, 263–88.

Phillips, M.L., Young, A.W., Scott, S.K. *et al.* (1998) Neural responses to facial and vocal expressions of fear and disgust. *Proceedings of the Royal Society of London, B: Biological Sciences*, **265**, 1809–17.

Preston, S.D. and de Waal, F.B. (2002) Empathy: its ultimate and proximate bases. *Behavioral and Brain Sciences*, **25**, 1–20.

Prinz, J. (2007) *The Emotional Construction of Morals*, Oxford University Press, New York.

Rainville, P. (2002) Brain mechanisms of pain affect and pain modulation. *Current Opinion in Neurobiology*, **12**, 195–204.

Rizzolatti, G., Fogassi, L. and Gallese, V. (2001) Neurophysiological mechanisms underlying the understanding and imitation of action. *Nature Reviews. Neuroscience*, **2**, 661–70.

Rolls, E.T. (1999) *The Brain and Emotion*, Oxford University Press, Oxford.

Rozin, P., Haidt, J. and McCauley, C.R. (1993) Disgust, in *Handbook of Emotions* (eds M. Lewis and J.M. Haviland), Guilford, New York, pp. 575–94.

Schoenbaum, G. and Roesch, M. (2005) Orbitofrontal cortex, associative learning, and expectancies. *Neuron*, **47**, 633–6.

Singer, T., Seymour, B., O'Doherty, J. *et al.* (2004) Empathy for pain involves the affective but not sensory components of pain [see comment]. *Science*, **303**, 1157–62.

Singer, T., Seymour, B., O'Doherty, J.P. *et al.* (2006) Empathic neural responses are modulated by the perceived fairness of others. *Nature*, **439**, 466–9.

Sprengelmeyer, R., Rausch, M., Eysel, U.T. and Przuntek, H. (1998) Neural structures associated with the recognition of facial basic emotions. *Proceedings of the Royal Society of London, B: Biological Sciences*, **265**, 1927–31.

Viding, E. (2004) Annotation: understanding the development of psychopathy. *Journal of Child Psychology and Psychiatry and Allied Disciplines*, **45**, 1329–37.

Vuilleumier, P., Armony, J.L., Driver, J. and Dolan, R.J. (2003) Distinct spatial frequency sensitivities for processing faces and emotional expressions. *Nature Neuroscience*, **6**, 624–31.

Whalen, P.J. (1998) Fear, vigilance, and ambiguity: initial neuroimaging studies of the human amygdala. *Current directions in psychological science*, **7**, 177–88.

Wicker, B., Keysers, C., Plailly, J. *et al.* (2003) Both of us disgusted in *my* insula: the common neuron basis of seeing and feeling disgust. *Neuron*, **40**, 655–64.

Winston, J.S., O'Doherty, J. and Dolan, R.J. (2003) Common and distinct neural responses during direct and incidental processing of multiple facial emotions. *Neuroimage*, **20**, 84–97.

Chapter 10

ANGRY AFFECT, AGGRESSION AND PERSONALITY DISORDER

KEVIN HOWELLS

University of Nottingham, UK

> You will not be punished for your anger, you will be punished by your anger
> Gautama Siddhartha, the founder of Buddhism, 563–483 BC

Why should anger be a focus of attention in clinical and forensic psychology and psychiatry and in considering the interpersonal problems of people with personality disorder? Anger is, after all, a normal experience and a common one for the vast majority of people, as revealed by studies in which community residents are asked to keep diaries of their anger experiences (Averill, 1982). Within psychology, anger has virtually always been identified by theorists and researchers as one of the 'core' emotions, which is universally experienced and recognized (Power and Dalgleish, 1999).

Like other emotions, anger is commonly viewed within psychology as functional and adaptive in the evolutionary sense (Power and Dalgleish, 1999) and as having positive as well as negative consequences. Given that one of the elicitors of anger is the perception of an 'is-ought discrepancy', as in a perceived injustice (Berkowitz and Harmon-Jones, 2004), anger clearly has a role in motivating moral and adaptive behaviour in the form of attempts to correct and change unsatisfactory and unjust states of affairs. Anger becomes a problem for the individual (in terms of mental health and criminal behaviour) when the self-regulation and control of angry experiences, thoughts and impulses are impaired. Impairment of this sort may be an enduring trait or disposition on the part of the person, as in the person with long-term problems of temper control, or may be a temporary state brought about by external situations and recent experiences, for example a family crisis or states of intoxication. Use of the term *impairment* involves a value judgement, either on the part of the angry person that the emotion, or, more likely, the behavioural expression of anger, is 'bad' or dysfunctional for them in pursuing their personal goals, or by other people, who may judge the expression of anger to be harmful to themselves or to society in general.

Anger has become a major focus in forensic clinical settings for two reasons. Firstly, anger and anger regulation have been observed to be common problems in offender populations; indeed anger and hostility are a recognized risk factor for the development of offending behaviour (Novaco, Ramm and Black, 2001). Secondly, anger has been proposed to be functionally related to important behaviours, notably, violence, sex offending, arson, self-harm in prisoners and disruptiveness in prison. In this chapter, I will expand on the thesis that anger is important for aggressive behaviours, with a particular focus on aggression in the form of violent offending and sexual offending.

The role of anger in relation to personality disorder has received relatively little attention in the research literature, though anger appears to be a major focus in clinical and lay observations and amongst users of services for people with personality disorders. In this chapter, I will review what is known about links between anger and personality disorder. Finally, I will discuss issues arising in attempts to treat dysfunctional anger in people with personality disorders who are at risk of aggression and violence.

SOME DEFINITIONS

The definition of anger and the location of related subcategories of anger (rage, fury, annoyance, frustration, etc.) within the overall concept of aggression are not without their problems (Parrott and Giancola, 2006; Russell and Fehr, 1994). Anger needs to be distinguished from *hostility*, which refers to the *negative cognitive evaluation of people or events*. Both anger and hostility can give rise to the *expression* of anger in the form of *behavioural aggression*, but need not do so. *Anger* refers to an *internal emotional response*, with typical psychophysiological and facial components. Berkowitz and Harmon-Jones (2004) define anger as 'a syndrome of relatively specific feelings, cognitions and physiological reactions linked associatively with an urge to injure some target' (p. 108).

The title of this chapter refers to angry affect rather than angry emotion. I will follow Berkowitz (2000) in using angry affect as a broad term, which includes angry emotions, moods and feelings. From this perspective, emotion refers to relatively brief event-specific affective reactions (e.g. an emotional response to a social event involving verbal abuse by another person). An angry mood would refer to an ongoing general state of anger, with no specific triggering event. Emotions typically involve not only the conscious phenomenological experience of anger (feelings) but also the full array of component processes, including exposure to the aversive event, cognitive appraisals of a distinctive sort (e.g. of having been deliberately offended against), physiological activation of the autonomic nervous system (heart rate changes or facial flushing), action tendencies (e.g. to punish for the misgiving or to shut up the offensive person) and overt behaviours such as aggression (Berkowitz, 2000; Frijda, 1986; Power and Dalgleish, 1999). One of the themes to emerge in the chapter is that specific anger emotion may occur in the context of, and be influenced by, broader negative affective states and thus needs to be construed as 'embedded' within broader aspects of the person (Novaco, 1996).

ANGER AS A DEPENDENT VARIABLE

A number of environmental, cognitive and appraisal processes and biases have been identified as significant antecedents for states of anger (Berkowitz and Harmon-Jones, 2004; Hazebroek, Howells and Day, 2001; Novaco and Welsh, 1989; Ortony, Clore and Collins, 1988; Smith and Elsworth, 1985). Anger is typically a response to aversive environmental events, with hostile attributions, perceptions and expectation biases influencing whether subsequent emotional arousal is experienced as anger (Berkowitz and Harmon-Jones, 2004; Crick and Dodge, 1994). The central importance given to cognitive and appraisal processes is congruent with the fact that cognitive–behavioural treatments, with their emphasis on changing anger-generating appraisals, beliefs and underlying schema, have become the dominant treatment approach for anger problems (Howells, 1998).

There is some recent evidence that perspective-taking deficits are associated with high anger arousal following exposure to an interpersonal provocation (Mohr, Howells and Gerace, 2007). This association has a number of possible explanations. One obvious explanation is that being able to take the perspective of the perpetrator of the transgression may inhibit cognitive appraisals and attributions which are likely to lead to blaming and to elicit anger and thus may promote forgiveness of the transgression (Day et al., 2008; Zechmeister and Romero, 2002).

ANGER AS AN INDEPENDENT VARIABLE

Anger, like other emotions and affective states, has significant and distinctive effects on the person's subsequent cognitive processing, appraisals of subsequent events, emotions and behaviours. There is some evidence that angry states, once present, result in a tendency to appraise subsequent events in ways consistent with the appraisals that originally elicited the emotion (Forgas, 2001; Hemenover and Zhang, 2004). Thus, for example, a person may be made angry by the perception that he or she was unjustly treated by another person and the effect of the anger is to sensitize him or her to subsequent instances of unjust treatment. Anger has been linked to violence in general, to violence towards children and to homicide (Howells, 1998; Novaco, 1997). It has been estimated that as many as two thirds of homicide offences may be mediated by anger and negative affective arousal (Howells, submitted). The types of aggression associated with anger appear to be broader than conventional assault, including, for example, behaviours such as dangerous driving (Nesbit, Conger and Conger, 2006). State anger, trait anger and driving-related anger are all strong predictors of aggressive driving, with correlations of circa +0.4 (Nesbit, Conger and Conger, 2006).

Although aggressive action tendencies (physical and verbal aggression to others) in relation to angry emotions are commonly described in the literature, it is clear that a wide range of other behavioural responses to anger can occur, including attempts at tension reduction, communication or talking about anger, 'turning away' from the provoker, self-aggression and 'letting anger fade away' (Averill, 1984; Van Coillie, Van Mechelen and Ceulemans, 2006). Not only is the experience of anger not a *sufficient condition* for aggression it is also not a *necessary condition*. Thus, aggression can occur without anger being an antecedent.

Hostile (or angry) and instrumental aggression have long been distinguished in the literature and the distinction is consistent with the proposition that anger is not necessary for aggression to occur. Hostile (the term 'angry' will be used henceforth) aggression typically involves a triggering frustrating event, an internal state of anger arousal and an impulse to hurt or harm the perpetrator of the frustration. In instrumental aggression, the intention is to obtain some reward, usually material, and the perpetrator does not show emotional arousal (or cognitions) of an angry sort. A homicide in the course of an angry row provides an example of angry aggression and the predatory use of aggression to extort money from cashier at a service station, an example of instrumental aggression. An unhelpfully wide range of terms has been used to describe the angry/instrumental distinction ('impulsive', 'defensive', 'angry', 'hostile', 'affective', 'hot-blooded' vs. 'predatory', 'offensive', 'attack', 'instrumental', 'proactive', etc.) allowing for conceptual drift and confusion (McEllistrem, 2004).

Although the angry/instrumental distinction has been subject to a major critique (Bushman and Anderson, 2001) and despite acknowledged difficulties in categorizing acts as clearly angry or instrumental (Barratt and Slaughter, 1998), it endures as a useful distinction for theorists, researchers and clinicians in the field of aggression, albeit with variations in the terminology used (Berkowitz, 1993, 2003; Bettencourt *et al.*, 2006; Blair, 2004; Crick and Dodge, 1996; Dodge and Coie, 1987). A useful refinement of the distinction is offered by Howard (this volume, Chapter 8), with an important teasing apart of impulsiveness as a dimension orthogonal to the angry/instrumental one. Howard's analysis also usefully stresses the potential positive affect aspect of instrumental anger and aggression, draws attention to the possible positive hedonic tone of some anger experiences and reminds clinicians and theorists of the non-impulsive but angry aggressor (see discussion of overcontrol below).

Despite the problems of the angry instrumental/dichotomy, the presence or absence of anger as an antecedent for aggressive and violent acts remains an important clinical issue. Some aggressive and violent acts can clearly occur in a 'cool' state of mind and a perpetrator whose acts were always of this sort would not require forms of clinical intervention predicated on the assumption that heightened anger had lead to impulsive aggression and that angry impulses need to be controlled.

The angry/instrumental distinction is most appropriately applied to acts rather than to actors. Perpetrators of aggression may engage in both angry and instrumental acts on different occasions or may have multiple goals and functions for any one aggressive act. This latter possibility is addressed in the functional analytic methodology adopted by Daffern *et al.* (2007) discussed in more detail below. In a study of 502 aggressive incidents, Daffern, Howells and Ogloff (2007) found that anger expression was the most frequent function for aggressive acts committed by patients in a high security forensic hospital, but that functions differed for aggressive behaviours towards staff and those towards patients. Demand avoidance was a common function for aggression towards staff but rare for aggression towards patients. To obtain tangibles (an instrumental function) was rare for both types of incident.

Anger has dispositional (trait) as well as state aspects. In considering whether anger is an independent variable that influences the dependent variable of aggressive behaviour, the issue of whether anger-related traits predict aggression is therefore important. In a meta-analytic investigation, Bettencourt *et al.* (2006) have demonstrated that trait anger (defined by intensity, frequency and duration of anger reactions), Type-A personality, rumination, narcissism and impulsivity all predicted aggression. However, an important distinction is made between aggression in 'neutral' conditions and in 'provocation' situations. These anger-related traits predict only provocation-linked aggression. The work of Bettencourt and colleagues has important potential clinical implications, indicating as it does that being anger prone, a ruminator about bad events, narcissistically vulnerable to threats to self-esteem and a poor regulator of impulses require an *interaction* with provoking and frustrating circumstances if these traits are to influence the probability of aggressive behaviour occurring.

SEXUAL AGGRESSION

Although anger has most typically been construed as an important antecedent for general aggression and violence there is also some evidence to support the notion that it is important too, along with other negative emotions, for sexual aggression (for a review, see Howells, Day and Wright, 2004). Clinical descriptions of rapists, for example, have identified angry emotion as a common antecedent in some offenders (Groth, 1979; Langton and Marshall, 2000; Pithers *et al.*, 1988). Anger-mediated offending also appears as a subgroup in taxonomic studies. Amongst the nine sub-types of sex offenders identified by Knight and Prentky (1990), for example, are a globally and undifferentiated angry type and a vindictive group for whom anger is present but more sharply focused on women. In a laboratory study, the induction of anger led to a disinhibition of sexual arousal to rape depictions (Yates, Barbaree and Marshall, 1983) and recent anger experiences have been shown to predict re-offending in sex offenders in the community (Hanson and Harris, 2000).

Offence pathway analyses (Hudson, Ward and McCormack, 1999; Ward *et al.*, 1995) clearly indicate the importance of anger for some sexual offences. In Polaschek *et al.*'s (2001) model of offence pathways in rape, mood and emotion shape and determine goal formation with the two predominant goals being either sexual gratification or redressing harm to self. The sexual gratification goal involves either the enhancement of positive mood or escaping negative mood. Redressing harm to self involves harming the other. The redressing harm process clearly indicates an angry route to sexual aggression.

In understanding anger–sex offending links, the state versus trait distinction is, again, important. One way of formally evaluating the theory that the sexual aggression offence may be functionally related to anger would be to investigate levels of trait anger in sex offenders. The question becomes whether such offenders are more angry than those without sexual aggression. There have not been many studies along these lines, but the results have not provided convincing support. Loza and Loza-Fanous (1999), for example, seriously question the evidence for the anger–rape link and also raise doubts about the use of anger management methods with this group. In the sample they studied, 81% of the rapists had been referred to anger management programmes. These authors also make the important point that previous studies showing anger–rape links are open to the possibility that anger motives may be post-hoc explanations and justifications rather than genuine antecedents.

Howells, Day and Wright (2004) have suggested that before dismissing the high trait anger theory, we should consider alternative interpretations. (1) That a subset of trait angry individuals is swamped by a larger number of more instrumental sexual aggressors in the populations studied. (2) That the effects of anger on sex offending cannot be observed at the trait level. A sex offender need not have a high level of trait anger for state anger to be, nevertheless, an important and even necessary condition for the offence to occur. (3) It may be that the degree of relevance of anger depends on the risk characteristics of the population being studied. The high risk end of the spectrum (e.g. repeated offending with very high, even life-threatening, levels of violence) may be a more affect-driven population.

ANGER AND THEORIES OF AGGRESSION

Contemporary theories of aggression identify angry states as important antecedents for acts of aggression. There is some variation within theories as to how the affective state is to be described. Anderson and Bushman use the term anger in their General Aggression model (Anderson and Bushman, 2002) but Berkowitz's influential theory (2003) locates anger within a broader state of negative affect which influences the occurrence of aggression. For Berkowitz, aversive events elicit, in an automatic and 'wired-in' way, an initial state of general negative affective arousal which creates two 'primitive' inclinations to escape (flight) or attack and destroy (fight) the aversive stimulation. These two inclinations lead to corresponding states of 'rudimentary anger ' and 'rudimentary fear', which require higher order and deeper cognitive processing before full and differentiated anger and fear reactions are produced. Berkowitz's theory would appear to be consistent with the effects of general distress and negative affect on anger reactions. Depression, for example, or general stress would be predicted to amplify anger experience and expression (see discussion below). Cognition has a role in Berkowitz's theory but it is a secondary rather than a primary process. Therapy-derived theories of anger (Deffenbacher, 1999; Novaco, 1997) put far greater emphasis on cognitive processing, consistent with cognitive–behavioural therapeutic approaches.

In Anderson and Bushman's (2002) General Aggression model, a wide range of explanatory mechanisms for the effects of anger in determining aggression are specified:

(1) Anger reduces inhibitions against aggression, through (a) providing a justification for aggressive retaliation, and (b) interfering with higher level cognitive processes (e.g. re-appraisal or moral reasoning).
(2) Anger allows the person to maintain an aggressive intention over time by facilitating attention to the provoking events, increasing the depth of processing of those events and improving recall of these events.
(3) Anger is used as an information cue about causes, culpability and ways of responding.
(4) Anger primes aggressive thoughts, scripts and expressive motor behaviours (what they call 'anger-related knowledge structures' (p. 45) and
(5) Anger energizes behaviour by increasing arousal.

SELF-REGULATION

The difference between aggressive and non-aggressive individuals, or between occasions on which an individual is aggressive as compared with occasions on which s/he is not, may lie in either instigatory or in inhibitory factors, or in both. Aversive environmental events, hostile appraisals and psychophysiological factors and subsequent anger are all potential instigators but it is theoretically possible that aggressive people are normal in relation to such factors but are lacking in inhibitory or self-regulatory skills. The definition of internal inhibition is problematic and a range of other explanations needs to be examined before resorting to inhibition as an explanation of why aggression has not occurred following the arousal of anger (Megargee, 1997). It is also important to distinguish the failure to *acquire* inhibitions about anger expression (e.g. from the failure of socialization) from the *breakdown* of inhibitions (e.g. the effects of fatigue or alcohol or the suspension of normal rules or values). Again, the aggressive individual with high scores on anger instigation may show inhibitory deficits for a range of reasons, some being intrapersonal and others environmental (Baumeister, Heatherton and Tice, 1994).

Some aggressive individuals have characteristics which are the opposite to those of the high anger, high impulsivity individual. Tsytsarev and Grodnitsky (1995), for example, have described what they refer to as 'prolonged' anger arousal and an 'accumulation of affective tension which turns into an explosion of anger and rage, and is usually accompanied, or preceded, by intense feelings of humiliation and despair' (p. 104). See also Howard's (this volume, Chapter 8) defensive/controlled type. It has been suggested that such individuals may normally have high inhibitions about anger experience and expression, hence the 'overcontrolled' (vs. 'undercontrolled') description. This group has received some, though not extensive, attention in empirical studies (Blackburn, 1971, 1993; Lang et al., 1987; Megargee, 1966). Davey, Day and Howells (2005) have proposed that the overcontrolled violent offender type falls into two sub-types, distinguishing the *phenomenologically overcontrolled* offender, who does not report either anger-eliciting cognitions or angry emotional arousal following exposure to a frustration, from the *behaviourally overcontrolled* individual, who may experience intense anger, ruminate on and rehearse grievances but strongly inhibits behavioural expression (a distinction resembling Blackburn's (1986, 1993) *conforming* and *inhibited* types).

General models of emotion regulation are likely to be important in understanding the pathologies of anger regulation. Gross (1998a, 1998b, 2002), for example, has described a process model of emotion regulation, which identifies regulation strategies that may be employed at different stages of the emotion response. *Antecedent-focused* emotion regulation occurs prior to the full activation of the emotion, while *response-focused* regulation occurs after the emotion is underway, in an attempt to control the emotional response. Potential regulatory strategies can include selection/avoidance of the situation to which the person will be exposed, modification of the situation, interrupting rumination, distraction, re-appraisal, seeking social support, suppression or masking of the emotional reaction and self-soothing (Barrett *et al.*, 2001). A major lesson to be derived from theoretical models such as those of Gross (2002) is that treatment needs to increase the flexibility and variety of self-regulatory strategies used by the individual with an anger pathology.

ANGER IN PERSONALITY DISORDERED PEOPLE

Some theorists have argued that abnormalities in trait anger and related neuroanatomical and biochemical systems are fundamental determinants of psychiatric disorder. Lara and Akiskal (2006), for example, proposed that mood, behavioural and personality disorders are produced by fear and anger-prone temperaments and their interactions. There is certainly an argument that anger problems have been severely neglected in understanding the problems associated with mental disorders. In an important and large-scale study, Posternak and Zimmermann (2002) evaluated the degree of anger experienced in a sample of 1300 psychiatric outpatients. These authors evaluated both levels of subjective anger experienced during the preceding week and also level of overt expression of anger in the preceding week. At least moderate levels of subjective anger were experienced by more than half of the patients and over a quarter reported marked or extreme anger; 'marked' defined as 'most of the time aware of feeling quite angry or often feeling very angry' and 'extreme' as 'almost constantly aware of feeling very angry' p. 667). Nearly one quarter reported at least moderate expression of angry aggression. Subjective anger was as frequent as depressed mood and anxiety, affective states more widely recognized as important in mentally disordered populations. In this study, anger had strong associations with some Axis I disorders (intermittent explosive disorder, post-traumatic stress disorder, bipolar disorder, major depressive disorder and somatoform disorders). Patients diagnosed with any personality disorder were 2.6 times more likely to report subjective anger. Patients with Cluster B disorders were 4.6 times more likely to report anger. Cluster B also had a strong association with angry aggression.

Sophisticated psychometric measures now exist to assess components of anger (DiGiuseppe and Tafrate, 2004). Some indirect evidence relating to anger in personality disorder has been provided by DiGiuseppe and Tafrate (2004) in their validation of the Anger Disorders Scale (ADS). These authors correlated the various scales of the ADS with a measure of personality disorders – the MCMI-III (Millon, 1993) and with a measure of Axis I disorders in 230 psychotherapy clients. The anger scales correlated significantly, though modestly, with many personality disorders. Choosing for comment a somewhat arbitrary cut-off of a correlation of 0.40 or above, the ADS total anger score correlated strongly not only with 'negativistic' (+0.58) and 'sadistic' (+0.52) personality disorders (neither of which is included in DSM-IVTR) but also significantly with borderline (+0.53), schizotypal (+0.43), paranoid (+0.44) and antisocial (0.41). Interestingly, there was a significant negative correlation (−0.46) between compulsive personality disorder (PD) and anger. Contrary to expectations, there was no significant correlation between narcissistic PD and anger in this study. Particular components of anger (as reflected in subscales) were also associated with PDs. The borderline scale correlated positively with brooding, suspiciousness and passive aggression. The antisocial scale had only modest correlations with any anger subscales. Paranoid PD was associated with suspiciousness and resentment.

Gould *et al.* (1996) have also reported an association between 'anger attacks' and Cluster B and Cluster C PD traits and also with self-defeating traits. Fava *et al.* (1993) reported an association between anger attacks and the frequency of borderline, narcissistic, histrionic and antisocial PDs. In a depressed group, Tedlow *et al.* (1999) reported an association between anger attacks and borderline, avoidant, dependent, antisocial and narcissistic PDs.

In some recent work (Daffern and Howells, in press), a functional analysis was conducted with dangerous and severe personality disordered patients in a high secure unit at Rampton Hospital, UK. As in previous work with aggressive incidents in psychotic patients (Daffern, Howells and Ogloff, 2007), anger expression was the most common function for aggressive acts, both those occurring in the institution and those involved in the index offence, prior to admission. Given the expected high prevalence of psychopathic features in this latter population, the high frequency of anger expression and low frequency of instrumental functions are surprising. Psychopathy is typically construed as associated with instrumental aggression (Cornell *et al.*, 1996). (See discussion of psychopathy and anger below.)

THE DSM AND ANGER

Of the PDs described in DSM-IV, only four include significant reference to anger as a defining feature: antisocial personality disorder (APD), borderline personality disorder (BPD), narcissistic personality disorder (NPD) and paranoid personality disorder (PPD).

The diagnostic criteria for APD include 'irritability and aggressiveness, as indicated by repeated physical fights and assaults'. There is a tautological aspect to this criterion in that aggressiveness and fights and assaults refer to essentially the same behaviours. The attribution of irritability (a trait generally seen as overlapping with trait anger, though not synonymous with it) is consistent with the notion that the person with APD is prone to angry aggression, though it is aggression rather than anger that is emphasized. Commentators on the DSM PDs generally confirm that this is so. Sperry (1995), for example, suggests that 'persons with antisocial personality disorders are... noted for their impulsive anger, deceitfulness and cunning' (p. 16) and that they have an 'ill-tempered' temperament resulting in 'antagonistic and belligerent' interpersonal behaviours. According to Sperry, those with APD 'avoid softer emotions such as warmth and intimacy'. 'Lack of remorse' and 'impulsivity' are also diagnostic criteria for APD in DSM-IV. These latter traits would be consistent with poor regulation and inhibition of angry behaviours.

Of the four PDs being discussed, BPD has the strongest association with anger, in terms of the DSM-IV account. One criterion is 'inappropriate intense anger or difficulty controlling anger (e.g. frequent displays of temper, constant anger, recurrent physical fights'. This criterion suggests that people with BPD have high trait anger, the latter normally being defined in terms of high intensity and frequency of anger. The criterion suggests both high inner experience of angry emotion plus high behavioural expression.

In addition to this specific anger-related criterion, another criterion specified is 'affective instability due to a marked reactivity of mood (e.g. intense episodes of dysphoria, irritability or anxiety usually lasting a few hours, and only rarely more than a few days'. Given the argument (below) that anger has some relationship to broader negative affect, the affective instability criterion is consistent with high state anger being influenced by negative affect. Sperry (1995) comments on the 'high autonomic reactivity' and 'hyperresponsiveness' associated with BPD and on the general pattern of a 'combination of intense emotional responses, inadequate emotional regulation skills (and) impulsive behaviour' (p. 60). Poor emotion regulation skills are a core feature of Linehan's (1993) and Livesley's (2003) account of BPD. Thus, BPD (by DSM definition) involves intense and frequent angry emotion, in combination with poor self-regulation (Gardner et al., 1991). There is some similarity in the APD and BPD anger profile, though anger is clearly seen as more central to BPD. The triggers eliciting anger responses are likely to differ for APD and BPD, the latter being assumed to be particularly sensitive to rejection, thwarted dependency and abandonment, as a result of insecure attachments (Dutton and Starzomski, 1993). The latter authors suggest that 'anger is an unavoidable aspect of intimacy for borderlines' (p. 334). The triggers for anger in APD are less clear cut and might be expected to be of a general frustration nature or to be characterized by threats to dominance. Formal mapping of the nature of the provoking event for both APD and BPD is required, in that people with both disorders appear to be 'provocation sensitive' (Bettencourt et al., 2006) but in different ways.

The involvement of anger in NPD is less explicit, but certainly implied in the DSM-IV account. The criterion 'has a sense of entitlement, that is, unreasonable expectations of especially favourable treatment and automatic compliance with his or her expectations' leaves the narcissist inevitably prone to anger, or at least frustration, when such expectations are not met (Hart and Joubert, 1996). Sperry (1995) describes the person with NPD as 'likely to respond to criticism with rage' (p. 114) and identifies narcissistic rage as the characteristic emotional style of NPD. Millon (1996) proposes that the affective tone of NPD is cheerful, carefree and nonchalant but that 'should the balloon be burst . . . there is a rapid turn to either an edgy irritability and arrogance with others or to repeated bouts of dejection that are characterized by feeling humiliated and empty. Shaken by these circumstances, the narcissist is likely to briefly display a vacillation between rage, shame and feelings of emptiness' (p. 408). The narcissist, therefore, is seen as vulnerable, but as showing rage only when particular triggering events, for example, threats to ego, arise (Baumeister, Smart and Boden, 1996). This is clearly outlined in Sperry's (1995) formulation of NPD.

There is also support for the links between narcissism and anger in studies of personality in non-clinical populations (McCann and Biaggio, 1989). Papps and O'Carroll (1998) reported an association between both narcissism and high self-esteem and anger traits. Particular aspects of narcissism, for example, perceived authority and sense of entitlement may have stronger associations with anger than others (Witte, Callahan and Perez-Lopez, 2002).

The anger-relevant DSM-IV criteria for paranoid PD are the following: 'suspects, without sufficient basis, that others are exploiting, harming or deceiving him or her'; 'reads hidden, demeaning or threatening meanings into benign remarks or events'; 'persistently bears grudges, that is, unforgiving of insults, injuries or slights'; 'perceives attacks on his or her character or reputation that are not apparent to others and is quick to react angrily and counterattack'; 'has recurrent suspicions, without justification, regarding fidelity of spouse or sexual partner'. What is striking about these (essentially cognitive) features of PPD is that they mirror almost exactly the cognitive and attributional biases shown to characterize angry aggressive reactions – the attribution of malevolent intent, the rehearsal of grudges, blaming and unforgivingness are all found in angry aggressors (Dodge, 1991; Dodge and Coie, 1987; Hazebroek, Howells and Day, 2001; Novaco and Welsh, 1989; Ortony, Clore and Collins, 1988). Similarly, the triggering events identified in PPD (insults, slights, injuries) resemble those for angry aggression (Berkowitz and Harmon-Jones, 2004). Sperry (1995) comments that the two emotions expressed in depth in PPD are 'anger and intense jealousy' (p. 156) and that 'paranoid individuals are exquisitely sensitive to and angry about exclusion, slights and even whispering' (p. 161). Bentall and Taylor (2006) have suggested that attribution of malicious intent by others is an important process in paranoid states, while Millon (1996) describes individuals with PPD as 'typically edgy, envious, jealous and quick to take personal offence, reacting angrily with minimal provocation' (p. 704).

Given the clear relevance of anger to (at least) these four PDs, it is surprising that the anger component receives little or only very brief analysis in major texts on PD, reflecting perhaps the damaging separation of theories of PDs from mainstream psychological analyses of emotion. This parallels the separation, until recently, of PD from personality theory in general (Blackburn, 2007; Day and Bryan, 2007; Livesley, 2007; Widiger *et al.*, 2002).

ANGER AND PERSONALITY

Recent attempts to plot PDs onto the core dimensions of normal personality (Costa and Widiger, 2002) are useful in two respects. Firstly, the location of anger proneness within the dimensional space of normal personality is elucidated and, secondly, the links between particular PDs and constellations of normal traits can be investigated. One clear lesson from this work is that anger proneness (termed 'angry hostility' in this context) is a facet of a broader dimension of neuroticism (Widiger *et al.*, 2002) within the five-factor model. The association with neuroticism confirms the anger-negative affect connection posited by Berkowitz (2003). See also the study by Hicks and Patrick (2006) discussed below. The association between anger and negative affect is also consistent with evidence that anger 'attacks' are more common in those with depression, anxiety disorders and panic attacks (Gould *et al.*, 1996).

High scores on the 'angry hostility' facet reflect that the individual has 'episodes of intense and out of control rage and fury; is hypersensitive and touchy; easily reacts with anger and hostility towards annoyances, rebukes, criticisms, rejections, frustrations or other minor events; hostility provoking arguments, disputes and conflicts' (Costa and Widiger, 2002, p. 438). The suggested links between anger and PDs outlined above are also confirmed by Widiger *et al.*'s (2002) attempt to plot the five-factor model onto PDs. The latter authors suggest the 'angry–hostility' facet of neuroticism is high in BPD, NPD, APD and PPD, as proposed above. These four PDs share high anger but can then be differentiated in terms of other dimensions and facets of the five-factor model.

In a study of child molesters, Madsen, Parsons and Grubin (2006) found that those with PDs could be distinguished from those without PDs by their higher scores on domains and facets of the five-factor model, particularly on measures of neuroticism (high) and agreeableness (low). Of interest for the present chapter is that the anger–hostility facet was the best discriminator between PD and no PD, though other facets (impulsiveness, trust) also discriminated.

PSYCHOPATHY AND ANGER

Psychopathy, as defined by the Psychopathy Checklist Revised (PCL-R), has been reliably demonstrated to be linked to aggressive and violent behaviour and is believed to be one of the best predictors of reconviction for violent offences (Hare, 2006; Patrick and Zempolich, 1998). It is likely that the lay public, and even clinicians, associate the term psychopath with a disposition to extreme acts of violence. The demonstration, however, that amongst offenders, psychopathic individuals are more violent than non-psychopathic individuals, or more likely to be reconvicted for violence does not necessarily imply that psychopathy *per se* is inherently associated with aggression. It would appear likely that psychopathy (Hare, 2006) would be associated more strongly with instrumental than with angry aggressive acts, given the 'cold', affectless nature of psychopathic individuals (Hare, 2006). Consistent with this notion, Cornell *et al.* (1996) compared violent offenders who had committed at least one instrumental offence with those with a history of reactive violent offences. In both the samples studied, the two violent groups could be distinguished on the basis of their Hare Psychopathy score. Such studies have clear implications for treatment interventions, suggesting that the instrumentally violent psychopath has no need for anger interventions, requiring, perhaps, to learn to overcome his or her inhibitory deficits and related impairments in moral development (Blair, 2006).

Patrick (2006) has very usefully explored the construct of aggression in Cleckley's (1976) seminal account of psychopathy. He points out that Cleckley's criteria do not include indicators of hostility or aggression and that serious violent behaviour is not seen as characteristic of the disorder, though aggression and violence did occur in some of Cleckley's 15 prototypic cases. Of most relevance to the present chapter is that Cleckley's account also suggested that where aggression did occur it was not of an angry type. Two quotes (by Patrick) from Cleckley's text make this clear: '(His) fights always started over trifles. . . . He never attacked others suddenly or incomprehensibly. . . . The causes of his quarrels were readily understandable and were usually found to be similar to those which move such types as the familiar schoolboy bully. . . . No signs of towering rage appeared or even of impulses too strong to be controlled . . . the desire to show off appeared to be a strong motive behind many of his fights' (pp. 32–33 in Cleckley, 1976 and p. 601 in Patrick, 2006). 'It is my opinion that when the typical psychopath . . . occasionally commits a major deed of violence, it is usually a casual act done not from tremendous passion or as a result of plans persistently followed with earnest, compelling fervour. . . . The psychopath is not volcanically explosive, at the mercy of irresistible drives and overwhelming rages of temper. Often he seems scarcely wholehearted even in wrath or wickedness' (Cleckley, 1976, p. 263; Patrick, 2006, p. 607).

It would seem that the psychopath, as identified by the PCL-R, readily engages in aggression, but that aggression may not be central to the disorder. More importantly for our present purposes, there is little to suggest that (primary) psychopaths are anger prone, though the dearth of empirical studies into the psychopath's experience and expression of anger is striking (see Steuerwald and Kosson, 2000). Low experience of anger would be consistent with what has been proposed to be part of a general low experience of negative affect, including anxiety, fear, sadness, guilt and shame, as well as anger, in psychopaths, what Hicks and Patrick (2006) term negative emotionality. As Hicks and Patrick (2006) point out, the evidence relating to whether psychopaths do indeed have theory-predicted low negative emotionality (NEM) is inconsistent, with some studies reporting differences between Factor 1 and Factor 2 of the PCL-R, F1 correlating negatively with stress and positively with positive emotions, and Factor 2 positively with emotionality and impulsive aggression.

NEM appears to be a multi-faceted dimension with some differentiation of components of fear, emotional distress and anger, while anger shows a moderately large correlation with emotional distress (Hicks and Patrick, 2006). In the study by the latter authors, the unique variance in PCL-R F1 showed a weak negative association with anger/hostility while the unique variance in F2 showed a strong association with anger/hostility. This would appear to allow for angry aggression having some association with psychopathy, though this is specific to the F2 dimension of PCL-R-defined psychopathy. Indeed, Hicks and Patrick go so far as to suggest that 'the PCL-R taps two distinctive entities – one corresponding phenotypically to low stress reaction and an agentic interpersonal style and genotypically to a core weakness in defensive (fear) reactivity, and the other phenotypically to an impulsive-aggressive (externalizing) behavioural style and genotypically to a basic weakness in inhibitory control systems' (p. 284). (See also Patrick and Zempolich, 1998 and Hicks *et al.*, 2004). Such work implies that aggression in the 'pure' Cleckley psychopath is more likely to be appetitively oriented (i.e. 'instrumental' or 'proactive') then defensively motivated. (p. 313). (See also Howard's Chapter 8 in this volume.)

CONCLUSIONS ON ANGER LINKS TO PERSONALITY DISORDER

The conclusion that anger is high in the PDs described above is unsurprising, in the main. It is true *a priori* for BPD and APD in that anger is a criterion for the diagnosis, though this is inferential for APD. Anger appears to be too important a problem in people with PDs for it to remain unaddressed. Nevertheless, it is essential that empirical investigations assess more formally the extent and, particularly, the nature of anger in these populations. Anger has many environmental, cognitive, affective, psychophysiological and self-regulatory components and the patterns of such components for particular PDs need to be established.

If PDs do indeed influence aggression it is useful, even necessary, to map the possible effects of such disorders onto current models of the causation of aggression. Given the centrality of exposure to aversive (frustrating or 'provoking') events and subsequent anger (or broader negative affect) as a mediator of aggression in many theories of aggression (Berkowitz, 2003), obvious questions to ask are the following: Are those with PDs: (1) exposed to high levels of aversive 'provocation' (the term provocation here does not imply that the responsibility for the aversive events lies with others nor that others are to be blamed for them)? It may also be that the personality disordered cause their aversive experiences because of the negative effects on others of their impulsive and antisocial behaviours. (2) More likely to engage in the cognitive appraisals, evaluations and beliefs that are known to induce angry and aggressive responses to aversive stimulation (appraisals of negative intent, blaming, hostile attributions, etc.)? (3) More likely to show stronger physiological activation to aversive social events? (4) More likely to show more intense and frequent anger reactions? or (5) Are they the same as non-personality disordered on mechanisms (1)–(4) but are deficient in the self-regulatory skills that are required to inhibit the aggressive action tendencies that arise from (1) to (4)? In lay terms, those with PDs may be no more or less angry than the rest of us but control the emotion less effectively. Where anger is high in those with PDs, there is a need to understand in detail the particular processes and components that are leading to elevated anger.

Steuerwald and Kosson (2000) have described some of the many methodological difficulties in this field, including high reliance on self-report measures of anger, which are suspect in this clinical group, the use of analogue populations (e.g. students high and low in socialization), the use of methodologies such as filmed vignettes which confound anger measures with empathy deficits, disjunction between subjective and overt measures of anger, the failure to distinguish between intensity and frequency of anger responses and the low ecological validity of study settings.

TREATMENT OF ANGER IN PERSONALITY DISORDERS

In some respects anger treatment (the term used here rather than anger manage-ment) has been one of the success stories of contemporary cognitive–behavioural therapy. It has been a success in two senses of the term. Firstly, anger treatment has been one of the most widely delivered cognitive–behavioural treatments, partic-ularly in correctional and forensic settings (Howells *et al.*, 2005). 'Anger manage-ment' would seem to have entered the public lexicon to the extent of stimulating a feature film with this title and being a common newspaper headline ('Judge orders wife batterer to undertake anger management . . .'). The second and more important aspect of success has been accumulating evidence as to its effectiveness. Meta-analyses (Del Vecchio and O'Leary, 2004; DiGiuseppe and Tafrate, 2003) have demonstrated that cognitive–behavioural anger treatment significantly reduces anger problems compared to control conditions, with an at least moderate effect size.

There are however two qualifications to this general statement of effective-ness which are particularly pertinent to the present chapter and volume. The first is that severe or high risk violent offenders do not appear to consistently show the same positive response to anger treatments as do individuals who have anger problems but less severe problems of aggression and offending (Heseltine, Howells and Day, submitted; Howells *et al.*, 2005; Watt and Howells, 1999). Howells *et al.* (2005) and Watt and Howells (1999) have discussed possible rea-sons for reduced effectiveness with violent offender populations, including the effects of co-morbid psychological, social and psychiatric problems, insufficiently intensive treatment, poor selection of treatment participants and low readiness for treatment, in moderating treatment effects.

The second qualification is that evaluations of anger treatments with personality-disordered aggressors are rare indeed in the published literature. This however may be less of a problem than at first appears in that PD is rarely screened for in prison and community corrections settings. Given the known high prevalence of PD, particularly APD, in offender and high risk populations (Coid, 2002; Fazel and Danesh, 2002), it is likely that populations such as those studied by Dowden, Blanchette and Serin (1999) and others include a large proportion of participants with PDs.

It has been suggested that anger treatment has received only cursory attention in mentally disordered offender populations, in part because of the low profile of anger problems in taxonomic systems such as the DSM and the ICD-10 where they have a peripheral formal role (see above) (Jones and Hollin, 2004). The latter authors have reported a treatment programme for anger in personality-disordered offenders in a high security setting. The content of the programme was described in some detail and particular attention was paid to maintaining motivation and readiness. Encouragingly, the treatment was substantial (33 sessions), thus dealing with suggestions (Howells *et al.*, 2005) that some programmes are too brief and that this might contribute to low effectiveness. Encouraging reductions in anger and anger-related behaviours were shown, though the authors acknowledge the numbers were small and there was no untreated control group.

If the hypothesis (above) that different PDs have different constellations of anger features proves to be correct, then there is a clear implication that different PDs will require different therapeutic strategies to reduce their anger. Treatment of the anger 'symptom' will also need to occur at the appropriate point in the integrative and sequential treatment programmes advocated for PDs (Livesley, 2007).

There is some evidence that the effectiveness of anger treatments for violent offenders is impaired by the low readiness or motivation of some participants for treatment (Heseltine, Howells and Day, submitted; Howells and Day, 2003; Howells *et al.*, 2005; Howells and Day, 2006; Williamson, Day and Howells, 2003). The presence of other features of PD (e.g. impulsivity, low compliance) may well exacerbate problems of low treatment readiness and engagement (Howells and Day, 2007)

Finally, there are other implications for anger treatment planning from some of the research and clinical findings discussed in this chapter. The association of anger with broader negative affect suggests the desirability of a broader, more systemic approach to reduce angry aggression by ameliorating the affective state of the individual in treatment. This could have environmental, cognitive, behavioural, physiological and even psychopharmacological aspects (Lara and Akiskal, 2006). The strategy of improving regulation of negative affect and subsequent dysfunctional impulses is already well developed in relation to BPD (Linehan, 1993; Livesley, 2003). Skills in 'identifying emotions', 'affect and distress tolerance', 'self-soothing', 'grounding', 'attention control' and 'mindfulness' (commonly addressed in such programmes) may well have much to contribute to assisting people regulate their anger experience, so they are not punished by it (see the Buddhist quotation at the beginning of the chapter.)

REFERENCES

Anderson, C.A. and Bushman, B.J. (2002) Human aggression. *Annual Review of Psychology*, **53**, 27–51.

Averill, J.R. (1982) *Anger and Aggression: An Essay on Emotion*, Springer Verlag, New York.

Barratt, E.S. and Slaughter, L. (1998) Defining, measuring and predicting impulsive aggression: a heuristic model. *Behavioral Sciences and the Law*, **16**, 285–302.

Barrett, L.F., Gross, J., Christenson, T.C. and Bienvenuto, M. (2001) Knowing what you're feeling and knowing what to do about it: mapping the relation between emotion differentiation and emotion regulation. *Cognition and Emotion*, **15**, 713–24.

Baumeister, R.F., Heatherton, T.F. and Tice, D.M. (1994) *Losing Control: How and Why People Fail at Self Regulation*, Academic, San Diego.

Baumeister, R.F., Smart, L. and Boden, J.M. (1996) Relation of threatened egotism to violence and aggression: the dark side of high self esteem. *Psychological Review*, **103**, 5–33.

Bentall, R.P. and Taylor, J.L. (2006) Psychological processes and paranoia: implications for forensic behavioural science. *Behavioral Sciences and the Law*, **24**, 277–94.

Berkowitz, L. (1993) *Aggression: Its Causes, Consequences and Control*, McGraw-Hill, New York.

Berkowitz, L. (2000) *Causes and Consequences of Feelings*, Cambridge University Press, Cambridge.

Berkowitz, L. (2003) Affect, aggression and antisocial behavior, in *Handbook of Affective Sciences* (eds R.J. Davidson, K.R. Scherer and H.H. Goldsmith), Oxford University Press, Oxford, pp. 804–23.

Berkowitz, L. and Harmon-Jones, E. (2004) Towards an understanding of the determinants of anger. *Emotion*, **4**, 107–30.

Bettencourt, B.A., Talley, A., Benjamin, A.J. and Valentine, J. (2006) Personality and aggressive behaviour under provoking and neutral conditions: a meta-analytic review. *Psychological Bulletin*, **132**, 751–77.

Blackburn, R. (1971) Personality types among abnormal homicides. *British Journal of Criminology*, **37**, 166–78.

Blackburn, R. (1986) Patterns of personality deviation among violent offenders: replication and extension of an empirical taxonomy. *British Journal of Criminology*, **26**, 254–69.

Blackburn, R. (1993) *The Psychology of Criminal Conduct*, John Wiley & Sons, Ltd, Chichester.

Blackburn, R. (2007) Personality disorder and psychopathy: conceptual and empirical integration. *Psychology, Crime and Law*, **13**, 7–18.

Blair, R.J.R. (2004) The roles of orbital frontal cortex in the modulation of antisocial behaviour. *Brain and Cognition*, **55**, 198–208.

Blair, R.J.R. (2006) The emergence of psychopathy: implications for the neuropsychological approach to developmental disorders. *Cognition*, **101**, 414–42.

Bushman, B.J. and Anderson, C.A. (2001) Is it time to pull the plug on the hostile versus hostile versus instrumental aggression dichotomy? *Psychological Review*, **108**, 273–9.

Cleckley, H. (1976) *The Mask of Sanity*, 5th edn, Mosby, St. Louis MO.

Coid, J. (2002) Personality disorders in prisoners and their motivation for dangerous and disruptive behaviors. *Criminal Behaviour and Mental Health*, **12**, 209–26.

Cornell, D.G., Warren, J., Hawk, G. *et al.* (1996) Psychopathy in instrumental and reactive violent offenders. *Journal of Consulting and Clinical Psychology*, **64**, 783–90.

Costa, P.T. and Widiger, T.A. (eds) (2002) *Personality Disorders and the Five-Factor Model of Personality*, 2nd edn, American Psychological Association, Washington DC.

Crick, N.R. and Dodge, K.A. (1994). A review and reformulation of social information-processing mechanisms in children's social adjustment. *Psychological Bulletin*, **115** (1), 74–101.

Crick, N.R. and Dodge, K.A. (1996) Social information-processing mechanisms in reactive and proactive aggression. *Child Development*, **67**, 993–1002.

Daffern, M. and Howells, K. (in press) The functions of aggression in personality disordered offenders. *Journal of Interpersonal Violence*.

Daffern, M., Howells, K. and Ogloff, J.R.P. (2007) What's the point? Towards a methodology for assessing the function of psychiatric inpatient aggression. *Behavior Research and Therapy*, **45**, 101–11.

Davey, L., Day, A. and Howells, K. (2005) Anger, over-control and serious violent offending. *Aggression and Violent Behavior*, **10**, 624–35.

Day, A. and Bryan, J. (2007) Personality change and personality disorder: some initial thoughts on the application of McAdams' triarchic model to the treatment of personality disorders. *Psychology, Crime and Law*, **13**, 19–26.

Day, A., Gerace, A., Wilson, C. and Howells, K. (2008) Promoting forgiveness in violent offenders: a more positive approach to offender rehabilitation. *Aggression and Violent Behavior*, **13** (3), 195–200.

Deffenbacher, J.L. (1999) Cognitive-behavioral conceptualization and treatment of anger. *Journal of Clinical Psychology*, **53**, 295–309.

Del Vecchio, T. and O'Leary, D. (2004) Effectiveness of anger treatments for specific anger problems: a meta-analytic review. *Clinical Psychology Review*, **24**, 15–34.

DiGiuseppe, R. and Tafrate, R. (2003) Anger treatment for adults: a meta-analytic review. *Clinical Psychology: Science and Practice*, **10**, 70–84.

DiGiuseppe, R. and Tafrate, R.C. (2004) *Anger Disorders Scale: Manual*, Multi-Health Systems Inc.

Dowden, C., Blanchette, K. and Serin, R. (1999) *Anger Management Programming for Offenders: An Effective Intervention*, Correctional Service of Canada Report, Ottowa.

Dodge, K.A. (1991) The structure and function of reactive and proactive aggression, in *The Development and Treatment of Childhood Aggression* (eds D.J. Pepler and K.H. Rubin), Lawrence Erlbaum Associates, Hillsdale, NJ, pp. 201–18.

Dodge, K.A. and Coie, J.D. (1987) Social information-processing factors in reactive and proactive aggression in children's peer groups. *Journal of Personality and Social Psychology*, **53** (6), 1146–58.

Dutton, D.G. and Starzomski, A.J. (1993) Borderline personality in perpetrators of psychological and physical abuse. *Violence and Victims*, **8**, 327–37.

Fava, M., Rosenbaum, J.F., McCarthy, M.K. *et al.* (1993) Anger attacks in unipolar depression-Part 1: clinical correlates and response to fluoxetine treatment. *American Journal of Psychiatry*, **150**, 1158–63.

Fazel, S. and Danesh, J. (2002) Serious mental disorder in 23000 prisoners: a systematic review of 62 surveys. *The Lancet*, **359**, 545–50.

Forgas, J.P. (2001) *Handbook of Affect and Social Cognition*, Erlbaum, Mahwah, NJ.

Frijda, N.H. (1986) *The Emotions*, Cambridge University Press, Cambridge.

Gardner, D.L., Leibenluft, E., O'Leary, K.M. and Cowdry, R.W. (1991) Self-ratings of anger and hostility in borderline personality disorder. *Journal of Nervous and Mental Disease*, **179**, 157–61.

Gould, R.A., Ball, S., Kaspi, S.P. *et al.* (1996) Prevalence and correlates of anger attacks: a two-site study. *Journal of Affective Disorders*, **39**, 31–8.

Gross, J. (1998a) Antecedent and response focused emotion regulation: divergent consequences for experience, expression and physiology. *Journal of Personality and Social Psychology*, **74**, 224–37.

Gross, J. (1998b) The emerging field of emotion regulation: an integrative review. *Review of General Psychology*, **2**, 271–99.

Gross, J. (2002) Emotion regulation: affective, cognitive and social consequences. *Psychophysiology*, **39**, 281–91.

Groth, A.N. (1979) *Men Who Rape*, Plenum, New York.

Hanson, R.K. and Harris, A.J.R. (2000) Where should we intervene? Dynamic predictors of sexual offense recidivism. *Criminal Justice and Behavior*, **27**, 6–35.

Hare, R.D. (2006) Psychopathy: a clinical and forensic overview. *Psychiatric Clinics of North America*, **29**, 709–24.

Hart, P.L. and Joubert, C.E. (1996) Narcissism and hostility. *Psychological Reports*, **79**, 161–2.

Hazebroek, J., Howells, K. and Day, A. (2001) Cognitive appraisals associated with high trait anger. *Personality and Individual Differences*, **30**, 31–45.

Hemenover, S.H. and Zhang, S. (2004) Anger, personality and optimistic stress appraisals. *Cognition and Emotion*, **18**, 363–82.

Heseltine, K., Howells, K. and Day, A. (submitted) Brief anger interventions with offenders may be ineffective: a replication and extension. *Behaviour Research and Therapy*.

Hicks, B.M., Markon, K.E., Patrick, C.J. *et al.* (2004) Identifying psychopathy subtypes on the basis of personality structure. *Psychological Assessment*, **16**, 276–88.

Hicks, B.M. and Patrick, C.J. (2006) Psychopathy and negative emotionality: analyses of suppressor effects reveal distinct relations with emotional distress, fearfulness and anger-hostility. *Journal of Abnormal Psychology*, **115**, 276–87.

Howells, K. (1998) Cognitive-behavioural interventions for anger, aggression and violence, in *Treating Complex Cases: The Cognitive Behavioural Therapy Approach* (eds N. Tarrier, A. Wells and G. Haddock), John Wiley & Sons, Ltd, Chichester, pp. 295–318.

Howells, K. (2008) The treatment of anger in offenders, in *Anger and Indigenous Men* (eds A. Day, M. Nakata and K. Howells), The Federation Press, Annandale NSW, pp. 20–30.

Howells, K. (submitted) The treatment of anger in offenders.

Howells, K. and Day, A. (2003) Readiness for anger management: clinical and theoretical issues. *Clinical Psychology Review*, **23**, 319–37.

Howells, K. and Day, A. (2006) Affective determinants of treatment engagement in violent offenders. *International Journal of Offender Therapy and Comparative Criminology*, **50**, 174–86.

Howells, K. and Day, A. (2007) Readiness for treatment in high risk offenders with personality disorders. *Psychology, Crime and Law*, **13**, 47–56.

Howells, K., Day, A., Williamson, P. *et al.* (2005) Brief anger management programs with offenders: outcomes and predictors of change. *Journal of Forensic Psychiatry and Psychology*, **16**, 296–311.

Howells, K., Day, A. and Wright, S. (2004) Affect, emotions and sex offenders. *Psychology, Crime and Law*, **10**, 179–95.

Hudson, S.M., Ward, T. and McCormack, J.C. (1999) Offense pathways in sexual offenders. *Journal of Interpersonal Violence*, **14**, 779–98.

Jones, D. and Hollin, C.R. (2004) Managing problem anger: the development of a treatment program for personality disordered patients in high security. *International Journal of Forensic Mental Health*, **3**, 197–210.

Knight, R.A. and Prentky, R.A. (1990) Classifying sexual offenders: the development and corroboration of taxonomic models, in *Handbook of Sexual Assault: Issues, Theories and Treatment of the Offender* (eds W.L. Marshall, D.R. Laws and H.E. Barbaree), Plenum, New York, pp. 23–52.

Lang, R., Holden, R., Langevin, R. *et al.* (1987) Personality and criminality in violent offenders. *Journal of Interpersonal Violence*, **2**, 179–95.

Langton, C.M. and Marshall, W.L. (2000) The role of cognitive distortions in relapse prevention programs, in *Remaking Relapse Prevention with Sex Offenders* (eds D.R. Laws, S.M. Hudson and T. Ward), Sage, Thousand Oaks, CA, pp. 167–86.

Lara, D.R. and Akiskal, H.S. (2006) Toward an integrative model of the spectrum of mood, behavioral and personality disorders based on fear and anger traits: II: implications for neurobiology, genetics and psychopharmacological treatment. *Journal of Affective Disorders*, **94**, 89–103.

Linehan, M.M. (1993) *Cognitive-Behavioral Treatment of Borderline Personality Disorder*, Guilford, New York.

Livesley, W.J. (2003) *Practical Management of Personality Disorder*, Guilford, New York.

Livesley, W.J. (2007) The relevance of an integrated approach to the treatment of personality disordered offenders. *Psychology, Crime and Law*, **13**, 27–46.

Loza, W. and Loza-Fanous, A. (1999) The fallacy of reducing rape and violent recidivism by treating anger. *International Journal of Offender Therapy and Comparative Criminology*, **43**, 492–502.

Madsen, L., Parsons, S. and Grubin, D. (2006) The relationship between the five-factor model and DSM personality disorder in a sample of child molesters. *Personality and Individual Differences*, **40**, 227–36.

McEllistrem, J.E. (2004) Affective and predatory violence: a bimodal classification system of human aggression and violence. *Aggression and Violent Behavior*, **10**, 1–30.

Megargee, E. (1966) Undercontrolled and overcontrolled personality types in extreme antisocial aggression. *Psychological Monographs*, **80**, 1–116.

Megargee, E.I (1997) Internal inhibitions and controls, in *Handbook of Personality Psychology*, Academic.

McCann, J.T. and Biaggio, M.K. (1989) Narcissistic personality features and self-reported anger. *Psychological Reports*, **64**, 55–8.

Millon, T. (1993) *Millon Clinical Multiaxial Inventory – III Manual*, National Computer Sustems, Minneapolis.

Millon, T. (1996) *Disorders of Personality: DSM-IVtm and Beyond*, John Wiley & Sons, Ltd, New York.

Mohr, P., Howells, K., Gerace, A. *et al.* (2007) The role of perspective taking in anger arousal. *Personality and Individual Differences*, **43** (3), 507–17.

Nesbit, S.M., Conger, J.C. and Conger, A.J. (2006) A quantitative review of the relationship between anger and aggressive driving. *Aggression and Violent Behavior*, **12** (2), 156–76.

Novaco, R.W. (1996) Clinicians ought to view anger contextually. *Behaviour Change*, **10**, 208–18.

Novaco, R.W. (1997) Remediating anger and aggression with violent offenders. *Legal and Criminological Psychology*, **2**, 77–88.

Novaco, R.W., Ramm, M. and Black, L. (2001) Anger treatment with offenders, in *Handbook of Offender Assessment and Treatment* (ed. C.R. Hollin), John Wiley & Sons, Ltd, Chichester, pp. 281–96.

Novaco, R.W. and Welsh, W.N. (1989) Anger disturbances: cognitive mediation and clinical prescription, in *Clinical Approaches to Violence* (eds K. Howells and C.R. Hollin), John Wiley & Sons, Ltd, Chichester.

Ortony, A., Clore, G.L. and Collins, A. (1988) *The Cognitive Structure of Emotions*, Cambridge University Press, New York.

Papps, B.J. and O'Carroll, R.E. (1998) Extremes of self-esteem and narcissism and the experience and expression of anger and aggression. *Aggressive Behavior*, **24**, 421–438.

Parrott, D.J. and Giancola, P.R. (2006) Addressing "the criterion problem" in the assessment of aggressive behaviour: development of a new taxonomic system. *Aggression and Violent Behavior*, **12** (3), 280–99.

Patrick, C.J. (2006) Back to the future: Cleckley as a guide to the next generation of psychopathy research, in *Handbook of Psychopathy* (ed. C.J. Patrick), Guilford, New York, pp. 605–17.

Patrick, C.J. and Zempolich, K.A. (1998) Emotion and aggression in psychopathic personality. *Aggression and Violent Behavior*, **3**, 303–38.

Pithers, W.D., Kashima, K.K., Cumming, G.F. *et al.* (1988) Relapse prevention of sexual aggression, in *Human Sexual Aggression: Current Perspectives* (eds R.A. Prentky and V.L. Quinsey), Annals of the New York Academy of Sciences, Vol. **528**, New York Academy of Sciences, New York, pp. 244–60.

Polaschek, D.L.L., Hudson, S.M., Ward, T. and Siegert, R.J. (2001) Rapists' offence processes: a preliminary descriptive model. *Journal of Interpersonal Violence*, **16**, 523–44.

Posternak, M.A. and Zimmermann, M. (2002) Anger and aggression in psychiatric outpatients. *Journal of Clinical Psychiatry*, **63**, 665–72.

Power, M. and Dalgleish, T. (1999) *Cognition and Emotion: From Order to Disorder*, Psychology Press, Hove.

Russell, J.A. and Fehr, B. (1994) Fuzzy concepts in a fuzzy hierarchy: varieties of anger. *Journal of Personality and Social Psychology*, **67**, 186–205.

Smith, C.A. and Elsworth, P.C. (1985) Patterns of cognitive appraisal in emotion. *Journal of Personality and Social Psychology*, **48**, 813–38.

Sperry, M. (1995) *Handbook of Diagnosis and Treatment of the DSM-IV Personality Disorders*, Brunner/Mazel, Levittown, PA.

Steuerwald, B.L. and Kosson, D.S. (2000) Emotional experiences of the psychopath, in *The Clinical and Forensic Assessment of Psychopathy: A Practitioner's Guide* (ed. C.B. Gacono), Erlbaum, Mahwah, NJ, pp. 111–35.

Tedlow, J., Leslie, V., Keefe, B.R. *et al.* (1999) Axis I and Axis II disorder comorbidity in unipolar depression with anger attacks. *Journal of Affective Disorders*, **52**, 217–23.

Tsytsarev, S. and Grodnitsky, G. (1995) Anger and criminality, in *Anger Disorders* (ed. H. Kassinove), Taylor and Francis, Philadelphia, PA, pp. 91–108.

Van Coillie, H., Van Mechelen, I. and Ceulemans, E. (2006) Multidimensional individual differences in anger-related behaviours. *Personality and Individual Differences*, **41**, 27–38.

Ward, T., Louden, K., Hudson, S.M. and Marshall, W.L. (1995) Descriptive model of the offence chain for child molesters. *Journal of Interpersonal Violence*, **10**, 452–72.

Watt, B. and Howells, K. (1999) Skills training for aggression control: evaluation of an anger management program for violent offenders. *Legal and Criminological Psychology*, **4**, 285–300.

Widiger, T.A., Trull, T.J., Clarkin, J.F. *et al.* (2002) A description of the DSM-IV personality disorders with the five-factor model of personality, in *Personality Disorders and the Five-Factor Model of Personality*, 2nd edn (eds P.T. Costa and T.A. Widiger), American Psychological Association, Washington DC.

Williamson, P., Day, A. and Howells, K. (2003) Assessing offender readiness to change problems with anger. *Psychology, Crime and Law*, **9**, 295–307.

Witte, T.H., Callahan, K.L. and Perez-Lopez, M. (2002) Narcissism and anger: an exploration of underlying correlates. *Psychological Reports*, **90**, 871–5.

Yates, E., Barbaree, H.E. and Marshall, W.L. (1983) Anger and deviant sexual arousal. *Behaviour Therapy*, **15**, 287–94.

Zechmeister, J.S. and Romero, C. (2002) Victim and offender accounts of interpersonal conflicts: autobiographical narratives of forgiveness and unforgiveness. *Journal of Personality and Social Psychology*, **82**, 675–86.

Chapter 11

ATTACHMENT DIFFICULTIES

ANTHONY R. BEECH AND IAN J. MITCHELL

University of Birmingham, UK

INTRODUCTION

Gilbert and Proctor (2006) suggest that one of the key evolutionary changes that emerged in the evolution of mammals was attachment and general care giving for infants. They also noted that many mammals (particularly humans) need, and respond to, signals of care and affection and have evolved 'attachment' systems that are responsive to these signals. Nelson and Panksepp (1998) noted that the neural mechanisms which underlie attachment are organised into a *socially directed motivational system* within the brain. This neural system emerges in infancy and continues to modulate affiliative behaviours throughout an individual's lifespan. Affiliation and affiliative interactions have a soothing effect, alter pain thresholds and create experiences of safeness, and impact upon affect, and affect regulation (self-soothing) systems within the brain (Gilbert and Proctor, 2006). These systems involve the neuropeptides, oxytocin and vasopressin, and are instantiated in the limbic system in the brain, particularly the amygdala and the hippocampus (Panksepp, 1998).

The concept of attachment in humans was originally described by Bowlby (1969, 1973, 1980) as the process by which an infant has an inborn biological need to maintain close contact with its mother, or other main caretaker (Crittenden, 1985). Chapple (2003) described attachment in adulthood as 'connectedness' with others. Attachment theorists working in the area of adult personal relationships suggest that the caretaker–child relationship provides a model or template for future personal and intimate relationships with others (Collins and Read, 1994). This operates throughout that individual's lifespan irrespective of whether the relationship between the individual as a child and its primary carer/s was positive or negative. Therefore, attachment style can be seen as a set of enduring characteristics for making sense of one's life experiences and interactions with others (Young, Klosko and Weisharr, 2003). Ward, Hudson and Marshall (1996) argued that this is how expectations are developed about interpersonal relationships in that individuals may see themselves as worthy and deserving of another's attention, or conversely as worthless and undeserving of anybody's attention. Secure attachments give rise to internal working models of others as safe, helpful and supportive (Baldwin, 2005), while insecure attachments cause the individual to become focused on the power of others to control or reject them (Gilbert, 2005).

Attachment difficulties may represent a key determinant in explaining why some forms of interpersonal violence and abuse occur. Bowlby (1944), for example, postulated that psychopathy, violence and crime were primarily related to disorders of attachment, and that antisocial acts represent distorted attempts at interpersonal emotional exchanges. Others have observed that violent criminals' lives are associated with extremely disturbed attachment representations, a history of abuse and a marked lack of empathy (e.g. Craissati, in press). Continuity of antisocial behaviour over the lifespan has also been shown to be related to poor parental attachment (Fergusson and Lynskey, 1998). However, it is important to note that only a small proportion of individuals with an insecure attachment style would appear to engage in criminal activity. Consequently, attachment difficulties should only be viewed as one aspect of why violence occurs.

The purpose of this chapter is to explore the relationship between attachment difficulties and some aspects of interpersonal violence. In particular we aim to examine first, how personality traits and dysfunctional responding emerge from different attachment styles, and second, how these may lead, in part, to different types of offending, that is, *generalists/specialists* (Soothill *et al.*, 2000). We will briefly outline some of the neurobiological and psychological processes thought to underpin dysfunctional attachment in these groups, and finally suggest some therapeutic interventions to address attachment-related problems.

ATTACHMENT PROBLEMS AND VIOLENCE

Four adult attachment styles have been broadly identified in adulthood, one 'secure' and three 'insecure' styles:

1. *Secure/autonomous*, which is characterised by evaluations of attachment-related experiences, whether those be favourable or unfavourable. Individuals identified as having this style have high levels of self-esteem, view others as warm and accepting and report high levels of intimacy in close adult relationships (Ward, Hudson and Marshall, 1996). This pattern is associated with sensitive and responsive parenting in childhood.
2. *Preoccupied* (confusingly, the childhood version of this style is termed *ambivalent*), which is characterised as being preoccupied with past attachment experiences, and having an inability to report a coherent view of interactions with others (Holmes, 1993). Therefore, this style is associated with an increased risk of social withdrawal and rejection, and feelings of incompetence (Finzi *et al.*, 2001). This style has been found to be associated with an inconsistent parenting style in childhood where the parent is seen as behaving in ways that 'interfere with the child's autonomy or exploration' (Cassidy and Berlin, 1994, p. 981), leading

the individual to being uncertain of the quality of relationships, and living in fear of rejection (Henry and Wang, 1998).

3. *Dismissive* (the childhood version of this style is termed *avoidant*), which is characterised by an emphasis on achievement and self-reliance at the expense of intimacy. This pattern is associated with a rejecting or interfering parenting style, epitomised by the parent behaving in a remote, cold and controlling way, and discouraging independence (Belsky, 1999). Henry and Wang (1998) suggested that such an attachment style will cause the deactivation of the 'attachment mechanism', ultimately resulting in an adult who is emotionally autonomous and ready to express self-preservative behaviours. Such persons may be expected to show some antisocial characteristics, are often self-absorbed and unwilling to approach others for support (Sawle and Kear-Colwell, 2001) and have accepting attitudes about casual sex (Feeney, Noller and Patty, 1993). They are consequently more likely to engage in 'one night stands' (Brennan and Shaver, 1995) and to visit prostitutes and/or engage in coercive sex (Ward, Hudson and Marshall, 1996).

4. *Disorganised* (sometimes termed *Unresolved*), which is more often associated with parental maltreatment than the other insecure attachment styles (Carlson *et al.*, 1989; van Ijzendoorn, Schuengel and Bakermans-Kranenberg, 1999), and/or where the primary caregivers have experienced an unresolved loss or trauma of their own (Ainsworth and Eichberg, 1991; Main and Hesse, 1990). Here, it is argued that the parenting style is frightening or frightened, so that the individual, as a child, is caught in a conflict where what should be their source of security becomes a source of fear. Individuals with this style may not be actively hostile in their interactions with others, but may behave in a passive–aggressive manner. While, in intimate relationships their fear of rejection and avoidance of closeness may lead them to seek sex in an impersonal manner (Ward, Hudson and Marshall, 1996).

We should also note that in some studies the term 'unclassifiable' is used where no identifiable attachment style can be identified.

As for the diagnostic classification of insecure attachment, DSM-IV-TR (American Psychiatric Association, 2000) describes *Reactive Attachment Disorder of Infancy and Early Childhood* where two types of disturbance are reported: the *Inhibited* type where there is the persistent failure to initiate and respond to most social interactions in an appropriate way; and the *Disinhibited* type where there is an indiscriminate sociability or lack of selectivity in the choice of attachment figures.

Given the wealth of evidence in the offender literature concerning a history of adverse childhood events and attachment-related problems, for example, a history of trauma and abuse (Heide, 1999), it would not be unreasonable to suggest that many offenders would have difficulties establishing and maintaining interpersonal relationships and appropriate sexual relationships with adults. For example, discussing the development of disruptive behaviours and aggressive/violent behaviours, a number of authors have noted the role of coercive parent–child interactions and the absence of a positive and affectionate bond between parent and child, neglect, inconsistent parenting and severity of punishments (Frodi *et al.*, 2001; Greenberg, Speltz and DeKlyen, 1993; Sampson and Laub 1990). Lyons-Ruth,

Alpern and Repacholi (1993) reported that disorganised attachment, together with maternal psychosocial problems, was highly predictive of hostile–aggressive behaviours at a very young age. A similar conclusion was reached by Finzi *et al.* (2001) who reported that physically abused children were characterised by an avoidant attachment style, were aggressive, and suspicious of others. While Bowlby (1944), over half a century ago, suggested that early separations from, or absence of, attachment figures predispose individuals to develop emotional coldness or the 'affectionless' characteristic of psychopathy and a variety of other kinds of psychopathology.

As for how insecure attachment in part leads to antisocial behaviours in adulthood, Bowlby (1973) proposed that when children experience separations from parents, and when parents threaten abandonment, children feel intense anger. Dozier, Stovall and Albus (1999) noted that ordinary separations between children and parents can cause anger, but when prolonged separations are combined with frightening threats from parents/caregivers, children are likely to feel a dysfunctional level of anger towards the parents/primary caregivers often involving intense hate. Initially, the anger may be directed towards the parents, but this is seen as a dangerous strategy (given the parents' behaviour), and hence anger is often reprised and directed at other targets (Bowlby, 1973). Craissati (in press) observed that, for the delinquent adolescent, the early absence of a strong attachment to the parent may have been masked by the adult's physical capacity to control the child. The absence of parental control through emotional ties may not become clear until early adolescence when the life task is to transfer bonds to peers and social institutions (such as school) and there is a need for strongly internalised controls through morality, empathy, caring and commitment (Fonagy *et al.*, 1997).

The mechanism by which such childhood problems can lead to neurobiological problems and subsequent disturbances in social functioning is outlined by Joseph (2003) as:

> Deprived or abnormal rearing conditions induce severe disturbance in all aspects of social and emotional functioning, and affect the growth and survival of dendrites, axons, synapses, interneurons, neurons, and glia. The amygdala, cingulate, and septal nuclei develop at different rates which correlate with the emergence of wariness, fear, selective attachments, play behavior, and the oral and phallic stages of development. . . . The medial amygdala and later the cingulate and septal nuclei are the most vulnerable during the first three years of life. If denied sufficient stimulation these nuclei may atrophy, develop seizure-like activity or maintain or form abnormal synaptic interconnections, resulting in social withdrawal, pathological shyness, explosive and inappropriate emotionality, and an inability to form normal emotional attachments (p. 189).

As regards the genesis of sexual offending, Marshall (1989) was one of the first to suggest that insecure attachment in childhood would lead to difficulties in establishing intimate adult relationships and in the pursuit of intimacy through inappropriate sexual behaviour, while Craissati, McClurg and Browne (2002) found that sexual offenders commonly reported an 'affectionless control' style of parenting. Physical and sexual abuse are also highly likely to occur when there is a home life characterised by poor parental relationships and where there is a history of parental aggression, alcohol abuse and criminality (Dhaliwal *et al.*, 1996; Langevin, Wright and Handy, 1989; Weeks and Widom, 1998). Sexual offenders who reported an insecure attachment style were also more likely to report being sexually abused than those with a secure attachment style (Smallbone and McCabe, 2003). This may be due to them being less well looked after than securely attached children.

We will now look in more specific detail at the kinds of disorder associated with violent and sexual crime. We will first examine attachment problems in what can be regarded as *generalist* offenders, particularly in those with disorders where antisocial behaviour is a prominent feature (i.e. conduct disorder, psychopathy and antisocial personality disorder), and secondly in a more *specialist* offending group–those who commit paedophilic child sex offences.

Attachment and General Antisociality

In the literature, there are strong indications that dismissive attachment is related to antisocial disorders. Rosenstein and Horowitz (1996), for example, found that a sample of young people with a diagnosis of conduct disorder, a repetitive and persistent pattern of behaviour in which the basic rights of others or societal conventions are flouted, were generally classified as having a dismissing attachment style.

There also appears to be a strong association between disorganised and dismissive attachment and criminality more generally. Evidence for this assertion comes from Allen, Hauser and Borman-Spurell (1996). They measured states of mind among adolescents who were either psychiatric inpatients or high school students, finding that attachment predicted criminality 10 years later, even when psychiatric hospitalisation was taken into account. More specifically, criminality was predicted by 'derogation of attachment', a form of dismissing attachment in which the person belittles or negatively criticises attachment figures, or attachment-related experiences. Van Ijzendoorn *et al.* (1997) found an over-representation of disorganised or unclassifiable attachment in a group of offenders incarcerated in forensic mental health institutions for serous crimes such as murder and/or sexual offences. Baker and Beech (2004) reported high rates of disorganised attachment in a forensic psychiatric population of violent offenders, and sexually violent rapists, in comparison with non-clinical samples and non-sexual/non-violent offenders.

As for a relationship between insecure attachment and psychopathy, in a small study of 26 criminal offenders, just under two-thirds of their sample of psychopaths, defined by the Psychopathy Checklist Revised – Screening Version (PCL: SV; Hart, Cox and Hare, 1997), Frodi *et al.* (2001) found that most reported a dismissing attachment style, with the rest reported as 'unclassifiable'. The high levels of dismissive attachment reported by Frodi *et al.* do not necessarily suggest that psychopathy evolves from dismissive attachment. However, the seeming unfamiliarity the sample had with the concept of attachment *per se*, and the fact that these individuals did not have a good relationship with parents/carers (as evidenced by reports of severe childhood abuse, extensive neglect, early foster placements and institutionalisation) suggests a possible link.

Lang, af Klinteberg and Alm (2002) reported a relationship between victimisation as a child and later violence evidenced by the frequency of psychopaths having alcoholic or antisocial fathers. Ullrich and Marneros (2007), in a study looking at the factor analysis personality disorder dimensions scores of the of the ICD-10 as measured by the International Personality Disorder Examination (IPDE; Mombour et al., 1996), found that in those scoring highly on Factor 1 (dissocial, paranoid, histrionic and impulsive traits) were much more likely to have grown up with only one primary carer, or had frequent change of carers, violent carers and/or there was substance misuse by carers. Factor 1, as identified in the Ullrich and Marneros study, was found to have a strong correlation with psychopathy (as measured by the PCL: SV, Hart, Cox and Hare, 1997). Blair, Mitchell and Blair (2005) noted that such an adverse upbringing leading to poor attachment disrupts the process that leads to the development of morality, and therefore the development of psychopathic characteristics. This argument is in part based on the observation that elements of psychopathic traits can be seen before the age of eight (Blair et al., 2006; Saltaris, 2002).

The attachment model of the development of psychopathic behaviours is also supported by two case studies reported by Anderson et al. (1999, 2000) where damage to the ventromedial prefrontal cortex was incurred during very early childhood. This traumatic brain damage would be expected to have mirrored some of the neuronal changes that result from early psychological trauma as reported by Solomon and Heide (2005). The traumatic brain damage in these two cases resulted in a syndrome which can be termed 'pseudopsychopathy' which persisted into adulthood. Therefore, these cases did not exhibit all the features of psychopathy, but their moral reasoning was extremely limited, they were verbally and physically abusive, they had an inability to plan, never expressed guilt or remorse for their behaviour, nor were they responsive to verbal or physical punishment.

As for the presence of an adverse upbringing and attachment problems in anti-social personality disorder (APD), Zanarini et al. (1989) found that 89% of individuals in their sample meeting DSM-III (American Psychiatric Association, 1987) criteria for APD reported experiencing prolonged separations from a parent/caregiver at some point during their childhood, specifically through divorce or separation (Robins, 1996), although this finding has not been confirmed by Ullrich and Marneros (2007) in their IPDE psychopathic factor group. McCord (1979) found that APD was the most likely outcome when the individual's mother was unaffectionate and did not provide adequate supervision, and when their father was 'deviant'. Zanarini et al. reported that many of those diagnosed with APD also reported experiencing physical abuse or harsh discipline in childhood. Fonagy et al. (1996) reported an over-representation of disorganised attachment style in their sample of 82 non-psychotic inpatients compared to case matched controls.

Therefore, what we are moving towards here is a general association between dismissive, and in some cases disorganised attachment, in those disorders associated with antisocial behaviour and criminality more generally. We would note that Kendler, Davis and Kessler (1997) have described a hypothetical factor which they label as externalising which may unite these antisocial behaviour disorders (together with substance dependence). However, it is also worth noting that disorganised and dismissive attachment are also over-represented in other disorders such as borderline personality disorder (Fonagy et al., 1996) and schizophrenia

(Tyrell and Dozier, 1997, reported in Dozier, Stovall and Albus, 1999). We will now consider attachment problems in sexual offenders.

Problematic Attachment and Child Sexual Abuse

Ward, Hudson and Marshall (1996) found some evidence that child sexual abusers were more likely to report having a *preoccupied* attachment style, compared to rapists, violent offenders and non-violent offenders while rapists were more likely to report a *dismissing* style than child abusers and non-violent offenders. Stirpe *et al.* (2006) reported that a preoccupied attachment style is particularly prevalent in extrafamilial child sexual offenders[1] (paedophilic offenders). This style can cause problems in the way that they relate to others, cause feelings of inadequacy and loneliness (Ward and Beech, 2006). Baxter *et al.* (1984) similarly observed paedophiles are characteristically socially inadequate, lacking in interpersonal skills and confidence, and ill at ease in adult interactions. This pattern is not surprising given that a number of studies have reported that a larger proportion of paedophiles suffer from anxiety disorders and, in particular, social phobia compared to other groups of offenders (Hoyer, Kunst and Schmidt, 2001; McElroy *et al.*, 1999; Raymond *et al.*, 1999).

People with social phobia find interactions with adults, extremely threatening, especially when they run the risk of negative evaluation. Social anxiety and social phobia are thought to reflect fear precipitated by social evaluation and result in social avoidance (Rapee and Spence, 2004), which can arise from an ambivalent attachment style in childhood leading to fear of rejection. This style is associated with an increased risk of social withdrawal, social rejection and feelings of incompetence in adulthood (Finzi *et al.*, 2001). In keeping with these observations, Eastwood *et al.* (2005) demonstrated that patients with social phobia are adept at picking out negative, but not positive, facial expressions from neutral face distractors. However, socially anxious people may paradoxically also show high levels of interpersonal dependency (Darcy, Davila and Beck, 2005). Therefore, the socially phobic paedophile may find children less threatening and more interpersonally dependable.

Having briefly examined the relationship between attachment difficulties in generalist, antisocial offenders and what can be termed as the more specialist paedophilic offenders, we would argue that what is lacking in much of this work is a theoretically persuasive explanation of the relationship between interpersonal deficits and these particular types of antisocial behaviour. We are not saying we can provide one, but in the next section we will advance a tentative biological model to account for these offending behaviours.

TOWARDS A NEUROBIOLOGICAL MODEL OF ATTACHMENT-RELATED PROBLEMS IN OFFENDERS

When postulating neurobiologically inspired models of attachment-related problems in personality-disordered offenders we have focused on the contrasts between psychopathic offenders and fixated paedophiles, in that they would seem to represent both the extreme ends of the generalist–specialist distinction, and attachment-related problems. This view is advanced by Blair, Mitchell and Blair (2005), who observe that 'patients with this disorder [social phobia] exhibit some characteristics that are the antithesis of psychopathy' (p. 89). However, others would question this distinction.

Differences in Amygdala Function

One major difference between the two groups could be a difference in amygdala function. Blair *et al.* (2006) have argued that psychopathy is a developmental disorder, the psychological/behavioural characteristics of which reflect abnormal functioning in the neural circuitry involving the amygdala and the orbitofrontal cortex. More specifically, psychopaths show reduced amygdala activation during emotional memory and aversive conditioning tasks, and show deficits in the recognition of fearful facial expression, a task which is sensitive to amygdala damage.

In contrast, individuals with social phobia show abnormally increased amygdala activation when looking at angry and contemptuous faces (Killgore and Yurgelun-Todd, 2005; Phan *et al.*, 2006; Schneider *et al.*, 1999; Stein *et al.*, 2002). Furthermore, this increased amygdala activation correlates with the severity of social anxiety symptoms, but not general state or trait anxiety levels (Phan *et al.*, 2006). Veit *et al.* (2002) probably show the clearest distinction between these two groups by demonstrating that psychopaths and social phobics are the diametric opposites of each other with regard to amygdala-prefrontal function in a scanning experiment involving aversive conditioning to neutral faces.

The lack of recognition of fear in psychopaths, due to lack of amygdala function would suggest that this would make it easier to offend, as a key component of committing interpersonal violence towards others is the requirement to not recognise or understand the mental state of the other (the potential victim). These preconditions therefore make generalist offending that much easier.

As for fixated paedophiles, we have unpublished data suggesting that these show an abnormal fear of contamination from the bodily fluids of others. These fears, however, are reduced if the bodily fluids originate from children rather than adults. These abnormal contamination fears are most likely mediated by the amygdala as increased amygdala activity is associated with exposure to images relating to contamination threats (van den Heuvel *et al.*, 2004). These factors acting in concert, we would argue, cause the fixated paedophile to be driven to form intimate attachments but to be afraid of approaching adult women for fear of negative evaluation and rejection combined with a fear of contamination from them. Children therefore would represent less of an apparent health threat as well as being less of a social threat.

Differences in Neuropeptide Function

As for neurochemical differences between the groups, the most salient neurobiological system correlates of attachment are the central release of the neuropeptides, oxytocin and vasopressin. During attachment-related behaviours, neurones located mainly within the hypothalamus and amygdala release the neuropeptides into a variety of brain structures[2] as a consequence of socially pleasant sensory experiences, such as comforting touches and smells (Wismer Fries *et al.* 2005). Wismer Fries *et al.* (2005) noted that, 'these neuropeptides are associated with the emergence of social bonding, parental care, stress regulation, social communication, and emotional reactivity' (p. 17237). More specifically: *Oxytocin* is involved in social recognition and bonding. Evidence suggests that oxytocin is linked to social support, regulates stress hormone release and buffers stress (Heinrichs *et al.*, 2003). In women, it is released during labour and following stimulation of the nipples, so facilitating birth and breastfeeding. Oxytocin is also released during orgasm in both sexes. *Vasopressin* is involved in forming memories of social interactions (Popik, Vos and Vanree, 1992). It plays a role in social behaviour, initiates and sustains patterns of activity that support the pair bond in that it is released into the brain during sexual activity. The presence of vasopressin also appears to predispose males to become aggressive towards other males (Wismer Fries *et al.*, 2005). Furthermore, evidence from animal work suggests that strains of rodent specifically bred to show high levels of anxiety-related behaviours have elevated levels of vasopressin expression within limbic structures (Landgraf and Holsboer 2005).

The oxytocin system can interact with *corticosteroids* (Legross, 2001). For example, neonatal stress can result in long-term changes in the sensitivity of the oxytocin system (Carter, 1998). High levels of oxytocin are related to decreases in stress and related corticosteroid levels (Witt, Carter and Walton, 1990). These observations suggest the potential for stress to exert fairly direct effects upon the mechanisms that underlie attachment.

Psychopathy is characterised by emotional detachment and an inability to anticipate punishment (Blair *et al.*, 2006). The condition is associated with a *dismissive* attachment style (Frodi *et al.*, 2001). This lack of motivation to form long-lasting intimate relationships would be predicted to reflect low levels of oxytocin, and vasopressin release. This hypothesis has not been formally tested. However, it should be noted that the development of psychopathy is associated with early neglect and this is known to have a lasting impact on the oxytocin systems. Thus, being in foster care is a psychosocial factor which predicts high psychopathy scores (Campbell, Porter and Santor, 2004). Children who were placed in orphanages immediately after birth and neglected therein later showed both reduced basal levels of vasopressin and an inability to release oxytocin in response to normally pleasant social stimuli (Wismer Fries *et al.*, 2005). Similarly, Meinlschmidt and Heim (2007) have shown that the oxytocin system in men who had experienced early parental separation was abnormally ineffective in reducing corticosteroid levels. This suggests that early neglect could induce reduced oxytocin and vasopressin function which would lead to an inability to develop 'normal' emotional attachments, and perhaps produce a lack of empathy towards others (Solomon and Heide, 2005), which would make it easier to offend against others.

We would also tentatively argue that the neuropeptide functioning in fixated paedophiles will be the opposite of that seen in the psychopath. More specifically we argue that vasopressin function in fixated paedophiles will be elevated. Accordingly, raised vasopressin function would both drive the need to form long-lasting intimate social relationships whilst simultaneously resulting in excessive anxiety, which would interfere with the attachment process. This scenario captures something of the preoccupied style of attachment shown by many fixated paedophiles (Ward, Hudson and Marshall, 1996; Stirpe *et al.*, 2006).

These observations are of necessity brief and we are in the process of developing these ideas in more depth (Mitchell and Beech, in preparation).

TREATMENT FOR ATTACHMENT-RELATED PROBLEMS IN OFFENDERS

The aim of this section is to suggest treatment approaches that will act as an adjunct to the successful therapies, based on the 'What Works' risk, need and responsivity principles (Andrews and Bonta, 2003). The *risk* principle is concerned with the match between an individual's level of risk for reoffending and the amount of treatment they should receive. The *need* principle is that treatment for offenders should focus on changing criminogenic needs, and the *responsivity* principle is used to refer to the style and mode of intervention that engages the interest of the client group. Responsivity is concerned with how the individual interacts with the treatment environment with the specific aim of motivating and engaging an individual in the treatment process. Therefore, taking individual's attachment style would appear to be an important aspect of the treatment approach regardless of what particular offence-related work is being carried out.

Meyer and Pilkonis (2002) noted that attachment style has an influence upon the relationship formed in therapy. Specifically, they state that securely attached people formed effective therapeutic relationships, while people with a preoccupied style of attachment progressed from a poor alliance to strong alliance in the later stages of treatment, while patients with a dismissive attachment style reported deteriorating alliances towards the end of treatment. As for personality-disordered patients, the pattern of results is mixed. Fonagy *et al.* (1996) reported that patients who were dismissively attached exhibited the most improvement through treatment, compared to other attachment styles. In contrast, Meyer *et al.* (2001) found that secure attachment predicted improvement whereas non-secure attachment did not. There is also some limited research that suggests that treatment may be more effective when certain patient and therapists attachment styles are paired (Fernàndez-Alverez *et al.*, 2006). In contrast, Tyrell *et al.* (1999) found that complementary combinations of attachment were the most productive, for example, preoccupied patients did better working with dismissive therapists.

Generally, the approach to attachment-related problems can be said to have involved traditional psychotherapy approaches, including insight-oriented individual psychotherapy, cognitive therapy, family therapy and milieu therapy. However, these talking therapies, as Solomon and Heide (2005) note, depend upon top-down processing in which 'the client is taught to use cognitive strategies to manage or inhibit problematic feelings, thoughts and behaviours . . . [to] help them change erroneous beliefs or maladaptive ways of thinking and behaving . . .' (p. 56). However, it can be argued that clients with attachment problems may (when their threat systems are activated) respond in ways that cannot be modulated by the neocortex.

For example, some individuals with a preoccupied attachment style can be highly self-critical and construe many things as threatening. Therefore, they can understand the logic of what is being said in therapy, and generate alternative thoughts to self-criticism, but are rarely reassured by such efforts (Lee, 2005).

Therefore, as an adjunct to successful cognitive–behavioural therapies we would suggest that it is worth considering working with offenders in ways that tap more into the emotional (limbic) areas of the brain. Some useful ideas have been reported by Gilbert and colleagues (e.g. Gilbert, 2005; Gilbert and Proctor, 2006) in their compassion-focused work with people with borderline personality disorder. Their basic argument is that individuals who cannot feel compassion towards themselves will be unable to feel compassion for others, which we would suggest is a necessary part of victim empathy work, a common component of treatment for offenders.

A number of approaches to psychotherapy stress the importance of the development of inner compassion and self-soothing abilities, especially dialectical behaviour therapy (Linehan, 1993) and mindfulness work (e.g. Segal, Williams and Teasdale, 2002). However, the Compassionate Mind Training approach advocated by Gilbert (2005) may be especially worth considering here, in that it is a form of therapy where clients with high levels of shame and self-criticism (associated with insecure attachment) learn to self-soothe, which potentially increases levels of oxytocin and the opiates (Carter, 1998; Depue and Morrone-Strupinsky, 2005; Uväns-Morberg, 1998). This enables individuals to feel better about themselves and about others.

An alternative pharmacological approach would be to make use of newly developed vasopressin antagonists to reduce anxiety (Landgraf and Neumann 2004), or the use of oxytocin itself, where the nasal application of oxytocin has been found to increase trust in humans (Kosfield et al., 2005).

CONCLUSIONS

In this chapter, we have attempted to explore the relationship between attachment difficulties and particular types of offending. We have noted evidence that there appears to be quite persuasive evidence that dismissive attachment is related to general APDs, while there is some fairly strong evidence that preoccupied attachment is over-represented in paedophilic child sexual abusers. Such attachment styles we would note can lead to problematic interactions with others. Therefore we would suggest that interventions, for identifiable problematic attachment styles, may be useful with these kinds of offenders, as an adjunct to therapies targeting particular offending behaviours. We have briefly described some types of interventions that may be worth considering in this chapter.

It is also becoming clear that attachment-related behaviours have a clear neurobiological basis and that attachment systems can become compromised if neglect and abuse occur in childhood. It seems to us that there are two clearly identifiable types of offenders, at opposite ends of a spectrum of offending, who differ in terms of neurobiological functioning. At one end of the spectrum is the type of offender characterised by a high level of antisocial behaviours and tendencies (conditions associated with early life stressors and physical abuse), where there is strong evidence of hypoactive amygdala functioning and we speculate that there may be low levels of central neuropeptide activity. At the other end of the offending spectrum there are fixated paedophiles (a condition often associated with early neglect and sexual abuse in later childhood), where we speculate that the opposite neurobiological pattern will be observed. There is more clearly evidence for some of these assertions than others; however, from this framework there are clear hypotheses that can be pursued in order to lead to an understanding of why sexual and violent offending is perpetrated.

NOTES

1. Incestuous (intra-familial) offenders are more likely to have a dismissive attachment style, indicating that these men are probably more generalist, antisocial offenders.
2. These target structures reside mainly within the limbic system, parts of the olfactory system and brain areas associated with controlling the autonomic nervous system.

REFERENCES

Ainsworth, M.D.S. and Eichberg, C.G. (1991) Effects on infant-mother attachment of mother's unresolved loss of an attachment figure or other traumatic experience, in *Attachment across the Life Cycle* (eds C.M. Parkes, J. Stevenson-Hinde and P. Marris), Routledge, London, pp. 160–83.

Allen, J.P., Hauser, S.T. and Borman-Spurell, E. (1996) Attachment theory as a framework for understanding sequelae of severe adolescent psychopathology: an 11-year follow-up study. *Journal of Consulting and Clinical Psychology*, **64**, 254–63.

American Psychiatric Association (1987) *Diagnostic and Statistical Manual of Mental Disorder*, 3rd edn, American Psychiatric Association, Washington DC.

American Psychiatric Association (2000) *Diagnostic and Statistical Manual of Mental Disorder*, *Text Revision*, 4th edn, American Psychiatric Association, Washington DC.

Anderson, S.W., Bechara, A., Damasio, H. *et al.* (1999) Impairment of social and moral behavior related to early damage in human prefrontal cortex. *Nature Neuroscience*, **2**, 1032–7.

Anderson, S.W., Damasio, H., Tranel, D. and Damasio, A.R. (2000) Long-term sequelae of prefrontal cortex damage acquired in early childhood. *Developmental Neuropsychology*, **18**, 281–96.

Andrews, D.A. and Bonta, J. (2003) *The Psychology of Criminal Conduct*, 3rd edn, Anderson, Cincinnati, OH.

Baker, E. and Beech, A.R. (2004) Dissociation and variability of adult attachment dimensions and early maladaptive schemas in sexual and violent offenders. *Journal of Interpersonal Violence*, **19**, 1119–36.

Baldwin, M.W. (2005) *Interpersonal Cognition*, Guilford, New York.

Baxter D.J., Marshall, W.L, Barbaree, H.E. *et al.* (1984) Deviant sexual behavior. Differentiating sex offenders by criminal and personal history, psychometric measures, and sexual-response. *Criminal Justice and Behavior*, **11**, 477–501.

Belsky, J. (1999) Patterns of attachment a modern evolutionary perspective, in *Handbook of Attachment; Theory Research and Clinical Applications* (eds J. Cassady and P.R. Shaver), Guilford, New York, pp. 141–61.

Blair, R.J.R., Mitchell, D. and Blair, K. (2005) *The Psychopath: Emotion and the Brain*, Blackwell, Oxford.

Blair, R.J.R., Peschardt, K.S., Budhani, S. *et al.* (2006) The development of psychopathy. *Journal of Child Psychology and Psychiatry*, **47**, 262–75.

Bowlby, J. (1944) Forty-four juvenile thieves: their characters and home-life. *International Journal of Psychoanalysis*, **25**, 19–53.

Bowlby, J. (1969) *Attachment and Loss: Attachment*, Basic Books, New York.

Bowlby, J. (1973) *Attachment and Loss: Separation, Anxiety and Anger*, Basic Books, New York.

Bowlby, J. (1980) *Attachment and Loss: Loss, Sadness and Depression*, Basic Books, New York.

Brennan, K.A. and Shaver, P.R. (1995) Dimensions of adult attachment, affect regulation, and romantic relationship functioning. *Personality and Social Psychology Bulletin*, **21**, 267–83.

Campbell, M.A., Porter, S. and Santor, D. (2004) Psychopathic traits in adolescent offenders: an evaluation of criminal history, clinical, and psychosocial correlates. *Behavioral Sciences and the Law*, **22**, 23–47.

Carlson, V., Cicchetti, D., Barnett, D. and Braunwald, K. (1989) Disorganized/disoriented attachment relationships in maltreated infants. *Developmental Psychology*, **25**, 525–31.

Carter, C.S. (1998) Neuroendocrine perspectives on social attachment and love. *Psychoneuroendocrinology*, **23**, 779–818.

Cassidy, J. and Berlin, L. (1994) The insecure/ambivalent pattern of attachment: theory and research. *Child Development*, **65**, 971–91.

Chapple, C.L. (2003) Examining intergenerational violence: violent role modeling or weak parental controls? *Violence and Victims*, **18**, 143–61.

Collins, N.L. and Read, S.J. (1994) Cognitive representations of attachment. The structure and function of working models, in *Advances on Personal Relationships, Volume 5: Attachment Processes in Adulthood* (eds D. Perlman and K. Bartholomew), Jessica Kingsley, London, pp. 53–90.

Craissati, J. (in press) Attachment problems and sex offending, in *Handbook of Assessment and Treatment of Sexual Offenders* (eds A.R. Beech, L. Craig and K.D. Browne), John Wiley & Sons, Ltd, Chichester.

Craissati, J., McClurg, G. and Browne, K.D. (2002) Characteristics of perpetrators of child sexual abuse who have been sexually victimized as children. *Sexual Abuse: A Journal of Research and Treatment*, **14**, 225–40.

Crittenden, P.M. (1985) Mother and infant patterns of interaction: developmental relationships. *Dissertation Abstracts International*, **45**, 2710.

Darcy, K., Davila, J. and Beck, J.G. (2005) Is social anxiety associated with both interpersonal avoidance and interpersonal dependence? *Cognitive Therapy and Research*, **29**, 171–86.

Depue, R.A. and Morrone-Strupinsky, J.V. (2005) A neurobehavioral model of affiliative bonding. *Behavioral and Brain Sciences*, **28**, 313–95.

Dhaliwal, G.K., Gauzas, L., Antonowicz, D.H. and Ross, R.R. (1996) Adult male survivors of childhood sexual abuse: prevalence, sexual characteristics, and long-term effects. *Clinical Psychology Review*, **16**, 619–39.

Dozier, M., Stovall, K.C. and Albus, K. (1999) Attachment and psychopathology in adulthood, in *Handbook of Attachment Theory and Research* (eds J. Cassidy and P.R. Shaver), Guilford, New York, pp. 497–519.

Eastwood, J.D., Smilek, D., Oakman, J.M. *et al.* (2005) Individuals with social phobia are biased to become aware of negative faces. *Visual Cognition*, **12**, 159–79.

Feeney, J.A., Noller, P. and Patty, J. (1993) Adolescents interactions with the opposite sex – influence of attachment style and gender. *Journal of Adolescence*, **16**, 169–86.

Fergusson, D.M. and Lynskey, M.T. (1998) Conduct problems in childhood and psychosocial outcomes in young adulthood: a prospective study. *Journal of Emotional and Behavioral Disorders*, **6**, 2–18.

Fernàndez-Alverez, H., Clarkin, J.F., del Carmen Salgueiro, M. and Critchfield, K.L. (2006) Participant factors in treating personality disorders, in *Principles of Therapeutic Change that Work* (eds L.G. Castonguay and L.E. Beutler), Oxford University Press, Oxford, pp. 203–18.

Finzi, R., Ram, A., Har-Even, D. *et al.* (2001) Attachment styles and aggression in physically abused and neglected children. *Journal of Youth and Adolescence*, **30**, 769–86.

Fonagy, P., Leigh, T., Steel, M. *et al.* (1996) The relation of attachment status, psychiatric classification, and response to psychotherapy. *Journal of Consulting and Clinical Psychology*, **64**, 22–31.

Fonagy, P., Target, M., Steele, M. and Steele, H. (1997) The development of violence and crime as it relates to security of attachment, in *Children in a Violent Society* (ed. J. Osojsky), Guilford, New York, pp. 150–77.

Frodi, A., Dernevik, M., Sepa, A. *et al.* (2001) Current attachment representations of incarcerated offenders varying in degree of psychopathy. *Attachment and Human Development*, **3**, 269–83.

Gilbert, P. (2005) Compassion and cruelty: a biopsychosocial approach, in *Compassion: Conceptualisations, Research and Use in Psychotherapy* (ed. P. Gilbert), Routledge, London, pp. 9–74.

Gilbert, P. and Proctor, S. (2006) Compassionate mind training for people with high shame and self-criticism: overview and pilot study of a group therapy approach. *Clinical Psychology and Psychotherapy*, **13**, 353–79.

Greenberg, M.T., Speltz, M.L. and DeKlyen, M. (1993) The role of attachment in the early development of disruptive behavior problems. *Development and Psychopathology*, **5**, 191–213.

Hart, S.D., Cox, D. and Hare, R. (1997) *Psychopathy Checklist – Screening Version*, Multi-Health Systems, Toronto.

Heide, K.M. (1999) *Young killers: The Challenge of Juvenile Homicide*, Sage, Thousand Oaks, CA.

Heinrichs, M., Baumgartner, T., Kirschbaum, C. and Ehlert, U. (2003) Social support and oxytocin interact to suppress cortisol and subjective responses to psychosocial stress. *Biological Psychiatry*, **54**, 1389–98.

Henry, J.P. and Wang, S. (1998) Effects of early stress on adult affiliative behavior. *Psychoneuroendocrinology*, **23**, 863–75.

Holmes, J. (1993) Attachment theory: a biological basis for psychotherapy? *British Journal of Psychiatry*, **163**, 430–8.

Hoyer, J., Kunst, H. and Schmidt, A. (2001) Social phobia as a comorbid condition in sex offenders with paraphilia or impulse control disorder. *Journal of Nervous and Mental Disease*, **189**, 463–70.

Joseph, R. (2003) Environmental influences on neural plasticity, the limbic system, emotional development and attachment: a review. *Child Psychiatry and Human Development*, **29**, 189–208.

Kendler, K.S., Davis, C.G. and Kessler, R.C. (1997) The familial aggregation of common psychiatric and substance use disorders in the National Comorbidity Survey: a family history study. *British Journal of Psychiatry*, **170**, 541–8.

Killgore, W.D.S. and Yurgelun-Todd, D.A. (2005) Social anxiety predicts amygdala activation in adolescents viewing fearful faces. *Neuroreport*, **16**, 1671–5.

Kosfield, M., Heinrichs, M., Zak, P.J. *et al.* (2005) Oxytocin increases trust in humans. *Nature*, **435**, 673–6.

Landgraf, R. and Holsboer, F. (2005) The involvement of neuropeptides in evolution, signaling, behavioral regulation and psychopathology: focus on vasopressin. *Drug Development Research*, **65**, 185–90.

Landgraf, R. and Neumann, I.D. (2004) Vasopressin and oxytocin release within the brain: a dynamic concept of multiple and variable modes of neuropeptide communication. *Frontiers in Neuroendocrinology*, **25**, 150–76.

Lang, S., af Klinteberg, B. and Alm, P.O. (2002) Adult psychopathy and violent behavior in males with early neglect and abuse. *Acta Psychiatrica Scandinavica*, **106** (Suppl. 412), 93–100.

Langevin, R., Wright, P. and Handy, L. (1989) Characteristics of sex offenders who were sexually victimized as children. *Annals of Sex Research*, **2**, 227–53.

Lee, D.A. (2005) The perfect nurturer: a model to develop a compassionate mind within the context of cognitive therapy, in *Compassion: Conceptualisations, Research and Use in Psychotherapy* (ed. P. Gilbert), Routledge, London, pp. 326–51.

Legross, J.J. (2001) Inhibitory effect of oxytocin on corticotrope function in humans, are vasopressin and oxytocin ying-yang neurohormones? *Psychoneuroendocrinology*, **26**, 649–55.

Linehan, M. (1993) *Cognitive Behavioural Treatment of Borderline Personality Disorder*, Guilford, New York.

Lyons-Ruth, K., Alpern, L. and Repacholi, B. (1993) Disorganized infant attachment classification and maternal psychosocial problems as predictors of hostile aggressive behavior in the preschool classroom. *Child Development*, **64**, 572–85.

Main, M. and Hesse, E. (1990) Parent's unresolved traumatic experiences are related to infant disorganization status: is frightened and/or frightening behavior the linking mechanism? in *Attachment in the Pre-School Years* (eds M.T. Greenberg, D. Cicchetti and E.M. Cummings), University of Chicago Press, Chicago, pp. 161–82.

Marshall, W.L. (1989) Invited essay: intimacy, loneliness and sexual offenders. *Behaviour Research and Therapy*, **27**, 491–503.

McCord, J. (1979) Some child-rearing antecedents of criminal behavior in adult men. *Journal of Personality and Social Psychology*, **37**, 1477–86.

McElroy, S.L., Soutullo, C.A., Taylor, P. *et al.* (1999) Psychiatric features of 36 men convicted of sexual offenses. *Journal of Clinical Psychiatry*, **60**, 414–20.

Meinlschmidt, G. and Heim, C. (2007) Sensitivity to intranasal oxytocin in adult men with early parental separation. *Biological Psychiatry*, **61**, 1109–11.

Meyer, B. and Pilkonis, P. (2002) Attachment style, in *Psychotherapy Relationships That Work: Therapist Contributions and Responsiveness to Patients* (ed. J. Norcross), Oxford University Press, Oxford, pp. 367–82.

Meyer, B., Pilkonis, P., Proietti, J.M. *et al.* (2001) Attachment styles and personality disorders as predictors of symptom course. *Journal of Personality Disorders*, **15**, 371–89.

Mitchell, I.J. and Beech, A.R. (in preparation) The neurobiology of psychopathy and socially phobic paedophilia.

Mombour, W., Zaudig, M., Berger, P. *et al.* (1996) *International Personality Disorder Examination ICD-10 Module*, Huber, Bern.

Nelson, E.E. and Panksepp. J. (1998) Brain substrates of infant-mother attachment, contributions of opioids, oxytocin, and norepinephrine. *Neuroscience and Biobehavioral Reviews*, **22**, 437–52.

Panksepp, J. (1998) *Affective Neuroscience*, Oxford University Press, Oxford.

Phan, K.L., Fitzgerald, D.A., Nathan, P.J. and Tancer, M.E. (2006) Association between amygdala hyperactivity to harsh faces and severity of social anxiety in generalized social phobia. *Biological Psychiatry*, **59**, 424–9.

Popik, P., Vos, P.E. and Vanree, J.M. (1992) Neurohypophyseal hormone receptors in the septum are implicated in social recognition in the rat. *Behavioral Pharmacology*, **3**, 351–8.

Rapee, R.M. and Spence, S.H. (2004) The etiology of social phobia: empirical evidence and an initial model. *Clinical Psychology Review*, **24**, 737–67.

Raymond, N.C., Coleman, E., Ohlerking, F. *et al.* (1999) Psychiatric comorbidity in pedophilic sex offenders. *American Journal of Psychiatry*, **156**, 786–8.

Robins, L. (1996) *Deviant Children Grown Up*, Williams & Wilkins, Baltimore, MD.

Rosenstein, D.S. and Horowitz, H.A. (1996) Adolescent attachment and psychopathology. *Journal of Consulting and Clinical Psychology*, **64**, 244–53.

Saltaris, C. (2002) Psychopathy in juvenile offenders: can temperament and attachment be considered as robust developmental precursors. *Clinical Psychology Review*, **22**, 729–52.

Sampson, R.J. and Laub, J.H. (1990) Crime and deviance over the life course: the salience of adult social bonds. *American Sociological Review*, **55**, 609–27.

Sawle, G.A. and Kear-Colwell, J. (2001) Adult attachment style and pedophilia: a developmental perspective. *International Journal of Offender Therapy and Comparative Criminology*, **45**, 32–50.

Schneider, F., Weiss, U., Kessler, C. *et al.* (1999) Subcortical correlates of differential classical conditioning of aversive emotional reactions in social phobia. *Biological Psychiatry*, **45**, 863–71.

Segal, Z., Williams, J.M.G. and Teasdale, J. (2002) *Mindfulness-Based Cognitive Therapy for Depression: A New Approach to Preventing Relapse*, Guilford, New York.

Smallbone, S.W. and McCabe, B.A. (2003) Childhood attachment, childhood sexual abuse, and onset of masturbation among adult sexual offenders. *Sexual Abuse: A Journal of Research and Treatment*, **51**, 1–10.

Solomon, E.P. and Heide, K.M. (2005) The biology of trauma. *Journal of Interpersonal Violence*, **20**, 51–60.

Soothill, K., Francis, B., Sanderson, E. and Ackerley, E. (2000) Sex offenders: specialists, generalists or both. *British Journal of Criminology*, **40**, 56–67.

Stein, M.B., Goldin, P.R., Sareen, J. *et al.* (2002) Increased amygdala activation to angry and contemptuous faces in generalized social phobia. *Archives of General Psychiatry*, **59**, 1027–34.

Stirpe, T., Abracen, J., Stermac, L. and Wilson, R. (2006) Sexual offenders' state-of-mind regarding childhood attachment: a controlled investigation. *Sexual Abuse: A Journal of Research and Treatment*, **18**, 289–302.

Tyrell, C.L. and Dozier, M. (1997) *The Role of Attachment in Therapeutic Process and Outcome For Adults with Serious Psychiatric Disorders*. Paper presented at the Biennial Meeting of the Society for Research in Child Development.

Tyrell, C.L., Dozier, M., Teague, G.B. and Fallott, R.D. (1999) Effective treatment relationships for persons with serous psychiatric disorder: the importance of attachment states of mind. *Journal of Consulting and Clinical Psychology*, **67**, 725–33.

Ullrich, S. and Marneros, A. (2007) Underlying dimensions of ICD-10 personality disorders: risk factors, childhood antecedents, and adverse outcomes in adulthood. *Journal of Forensic Psychiatry and Psychology*, **18**, 44–58.

Uväns-Morberg, K. (1998) Oxytocin may mediate the benefits of positive social interaction and emotions. *Psychoneuroendocrinology*, **23**, 819–35.

Van Den Heuvel, O.A., Veltman, D.J., Groenewegen, H.J. *et al.* (2004) Amygdala activity in obsessive-compulsive disorder with contamination fear: a study with oxygen-15 water positron emission tomography. *Psychiatry Research: Neuroimaging*, **132**, 225–37.

van Ijzendoorn, M.H., Feldbrugge, J.T., Derks, F.C. *et al.* (1997) Attachment representations of personality-disordered criminal offenders. *American Journal of Orthopsychiatry*, **67**, 449–59.

van Ijzendoorn, M.H., Schuengel, C. and Bakermans-Kranenberg, M.J. (1999) Disorganized attachment in early childhood: meta-analysis of precursors, concomitants, and sequelae. *Development and Psychopathology*, **11**, 225–50.

Veit, R., Flor, H., Erb, M. *et al.* (2002) Brain circuits involved in emotional learning in antisocial behavior and social phobia in humans. *Neuroscience Letters*, **328**, 233–6.

Ward, T. and Beech, A.R. (2006) An integrated theory of sex offending. *Aggression and Violent Behavior*, **11**, 44–63.

Ward, T., Hudson, S.M. and Marshall, W.L. (1996) Attachment style in sex offenders: a preliminary study. *The Journal of Sex Research*, **33**, 17–26.

Weeks, R. and Widom, C. (1998) Self-reports of early childhood victimization among incarcerated adult male felons. *Journal of Interpersonal Violence*, **13**, 346–61.

Wismer Fries, A.B., Ziegler, T.E., Kurain, J.P. *et al.* (2005) Early experience in humans is associated with changes in neuropeptides critical for regulating social behavior. *Proceedings of the National Academy of Sciences of the United States of America*, **102**, 17237–40.

Witt, D.M., Carter, C.S. and Walton, D.M. (1990) Central and peripheral effects of oxytocin administration in prairie voles (Microtus ochrogaster). *Pharmacology Biochemistry and Behavior*, **37**, 63–9.

Young, J.E., Klosko. J.S. and Weisharr, M.E. (2003) *Schema Therapy: A Practitioner's Guide*, Guilford, London.

Zanarini, M.C., Gunderson, J.G., Marino, M.F. *et al.* (1989) Childhood experiences of borderline patients. *Comprehensive Psychiatry*, **30**, 18–25.

Chapter 12

EMPATHY AND OFFENDING BEHAVIOR

WILLIAM L. MARSHALL, LIAM E. MARSHALL, AND GERIS A. SERRAN

Rockwood Psychological Services, Canada

Psychologists (e.g. Batson, 1991; Eisenberg and Miller, 1987; Hoffman, 1982; Penner *et al.*, 1995) have often claimed that empathy underlies prosocial behavior and that its absence typically results in aggressive and acquisitive behaviors that ignore the rights or suffering of others (Fesbach, 1987; Miller and Eisenberg, 1988). Presently available evidence supports the idea that empathic people are more prosocial than those who have a relative lack of empathy (Zahn-Waxler and Robinson, 1995), and that the latter group tend to be more aggressive (Eisenberg, 2000). In that case, the issue of empathy, or lack thereof, should be a central feature in the assessment and treatment of those who commit criminal offenses. As we will see, however, empathy research with offenders has, for the most part, been restricted to those who commit either violent or sexual offenses and in those offenders who are found to be psychopathic.

In the chapter, we will begin by examining the concept of empathy, and then we will evaluate some of the most commonly employed measures of empathy, before we turn to a review of the evidence on empathy deficits in offenders. Finally, we will examine approaches to the enhancement of empathy, and we will describe what little data there is on their effectiveness.

CONCEPTUAL ISSUES

The notion of sympathy and its influence on behavior first appeared in the writings of the Scottish philosopher, David Hume (Hume, 1739), and was taken up by his compatriot Adam Smith (Smith, 1759). Both these philosophers considered sympathy to be essential to moral development. As such their ideas foreshadow current research interests in the relationship between empathy or sympathy and such prosocial behaviors as altruism (Batson, 1987) and reparative responses to distress in others (Zahn-Waxler, Radke-Yarrow and King, 1979).

Personality, Personality Disorder and Violence   Edited by Mary McMurran and Richard C. Howard
© 2009 John Wiley & Sons, Ltd

Empathy and Sympathy

Many writers have used these terms interchangeably (Fesbach, 1978; Hogan, 1969; Ohbuchi, 1988) while others (Dymond, 1949; Fesbach, 1975) have described sympathy in terms identical to what others mean by empathy. It appears better to distinguish these terms and several authors have done so (Batson, Fultz and Schoenrade, 1987; Eisenberg, 2000; Hanson, 1997). Empathy, so Eisenberg (2000) declares, is an emotional response to the recognition of another person's state that is a near-enough match for the other's emotion. As such empathy does not necessarily lead to a sympathetic response which involves feelings of concern for the upset person and, where possible, leads to reparative behaviors meant to ameliorate the other's distress. As Batson, Fultz and Schoenrade (1987) note, in some people, or on some occasions in most people, the recognition of distress in others is so upsetting to the observer that, far from seeking to comfort the distressed person, they seek only to reduce their own discomfort.

Trait or State Response

Most discussions of empathy, and certainly the majority of measures (see Serran, 2002), construe empathy as a disposition that is manifest across situations, persons and time. Quite early on Cottrell (1942) challenged this idea declaring the trait approach to be inadequate. What Cottrell said was needed was 'a situational frame of reference' (p. 381). As Hoffman (1982) points out, if we were not able to readily suppress empathy, we would experience what he calls 'promiscuous empathy' which would overwhelm us. We have to be able to differentially suppress empathy in order to function effectively in social interactions. Everyday experience suggests that empathic responding is tempered, if not determined, by situational or personal features. Readers of novels have no trouble suspending empathy when an established villain is brought to a sorry end. Indeed, novelists, dramatists and film-makers rely on such responses. There is now extensive evidence indicating that, indeed, empathic responding is modified by a variety of situational (Batson, 1987; Fultz, Schaller and Cialdini, 1988; Strayer, 1993) and personal features (Davis and Kraus, 1997; Thomas and Fletcher, 1997). Researchers working with sexual offenders have similarly found differences in empathy depending upon who the identified distressed person is (Beckett and Fisher, 1994; Fernandez and Marshall, 2003; Fernandez et al., 1999; Hanson and Scott, 1995; McGrath, Cann and Konopasky, 1998). In these studies, it was found that sexual offenders did not lack empathy toward people in general but failed to display empathy toward their own victims.

MODELS OF EMPATHY

Empathy has come to be viewed as a multi-component process (Davis, 1983; Williams, 1990). In attempting to make sense of the general literature on empathy, Marshall et al. (1995) outlined a four-stage model that defined empathy as an unfolding process with each stage dependent upon the emergence of the former stage. In effective empathy, these stages involve the recognition of another person's distress, followed by the ability to take the perspective of the other person, then the observer experiences much the same emotion as the distressed person, and finally, the observer does (or does not) take action to ameliorate the distress of the other person. Surprisingly, the emotional recognition aspect of empathy has, with a few exceptions (Fesbach, 1987; Miller and Eisenberg, 1988), been largely neglected by researchers in general psychology.

In so far as Marshall *et al.*'s model has any value, it is that it allowed the prediction of possible deficits in offenders' capacity for empathy; that is, they may be deficient at any or all of the four stages. Hudson *et al.* (1993) detected deficits among sexual offenders in their capacity to recognize emotions in others (Stage 1 in the model), and Hanson and Scott (1995) showed that sexual offenders were deficient in perspective taking (Stage 2).

Despite the fact that Marshall *et al.*'s model did produce some novel findings, it has serious limits. As Pithers (1999) noted, some compassionate responses (Stage 4 in Marshall *et al.*'s model) occur so rapidly that they could not be preceded by the processes Marshall *et al.* suggested. Pithers also pointed out that empathic people are more able to accurately predict another person's response to what they might say or do and, as a result, they act to reduce the likelihood of upsetting the other person. This, along with correctly identifying another person's distress, is essentially what Ickes (1997) refers to as 'empathic accuracy'. Research by Batson and his colleagues (Batson, 1991; Batson, Fultz and Schoenrade, 1987; Batson *et al.*, 1983) has demonstrated that if the observer experiences a high level of distress in response to seeing someone else upset, then the observer will become self-focused and attempt to do whatever will reduce his or her own distress rather than respond sympathetically. Hanson (1997), basing part of his reasoning on Batson's findings, declares that a sympathetic response (i.e. an attempt to ameliorate the observed person's distress) will only occur if empathy is accurate, if there exists a benign or caring relationship between the observed and observer, and only if the observer can cope with his or her own feelings.

As a result of these challenges, we (Marshall and Marshall, 2001) have modified our model of empathy (see Figure 12.1). In this model, emotional recognition is still the first stage. An inability to recognize distress in others may result from poor emotional recognition skills (Buck, 1984) and at least some offenders appear to lack these basic skills (Hudson *et al.*, 1993). However, an apparent lack of emotional recognition may be the result of a deliberate decision to distort information. Many offenders deny they have done harm even when there is clear evidence of distress in their victim (Laws, 2002). In the experimental psychology literature, there are studies demonstrating that people typically engage in defensive strategies when faced with the damaging consequences of their actions (Janoff-Bulman, 1979; Shaver, 1970) and that these strategies are meant to obviate the negative emotions that would otherwise be activated in the observer or perpetrator (Thornton, 1984).

Hanson (2003) makes the point that when an offender has to confront the harm he has done, he may respond with either guilt or shame. A guilty person recognizes that his or her action caused problems but the offensive behavior is seen

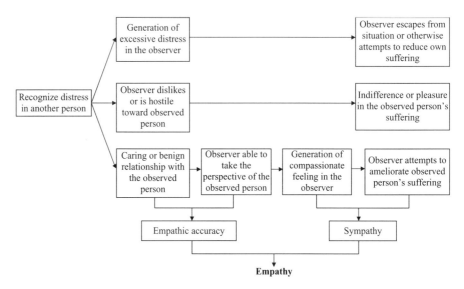

Figure 12.1   Model of empathy.

as a problem that can be avoided in the future. A person who responds to this situation with shame, however, attributes his or her actions as due to the fact that he or she is a bad person whose behavior is unchangeable. Applying descriptors to offenders such as *Antisocial Personality Disorder* or *Pedophilia* no doubt exacerbates this tendency among offenders to see their crimes as resulting from some constitutional, and unchangeable, defect. Thus, an offender experiencing shame will either block his recognition of the harm he has done (i.e. he will display poor emotional recognition), or he will be so upset that he will focus attention on reducing his own distress. In both cases, the offender should display cognitive distortions about the consequences of his offending or about the nature of his act. Thus, when the observer realizes that he or she may be emotionally overwrought if he or she identifies and accepts having caused distress, then self-protection will take over and no sympathetic response will emerge (top line of Figure 12.1).

In other cases, the observer might harbor negative feelings toward the distressed person, and, as a result, feel some pleasure at the observed person's suffering rather than responding empathically (middle line in Figure 12.1). On the other hand, when an offender responds in a callous or indifferent way to his victim's suffering, then we might think of him as psychopathic. When an offender responds with pleasure or satisfaction to his victim's suffering, it may be that he harbors anger toward the victim or it may be that he is a sadist. In our recent model, it is only when the observer has a positive disposition toward the suffering person that the full empathic process will unfold, including a sympathetic or compassionate response (bottom line in Figure 12.1).

Obviously this model has implications for how we might respond to offenders in treatment. For those offenders who do not have the capacity to deal with their victim's distress, treatment might be best directed at strengthening their emotional resilience before attempting to sensitize them to victim harm. When the response of an offender reflects psychopathic indifference or sadistic pleasure, treatment might best be directed at personalizing the victim in a way that is relevant to the offender (e.g. 'Imagine the victim is some one you care for'). Of course, both psychopaths and sadists stretch our resources, and perhaps our own capacity for empathy, but that should not cause us to exclude them from treatment.

MEASURES OF EMPATHY

Serran (2002), in her review of the literature on empathy measures, notes that what bedevils the development of agreed upon measures is the failure to agree on what empathy is. The problem with most measures is that they construe empathy as a trait that is displayed (or not) toward all people across all situations. In addition, the measures used are typically multi-factorial with some of the factors appearing to have little bearing on empathy. Finally, most measures have quite low test–retest reliability, poor internal consistency and weak construct validity (Cross and Sharpley, 1982; Dillard and Hunter, 1989; Langevin, Wright and Handy, 1988). In assessing offenders, we need to be more concerned with their capacity to empathically respond to their victims, and perhaps also to the class of people to whom their victims belong (e.g. women or children), rather than how they respond to people in general. In any case, general measures of empathy have not fared very well in the assessment of offenders. Victim-specific measures have revealed more valuable information.

EMPATHY DEFICITS IN OFFENDERS

Nonsexual Offenders

Numerous authors have claimed that people who commit crimes must necessarily have less empathy than those who do not offend (Blackburn, 1993; Burke, 2001; Bush, Mullis and Mullis, 2000; Hogan, 1969; Marcus and Gray, 1998). As Farrington (1998) has suggested, a lack of empathy impairs the ability of offenders 'to appreciate the effects of their behavior on other people' (p. 257). In this view, empathic people refrain from crime because they anticipate experiencing emotional discomfort if they cause harm to another person. These suggestions are consistent with observations in the general psychological literature that empathy inhibits aggression (Miller and Eisenberg, 1988). However, Farrington's suggestion that it is a lack of empathy that allows offenders to commit crimes ignores the fact that empathic people can readily suspend empathy when they chose to do so. It seems more likely that offenders choose to withhold empathy specifically for their victims rather than that they completely lack empathy.

In their meta-analytic examination of studies assessing empathy in offenders, Jolliffe and Farrington (2004) identified 35 studies that compared offenders ($N = 3\,168$) with nonoffenders ($N = 2\,253$). Jolliffe and Farrington concluded that their results 'suggest that empathy and offending are negatively related' (p. 467). Overall, they found that cognitive empathy was more strongly related to offending in the expected way than was affective empathy. Since 12 of the 20 studies contributing to this conclusion employed *Hogan's Empathy Scale* (Hogan, 1969), the psychometric properties of which are seriously lacking (Cross and Sharpley, 1982; Johnson, Cheek and Struther, 1983), this conclusion needs to be tempered by caution. Jolliffe and Farrington also found that low affective empathy was related (albeit weakly) to offending but this relied heavily on scores on the *Questionnaire Measure of Emotional Empathy* (Mehrabian and Epstein, 1972) which, like Hogan's scale, has serious psychometric problems (Dillard and Hunter, 1989; Langevin, Wright and Handy, 1988).

Jolliffe and Farrington (2004) also found that empathy differences between offenders and nonoffenders vanished when either socio-economic status or intelligence was controlled for. Seto (1992) found that when he partialled out educational attainment, the differences in empathy between sexual offenders and nonoffenders disappeared. Clearly, any studies of offenders' empathy need to control for these factors. Since empathy has a significant maturational component (see L.E. Marshall (2002) for a description of the developmental bases of empathy), and since many offenders present as quite immature, we might also expect age to be a factor influencing scores on measures of empathy. No doubt the tendency to present in a prosocial way, which is likely to be strongly present in offenders, will also influence offenders' reports of their empathic capacity.

It seems obvious, then, that simply asking offenders to complete self-report measures of empathy is not likely to reveal their actual capacity for empathy. However, perhaps the most important problem with the research conducted so far on offenders is that the measures employed are trait measures that assume the scores will reflect the person's persistent disposition to be empathic toward most, if not all, people. With sexual offenders, however, it is a lack of victim-specific empathy, not a lack of empathy toward all people, that is the problem.

Sexual Offenders

It is perhaps not surprising that clinicians working with sexual offenders have been concerned to develop empathic responding in their clients given that the effects of sexual abuse extends into every aspect of the victims' lives and these damaging consequences can be quite prolonged (Beitchman *et al.*, 1992; Conte, 1985; Koss and Harvey, 1991). Indeed, the most recent survey of sexual offender treatment programs in North America revealed that over 90% of all programs target the enhancement of empathy (McGrath, Cumming and Burchard, 2003). Enhancing empathy is also a core feature of British sexual offender treatment programs (Beckett *et al.*, 1994; Beech, Fisher and Beckett, 1999) and of Canadian programs (Wormith and Hanson, 1992).

Like the research with offenders in general, the early research on presumed empathy deficits in sexual offenders employed general trait measures. These studies produced inconsistent findings. For example, among adolescent sexual offenders, some researchers reported significant deficits compared to nonoffending adolescents (Burke, 2001; Knight and Prentky, 1993; Lindsey, Carlozzi and Eells, 2001), whereas others found no differences (Farr, Brown and Beckett, 2004; Monto *et al.*,

1994; Moriarty *et al.*, 2001). Similarly with adult sexual offenders some researchers have reported general empathy deficits (Rice *et al.*, 1994) while others have not (D'Orazio, 2002; Hayashino, Wurtele and Klebe, 1995; Hoppe and Singer, 1976; Langevin, Wright and Handy, 1988; Marshall and Maric, 1996; McGrath, Cann and Konopasky, 1998; Rapaport and Burkhart, 1984; Seto, 1992). Most importantly, Hanson and his colleagues (Hanson and Bussière, 1998; Hanson and Morton-Bourgon, 2004), as well as Smallbone, Wheaton and Hourigan (2003), found empathy to be unrelated to actual sexual offending as evident in either the offenders' prior convictions or in their subsequent recidivism.

As a result of examining available studies, we (Marshall *et al.*, 1995) concluded that the confusion in the literature about whether sexual offenders did or did not lack empathy was due to (a) the use of measures whose psychometric properties were dubious at best; and (b) to what we saw as the mistaken expectation that sexual offenders would lack empathy toward all people. We concluded that sexual offenders were more likely to simply lack empathy toward their victims and recent evidence has offered support for this idea.

Fernandez *et al.* (1999) generated vignettes describing three different children who had experiences that would be expected to distress them: (1) a child injured in a motor accident that left him or her disfigured; (2) a child who had been sexually abused by an unknown assailant; and (3) the offender's own victim. In this study, child molesters were asked to respond to a list of statements indicative of distress or harm to the identified child as well as to a list describing how they felt when reading the vignette. Compared to a matched group of nonoffenders, the child molesters did not show empathy deficits toward the disfigured child (taken as an indication of general empathy toward children) but they did display less empathy toward the hypothetical victim of an unknown offender. However, the child molesters displayed their greatest deficits toward their own victim. Fernandez and Marshall (2003), using a similar methodology, found victim-specific empathy deficits in rapists. These findings were repeated in two other studies (Marshall *et al.*, 1997a; Marshall and Moulden, 2001), and in a series of studies by other researchers (Farr, Brown and Beckett, 2004; Fisher, 1997; Fisher, Beech and Browne, 1999; Webster and Beech, 2000; Whittaker *et al.*, 2006). In fact, Webster and Beech (2000) found that victim-specific deficits among sexual offenders were unrelated to scores on a general empathy measure but were strongly related to the offenders' cognitive distortions.

What then to make of these victim-specific deficits? Quite clearly they mean that sexual offenders do not lack general empathy. They simply do what the rest of us do; they distribute empathy to some but not all people. Why do they specifically withhold it from their victims? The simple answer is because they choose not to allow themselves to experience empathy toward their victim because otherwise they would either not be able to continue offending or they would experience shame for the harm they had done. It is not so much that they withhold empathy as it is that they refuse to acknowledge harm. As a result, they have no reason to feel empathy. If this interpretation is true, then apparent victim-specific empathy deficits in sexual offenders are no more than instances of the various cognitive distortions that characterize these offenders (Ward *et al.*, 1997). In fact, Marshall, Hamilton and Fernandez (2001) found that the cognitive distortions of sexual offenders were highly correlated ($r = .85$) with their lack of victim empathy.

Why then would sexual offenders distort or block information accessible to them that indicate their victims are suffering? We (Marshall, Anderson and Fernandez, 1999) suggested that these distortions (and consequent lack of victim empathy) were generated in order to preserve what little self-esteem they had. Blaine and Crocker (1993), in their analysis of self-esteem, demonstrated that all people engage in self-serving biases in the way they process information in order to maintain their current sense of self-worth. Low self-esteem also predicts a strong sense of shame (Tangney, Burggraf and Wagner, 1995) and people who feel shame make efforts to protect themselves from information that would further increase their sense of shame (Harder, 1995). Not surprisingly, then, shame has been shown to reduce a person's capacity for empathy (Tangney, Burggraf and Wagner, 1995).

We noted earlier that some people respond to another's distress by becoming so distressed themselves that they either cannot respond empathically or distort information about harm. Available evidence indicates that people low in self-esteem have poor emotional self-regulatory skills (Baumeister, Zell and Tice, 2007), as do those who typically experience shame (Ferguson and Stegge, 1995). Such poor emotional regulation enhances the likelihood that people observing another's distress will themselves respond with overwhelming emotions. Sexual offenders have been shown to be low in self-esteem (Marshall, Anderson and Champagne, 1997), to have poor self-regulatory skills (Keenan and Ward, 2003) and to characteristically experience shame (Bumby, Marshall and Langton, 1999). Most importantly, Bumby, Levine and Cunningham (1996) have shown that those sexual offenders who score highly on measures of shame display little or no empathy for their victims. Thus, all the features (i.e. low self-esteem, shame, poor emotional regulation) that generate attempts to protect the self by distorting or avoiding processing available information are present in sexual offenders. We should, therefore, expect sexual offenders to resist accepting information regarding the harm they may have caused their victims, or to distort this information, and, as a result, appear to lack victim empathy. Thus, the apparent lack of victim empathy among sexual offenders may simply be due to tactics designed to deny harm.

TREATMENT OF EMPATHY DEFICITS

It has been said that empathy training is essential for all types of offenders (Mulloy, Smiley and Mawson, 1999; Ross and Ross, 1995; Serin and Kuriychuk, 1994). This seems sensible since numerous researchers in the broader literature have demonstrated that training people to experience empathy results in reduced aggression and less self-interested behaviors while at the same time enhancing general prosocial behavior (Eisenberg and Fabes, 1990; Fesbach, 1978; Iannotti, 1978).

Our discussion of the features that motivate sexual offenders to avoid recognizing harmful effects on their victims indicates that directly training empathy in such clients may be somewhat futile unless prior strategies are adopted that aim at enhancing self-esteem, reducing shame and instilling some degree of emotional regulation. Beech and Fisher (2002) make this same point. They note that if sexual offenders are required to face the harm they have done too early in treatment, they may not have the capacity to cope with these negative messages. Since we have shown that low self-esteem in sexual offenders occurs in conjunction with feelings of shame (Sparks *et al.*, 2003) and with a lack of victim empathy (Marshall *et al.*, 1997a), we expect that increasing self-esteem will reduce shame and thereby allow sexual offenders to confront the harm they have done to their victims. However, as Hanson (2003) correctly points out that increasing the capacity of sexual offenders to cope with distressing events will also be valuable in facilitating the offenders' acceptance of, and enable them to deal with, the harm they have done. Training in coping skills may, therefore, also be valuable prior to addressing issues of victim harm and empathy.

While we have not directly appraised these expectations, we have shown that our program effectively raises our clients' sense of self-worth (Marshall *et al.*, 1997b), enhances their coping skills (Serran *et al.*, 2007) and increases their empathy for their victims (Marshall, O'Sullivan and Fernandez, 1996). With respect to sexual offenders, therefore, we strongly recommend that self-esteem be enhanced, shame reduced and coping skills improved, prior to addressing victim harm and empathy.

Our specific strategies for enhancing victim empathy have been outlined in detail elsewhere (see, e.g., Fernandez and Serran, 2002; Marshall, O'Sullivan and Fernandez, 1996; Marshall, Anderson and Fernandez, 1999; Marshall *et al.*, 2006). As a first step, we attempt to attune our clients to the nature of the empathic process while at the same time training them to be better at detecting emotions in others and in themselves. Carich, Henderson-Odum and Metzger (2001) describe a similar approach aimed at enhancing the emotional recognition skills of sexual offenders, both in themselves and in others.

The therapist then asks the group to brainstorm what they believe is typically experienced by the victims of sexual abuse as perpetrated by some unknown offender (i.e. not the experiences of their own victim). When we first did this exercise, we were quite surprised by how many details across cognitive, emotional and behavioral functioning were identified by our clients. Apparently sexual offenders are not characteristically naïve about the consequences of sexual abuse on the victims; as we have suggested, they appear to simply block the recognition of these consequences when it comes to their own victims. Once a list of negative sequelae is generated, we discuss with each client the likelihood that these problems may occur should they offend again.

Note that we avoid, at this point, any discussion of the possible consequences to their own past victim(s). We do this partly because we expect initial resistance, but also because our focus is on reducing future offending, not punishing our clients for their past. Clinical experience suggests that exploring sexual offenders' past offending is, particularly early in treatment, likely to be seen by them as punitive and thereby likely to produce resistance, denial and minimizations. Having sexual offenders articulate the known consequences to victims of being sexually abused, and combining this with illustrative cases where several consequences have followed rather benign offending, is meant to encourage them to see that when they offend they cannot know in advance how damaging their behavior will be. We are not, therefore, attempting to enhance directly their empathy for their past victims, but rather to sensitize them to the likelihood that, should they offend again, then their future victim may suffer extensively.

Finally, we have our clients write two hypothetical letters: one supposedly from their victim to the offender describing a variety of likely harmful effects; while the other represents the offender's response to the victim's letter. These are read out to the group who provide feedback, and, as a result, the offender may be required to rewrite these letters before they are deemed adequate.

Some programs have offenders role-play a re-enactment of their offense with the goal of developing their perspective-taking skills and to enhance their sensitivity to their victim's distress. Unfortunately, as Pithers (1997) reports, such offense re-enactments can spiral out of hand and cause all manner of problems. As a consequence of Pithers' comments, Webster et al. (2005) compared the effects on empathy of having sexual offenders either re-enact the offense or role-play the short and long-term effects of sexual abuse. They found little in the way of differences between these two strategies and so they recommended not using offense re-enactments due to the possibility that the problems Pithers described might emerge. As we mentioned above, our procedures have been shown to enhance sexual offenders' sensitivity to victim harm and thereby increase their feelings of empathy toward their past victims (Marshall, O'Sullivan and Fernandez, 1996).

While these procedures may be effective with other criminals, they have not yet been tested and there may be reasons to suppose in advance that they may not be appropriate for all types of offenders. For example, Hudson et al. (1993) found that violent, nonsexual offenders were remarkably accurate in detecting distress in others. This is perhaps not surprising since presumably the goal of these offenders in their violent attacks on others is to produce distress; they, therefore, have every reason to be hyper-alert to the generation of distress in their victims rather than disposed to adopt distortions that protect them from such recognition. Violent offenders, then, may fit into the central track of our model of empathy; that is, they will respond to the distress of their victims with satisfaction in the same way the rest of us might respond to harm befalling someone we construe as a villain. Sexual sadists can be expected to respond in similar ways to their victims. However, this does not mean that empathy training will not be effective with violent or sadistic offenders. Indeed, we (Marshall and Hucker, 2006) suggested that it may be only *during* their offenses that sadists (and, as a corollary, violent offenders) take pleasure in the harm they do. It may be that post-offense consequences are irrelevant to a sadistic intention. If this is so, then it may be possible to generate victim empathy in such offenders if the focus is on long-term consequences. To date, empirical evaluations of empathy, or its training, with these specific offenders had not been sufficiently explored.

Offenders who commit crimes that do not directly injure, or do not quite so obviously emotionally scar their victims, should also be involved in training to sensitize them to harm. The loss of a person's sense of security as a result of someone breaking into his her home to steal possessions can be quite profound and long-lasting and have spill-over effects on the person's trust in others. If the loss of money or property is extensive, then further harm will be experienced by the victims and their families. Consequently, any treatment of such offenders should have a component that attempts to develop victim empathy. Again the focus should be upon future potential victims.

These suggestions for empathy enhancement among offenders imply a need to be flexible when dealing with different types of offenders. This flexibility is precisely what is meant by Andrews and Bonta's (2003) notion of 'responsivity', which is one of the three principles of effective offender treatment generated by their earlier meta-analysis (Andrews *et al.*, 1990). We believe that our strict adherence to this responsivity principle is what has made our treatment program for sexual offenders so uniformly effective: only 3.2% of 534 treated sexual offenders released for 5.4 years have re-offended and the rates are much the same across all the types of sexual offenders included in our treatment program. It is interesting in this context to note that among the re-offenders in our study, not one scored above 25 on Hare's (1991) *Psychopathy Checklist-Revised* despite the fact that in excess of 60 of the total group scored within the psychopathic range. Whether these psychopaths developed true empathy for their victims or decided for other reasons to cease offending, we cannot say but the results do suggest that a more optimistic approach may be justified toward these offenders who have been characteristically dismissed as untreatable.

CONCLUSIONS

A wide range of people who engage in criminal behavior appear to have problems recognizing the harm they cause or feeling empathy for their victims. As a result, treatment addressing these deficits should be an essential component of any rehabilitation program. However, researchers examining empathy in offenders need to develop far better measures than have been employed to date. In addition, researchers need to specify precisely what it is that is lacking in offenders who appear to be devoid of empathy. Are some of them simply so overwhelmed with distress when they contemplate the harm they have done, or are they disposed to be antagonistic toward, or indifferent toward, their victims? Our current model of empathy has served as a guide to our formulations of these questions and it may assist in generating ways to examine differences in empathic responding among a diversity of offenders. Until more precise research is conducted, much of what we have to say about the empathic ability of offenders, and its treatment-based enhancement, will remain speculative. We encourage the expansion of research on these issues using more sophisticated methodology than has been true to date.

REFERENCES

Andrews, D. and Bonta, J. (2003) *The Psychology of Criminal Conduct*, 3rd edn, Anderson, Cincinnati, OH.

Andrews, D.A., Zinger, I., Hoge, R.D. *et al.* (1990) Does correctional treatment work? A clinically relevant and psychologically informed meta-analysis. *Criminology*, **28**, 369–404.

Batson, C.D. (1987) Prosocial motivation: is it ever truly altruistic, in *Advances in Experimental Social Psychology*, Vol. 20 (ed. L. Berkowitz), Academic, New York, pp. 65–122.

Batson, C.D. (1991) *The Altruism Question: Toward a Social-Psychological Answer*, Erlbaum, Hillsdale, NJ.

Batson, C.D., Fultz, J. and Schoenrade, P.A. (1987) Distress and empathy: two qualitatively distinct vicarious emotions with different motivational consequences. *Journal of Personality*, **55**, 19–39.

Batson, C.D., O'Quin, K., Fultz, J. *et al.* (1983) Influence of self-reported distress and empathy on egoistic versus altruistic motivation to help. *Journal of Personality and Social Psychology*, **45**, 706–718.

Baumeister, R.F., Zell, A.L. and Tice, D.M. (2007) How emotions facilitate and impair self-regulation, in *Handbook of Emotion Regulation* (ed. J.J. Gross), Guilford, New York, pp. 408–26.

Beckett, R.C., Beech, A.R., Fisher, D. and Fordham, A.S. (1994) *Community-Based Treatment for Sex Offenders. An Evaluation of Seven Treatment Programs*, Home Office Publications Unit, London.

Beckett, R. and Fisher, D. (1994, November) *Assessing Victim Empathy: A New Measure*. Paper presented at the 13th Annual Research and Treatment Conference of the Association for the Treatment of Sexual Abusers. San Francisco.

Beech, A.R. and Fisher, D.D. (2002) The rehabilitation of child sex offenders. *Australian Psychologist*, **37**, 206–14.

Beech, A.R., Fisher, D. and Beckett, R.C. (1999) *Step 3: An Evaluation of the Prison Service Sex Offender Treatment Programme*, Home Office Publications Unit, London.

Beitchman, J.H., Zucker, K.J., Hood, J.E. *et al.* (1992) A review of the long-term effects of child sexual abuse. *Child Abuse and Neglect*, **16**, 101–18.

Blackburn, R. (1993) *The Psychology of Criminal Conduct*, John Wiley & Sons, Ltd, Chichester.

Blaine, B. and Crocker, J. (1993) Self-esteem and self-serving biases in reactions to positive and negative events: an integrative review, in *Self-Esteem: The Puzzle of Low Self-Regard* (ed. R.F. Baumeister), Plenum, New York, pp. 55–85.

Buck, R. (1984) *The Communication of Emotion*, Guilford, New York.

Bumby, K.M., Levine, H. and Cunningham, D. (1996, November) *Empathy Deficits, Shame, Guilt, and Self-Consciousness*. Paper presented at the 15th Annual Research and Treatment Conference of the Association for the Treatment of Sexual Abusers. Chicago.

Bumby, K., Marshall, W.L. and Langton, C. (1999) A theoretical model of the influence of shame and guilt on sexual offending, in *The Sex Offender: Theoretical Advances, Treating Special Populations and Legal Developments*, Vol. 3 (ed. B.K. Schwartz), Civic Research Institute, Kingston, NJ, pp. 5.1–5.12.

Burke, D.M. (2001) Empathy in sexually offending and nonoffending adolescent males. *Journal of Interpersonal Violence*, **16**, 222–33.

Bush, C.A., Mullis, R.L. and Mullis, A.K. (2000) Differences between offender and nonoffender youth. *Journal of Youth and Adolescence*, **29**, 467–78.

Carich, M.S., Henderson-Odum, N.V. and Metzger, C. (2001, October) *Enhancing Victim Empathy: A Treatment Context and Selected Victim Empathy Techniques*. Poster presentation at the Annual Research and Treatment Conference of the Association for the Treatment of Sexual Abusers. San Antonio, Texas.

Conte, J.R. (1985) Clinical dimensions of adult sexual abuse of children. *Behavioral Sciences and the Law*, **3**, 341–54.

Cottrell, L.S. (1942) The analysis of situational fields in social psychology. *American Sociological Review*, **7**, 374.

Cross, D.G. and Sharpley, C.F. (1982) Measurement of empathy with the Hogan Empathy Scale. *Psychological Reports*, **50**, 62.

Davis, M.H. (1983) Measuring individual differences in empathy: evidence for a multidimensional approach. *Journal of Personality and Social Psychology*, **44**, 113–26.

Davis, M.H. and Kraus, L.A. (1997) Personality and empathic accuracy, in *Empathic Accuracy* (ed. W. Ickes), Guilford, New York, pp. 144–68.

Dillard, J.P. and Hunter, J.E. (1989) On the use and interpretation of the Emotional Empathy Scale, the Self-consciousness Scale, and the Self-monitoring Scale. *Communication Record*, **16**, 104–29.

D'Orazio, D. (2002) *A Comparative Analysis of Empathy in Sexually Offending and Non-Offending Juvenile and Adult Males*. Unpublished doctoral dissertation. California School of Professional Psychology at Alliant University, Fresno.

Dymond, R.F. (1949) A scale for the measurement of empathic ability. *Journal of Consulting Psychology*, **13**, 127–33.

Eisenberg, N. (2000) Empathy and sympathy, in *Handbook of Emotions*, 2nd edn (eds M. Lewis and J.M. Haviland-Jones), Guilford, New York, pp. 677–92.

Eisenberg, N. and Fabes, R.A. (1990) Empathy: conceptualization, assessment, and relation to prosocial behavior. *Motivation and Emotion*, **14**, 131–49.

Eisenberg, N. and Miller, P. (1987) The relation of empathy to prosocial and related behaviors. *Psychological Bulletin*, **101**, 91–119.

Farr, C., Brown, J. and Beckett, R. (2004) Ability to empathise and masculinity levels: comparing male adolescent sex offenders with a normative sample of non-offending adolescents. *Psychology, Crime and Law*, **10**, 155–68.

Farrington, D.P. (1998) Individual differences and offending, in *The Handbook of Crime and Punishment* (ed. M. Tonry), Oxford University Press, New York, pp. 241–68.

Ferguson, T.J. and Stegge, H. (1995) Emotional states and traits in children: the case of guilt and shame, in *Self-Conscious Emotions: The Psychology of Shame, Guilt, Embarrassment, and Pride* (eds J.P. Tangney and K.W. Fischer), Guilford, New York, pp. 174–97.

Fernandez, Y.M. and Marshall, W.L. (2003) Victim empathy, social self-esteem and psychopathy in rapists. *Sexual Abuse: A Journal of Research and Treatment*, **15**, 11–26.

Fernandez, Y.M., Marshall, W.L., Lightbody. S. and O'Sullivan, C. (1999) The Child Molester Empathy Measure: description and an examination of its reliability and validity. *Sexual Abuse: A Journal of Research and Treatment*, **11**, 17–31.

Fernandez, Y.M. and Serran, G. (2002) Empathy training for therapists and clients, in *In Their Shoes: Examining the Issue of Empathy and its Place in the Treatment of Offenders* (ed. Y. Fernandez), Wood 'N' Barnes Publishing, Oklahoma City, OK, pp. 110–31.

Fesbach, N.D. (1975) Empathy in children: some theoretical and empirical considerations. *The Counseling Psychologist*, **5**, 25–30.

Fesbach, N.D. (1978) Studies of empathic behavior in children, in *Progress in Personality Research*, Vol. 8 (ed. B.A. Maher), Academic, New York, pp. 1–47.

Fesbach, N.D. (1987) Parental empathy and child adjustment/maladjustment, in *Empathy and its Development* (eds N. Eisenberg and J. Strayer), Cambridge University Press, Cambridge, UK, pp. 292–316.

Fisher, D. (1997) *Assessing Sexual Offenders' Victim Empathy*, Unpublished PH.D. Thesis, University of Birmingham, Birmingham, England.

Fisher, D., Beech, A. and Browne, K. (1999) Comparison of sex offenders to nonoffenders on selected psychological measures. *International Journal of Offender Therapy and Comparative Criminology*, **43**, 473–91.

Fultz, J., Schaller, M. and Cialdini, R.B. (1988) Empathy, sadness, and distress: three related but distinct vicarious affective responses to another's suffering. *Personality and Social Psychology Bulletin*, **14**, 312–25.

Hanson, R.K. (1997) Invoking sympathy – assessment and treatment of empathy deficits among sexual offenders, in *The sex Offender: New Insights, Treatment Innovations and Legal Developments*, Vol. III (eds B.K. Schwartz and H.R. Cellini), Civic Research Institute, Kingston, NJ, pp. 1.1–1.12.

Hanson, R.K. (2003) Empathy deficits of sexual offenders: a conceptual model. *Journal of Sexual Aggression*, **9**, 13–23.

Hanson, R.K. and Bussière, M.T. (1998) Predicting relapse: a meta-analysis of sexual offender recidivism studies. *Journal of Consulting and Clinical Psychology*, **66**, 348–62.

Hanson, R.K. and Morton-Bourgon, K. (2004) *Predictors of Sexual Recidivism: An Updated Meta-Analysis*. (Catalog No. PS3-1/2004-2E-PDF), Public Works and Services, Ottawa.

Hanson, R.K. and Scott, H. (1995) Assessing perspective-taking among sexual offenders, nonsexual criminals and nonoffenders. *Sexual Abuse: A Journal of Research and Treatment*, **7**, 259–77.

Harder, D.W. (1995) Shame and guilt assessment, and relationships of shame-and guilt-proneness to psychopathology, in *Self-Conscious Emotions: The Psychology of Shame, Guilt, Embarrassment, and Pride* (eds J.P. Tangney and K.W. Fischer), Guilford, New York, pp. 368–92.

Hare, R.D. (1991) *Manual for the Revised Psychopathy Checklist*, Multi-Health Systems, Toronto.

Hayashino, D.S., Wurtele, S.K. and Klebe, K.J. (1995) Child molesters: an examination of cognitive factors. *Journal of Interpersonal Violence*, **10**, 106–16.

Hoffman, M.L. (1982) Development of prosocial motivation: empathy and guilt, in *The Development of Prosocial Behavior* (ed. N. Eisenberg), Academic, New York, pp. 281–313.

Hogan, R. (1969) Development of an empathy scale. *Journal of Consulting and Clinical Psychology*, **33**, 307–16.

Hoppe, C.M. and Singer, R.D. (1976) Overcontrolled hostility, empathy, and egocentric balance in violent and nonviolent psychiatric offenders. *Psychological Reports*, **39**, 405–45.

Hudson, S.M., Marshall, W.L., Wales, D. *et al.* (1993) Emotional recognition skills of sex offenders. *Annals of Sex Research*, **6**, 199–211.

Hume, D. (1739) *A Treatise of Human Nature*, Clarendon, Oxford.

Iannotti, L.A. (1978) Effect of role-taking experiences on empathy, altruism, and aggression. *Developmental Psychology*, **14**, 119–24.

Ickes, W. (1997) *Empathic Accuracy*, Guilford, New York.

Janoff-Bulman, R. (1979) Characterological versus behavioral self-blame: inquiries into depression and rape. *Journal of Personality and Social Psychology*, **37**, 1798–1809.

Johnson, J.A., Cheek, J.M. and Struther, R. (1983) The structure of empathy. *Journal of Personality and Social Psychology*, **45**, 1299–312.

Jolliffe, D. and Farrington, D.P. (2004) Empathy and offending: a systematic review and meta-analysis. *Aggression and Violent Behavior*, **9**, 441–76.

Keenan, T. and Ward, T. (2003) Developmental antecedents of sexual offending, in *Sexual Deviance: Issues and Controversies* (eds T. Ward, D.R. Laws and S.M. Hudson), Sage, Thousand Oaks, CA, pp. 119–34.

Knight, R.A. and Prentky, R.A. (1993) Exploring characteristics for classifying juvenile sex offenders, in *The Juvenile Sex Offender* (eds H.E. Barbaree, W.L. Marshall and S.M. Hudson), Guilford, New York, pp. 45–83.

Koss, M.P. and Harvey, M.R. (1991) *The Rape Victim: Clinical and Community Interventions*, 2nd edn, Sage, Newbury Park, CA.

Langevin, R., Wright, M.A. and Handy, L. (1988) Empathy, assertiveness, aggressiveness, and defensiveness among sex offenders. *Annals of Sex Research*, **1**, 533–47.

Laws, D.R. (2002) Owning your own data: the management of denial, in *Motivating Offenders to Change: A Guide to Enhancing Engagement in Therapy* (eds C.R. Hollin and M. McMurran), John Wiley & Sons, Ltd, Chichester, pp. 173–91.

Lindsey, R.E., Carlozzi, A.F. and Eells, G.T. (2001) Differences in dispositional empathy of juvenile sex offenders, non-sex-offending delinquent juveniles, and nondelinquent juveniles. *Journal of Interpersonal Violence*, **16**, 510–21.

Marcus, R.F. and Gray, L. (1998) Close relationships of violent and nonviolent African American delinquents. *Violence and Victims*, **13**, 31–46.

Marshall, L.E. (2002) The development of empathy, in *In Their Shoes: Examining the Issue of Empathy and its Place in the Treatment of Offenders* (ed. Y. Fernandez), Wood 'N' Barnes Publishing, Oklahoma City, OK, pp. 36–52.

Marshall, L.E. and Marshall, W.L. (2001) *A Revised Model of Empathy*. Unpublished manuscript, Rockwood Psychological Services, Kingston, Canada.

Marshall, W.L., Anderson, D. and Champagne, F. (1997) Self-esteem and its relationship to sexual offending. *Psychology, Crime and Law*, **3**, 161–86.

Marshall, W.L., Anderson, D. and Fernandez, Y.M. (1999) *Cognitive Behavioural Treatment of Sexual Offenders*, John Wiley & Sons, Ltd, Chichester.

Marshall, W.L., Champagne, F., Brown, C. and Miller, S. (1997a) Empathy, intimacy, loneliness, and self-esteem in nonfamilial child molesters. *Journal of Child Sexual Abuse*, **6**, 87–97.

Marshall, W.L., Champagne, F., Sturgeon, C. and Bryce, P. (1997b) Increasing the self-esteem of child molesters. *Sexual Abuse: A Journal of Research and Treatment*, **9**, 321–33.

Marshall, W.L., Hamilton, K. and Fernandez, Y. (2001) Empathy deficits and cognitive distortions in child molesters. *Sexual Abuse: A Journal of Research and Treatment*, **13**, 123–30.

Marshall, W.L. and Hucker, S.J. (2006) Sexual sadism: its features and treatment, in *Sex and Sexuality* (ed. R.D. McNulty), Greenwood, Westport, CT, pp. 227–50.

Marshall, W.L., Hudson, S.M., Jones, R. and Fernandez, Y.M. (1995) Empathy in sex offenders. *Clinical Psychology Review*, **15**, 99–113.

Marshall, W.L. and Maric, A. (1996) Cognitive and emotional components of generalized empathy deficits in child molesters. *Journal of Child Sexual Abuse*, **5**, 101–10.

Marshall, W.L., Marshall, L.E., Serran, G.A. and Fernandez, Y.M. (2006) *Treating Sexual Offenders: An Integrated Approach*, Routledge, New York.

Marshall, W.L. and Moulden, H. (2001) Hostility toward women and victim empathy in rapists. *Sexual Abuse: A Journal of Research and Treatment*, **13**, 249–55.

Marshall, W.L., O'Sullivan, C. and Fernandez, Y.M. (1996) The enhancement of victim empathy among incarcerated child molesters. *Legal and Criminological Psychology*, **1**, 95–102.

McGrath, M., Cann, S. and Konopasky, R.J. (1998) New measures of defensiveness, empathy, and cognitive distortions for sexual offenders against children. *Sexual Abuse: A Journal of Research and Treatment*, **10**, 25–36.

McGrath, R.J., Cumming, G.F. and Burchard, B.L. (2003) *Current Practices and Trends in Sexual Abuser Management: The Safer Society 2002 Nationwide Survey*, Safer Society Press, Brandon, VT.

Mehrabian, A. and Epstein, N. (1972) A measure of emotional empathy. *Journal of Personality*, **40**, 525–43.

Miller, P.A. and Eisenberg, M. (1988) The relation of empathy to aggressive and externalizing/antisocial behavior. *Psychological Bulletin*, **103**, 324–44.

Monto, M., Zgourides, G., Wilson, J. and Harris, R. (1994) Empathy and adolescent male sex-offenders. *Perceptual and Motor Skills*, **79**, 1598.

Moriarty, N., Stough, C., Tidmarsh, P. *et al.* (2001) Deficits in emotional intelligence underlying adolescent sex offending. *Journal of Adolescence*, **24**, 1–9.

Mulloy, R., Smiley, W.C. and Mawson, D.L. (1999) The impact of empathy training on offender treatment. *Forum on Corrections Research*, **11**, 15–8.

Ohbuchi, K. (1988) Arousal of empathy and aggression. *Psychologia: An International Journal of Psychology*, **31**, 177–86.

Penner, L.A., Fritzsche, B.A., Craiger, J.P. and Freifeld, T.S. (1995) Measuring the prosocial personality, in *Advances in Personality Assessment*, Vol. 10 (eds J. Butcher and C.D. Spielberger), Erlbaum, Hillsdale, NJ, pp. 147–63.

Pithers, W.D. (1997) Maintaining treatment integrity with sexual abusers. *Criminal Justice and Behaviour*, **24**, 34–51.

Pithers, W.D. (1999) Empathy: definition, enhancement, and relevance to the treatment of sexual abusers. *Journal of Interpersonal Violence*, **14**, 257–84.

Rapaport, K. and Burkhart, B.R. (1984) Personality and attitudinal characteristics of sexually coercive college males. *Journal of Abnormal Psychology*, **93**, 216–21.

Rice, M.E., Chaplin, R.E., Harris, G.E. and Coutts, J. (1994) Empathy for the victim and sexual arousal among rapists and nonrapists. *Journal of Interpersonal Violence*, **9**, 435–49.

Ross, R. and Ross, R. (1995) *Thinking Straight: The Reasoning and Rehabilitation Program for Delinquency Prevention and Offender Rehabilitation*, Air Training and Publications, Ottawa.

Serin, R.C. and Kuriychuk, M. (1994) Social and cognitive deficits in violent offenders. *International Journal of Law and Psychiatry*, **17**, 431–41.

Serran, G.A. (2002) The measure of empathy, in *In Their Shoes: Examining the Issue of Empathy and its Place in the Treatment of Offenders* (ed. Y. Fernandez), Wood 'N' Barnes Publishing, Oklahoma City, OK, pp. 16–35.

Serran, G.A., Firestone, P., Marshall, W.L. and Moulden, H. (2007) Changes in coping following treatment for child molesters. *Journal of Interpersonal Violence*, **9**, 1199–1210.

Seto, M.C. (1992) *Victim Blame, Empathy, and Discrimination of Sexual Arousal to Rape in Community Males and Incarcerated Rapists.* Unpublished M.A. Thesis, Queen's University, Kingston, Ontario, Canada.

Shaver, K.G. (1970) Defensive attribution: effects of severity and relevance on the responsibility assigned for an accident. *Journal of Personality and Social Psychology*, **14**, 101–13.

Smallbone, S.W., Wheaton, J. and Hourigan, D. (2003) Trait empathy and criminal versatility in sexual offenders. *Sexual Abuse: A Journal of Research and Treatment*, **15**, 49–60.

Smith, A. (1759) *The Theory of Moral Sentiments*, Strahan, London.

Sparks, J., Bailey, W., Marshall, W.L. and Marshalll, L.E. (2003, October) *Shame and Guilt in Sex Offenders.* Paper presented at the 22nd Annual Research and Treatment Conference of the Association for the Treatment of Sexual Abusers, St. Louis.

Strayer, J. (1993) Children's concordant emotions and cognitions in response to observed emotions. *Child Development*, **64**, 188–201.

Tangney, J.P., Burggraf, S.A., Wagner, P.E. (1995) Shame-proneness, guilt-proneness, and psychological symptoms, in *Self-Conscious Emotions: The Psychology of Shame, Guilt, Embarrassment, and Pride* (eds J.P. Tangney and K.W. Fischer), Guilford, New York, pp. 343–67.

Thomas, G. and Fletcher, G.J.O. (1997) Empathic accuracy in close relationships, in *Empathic Accuracy* (ed. W. Ickes), Guilford, New York, pp. 194–217.

Thornton, B. (1984) Defensive attribution of responsibility: evidence for an arousal-based motivational bias. *Journal of Personality and Social Psychology*, **46**, 721–34.

Ward, T., Hudson, S.M., Johnston, L. and Marshall, W.L. (1997) Cognitive distortions in sex offenders: An integrative review. *Clinical Psychology Review*, **17**, 479–507.

Webster, S.D. and Beech, A.R. (2000) The nature of sexual offenders' affective empathy: a grounded theory analysis. *Sexual Abuse: A Journal of Research and Treatment*, **12**, 249–61.

Webster, S.D., Bowers, L.E., Mann, R.E. and Marshall, W.L. (2005) Developing empathy in sexual offenders: the value of offence re-enactments. *Sexual Abuse: A Journal of Research and Treatment*, **17**, 63–77.

Whittaker, M.K., Brown, J., Beckett, R. and Gerhold, C. (2006) Sexual knowledge and empathy: a comparison of adolescent child molesters and non-offending adolescents. *Journal of Sexual Aggression*, **12**, 143–54.

Williams, C.A. (1990) Biopsychosocial elements of empathy: a multidimensional model. *Issues in Mental Health Nursing*, **11**, 155–74.

Wormith, J.S. and Hanson, R.K. (1992) The treatment of sexual offenders in Canada: an update. *Canadian Psychology/Psychologie canadienne*, **33**, 180–98.

Zahn-Waxler, C. and Robinson, J. (1995) Empathy and guilt: early origins of feelings of responsibility, in *Self-Conscious Emotions: The Psychology of Shame, Guilt, Embarrassment, and Pride* (eds J.P. Tangney and K.W. Fischer), Guilford, New York, pp. 143–73.

Zahn-Waxler, C., Radke-Yarrow, M. and King, R.A. (1979) Child rearing and children's prosocial initiations toward victims of distress. *Child Development*, **50**, 319–30.

PART III

COGNITION

Chapter 13

PSYCHOPATHIC VIOLENCE: A COGNITIVE-ATTENTION PERSPECTIVE

JENNIFER E. VITALE
Hampden-Sydney College, USA

JOSEPH P. NEWMAN
University of Wisconsin-Madison, USA

There is little doubt that any discussion of violence and violence prevention must include consideration of the psychopath. Characterized by impoverished interpersonal and affective experiences and by impulsive, often antisocial behavior, psychopathic individuals are responsible for a disproportionate amount of crime and violence and represent a significant drain on the financial and emotional resources of their families, friends and communities. Comprising nearly 25% of incarcerated offender populations, these individuals commit more violence within institutions than other offenders and engage in higher levels of violent recidivism than other offenders (see Hare and Hart, 1993; Hemphill, Hare and Wong, 1998; Hemphill *et al.*, 1998; Salekin, Rogers and Sewell, 1996). Psychopaths are also remarkable for their participation in diverse forms of violence. Traditionally a distinction is made between reactive violence (i.e. violence that is emotion based and impulsive) and instrumental violence (i.e. violence that is planned, deliberate and goal directed). Psychopaths commit not only reactive violence, but are also significantly more likely to engage in instrumental violence than non-psychopathic offenders (Blair, 2005; Cornell, Warren and Hawk, 1996; Serin, 1991).

Although there is agreement regarding the robust association between psychopathy and violence, there is less agreement regarding psychopaths' amenability to treatment. Historically, the prognosis for psychopathy has been poor, and although some suggest that the psychopath will respond to treatment (e.g. Salekin, 2002; Skeem, Monahan and Mulvey, 2002), many individuals in the field consider the syndrome to be relatively intractable (e.g. Hare, 1993; Lykken, 1995). For example, Ogloff, Wong and Greenwood (1990) assessed psychopaths' performance in a therapeutic community setting, and found that psychopaths assessed using an early version of the Psychopathy Checklist-Revised (PCL-R; Hare, 1991) were more likely to experience early discharge from the program, were less motivated, and showed less overall improvement. Similarly, Rice, Harris and Cormier (1992) examined psychopaths' performance in an intensive therapeutic community contained within a maximum security prison and found that, although treatment was associated with lower recidivism among non-psychopathic participants, the reverse was true for the psychopaths; psychopaths in the treatment group were actually more likely to violently recidivate (Rice, Harris and Cormier, 1992). This finding has been attributed to the possibility that the new social skills developed in the treatment setting merely improved the psychopaths' ability to manipulate and control others (Harris and Rice, 2006).

Consistently, research suggests that psychopaths are resistant to treatment. Compared to non-psychopaths, psychopaths in treatment demonstrate poor program adjustment (e.g. Hobson, Shine and Roberts, 2000; Ogloff, Wong and Greenwood, 1990; Rice, Harris and Cormier, 1992; Richards, Casey and Lucente, 2003) and lower levels of therapeutic gain (Hughes *et al.*, 1997). Further, treatment appears to be associated with heightened recidivism rates for psychopaths (e.g. Hare *et al.*, 2000; Rice, Harris and Cormier, 1992).

In light of these findings, several alternatives have been proposed. One is to de-emphasize treatments for psychopaths that are geared towards building social skills or empathy, and instead to create behavior modification programs with the goal of reducing harm (i.e. criminal recidivism) caused by psychopaths (Harris and Rice, 2006). A second alternative is to turn to research on the etiology of psychopathy in order to devise treatment strategies better suited to the particular deficits demonstrated by this group (Serin and Kuriychuk, 1994; Wallace *et al.*, 2000).

In this chapter, we opt to take this second approach. Specifically, we choose to focus on one theory of psychopathy that we believe has direct implications for treatment and intervention, and we argue that focusing on the specific psychobiological mechanisms that underlie the psychopaths' callous impulsivity will help clinicians and counselors to devise more effective interventions.

To this end, this chapter has three primary goals: First, we will trace the evolution of the response modulation model of psychopathy (Gorenstein and Newman, 1980; Patterson and Newman, 1993), which proposes that psychopaths are characterized by a cognitive-attention deficit that impairs their ability to inhibit behaviors and to reflect upon and learn from the consequences of those behaviors. Second, we will review the experimental evidence that supports the response modulation model. Third, we will tie the model to self-regulation to make the argument that the processes that underlie disinhibition in the laboratory are the same as those that underlie violence in the community, and that examination of these processes can help to elucidate mechanisms for treatment.

THE CLINICAL EVIDENCE

Psychopathy as a clinical syndrome has only recently been distinguished clearly from general criminality, from sociopathy and from antisocial personality disorder. In large part, this distinction resulted from the publication of 'The Mask of Sanity'

(Cleckley, 1988). The Mask of Sanity provided detailed case histories in addition to a set of specific criteria meant to distinguish the syndrome from the number of other disorders that had come to be included under the 'psychopathy' label. Thus, through this work, Cleckley (1988) provided a means for distinguishing the psychopath from the 'psychotic', the 'psychoneurotic', the 'mental defective' and the 'criminal and the alcoholic'.

The Mask of Sanity outlines 16 core traits of psychopathy that Cleckley formulated on the basis of case histories. Among these criteria, several have strongly influenced modern conceptualizations of the syndrome. First, Cleckley (1988) described the psychopath as 'lacking in remorse or shame (p. 337)'. The psychopath does not express genuine contrition for the antisocial acts he or she commits, and often cannot even appreciate the purpose of feeling such remorse. When remorse is expressed, it can seem hollow and forced. As Cleckley writes: 'Usually he denies emphatically all responsibility and directly accuses others as responsible, but often he will go through an idle ritual of saying that much of his trouble is his own fault. . . . More detailed questioning about just what he blames himself for and why may show that a serious attitude is not only absent but altogether inconceivable to him' (p. 343).

Second, the psychopath engages in 'inadequately motivated antisocial behavior' (p. 337). Among the behaviors Cleckley included in this category were minor infractions such as lying, cheating, brawling, as well as more serious offenses, such as theft, fraud and forgery. This range is crucial when considering the violence of the psychopath. Although violence is clearly a part of the behavioral repertoire of many psychopaths, this symptom need not be understood independently of the psychopath's general antisocial behavior and lack of inhibition. For example, we used a sample of male offenders from minimum, medium and maximum security prisons and conducted a mixed-model analysis of variance with charges for violent and non-violent crimes as the repeated measure and PCL-R group (≤20, 21–29, ≥30) as the between-participants variable. We z-scored the repeated measures so that they would have equal weight in the analysis. Although the main effect for psychopathy was highly significant ($F(2, 2255) = 182.9$, $p < 0.001$, $\eta^2 = 0.14$), the psychopathy by crime type interaction did not approach statistical significance ($F(2, 2255) < 1.0$, $\eta^2 = 0.000$). In other words, although psychopathy is associated with significantly more criminal behavior, this predilection is no more true for violent than for non-violent crime.

Third, the psychopath shows 'poor judgment and failure to learn by experience' (Cleckley, 1988; p. 337). Despite the fact that these individuals are characterized by average intelligence, they nevertheless repeatedly make poor choices and evidence poor judgment in their attempts at goal attainment. Further, although the psychopath will be able to explain 'what went wrong' in a particular situation (i.e. what he did that may have lead to the poor outcome), he seems incapable of using this knowledge in future situations.

Fourth, the psychopath 'exhibits general poverty in major affective reactions'. Although the psychopath may express himself in ways that suggest that he is experiencing affective reactions (e.g. a short temper, a declaration of affection), these expressions do not convey a sense of long-lasting, deep emotional experience. There is no 'mature, wholehearted anger, true or consistent indignation, honest, solid grief, sustaining pride, deep joy, and genuine despair' (Cleckley, 1988; p. 348).

Although the Cleckley criteria formed the basis for the identification of the psychopathy syndrome, it was the emergence of Hare's (1980) PCL and PCL-R (Hare, 1991) that enabled researchers and clinicians in the field to assess the syndrome reliably. The PCL-R is composed of 20 items, which are scored using interview and file review as 0 'not applicable to the individual', 1 'applicable only to a certain extent' or 2 'applicable to the individual'. Scores range from 0 to 40 and a diagnostic cut-off of 30 has become the accepted standard in North American, male samples.

Initial Exploratory Factor Analysis of the PCL-R revealed two correlated (0.50) factors (Hare, 1991; Harpur, Hakstian and Hare, 1988; Harpur, Hare and Hakstian, 1989). The first, Factor 1, was dubbed the affective/interpersonal factor as it included those items representing many of the deficient emotional and interpersonally manipulative characteristics of the syndrome (e.g. glib/superficial charm, manipulative, callous, shallow affect, etc.). The second, Factor 2, became known as the social deviance or impulsive/antisocial lifestyle factor on the basis of its inclusion of those items measuring the psychopath's irresponsible, antisocial and criminal behavior (e.g. poor behavioral controls, impulsivity, early behavior problems). Although there is currently some debate regarding the best fitting factor model (e.g. Cooke, Michie and Hart, 2006; Hare and Neumann, 2006), the tendency to conceptualize psychopathy as comprising both interpersonal/affective and impulsive/irresponsible components still dominates thinking in the field.

In summary, the psychopath as described in the clinical literature and assessed using the PCL-R is an individual with features distinct from an individual with antisocial personality disorder or sociopathy. The classic or 'primary' psychopath is distinguished by limited affective experiences, is known to act impulsively and often antisocially, but nevertheless seems calm and at ease in the presence of others. Psychopaths' over-representation in criminal samples provides strong, pragmatic motivation for understanding the factors that underlie the syndrome. In the following sections, we describe and discuss the response modulation model, a cognitive-attention model proposed to explain the psychopathy syndrome.

THE EVOLUTION OF THE RESPONSE MODULATION MODEL

The response modulation model emerged in the context of Lykken's (1957, 1995) low-fear hypothesis, which proposed that the psychopath is characterized by a dispositional fearlessness that impedes normal socialization and results in the cluster of symptoms characteristic of the syndrome (e.g. failure to learn from experience, lack of empathy, irresponsibility, manipulativeness). This proposal was based, in part, upon the results of Lykken's highly influential 1957 study of conditioning in psychopaths which showed that psychopaths (designated on the basis of their similarity to Cleckley's prototype) had lower scores on a self-report measure of fearfulness (i.e. the Activity Preference Questionnaire), showed poor electrodermal conditioning relative to controls in a paradigm wherein electric shock served as the unconditioned stimulus, and also exhibited deficient passive avoidance performance. Taken together, these data suggested deficient fear conditioning among psychopaths, and served as the basis for Lykken's 'low-fear' hypothesis.

The response modulation model emerged not as a refutation of psychopaths' fearlessness, but with the intent of explicating the psychobiological processes that underlay this fearlessness. In experimental terms, the response modulation model was meant to explain the psychopath's deficient passive avoidance performance, decreased physiological anticipatory responses to aversive stimuli and impaired ability to delay gratification.

According to Gorenstein and Newman (1980), the behavior of psychopathic individuals reflects a basic tendency towards disinhibition, which they defined as 'human behavior that has been interpreted as arising from lessened controls on response inclinations' (p. 302). Disinhibited individuals, then, are those who 'appear unable to control their immediate response inclinations as a means of achieving long-range goals' (p. 302). This disinhibition, which was characteristic of several pathological syndromes in addition to psychopathy, including alcoholism, hyperactivity and hysteria, had a parallel in the animal literature. Specifically, the behaviors that characterize human disinhibition are similar to the behaviors that are exhibited by animals with septal lesions, which involve impaired performance on passive avoidance tasks and delay of gratification tasks. Further, animals with septal lesions are significantly slower to suppress reward-seeking behavior in response to cues signaling imminent electric shock and are also slower to initiate active avoidance in anticipation of shock (Kaada, Rasmussen and Kveim, 1962; McCleary, 1961), behavioral responses that might be labeled 'fearlessness'.

These similarities lead Gorenstein and Newman to propose, not that psychopaths are characterized by gross deficits in the septal regions, but instead that an examination of the septal literature in animals might illuminate perceptual, motivational and learning parallels to disinhibited humans. Such parallels would generate novel hypotheses relevant to the psychological processes underlying human disinhibitory psychopathology, and lay the foundation for grounding these psychological processes in psychophysiology. Thus, initially, the goal of the response modulation model was to translate the neuropsychological consequences of septal lesions in animals into testable hypotheses for humans, with the aim of clarifying the processes that result in disinhibited behavior.

One key piece of evidence to emerge from the animal literature was that animals with septal lesions are not universally impaired. Septal animals show good avoidance of punishment when this avoidance is the primary task. For example, septal-lesion animals can avoid shocks as well as control animals on a Sidman avoidance paradigm, wherein avoidance of shock is the primary task requirement (Morgan and Mitchell, 1969; Sodetz, 1970). In addition, although septal animals are less able to withhold an immediate response in an appetitive differential reinforcement of low rates of behavior situation, which requires the animal to withhold responding until an interval of time has elapsed (Ellen and Butter, 1969; Ellen, Wilson and Powell, 1964), if the interval during which the animal must inhibit responding is signaled externally the animals perform normally (Ellen and Butter, 1969; Kelsey and Grossman, 1971). Using these data from the septal animal literature as a parallel for human psychopathy, Newman and colleagues (Newman and Kosson, 1986; Newman, Patterson and Kosson, 1987; Newman and Schmitt, 1998) proposed that the apparent 'fearlessness' of psychopaths does not reflect a generalized inability to respond to punishment, and that under the appropriate contexts, the psychopath could demonstrate normal punishment learning and avoidance responses.

To test this hypothesis, Newman and colleagues undertook a series of studies that tested the psychopaths' putative insensitivity to punishment across a variety of contexts. First, Newman and Kosson (1986) used a standard Go/No-go passive avoidance task. On this task, participants are asked to respond to a series of eight two-digit numbers. Four of these numbers are 'S+' numbers, and four are 'S−' numbers and participants must learn through trial and error which numbers are which. In the first condition, which was a mixed contingency reward/punishment condition, the participants would earn money for responding to an S+ number, but would lose money for responding to an S− number. Thus, in this condition, each of the participants' responses were either rewarded or punished. In this condition, psychopaths performed as was predicted on the basis of the prior passive avoidance literature. That is, they committed significantly more errors than controls, responding significantly more often to the punished S− numbers (Newman and Kosson, 1986).

On the basis of data from the septal animal literature, however, Newman and Kosson (1986) introduced a second task condition. In this condition, the 'punishment only' condition, there was no reward; instead participants would lose money if they responded to the S− numbers and would also lose money for *failing to respond* to the S+ numbers. Thus, in contrast to the reward/punishment condition, the only goal in this condition was to avoid punishment. Further, contrary to what would be predicted given the 'fearlessness' and punishment insensitivity explanations for psychopaths' performance, the psychopaths did not commit significantly more errors in this condition than controls. In fact, the psychopaths committed non-significantly fewer errors on average, than the non-psychopaths (Newman and Kosson, 1986). Thus, like the septal animals, the psychopaths were able to demonstrate responsiveness to punishment stimuli in a particular context. In a single-focus condition, the psychopaths' deficit disappeared.

In a second task, Newman, Patterson and Kosson (1987) showed that, when external constraints were placed on psychopaths' responding, they were able to show context appropriate response inhibition. The authors used a card-playing task during which, on each trial, participants may choose to either turn over (i.e. 'play') a single card from a deck of cards or quit the task. If the card played is a face card, participants earn money. If the played card is a number card, the participants lose money. Importantly, the deck is 'stacked' such that, in the first set of 10 trials, 90% are face cards, in the second set of 10 trials 80% are face cards, in the third set of 10 trials 70% are face cards, and so on until 100% of the cards in a 10-card series are number cards. When psychopaths' performance is compared to non-psychopaths' performance on this task, they play significantly more cards and lose significantly more money than controls. That is, they appear insensitive to the loss of money and continue to play beyond the point at which they could 'break even'. Importantly, however, when the authors utilized a version of this task on which participants were forced to pause for 5 seconds between each trial, psychopaths' performance was not significantly different from controls' (Newman, Patterson and Kosson, 1987). Thus, when forced to reflect on their performance, the psychopaths showed the ability to learn from the consequences of their actions and to use this information to guide subsequent responding.

The results from the mixed contingency passive avoidance tasks and the card-playing task provided evidence that 'fearlessness' was an insufficient label for the psychopathic deficit. Psychopaths' 'fearlessness' had been based, in large part, on their apparent deficiencies on the passive avoidance task, but the new data revealed that psychopaths were not universally deficient at learning to avoid punishment on this task. What had emerged as important in these studies were the specific task demands and the opportunities for reflection. In response to these new data, in their 1993 reformulation of the response modulation model, Patterson and Newman focused on the role of attention in the performance deficits of psychopaths and as the psychological process that best mirrors the 'septal syndrome' proposed by Gorenstein and Newman (1980). According to Patterson and Newman (1993), psychopaths are deficient in the ability to suspend a dominant response and enact a brief, concurrent shift of attention from the organization and implementation of goal-directed responding to the evaluation of its consequences. It is this shift that allows individuals to make adjustments to their responses, if needed, and it is the absence of this shift that contributes to psychopathic disinhibition.

This explanation is consistent with the behavior of the psychopaths on both the passive avoidance and card-playing tasks. In both cases, the task conditions that revealed poor performance by psychopaths require efficient response modulation – that is they require the ability to shift attention to the information in the situation signaling punishment, which would then enable response change. Conversely, in the two conditions wherein psychopaths showed normal performance, efficient response modulation was not required. In the punishment only version of the passive avoidance task, for instance, there is a single focus of attention which obviates the need to shift attention between competing contingencies. Similarly, on the version of the card-playing task where the participant is forced to pause between trials, the psychopath is provided with the opportunity for reflection and the response modulation process is thus less essential. As proposed by Patterson and Newman (1993), it is the particular circumstances of a task that can either exacerbate or compensate for the psychopaths' deficit in response modulation.

In their proposal, Patterson and Newman (1993) set forth a four-stage sequence for response modulation. At the first step, a dominant response set is established. This set then guides the effortful allocation of attention to goal-relevant environmental stimuli and creates an expectation that reward is likely given the current response set. At the second step, an unexpected or aversive event violates the expectancy for reward. At this step, the violated expectancy generates an automatic call for processing and results in an increase in general (i.e. non-specific) arousal. At the third step, the call for processing is either answered and the dominant response is suppressed in order to allow for the effortful initiation of information gathering or the call for processing fails to suppress behavior in which case the arousal from stage 2 will facilitate ongoing behavior rather than information gathering. In the first case, there is modulation of the dominant response in light of new information. In the second case, there is a paradoxical increase in the intensity of the dominant response set. This intensification of the dominant response set Patterson and Newman (1993) labeled 'disinhibition'. The psychopaths' deficit occurs at this third stage, when they fail to answer to automatic call for processing generated by the discrepancy between their dominant response and the consequences of that response. As a result, they fail to initiate information gathering and this lack of reflection undermines the associative learning (i.e. between the response and the unanticipated outcome) that would then enable them to adapt their dominant response (i.e. stage 4 of the sequence) (Patterson and Newman, 1993).

This reformulation of the response modulation model accomplished two things: First, it was able to account for the discrepant passive avoidance and card-playing task data and set forth the argument that deficits in attention processes and not general 'fearlessness' were the core of the psychopathic deficit. Second, it generated a crucial hypothesis that the psychopath would show performance abnormalities not only on tasks that involved punishment or other emotion-based stimuli, but on any task that involved the shift of attention from the implementation of a response to the processing of secondary information relevant to that response.

To test this crucial hypothesis, Newman and colleagues (Newman, Schmitt and Voss, 1997; Hiatt, Schmitt and Newman, 2004; Vitale et al., 2005, 2007) undertook a series of experiments that utilized variations on the classic Stroop paradigm, which enabled the use of emotionally neutral stimuli. The first of these tasks was a computerized picture word task (Gernsbacher and Faust, 1991). On this task, participants are presented with two consecutive pictures or words, and are instructed to indicate whether or not the two pictures (or words) are conceptually related. On word trials, the first word is presented with a superimposed picture. On picture trials, the first picture is presented with a superimposed word. In each case, participants are instructed to ignore this secondary (i.e. superimposed) stimulus. However, on half of the trials when the consecutively presented stimuli are conceptually unrelated, the superimposed picture (or word) presented over the first stimulus is conceptually related to the second stimulus. In these trials, the correct response is 'unrelated', but the response indicated by the secondary stimulus is incongruent with this response. Among healthy participants, responses on these trials are slower than responses to trials when the to-be-ignored stimuli are unrelated to the second stimulus (see Gernsbacher and Faust, 1991). Consistent with the performance of healthy participants, non-psychopathic male offenders responded significantly more slowly on incongruent versus neutral trials (i.e. interference). However, this effect was significantly smaller in psychopathic male offenders, thus demonstrating significantly less sensitivity to the secondary stimulus among this group (Newman, Schmitt and Voss, 1997).

Hiatt, Schmitt and Newman (2004) demonstrated reduced interference in response to emotionally neutral, secondary stimuli among low-anxious, psychopathic male offenders using a picture word Stroop (PW Stroop) task. The PW Stroop consists of four cards. The first card is printed with a series of object words, which participants are asked to read. The second card is printed with a series of line drawings of objects, which they are instructed to name. On the third card, the line drawings are presented with superimposed trigrams (three-letter, non-word combinations). On the fourth card, the line drawings are presented with superimposed, incongruent words from card one (e.g. the word 'hen' over a line drawing of a frog). On cards three and four, participants are instructed to name the drawings and ignore the superimposed trigrams and words. Consistent with findings from the PW task (Newman, Schmitt and Voss, 1997), Hiatt, Schmitt and Newman (2004) found that low-anxious, psychopathic men showed significantly less interference in response to the superimposed, incongruent words than low-anxious, non-psychopathic men. In addition, this result has been replicated among adolescents assessed using the Antisocial Process Screening Device (Frick and Hare, 2001), a measure designed to assess psychopathy traits in children and adolescents (Vitale *et al.*, 2005), and among female offenders assessed using the PCL-R (Vitale *et al.*, 2007). In each case, psychopathic individuals show significantly less interference on the PW and PW Stroop tasks than controls.

In the most recent reformulation of the response modulation model, MacCoon, Wallace and Newman (2004) reframe the deficit in neural-network terms. Specifically, the 'context appropriate balance of attention' (CABA) model proposes that the deficit is best conceptualized in terms of the top-down and bottom-up mediated foci of selective attention. 'Top-down' attention is capacity limited, goal directed and corresponds to the first stage of the Patterson and Newman (1993) model. It is crucial for the successful implementation of a dominant response set, especially when distraction is present. In neural-network terms, the dominant response is the – currently – most active network of coactivated neurons. Bottom-up processing, in contrast, corresponds to the 'call for processing' that Patterson and Newman invoked, and involves automatic conflict monitoring. From this perspective, the response modulation deficit represents the failure of limited capacity, selective attention to enhance the activation of alternative neural networks that underlie non-dominant, yet potentially more adaptive, responses.

Response modulation, in the CABA model, involves the interruption and transfer of top-down attentional resources in response to bottom-up calls for processing. If top-down attention is too readily co-opted, the quality of goal-directed behavior is likely to suffer from a lack of focus. Conversely, when top-down attention is over-committed to dominant responses, the quality of behavior is compromised by the failure to activate non-dominant responses related to changing circumstances, past learning and other broader considerations that might otherwise result in the activation of alternative responses and suppression of less adaptive behaviors. By this view, adaptive decision making and behavior is best served by a context-appropriate balance of attention which, in turn, depends upon the quality of response modulation (MacCoon, Wallace and Newman, 2004).

For example, consider the passive avoidance task. In the mixed contingency version of the task, there are two goals (win money, avoid losing money) that represent two different networks. Once one of the two networks becomes activated (i.e. becomes the dominant response set), it will continue until a discrepancy occurs and an automatic, bottom-up call for processing is initiated. Answering this call for processing requires top-down selective attention, which facilitates the activation of a competing, non-dominant network. Among psychopaths, the call for processing is never answered, sustained activation of the non-dominant network is undermined and the dominant response continues.

The CABA model presented by MacCoon, Wallace and Newman (2004) takes the response modulation model one step further by introducing a new, neural-network vocabulary to the model and by specifying even more clearly the point at which the response modulation deficit occurs. It is the latest step in the response modulation model's continuing evolution, and one that lends itself well to applying the response modulation deficit to existing models of self-regulation. In the next section, we consider how response modulation may represent a unique lens through which to view the self-regulation processes of psychopathic individuals and may present new points of intervention.

RESPONSE MODULATION AND PSYCHOPATHIC SELF-REGULATION

Traditional models of self-regulation emphasize the effortful inhibition of inappropriate behavior. According to Kanfer and Gaelick (1986), for instance, self-regulation involves the effortful monitoring, evaluating and, if necessary, modification of behavior. Similarly, Baumeister and Hetherton (1996) argue that the existence of standards and goals, the monitoring of progress towards these standards and goals, and correction, represent the three key elements of self-regulation. In each case, traditional models of self-regulation emphasize a top-down approach to behavior modification, wherein a discrepancy between the outcome of a behavior and an existing goal or standard initiates an effortful evaluation of the ongoing behavior and, if necessary, an adjustment of the behavior. Such approaches highlight the importance of self-regulation in novel situations and when habitual or pre-potent responses are not optimal, and there is an increased need for effortful monitoring, evaluating and modification of behavior.

In Figure 13.1, we present a representation of the standard model of self-regulation as it relates to violence. In the model, the self-regulating individual is able to use top-down resources to select a violent or non-violent response to a provocation. The individual who does not engage in self-regulation, however, will implement a pre-potent reaction to the provocation (i.e. dashed line).

This model, however, may not best explain the disinhibition of the psychopath, primarily because the self-regulation deficits associated with psychopathy do not occur at this stage. They occur at an earlier stage, when the 'call for processing' emerging from the existence of a discrepancy between the outcome of a behavior and a set of goals or standards is not answered by top-down attention processes. This position is exemplified well by Shapiro's (1965) noting that the psychopath

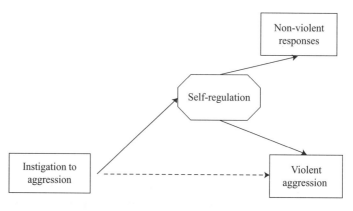

Figure 13.1 Self-regulation of aggression.

remains 'oblivious to the drawbacks or complications that would give another person pause and might otherwise give him pause as well' (p. 147–9).

Response modulation facilitates the processing of response conflict information and the evaluation of responses that initiates self-regulation. Thus, poor response modulation interferes, not by affecting the effortful self-regulatory process itself, but by inhibiting the initiation of this process. The psychopath's problem is not one of effortful self-regulation or cognitive control – that is mobilizing sufficient controlled resources to overcome the dominant response within the self-regulation model. Rather, the problem is a failure to register the response conflict that should initiate the self-regulation sequence. In fact, to the extent that a person fails to process the conflict, cognitive control skills become irrelevant.

In Figure 13.2a, we elaborate upon the standard model by inserting an earlier stage of information processing that incorporates conflict processing and the function of response modulation. In particular, automatic associations related to the

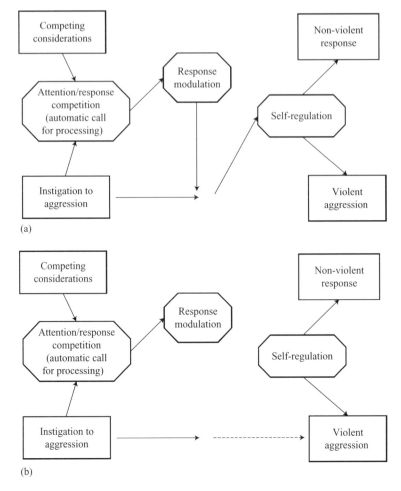

(a)

(b)

Figure 13.2   Elaborated model of self-regulation and aggression incorporating conflict monitoring and response modulation.

instigation of aggression give rise to response conflict and issue a call for more effortful or controlled processing. To the extent that response modulation occurs, there will be a brief and relatively automatic shift of attention from the implementation of goal-directed behavior to its evaluation (Patterson and Newman, 1993). Or, in other words, individuals will 'answer the call for processing' by elaborating upon the response conflict and then shifting to a control mode that involves the effortful evaluation and, if necessary, modification of behavior (i.e. self-regulation).

However, if response modulation does not occur (see Figure 13.2b), then the call for processing will not be answered, and there will little or no elaboration on the response conflict, in which case the pre-potent response will be expressed in a relatively automatic fashion (i.e. without the benefit for effortful evaluation) as illustrated by the dashed line.

According to this model, attempts to alter psychopathic behavior at the level of effortful self-regulation are likely to meet with failure. As Wallace *et al.* (2000) have argued, given that the deficit occurs at the point of automatic conflict monitoring, it would be unlikely that simply changing the content of psychopathic thought (e.g. teaching social skills and anger management, traditional cognitive therapy) would result in significant improvement in these individuals' behavior. Such techniques require the psychopath to engage in effortful self-regulation and the psychopath, as a result of his response modulation deficit, will fail to do so. Thus, he will be unable to access these new, more adaptive responses in key situations.

Rather than focusing primarily on changing the content of psychopaths' response repertoire or addressing their motivation to act appropriately, the model presented here places primary emphasis on developing and teaching strategies for compensating for the basic information processing deficit that makes accessing these alternative responses so challenging (Wallace *et al.*, 2000). It has been demonstrated that conditions exist under which, in experimental paradigms, the psychopaths' performance deficits disappear and they are able to perform as well as controls (Arnett, Smith and Newman, 1997; Newman and Kosson, 1986; Newman, Patterson and Kosson, 1987). These conditions need to be translated into 'real-world' terms, and our understanding of the parameters of the psychopaths' response modulation deficit utilized to craft interventions that will create these conditions.

In summary, according to the response modulation hypothesis and CABA model, psychopathic individuals are predisposed to act on urges once they become pre-potent because they do not allocate sufficient top-down attentional resources to process bottom-up associations that would otherwise serve to modify the behavior. According to this view, the problematic behavior of psychopaths reflects a general deficit in the flexibility of attention that directly impacts self-regulation and adaptive decision making, rather than specific drives toward violent action and reward seeking or a lack of motivation to avoid punishment. To the extent that a response modulation deficit will hinder the psychopathic individual's ability to engage in effortful self-regulation strategies, then their behaviors (both violent and non-violent) will lack the qualities of evaluation and deliberateness that are present in others.

One potential benefit of using the response modulation model to explain psychopaths' behavior is that it enables us to consider psychopaths' diverse criminality in a novel way. As noted above, the psychopathic offender is remarkable for his participation in both reactive and instrumental aggression. Current models of violence generally hold that that these two forms of aggression differ in their origin, mechanisms and management (Volavka, 1999). For example, impulsive–reactive aggression is associated with a potential dysfunction of inhibitory projections from the orbital/medial *prefrontal* cortex to the amygdala (e.g. Best, Williams and Coccaro, 2002; Davidson, Putnam and Larson, 2000). At a psychological level, impulsive aggression involves a problem mobilizing sufficient top-down resources to inhibit strong aggressive urges by activating alternative responses, particularly when such urges are fueled by negative affect (New *et al.*, 2002; Raine *et al.*, 1998). In contrast, because instrumental aggression is intentional, it is not normally attributed to deficient top-down control. Although there is less consensus regarding the psychobiological substrate of instrumental aggression, Blair's (2001) Violence Inhibition Mechanism Model suggests that instrumental aggression reflects psychopaths' inability to form associations between emotional, unconditioned stimuli (such as distress cues) and conditioned stimuli.

This dual-etiology approach appears well suited to psychopathy, which as assessed by the PCL-R, is comprised of two broad factors. For many investigators, the two-factor PCL-R model of psychopathy (e.g. Fowles and Dindo, 2006) indicates that psychopathy is an etiologically heterogeneous syndrome with some salient features of the disorder (e.g. the interpersonal callousness and shallow affect associated with PCL-R Factor 1) reflecting one set of psychobiological processes and other salient features (e.g. the impulsive behavior and antisocial lifestyle associated with PCL-R Factor 2) reflecting other psychobiological processes.

In contrast to this approach, the response modulation model suggests that both forms of violence stem from the same underlying deficit in response modulation. This alternative explanation, although preliminary at this time, does have some benefits to recommend it. First, it presents a more parsimonious explanation for psychopaths' behavior which is also consistent with the clinical observations of Cleckley and others. Cleckley, for example, conceptualized the diverse irresponsible and antisocial behaviors of the psychopath as reflecting a single, underlying deficit. According to Cleckley (1988): '[violence] should be regarded as the exception rather than the rule . . . [However], when serious criminal tendencies do emerge in the psychopath, they gain ready expression . . .' (p. 262), and that: 'there is less to indicate excessively violent rage than a relative weak emotion breaking through even weaker restraints' (p. 263). This view of psychopathic violence – as a result of weak 'restraints' – places it along the same continuum as their other impulsive, irresponsible behaviors. In all cases, psychopathic individuals appear to act on immediate urges without evaluating the implications of their actions for themselves or others.

Second, this approach accounts for the relative uniqueness of instrumental violence among psychopathic offenders. Although all instrumental violence is not perpetrated by psychopaths, psychopaths are more likely to engage in this behavior than other offenders (Blair, 2005; Cornell, Warren and Hawk, 1996; Serin, 1991). As a result, it is important for any model of psychopathic violence to explain this goal-directed aggression. The response modulation model presents a viable theoretical model, with maladaptive, goal-directed behavior enacted in the laboratory serving as a parallel for instrumental aggression occurring outside of the lab. For example, in both the passive avoidance and card-playing tasks, psychopathic individuals have demonstrated an inability to consider both long-term consequences and immediate punishments once they have initiated a dominant 'go' response set. In some ways, this behavior is similar to that exhibited by the psychopath who, once he has obtained a gun and decides to wield it during a robbery, is then apparently unable to consider that the punishment if he is caught will be increased as a result of the presence of the weapon.

Third, while much of the research on psychopathic violence has focused on explaining their – relatively unique – instrumental aggression, the response modulation model also sheds new light on the reactive aggression of psychopaths. Typically, impulsive aggression is conceptualized as the disinhibited expression of negative affect; however, this explanation seems paradoxical among psychopaths, who are characterized by a diminished capacity for affect (Cleckley, 1988; Hare, 1991). Indeed, psychopathic behavior is typically attributed to the failure of negative emotions such as fear and sadness to constrain their violent and other antisocial acts. Thus, the reactive aggression of psychopaths may differ in important ways from the reactive aggression of non-psychopaths. With its emphasis on cognitive-attention factors, the response modulation model can address psychopaths' reactive aggression without requiring heightened levels of negative affect. Rather, in this model, the reactive aggression reflects the intensification of the pre-potent response as a result of the failure of response modulation. That is, given an instigation to aggression, the psychopath will enact a pre-potent, aggressive response, not because anger has 'short circuited' the normal self-regulation sequence, but because the inability to enact a shift of attention to environmental cues signaling the need for regulation ensures that the self-regulation is never initiated.

At this time, it is unclear which theoretical model will best account for psychopathic violence. The dual-etiology approach is consistent with traditional conceptualizations of reactive and instrumental violence; however, the response modulation model offers a more parsimonious explanation for the impulsive and instrumental aggression of psychopathic individuals and acknowledges the potential uniqueness of psychopathic violence. Thus, it is worthy of continued exploration, particularly given the possibility that increasing our understanding of this model may enable us to address more effectively the impulsive and violent behaviors of the psychopath.

SUMMARY AND CONCLUSION

Regardless of whether the impulsive and instrumental aggression of psychopathic individuals reflect the same processes, we propose that the laboratory evidence on response modulation deficits in psychopathy and their established relevance for the passive avoidance learning deficits of psychopathic individuals commend the use of the response modulation model for conceptualizing the etiological processes that underlie the violent behavior of psychopathic individuals. Adoption of this perspective results in several implications. First, it suggests that the violent and non-violent, yet impulsive, behaviors of psychopaths reflect a single, underlying deficit. Second, it holds that this single, underlying deficit is cognitive attentional in nature, and may be understood as a failure of top-down attention processes to sufficiently activate non-dominant networks in the face of bottom-up calls for processing. Finally, this approach argues that treating the self-regulatory deficits of psychopathic individuals will require an emphasis on the response modulation process that initiates and motivates cue induced self-regulation, rather than on increasing the individual's effortful cognitive control processes. Thus, it is the intention of the authors that, by highlighting this model and by continuing to build upon the core experimental data that support it, researchers and clinicians alike will benefit from new insights into the assessment of the etiological processes underlying psychopathy, differential diagnosis and more specific and effective interventions.

REFERENCES

Arnett, P.A., Smith, S.S. and Newman, J.P. (1997) Approach and avoidance motivation in psychopathic criminal offenders during passive avoidance. *Journal of Personality and Social Psychology*, **72**, 1413–28.

Baumeister, R.F. and Hetherton, T.F. (1996) Self-regulation failure: an overview. *Psychological Inquiry*, **7**, 1–15.

Best, M., Williams, J.M. and Coccaro, E.F. (2002) Evidence for a dysfunctional prefrontal circuit in patients with an impulsive aggressive disorder. *Proceedings of the National Academy of Sciences of the United States of America*, **99** (12), 8448–53.

Blair, R.J.R. (2001) Neurocognitive models of aggression, the antisocial personality disorders, and psychopathy. *Journal of Neurology, Neurosurgery and Psychiatry*, **71**, 727–31.

Blair, R.J.R. (2005) The neurobiology of antisocial behaviour and psychopathy, in *The Cognitive Neuroscience of Social Behaviour* (eds A. Easton and N.J. Emery), Psychology Press, New York, pp. 291–324.

Cleckley, H. (1988) *The Mask of Sanity*, Mosby, St. Louis.

Cooke, D.J., Michie, C. and Hart, S.D. (2006) Facets of clinical psychopathy: towards clearer measurement, in *Handbook of Psychopathy* (ed. C. Patrick), Guilford, New York, pp. 91–106.

Cornell, D.G., Warren, J. and Hawk, G. (1996) Psychopathy in instrumental and reactive violent offenders. *Journal of Consulting and Clinical Psychology*, **64**, 783–90.

Davidson, R.J., Putnam, K.M. and Larson, C.L. (2000) Dysfunction in the neural circuitry of emotion regulation: a possible prelude to violence. *Science*, **298** (5479), 591–4.

Ellen, P. and Butter, J. (1969) External cue control of DRL performance in rats with septal lesions. *Physiology and Behavior*, **4**, 1–6.

Ellen, P., Wilson, A.S. and Powell, E.W. (1964) Septal inhibition and timing behavior in the rat. *Journal of Comparative Neurology*, **10**, 120–32.

Fowles, D.C. and Dindo, L. (2006). A dual-deficit model of psychopathy, in *Handbook of Psychopathy* (ed. C.J. Patrick), Guilford Press, New York, NY, pp. 14–34.

Frick, P.J. and Hare, R.D. (2001) *The Antisocial Process Screening Device*, Multi-Health Systems, Toronto.

Gernsbacher, M.A. and Faust, M.E. (1991) The mechanism of suppression: a component of general comprehension skill. *Journal of Experimental Psychology: Learning, Memory, and Cognition*, **17**, 245–62.

Gorenstein, E.E. and Newman, J.P. (1980) Disinhibitory psychopathology: a new perspective and a model for research. *Psychological Review*, **87**, 301–15.

Hare, R.D. (1980) A research scale for the assessment of psychopathy in criminal populations. *Personality and Individual Differences*, **1**, 111–9.

Hare, R.D. (1991) *Manual for the Hare Psychopathy Checklist-Revised*, Multi-Health Systems, Toronto.

Hare, R.D. (1993) *Without Conscience: The Disturbing World of the Psychopaths among Us*, Guilford, New York.

Hare, R.D., Clark, D., Grann, M. and Thornton, D. (2000) Psychopathy and the predictive validity of the PCL-R: an international perspective. *Behavioral Sciences and the Law*, **18**, 623–45.

Hare, R.D. and Hart, S.D. (1993) Psychopathy, mental disorder, and crime, in *Mental Disorder and Crime* (ed. S. Hodgins), Sage, Newbury Park, CA, pp. 104–15.

Hare, R.D. and Neumann, C.S. (2006) The PCL-R assessment of psychopathy: development, structural properties, and new directions, in *Handbook of Psychopathy* (ed. C. Patrick), Guilford, New York, pp. 58–90.

Harpur, T.J., Hakstian, A.R. and Hare, R.D. (1988) Factor structure of the Psychopathy Checklist. *Journal of Consulting and Clinical Psychology*, **56**, 741–7.

Harpur, T.J., Hare, R.D. and Hakstian, A.R. (1989) Two-factor conceptualization of psychopathy: construct validity and assessment implications. *Psychological Assessment*, **1**, 6–17.

Harris, G.T. and Rice, M.E. (2006) Treatment of psychopathy: a review of empirical findings, in *Handbook of Psychopathy* (ed. C. Patrick), Guilford, New York, pp. 555–72.

Hemphill, J.F., Hare, R.D. and Wong, S. (1998) Psychopathy and recidivism: a review. *Legal and Criminological Psychology*, **3**, 139–70.

Hemphill, J.F., Templeman, R., Wong, S. and Hare, R.D. (1998) Psychopathy and crime: recidivism and criminal careers, in *Psychopathy: Theory, Research and Implications for Society* (eds D.J. Cooke, R.D. Hare and A. Forth), Kluwer Academic, Dordrecht, pp. 375–99.

Hiatt, D.D., Schmitt, W.A. and Newman, J.P. (2004) Stroop tasks reveal abnormal selective attention among psychopathic offenders. *Neuropsychology*, **18**, 50–9.

Hobson, J., Shine, J. and Roberts, R. (2000) How do psychopaths behave in a prison therapeutic community? *Psychology, Crime and Law*, **6**, 139–54.

Hughes, G., Hogue, T., Hollin, C. and Champion, H. (1997) First stage evaluation of a treatment programme for personality disordered offenders. *Journal of Forensic Psychiatry*, **8**, 515–27.

Kaada, B.R., Rasmussen, E.W. and Kveim, O. (1962) Impaired acquisition of passive-avoidance behavior by subcallosal, septal, hypothalamic, and insular lesions in rats. *Journal of Comparative and Physiological Psychology*, **55**, 661–70.

Kanfer, F.H. and Gaelick, L. (1986) Self-management models, in *Helping People Change: A Textbook of Methods* (eds F.H. Kanfer and A.P. Goldstein), Pergamon, New York, pp. 283–345.

Kelsey, J.E. and Grossman, S. (1971) Non-perseverative disruption of behavioral inhibition following septal lesions in rats. *Journal of Comparative and Physiological Psychology*, **75**, 302–11.

Lykken, D.T. (1957) A study of anxiety in the sociopathic personality. *Journal of Abnormal Psychology*, **55**, 6–10.

Lykken, D.T. (1995) *The Antisocial Personalities*, Lawrence Erlbaum Associates, Hillsdale, NJ.

MacCoon, D.G., Wallace, J.F. and Newman, J.P. (2004). Self-regulation: Context-appropriate balanced attention, in *Handbook of Self-Regulation: Research, Theory, and Applications* (eds R.F. Baumeister and K.D. Vohs), Guilford Press, New York, NY, pp. 422–44.

McCleary, R.A. (1961) Response specificity in the behavioral effects of limbic system lesions in the cat. *Journal of Comparative and Physiological Psychology*, **54**, 605–13.

Morgan, J.M. and Mitchell, J.C. (1969) Septal lesions enhance the delay of responding on a free operant avoidance schedule. *Psychonotnic Science*, **16**, 10–11.

New, A.S., Hazlett, E.A., Buchsbaum, M.S. *et al.* (2002). Blunted prefrontal cortical 18 fluorodeoxyglucose positron emission tomography response to meta-chlorophenylpiperazine in impulsive aggression. *Archives of General Psychiatry*, **59** (7), 621–9.

Newman, J.P. and Kosson, D.S. (1986) Passive avoidance learning in psychopathic and nonpsychopathic offenders. *Journal of Abnormal Psychology*, **96**, 257–63.

Newman, J.P., Patterson, C.M. and Kosson, D.S. (1987) Response perseveration in psychopaths. *Journal of Abnormal Psychology*, **96**, 145–8.

Newman, J.P. and Schmitt, W.A. (1998) Passive avoidance in psychopathic offenders: a replication and extension. *Journal of Abnormal Psychology*, **107**, 527–32.

Newman, J.P., Schmitt, W.A. and Voss, W. (1997) Processing of contextual cues in psychopathic and nonpsychopathic offenders. *Journal of Abnormal Psychology*, **106**, 563–75.

Ogloff, J.R., Wong, S. and Greenwood, A. (1990) Treating criminal psychopaths in a therapeutic community program. *Behavioral Sciences and the Law*, **8**, 181–90.

Patterson, C.M. and Newman, J.P. (1993) Reflectivity and learning from aversive events: toward a psychological mechanism for the syndromes of disinhibition. *Psychological Review*, **100**, 716–36.

Raine, A., Meloy, J.R., Bihrle, S. *et al.* (1998) Reduced prefrontal and increased subcortical brain functioning assessed using positron emission tomography in predatory and affective murderers. *Behavioral Sciences and Law*, **16** (3), 319–32.

Rice, M.E., Harris, G.T. and Cormier, C. (1992) A follow-up of rapists assessed in a maximum security psychiatric facility. *Journal of Interpersonal Violence*, **5**, 435–48.

Richards, H.J., Casey, J.O. and Lucente, S.W. (2003) Psychopathy and treatment response in incarcerated female substance abusers. *Criminal Justice and Behavior*, **30**, 251–76.

Salekin, R.T. (2002) Psychopathy and therapeutic pessimisms: clinical lore or clinical reality? *Clinical Psychology Review*, **22**, 79–112.

Salekin, R.T., Rogers, R. and Sewell, K.W. (1996) A review and meta-analysis of the Psychopathy Checklist and Psychopathy Checklist-Revised: Predictive validity of dangerousness. *Clinical Psychology: Science and Practice*, **3**, 203–15.

Serin, R.C. (1991) Psychopathy and violence in criminals. *Journal of Interpersonal Violence*, **6**, 423–31.

Serin, R.C. and Kuriychuk, M. (1994) Social and cognitive processing deficits in violent offenders: implications for treatment. *International Journal of Law and Psychiatry*, **17**, 431–41.

Shapiro, D. (1965) *Neurotic Styles*, Basic Books, New York.

Skeem, J.L., Monahan, J. and Mulvey, E.P. (2002) Psychopathy, treatment involvement, and subsequent violence among civil psychiatric patients. *Law and Human Behavior*, **26** (6), 577–603.

Sodetz, F.J. (1970) Septal ablation and free operant avoidance behavior in the rat. *Physiology and Behavior*, **5**, 773–8.

Vitale, J.E., Hiatt, K.D., Brinkley, C.A. and Newman, J.P. (2007) Abnormal selective attention in psychopathic female offenders. *Neuropsychology*, **21**, 301–12.

Vitale, J.E., Newman, J.P., Bates, J.E. *et al.* (2005) Deficient behavioral inhibition and anomalous selective attention in a community sample of adolescents with psychopathic and low-anxiety traits. *Journal of Abnormal Child Psychology*, **33**, 461–70.

Volavka, J. (1999) The neurobiology of violence: an update. *Journal of Neuropsychiatry and Clinical Neurosciences*, **11** (3), 307–14.

Wallace, J.F., Schmitt, W.A., Vitale, J.E. and Newman, J.P. (2000) Experimental investigations of information processing deficiencies and psychopathy: implications for diagnosis and treatment, in *Clinical and Forensic Assessment of Psychopathy* (ed. C. Gacono), Lawrence Erlbaum Associates, Hillsdale, NJ, pp. 87–110.

Chapter 14

SOCIAL PROBLEM SOLVING, PERSONALITY DISORDER AND VIOLENCE

MARY MCMURRAN

University of Nottingham, UK

Social problem solving is 'the self-directed cognitive–affective–behavioral process by which an individual attempts to identify or discover solutions to specific problems encountered in everyday living' (D'Zurilla and Nezu, 2007, p. 11). A *problem* arises in a life situation where a response is required but none is available, and a *solution* is a situation-specific coping response that is the product of the problem-solving process (D'Zurilla and Nezu, 2007).

There are many kinds of problem in everyday living, but of most relevance to the subject of this chapter are interpersonal problems, since personality disorders are defined to a large degree by difficulties in interpersonal functioning. Furthermore, violence may be viewed as one type of solution to interpersonal problems, albeit a solution that is not effective according to D'Zurilla and Nezu's (2007) criteria:

> With specific reference to an interpersonal problem, an effective solution is one that resolves the conflict or dispute by providing an outcome that is acceptable or satisfactory to all parties. In other words, the solution minimizes negative consequences and maximizes positive consequences for the two or more people involved in the dispute. This outcome may involve a consensus, compromise, or negotiated agreement that accommodates the interests and well-being of all concerned parties (p. 14).

Violence is not respectful of the interests and well-being of other parties, and nor is it respectful of the law. In this chapter, the cognitive–behavioural–affective problem-solving process that is initiated when a problem arises will be examined. Aspects of this process that elevate the risk of violence will be identified.

In practical terms, social problem-solving theory and research are useful in developing interventions, with social problem-solving therapy proving effective in

---

Personality, Personality Disorder and Violence   Edited by Mary McMurran and Richard C. Howard
© 2009 John Wiley & Sons, Ltd

ameliorating a range of problems (Malouff, Thorsteinsson and Schutte, 2007). In this chapter, however, the focus will be on the treatment of violence and people with personality disorders.

SOCIAL PROBLEM SOLVING AND SOCIAL FUNCTIONING

Put simply, a model of social functioning featuring social problem solving may be described as follows. Innate temperament characteristics are the developmental start point for adult traits, which are stable patterns of interpersonal functioning. Social problem-solving abilities are one important mediator of the relationship between traits and social functioning. Early temperament in the form of varying levels of activity, attention and fear may directly impact upon the acquisition of social problem-solving skills, but over time there is also a reciprocal interaction between the individual and that individual's social environment. Hence, over the life span, the development of social problem-solving skills is influenced both directly by individual characteristics and through learning experiences.

Social problem solving consists of several types of abilities, which D'Zurilla and Nezu (2007) describe in three levels. First, *orienting responses* involve the ability to recognise a problem when one arises, the activation of beliefs about one's ability to solve problems, and the affective responses to the problematic situation and about one's problem-solving competencies. Second, there are specific *problem-solving skills* of defining the problem, setting goals, generating a range of possible solutions, thinking through the potential consequences of each solution, selecting the viable options, formulating a means-end action plan, carrying out that plan and evaluating progress towards goal attainment. Social problem solving is the real-life application of the higher order cognitive abilities of abstracting relevant information, reasoning, consequential thinking, planning and self-regulation that are collectively known as 'executive cognitive functioning' (Zelazo *et al.*, 1997). Finally, there are *basic cognitive abilities* that are fundamental to problem solving, such as perception, attention, information processing and memory. To these may be added language ability. These basic abilities are the building blocks of general intelligence, yet intelligence and social problem solving are not strongly associated, at least at higher levels of intellectual functioning (D'Zurilla and Nezu, 2007). Individuals within the normal and higher ranges of intelligence show great variability in social competence and this is not explained by their IQ. Research with offenders has not found an association between intelligence and social problem solving (Biggam and Power, 1999).

Individual differences will impact upon overall social problem solving effectiveness, and some of these variables will be examined in this chapter. While the process of social problem solving impacts upon social problem solving outcomes, external variables will also clearly have an effect. Although context is not emphasised in this chapter, social problem solving abilities cannot be understood in isolation from the context in which the person lives, the resources available to him or her and the characteristics of the other people involved in an interpersonal problem.

SOCIAL PROBLEM SOLVING, AGGRESSION AND VIOLENCE

Childhood externalising disorders, which are characterised by disruptive be-haviour and aggression, include conduct disorder, oppositional defiant disorder and attention deficit/hyperactivity disorder. These disorders are more common in boys and are associated with later antisocial personality disorder and substance abuse problems (Farrington, 1995; Fergusson and Horwood, 2002; Moffitt *et al.*, 2002). Children with externalising disorders have been shown to have social infor-mation processing deficits and biases. Compared with socially competent children, they encode fewer social cues, focus more on hostile cues, are more likely to at-tribute hostile intent to others, generate fewer problem-solving solutions, produce more aggressive behavioural options and evaluate aggression more positively (see review by Matthys and Lochman, 2005).

One correlate of externalising problems is verbal ability. Boys with externalising problems have significantly lower verbal IQ than those without and this corre-lates modestly with the production of aggressive solutions to social problems (Coy *et al.*, 2001). Zadeh, Im-Boulter and Cohen (2007) found that language competence in children with externalising problems explained the relationship between so-cial competence and externalising problems. As they noted, good social problem solving requires the ability to communicate with others.

In boys, low IQ is related to delinquency, with this being accounted for by low verbal IQ rather than performance IQ (Lynam, Moffitt and Stouthamer-Loeber, 1993). In a longitudinal study of a cohort of London boys, Farrington also found that low verbal IQ at age 8–10 was a predictor of persistent offending in later life (Farrington, 1995). Wong and Cornell (1999) identified a high prevalence (25%) of juvenile offenders who were relatively deficient in verbal IQ compared with performance IQ, and this was associated with a hostile attributional bias. Barratt *et al.* (1997) found that impulsive aggressive and non-impulsive aggressive adult prisoners did not differ on impulsivity but that they did differ on verbal skills.

How might verbal deficits relate to antisocial behaviour and aggression? Lynam, Moffitt and Stouthamer-Loeber (1993) suggested that verbal IQ was a broad index of executive cognitive functioning and tested this hypothesis by examining the contribution of impulsivity in explaining the relationship between verbal IQ and delinquency. Although impulsivity was found to be a strong predictor of delin-quency, the relationship between low verbal IQ and delinquency was *not* explained by impulsivity. One alternative suggestion is that verbal deficits lower efficacy in dealing with problematic situations, causing frustration which is expressed as ag-gression. This pathway is rehearsed repeatedly from very early on in life, and so aggressive behaviour becomes an entrenched learned response to frustration (Barratt *et al.*, 1997).

Interestingly, the relationship between verbal abilities, social competence and ag-gression may also explain gender differences in antisocial behaviour and violence. In their review of the role of social cognitive skills in explaining gender differ-ences in crime and violence, Bennett, Farrington and Huesmann (2005) highlight gender differences in left hemisphere maturation, the left hemisphere being the one responsible for language skills. The left hemisphere matures more quickly in females compared with males, girls develop language skills more rapidly, and males perform less well than females on test of verbal ability. This may confer an early advantage upon females in dealing with their social environment, which leads to the development of better and more pro-social information processing skills.

That social problem-solving abilities are learned is supported in a study by Jaffee and D'Zurilla (2003). If social problem-solving skills are learned, it would be expected that adolescents' social problem-solving skills would be worse than those of their parents because adolescents have had less practice. In their study, this hypothesis was supported. Furthermore, in these adolescents, dysfunctional social problem solving was related to aggression and delinquency, with aggression associated specifically with high scores on the Social Problem Solving Inventory-Revised (SPSI-R; D'Zurilla, Nezu and Maydeu-Olivares, 2002) scales of negative problem orientation (NPO) and avoidant style (AS). The authors recommended social problem-solving skills training for preventing adolescent behaviour problems, with the focus of training being not necessarily on the adolescent alone but conjointly with parents.

There are four main practical implications from research into verbal deficits, social problem solving and aggression. First, early social problem-solving interventions are necessary to enable young people to learn to cope effectively with interpersonal problems so that they avoid repeated incidents of frustration and aggression. Second, interventions could usefully focus on parents' skills as well as conjoint parent–child problem solving. Third, these interventions, which are often heavily verbally based, should be delivered with the recipients' verbal deficits in mind. Finally, improving verbal and communication skills should be a component of these interventions.

SOCIAL PROBLEM SOLVING, PERSONALITY AND AGGRESSION

Where antisocial behaviour and aggression are concerned, there are two highly relevant personality domains, these being impulsivity and callous–unemotional traits. These will be the focus here.

Impulsivity

Enticott and Ogloff (2006) note that there are many behavioural expressions of impulsivity and they offer a definition of impulsive behaviour: 'Impulsivity is expressed as rapid, spontaneous, ill-planned, excessive, and potentially maladaptive conduct' (p. 4). Aggression and violence are one type of behavioural expression of impulsivity. There are several proposed causal mechanisms, and three models of impulsivity prevail: (1) the inability to withhold a response, that is a decreased sensitivity to negative consequences of behaviour; (2) a preference for small immediate rewards over larger delayed rewards, that is an inability to delay gratification or a lack of regard for long-term consequences; and (3) making premature responses before complete processing of information (Moeller *et al.*, 2001). The last of these is of interest here.

Enticott and Ogloff (2006) describe one underlying process as 'rapid action with-out forethought' or 'lack of premeditation'. In a problematic situation, executive cognitive processes are deficient or lacking. These processes help a person attend to relevant cues, assimilate relevant information, identify potential actions, anticipate consequences and form and execute a means-end action plan that maximises the likelihood of positive outcomes and minimises the likelihood of negative outcomes.

While testing the hypothesis that people with poor executive cognitive func-tioning (ECF) are less able to inhibit behaviour, including aggression, Hoaken, Shaughnessy and Pihl (2003) found evidence in favour of social problem-solving deficits. They conducted a laboratory study of ECF and aggression using a compet-itive reaction time task paradigm where aggression is measured by the intensity of electric shock delivered to an unseen opponent (who is fictional) and the level of provocation is manipulated by the intensity of shock received by the experi-mental subject and supposedly selected by the 'opponent'. Hoaken, Shaughnessy and Pihl (2003) found that participants with low ECF responded more aggressively to provocation than did those with high ECF, and that this effect was more pro-nounced for men than women. Compared to those with high ECF, those with low ECF did not make significantly more errors of commission on a Go/No Go task (i.e. where a participant is asked to withhold a response to a stimulus previously paired with a reward). They did, however, take significantly longer to select the intensity of shock to be delivered to their opponent. Hoaken, Shaughnessy and Pihl (2003) interpreted these results as indicating the importance of a social component: peo-ple with low ECF make poor social decisions in that they are aggressive, but they make these decisions slowly. They are more aggressive because they are unable to cope with the number of response options, fail to access socially appropriate responses and make default aggressive responses when provoked. That is, people with low ECF are poor at social problem solving. This accords with evidence from the study by Lynam, Moffitt and Stouthamer-Loeber (1993) cited earlier.

In our own research surveying student populations, we have shown that impul-sivity, measured by the Barratt Impulsiveness Scale (Patton, Stanford and Barratt, 1995) predicts aggression, measured by the Buss–Perry Aggression Questionnaire (Buss and Perry, 1992). However, upon entering social problem solving into the analysis, measured by the SPSI-R (D'Zurilla, Nezu and Maydeu-Olivares, 2002), this relationship disappears, leaving social problem solving as the predictor of aggression (McMurran, Blair and Egan, 2002; Ramadan and McMurran, 2005). That is, the relationship between impulsivity and aggression is mediated by social problem-solving skills.

Callous–Unemotional Traits

Although one might expect callous–unemotional traits to impact adversely upon social problem solving, this may not be the case. Waschbusch et al. (2007) studied children with and without externalising problems to test the interaction effect of conduct problems and callous–unemotional traits on social problem solving. The expectation was that higher conduct problems would be associated with poorer social problem solving but that this relationship would be stronger in those with high callous–unemotional traits. The results were actually in the direction opposite to that expected: the relationship between high conduct problems and poor social problem solving was stronger for those who were *low* on callous–unemotional traits. The authors suggest that poor social problem solving may be associated with harsh discipline in childhood rather than emotion processing deficits.

This proposition is supported by research by Dodge *et al.* (1995), who found that physical harm in early childhood was associated with an increased risk for later conduct problems. The mechanisms suggested as explaining this connection were that the child becomes defensively hypervigilant for hostile cues, readily attributes hostile intent to others and acquires a repertoire of highly accessible aggressive responses. Recent evidence suggests that by early adolescence, of all these processes, retrieving aggressive response options from memory is the most strongly predictive of antisocial behaviour (Lösel, Bliesener and Bender, 2007).

These findings suggest that poor social problem solving and aggression may be linked through emotional hyper-reactivity, which describes the secondary rather than the primary psychopath (see Blackburn, Chapters 6) or the anxious type of antisocial personality disorder (De Brito and Hodgins, Chapter 7). In our investigations with mentally disordered offenders using the NEO-Five Factor Inventory (Costa and McCrae, 1992), we found that high neuroticism (N) predicted poor social problem solving (McMurran *et al.*, 2001a; McMurran, Egan and Duggan, 2005).

SOCIAL PROBLEM SOLVING, PERSONALITY DISORDER AND AGGRESSION

In our research using the SPSI-R (D'Zurilla, Nezu and Maydeu-Olivares, 2002), we have studied people with and without personality disorder. The SPSI-R has five scales. Two of these measure problem orientation – positive problem orientation (PPO) and NPO. PPO is a cognitive set in which problems are viewed as a challenge, there is optimism about finding solutions, and there is commitment to devoting effort to attaining a successful solution. NPO is a cognitive–emotional set where problems are seen as a threat, perceived self-efficacy in solving problems is low, and problems cause feelings of upset and frustration. The other three scales measure problem-solving style – rational problem solving (RPS), impulsive/careless style (ICS) and avoidant style (AS). A total social problem solving (SPS) score may also be calculated. Good SPS is indicated by higher scores on PPO, RPS and SPS, and lower scores on NPO, ICS and AS. Mean scale scores and standard deviations for male samples with personality disorder, prisoners and mature students are presented in Table 14.1. These data show that the samples with personality disorders score poorly on the SPSI-R.

For the purpose of this chapter, the focus will be on two specific personality disorders of which impulsivity and aggression are defining features: antisocial and borderline. As we have seen, poor SPS mediates between impulsivity and aggression, hence it is worth examining SPS in relation to these personality disorders.

In the development of adult personality disorders, there is an interplay between genetic factors and adverse childhood experiences; that is, basic characteristics or

Table 14.1   Mean scores and standard deviations on the Social Problem Solving Inventory-Revised for UK male samples

SPSI-R	Personality disordered offenders (N = 72)[a]	Personality disordered community adults (N = 80)[b]	Vulnerable prisoners on special location (N = 68)[c]	Prisoners on normal location (N = 47)[c]	Mature students (N = 70)[d]
Positive problem orientation	9.29 (4.63)	6.36 (4.38)	10.30 (5.43)	12.26 (5.03)	12.82 (4.14)
Negative problem orientation	22.33 (8.65)	25.35 (8.34)	23.48 (11.07)	15.53 (12.22)	10.95 (6.79)
Rational problem solving	29.19 (18.08)	24.20 (17.53)	38.43 (20.33)	37.49 (17.17)	44.78 (12.60)
Impulsive/careless style	23.32 (8.88)	19.64 (9.00)	21.65 (10.44)	15.02 (10.03)	10.97 (5.84)
Avoidant style	15.25 (6.48)	14.56 (6.31)	14.73 (7.27)	10.45 (7.62)	8.25 (5.42)
Social problem solving	8.52 (3.57)	7.92 (3.41)	9.36 (3.83)	11.78 (4.11)	13.39 (2.51)

[a] Unpublished data from the Personality Disorder Treatment Unit, Arnold Lodge, Leicester.
[b] Unpublished data from Huband *et al.*'s (2007) sample.
[c] Data from Hayward, McMurran and Sellen (2007).
[d] Data from McMurran, Blair and Egan (2002).

tendencies are expressed as characteristic adaptations or traits through the influence of the individual's life experiences (McCrae and Costa, 2003). The heritability of impulsivity (Baker, Bezdjian and Raine, 2006) means that a child with high impulsivity might be born to parents with impulsivity, which may increase the chances of adverse childhood experiences. These adverse experiences influence the development of social problem-solving skills.

Antisocial Personality Disorder

Over the lifespan, especially under circumstances of poor parental control and harsh discipline, impulsivity may lead to failure to learn self-regulation skills, poorly developed social problem-solving skills, learned aggression in response to problems, the use of drink and drugs and the development of values supportive of antisocial behaviour. This constellation of problems is one that describes antisocial personality disorder (ASPD). ASPD is a diagnosis markedly more common in men: in the UK general population, 1% men and 0.2% of women have ASPD (Coid *et al.*, 2006), and among prisoners 47% men and 21% women have ASPD (Fazel and Danesh, 2002). As people with these problems then become parents, so the family transmission of problems continues.

   In a factor analytic study of item scores on the International Personality Disorder Examination (Loranger, 1999) from 224 people with personality disorders, an antisocial personality factor was one of three factors found (Howard *et al.*, 2008). This factor was contributed to by antisocial, histrionic, narcissistic, paranoid and borderline items. Of all the SPSI-R scales, only ICS positively predicted this factor (N. Huband, personal communication, 31 July 2007). However, in our sample of 173 men and women, whereas most individual personality disorders were associated with social problem-solving deficits as measured by the SPSI-R, ASPD was not among them (McMurran *et al.*, 2007). This unexpected finding accords with research by Herrick and Elliott (2001), who found an association between social problem-solving deficits and Cluster A and Cluster C personality disorders but not Cluster B, which is the cluster within which ASPD lies. Herrick and Elliott (2001) suggested that Cluster B respondents might overestimate their social problem-solving abilities.

Assessment of social problem-solving skills in people who may not have sufficient self-awareness to recognise their strengths and weaknesses or who may wish to conceal problems is a general issue that needs to be addressed. We might wish to interpret self-report information in light of other evidence. Since impulsive aggression is a signature of ASPD, and, as explained earlier, social problem-solving deficits are known to mediate the impulsivity–aggression relationship, it seems fair to infer that social problem-solving deficits exist but that self-report measures are not picking these up in people with ASPD. The skills required for social problem solving depend upon the executive cognitive functions, and violent offenders and men with ASPD have poorer ECF than non-violent offenders and non-offenders (Giancola, 2000; Hoaken, Shaughnessy and Pihl, 2003). Quite simply, because of their deficits, people with ASPD may not be able to recognise or articulate how they solve problems, and consequently these are not detected by self-report measures. Of course, people with ASPD may also, for various reasons, fake good on self-reported problem-solving tests. The development of measures that are less reliant upon self-report and instead measure implicit processes is one potentially fruitful area of research.

An alternative explanation is that people with ASPD do, in fact, have good social problem-solving abilities but that they are unable to employ them under certain circumstances. In situations where there is a perceived threat and consequent high physiological arousal, social problem-solving abilities would be impaired. Given the effects of harsh childhood experiences, threat perception and physiological arousal may be elevated in this group. Additionally, the impact of threat is likely to be exacerbated when alcohol or certain illicit drugs have been taken (see review by McMurran, 2008).

Psychosocial treatments specifically for ASPD are scarce, and often the treatment target is substance abuse, which is a common co-occurring disorder (Duggan *et al.*, 2005). However, since ASPD is common among offenders (Fazel and Danesh, 2002), it is possible to infer that what works for offenders in general is likely to work for offenders with ASPD. Some of the most successful interventions for offenders have a strong focus on social problem-solving skills, as we shall see in the next section.

Borderline Personality Disorder

The main features of borderline personality disorder (BPD) are problems with affect regulation, impulse control, close personal relationships and self-image, and there is a high mortality rate from suicide (Lieb *et al.*, 2004). BPD is more common in women than men (ratio 70:30), in contrast to ASPD. The social antecedents of BPD are attachment difficulties, perhaps as a result of an invalidating social environment, neglect or even abuse (Lieb *et al.*, 2004; Linehan, 1993).

Most of the studies of social problem solving in relation to BPD focus on suicide and self-harm, which overlaps substantially but does not wholly equate with BPD. Other psychiatric disorders are also associated with suicide and self-harm. Additionally, suicidal and self-harming behaviour are likely to be evidence of an emotional crisis, which temporarily impairs problem solving. Bray, Barrowclough and Lobban (2007) teased out some of these confounds by comparing people diagnosed with BPD against a group of patients with primarily Axis I disorders and a group of people with no mental health problems. They found that both the BPD group and the clinical control group were poorer overall at social problem solving than the non-clinical control group, with the BPD group showing specific deficits compared with the clinical control group in that they produced less specific solutions to problems on the Means-End Problem-Solving (MEPS) test (Platt and Spivack, 1975), and higher NPO, ICS and SPS scores on the SPSI-R.

In our study of social problem solving and personality disorders, we found that BPD was predicted by high ICS and low AS (McMurran *et al.*, 2007). The ICS scale taps problem-solving attempts that are hurried and incomplete, and where there is a failure systematically to consider a range of alternatives and to weigh up the consequences. The AS scale taps procrastination, passivity and inaction, characteristics which were *not* associated with BPD.

One of the core components of dialectical behaviour therapy (Linehan, 1993), the best evaluated psychosocial therapy for people with BPD (Binks *et al.*, 2006), is teaching social problem-solving skills.

TREATMENT

Aggressive behaviour in children and adolescents has been successfully treated through social-cognitive skills training programmes (see reviews by Lösel and Beelmann, 2005; Matthys and Lochman, 2005). In a meta-analysis of child-focused cognitive–behavioural interventions for anger and angry aggression, social problem-solving interventions were noted as successfully reducing aggression with a medium effect size[1] ($d = 0.57$), although multimodal programmes that also included behavioural skills training were more effective ($d = 0.75$) (Sukhodolsky, Kassinove and Gorman, 2004). Interestingly, social problem-solving interventions were by far the most effective, in comparison with skills development, affect control training, and multimodal programmes, in reducing anger experience ($d = 1.05$).

In the criminal justice system, treatment is dominated by structured cognitive–behavioural programmes, based upon sound evidence that these are what work with offenders to reduce recidivism (McGuire, 2002). Among these are general cognitive skills programmes, of which *Reasoning and Rehabilitation* (Ross, Fabiano and Ross, 1986) and *Enhanced Thinking Skills* (Clark, 2000) are the most widely used. Within both of these programmes are components on interpersonal problem-solving skills. A recent meta-analysis of controlled evaluations of these programmes indicated that, overall, recidivism at 1 year was reduced by 14% for programme participants compared with controls (Tong and Farrington, 2008). A different programme that specifically targets offenders' social problem solving is *Think First* (McGuire, 2000). In an outcome evaluation, this programme has been shown to be more effective in reducing recidivism than more general cognitive skills training programmes (Hollin *et al.*, 2003).

A less structured, more therapeutic approach to developing the skills of social problem solving, following the work of D'Zurilla and Nezu (2007), is *Stop & Think!* The procedure may be described in seven separate steps:

1. *Problem orientation,* which is the recognition of negative emotions and viewing them as a cue to initiate the problem-solving process. Attention needs to be paid to problem orientation; problems are a normal part of life, and active and systematic problem solving produces the best chances of an effective resolution.
2. *Problem definition,* which is the ability to define a problem clearly and accurately.
3. *Goal setting,* which is identification of the desired outcome.
4. *Generation of alternatives,* which is the creative generation of a range of possible ways of achieving the goal.
5. *Decision making,* where, after examining the likely positive and negative consequences of each potential solution to both self and others, the best options are selected. These should then be arranged in logical sequence to form a means-end action plan.
6. *Action* is the implementation of the action plan over time.
7. *Evaluation* is a review of the success or otherwise of the action plan, either in progress or at its conclusion.

In *Stop & Think!* these steps are translated into six key questions that guide the problem-solving process in clinical practice: Bad feelings? What's my problem? What do I want? What are my options? What is my plan? How am I doing? These six key questions guide the *Stop & Think!* sessions, with a focus on the participant's current concerns, aiming not only to solve existing problems but also to teach people the problem-solving strategy.

A pilot study of a brief *Stop & Think!* intervention with nine male patients (six mentally ill and three personality disordered) in a UK regional secure unit for mentally disordered offenders produced improvements in patients' SPSI-R SPS scores and reductions in ICS and NPO (McMurran *et al.*, 1999). The effectiveness of *Stop & Think!* was then examined further with personality disordered offenders ($N = 14$) in the secure unit, with positive change evident on all scales of the SPSI-R except PPO after 3 months in treatment (McMurran *et al.*, 2001b). *Stop & Think!* has also shown positive effect with vulnerable prisoners, particularly in reducing NPO and AS, and improving overall SPS (Hayward, McMurran and Sellen, 2007).

More recently, a randomised controlled trial examined the effectiveness of a combination of *Stop & Think!* and psychoeducation, an individual component in which the nature of the patient's personality disorder and consequent problems was discussed (Huband *et al.*, 2007). Participants were 176 community-dwelling men and women with personality disorders in several sites across the East Midlands of England, who were randomly allocated to either treatment or a wait-list control. The treated group received, on average, nine group sessions and a further three individual sessions, and they showed significantly greater improvement on SPSI-R scales, on a Social Functioning Questionnaire (Tyrer *et al.*, 2005), which measures functioning in the domains of home, work, leisure and relationships, and on anger expression, as measured by the State-Trait Anger Expression Inventory (Spielberger, 1999). Improvement in social functioning is of key importance in that this has been empirically identified in several studies as integral component of personality disorder (Nur *et al.*, 2004; Seivewright, Tyrer and Johnson, 2004; Skodol *et al.*, 2005). Hence, improving social functioning is an important aspect of treating personality disorder *per se*. Further analysis showed that, after controlling for baseline social functioning, the best predictor of improvement was a positive change on NPO (McMurran, Huband and Duggan, 2008).

In summary, *Stop & Think!* is an intervention that seems to work well with offenders, offenders with personality disorders and non-offenders with personality disorders. Furthermore, it is viewed as an acceptable intervention by its recipients (McMurran and Wilmington, 2007). However, most of the outcome measures to date have been self-reported improvements, and evaluations need to be conducted with more robust outcomes measures.

CONCLUSION

The research summarised in this chapter provides evidence to support the targeting of deficits in the social problem-solving process as one way of reducing aggression and violence. In developing this work, several issues require further attention.

First, the content of social problem-solving therapies needs to be attentive to the needs of people who are impulsively aggressive or violent. Their main problem will likely be a negative problem orientation, which is a cognitive–emotional set whereby problems are seen as a threat, perceived self-efficacy in solving problems is low, and problems cause feelings of upset and frustration. In problem-solving therapy for people with aggression and antisocial behaviour problems, it is important to aim to reduce feelings of threat and frustration and to enhance self-efficacy. Many offenders will possess traits of anxiety and neuroticism, and so affect regulation skills will also be an important treatment component. People with different constellations of personality traits and personality disorders are likely to require emphasis on different aspects of the process.

Second, in the design and delivery of treatment, individual characteristics associated with social problem-solving deficits and aggression must be taken into account. Those who require treatment are likely to be of low verbal ability, but despite this, most offender treatment programmes require high verbal skills, abstract thinking and completion of a considerable amount of written work (Davies *et al.*, 2004). Additionally, while cognitive skills training is effective, the inclusion of skills practice improves treatment outcome in reducing aggression (Sukhodolsky, Kassinove and Gorman, 2004).

Third, additional methods of assessing an individual's social problem-solving processes are required. Some people may have difficulty recognising the process they use to solve problems and so self-report checklists are unsatisfactory. Furthermore, there may be differences in problem solving depending on the type of problem that needs to be solved. Contemporaneous diaries may be one useful additional method (Baker, 2006). For those who are disinclined to be candid about their abilities, implicit measures of social problem solving need to be developed.

Finally, attention needs to be paid to offenders' motivation to use more effective social problem-solving strategies through developing pro-social values and identifying valued goals in life that make the effort worthwhile.

ACKNOWLEDGEMENTS

My thanks to Christine Maguth Nezu and Arthur M. Nezu for their helpful comments on this chapter.

NOTE

1. Cohen's d effect size is calculated by dividing the difference between the pre-intervention and post-intervention means by the square root of the pooled standard deviations. Convention is that an effect size of 0.20 is considered small, 0.50 medium, and 0.80 large.

REFERENCES

Baker, S.R. (2006) Towards an idiothetic understanding of the role of social problem solving in daily event, mood and health experiences: a prospective daily diary approach. *British Journal of Health Psychology*, **11**, 513–31.

Baker, L.A., Bezdjian, S. and Raine, A. (2006) Behavioral genetics: the science of antisocial behavior. *Law and Contemporary Problems*, **69**, 7–46.

Barratt, E.S., Stanford, M.S., Kent, T.A. and Felthous, A. (1997) Neuropsychological and cognitive psychophysiological substrates of impulsive aggression. *Biological Psychiatry*, **41**, 1045–61.

Bennett, S., Farrington, D.P. and Huesmann, L.R. (2005) Explaining gender differences in crime and violence: the importance of social cognitive skills. *Aggression and Violent Behavior*, **10**, 263–88.

Biggam, F. and Power, K. (1999) Suicidality and the state-trait debate on problem-solving deficits: a re-examination with incarcerated young offenders. *Archives of Suicide Research*, **5**, 27–42.

Binks, C.A., Fenton, M., McCarthy, L. et al. (2006) Psychological therapies for people with borderline personality disorder. *Cochrane Database of Systematic Reviews* (1), CD005652. DOI: 10.1002/14651858.CD005652.

Bray, S., Barrowclough, C. and Lobban, F. (2007) The social problem solving abilities of people with borderline personality disorder. *Behaviour Research and Therapy*, **45**, 1409–17.

Buss, A.H. and Perry, M. (1992) The Aggression Questionnaire. *Journal of Personality and Social Psychology*, **63**, 452–9.

Clark, D. (2000) *Theory Manual for Enhanced Thinking Skills*, Home Office Prison and Probation Services, London.

Coid, J., Yang, M., Tyrer, P. et al. (2006) Prevalence and correlates of personality disorder in Great Britain. *British Journal of Psychiatry*, **188**, 423–31.

Costa, P.T. and McCrae, R.R. (1992) *Revised NEP Personality Inventory (NEO PI-R^{TM}) and NEO Five Factor Inventory (NEO-FFI)*, Psychological Assessment Resources, Odessa, FL.

Coy, K., Speltz, M.L., DeKlyen, M. and Jones, K. (2001) Social-cognitive processes in preschool boys with and without oppositional defiant disorder. *Journal of Abnormal Child Psychology*, **29**, 107–19.

Davies, K., Lewis, J., Byatt, J. *et al.* (2004) *An Evaluation of the Literacy Demands of General Offending Behaviour Programmes*, Home Office Research Findings, No. 233, Home Office, London.

Dodge, K.A., Pettit, G.S., Bates, J.E. and Valente, E. (1995) Social information-processing patterns partially mediate the effect of early physical abuse on later conduct problems. *Journal of Abnormal Psychology*, **104**, 632–43.

Duggan, C., Adams, C., McCarthy, L. *et al.* (2005) *A Systematic Review of the Effectiveness of Pharmacological and Psychological Treatments for Those with Personality Disorder*, National Programme on Forensic Mental Health Research and Development, Liverpool.

D'Zurilla, T.J. and Nezu, A.M. (2007) *Problem-Solving Therapy: A Positive Approach to Clinical Intervention*, 3rd edn, Springer, New York.

D'Zurilla, T.J., Nezu, A.M. and Maydeu-Olivares, A. (2002) *Social Problem-Solving Inventory – Revised (SPSI-R): Technical Manual*, Multi-Health Systems, North Tonawanda, NY.

Enticott, P.G. and Ogloff, J.R.P. (2006) Elucidation of impulsivity. *Australian Psychologist*, **41**, 3–14.

Farrington, D.P. (1995) The development of offending and antisocial behaviour from childhood: key findings from the Cambridge study in delinquent development. *Journal of Child Psychology and Psychiatry*, **36**, 929–64.

Fazel, S. and Danesh, J. (2002) Serious mental disorder in 23,000 prisoners: a systematic review of 62 surveys. *The Lancet*, **359**, 545–50.

Fergusson, D.M. and Horwood, L.J. (2002) Male and female offending trajectories. *Development and Psychopathology*, **14**, 159–77.

Giancola, P.R. (2000) Executive functioning: a conceptual framework for alcohol-related aggression. *Experimental and Clinical Psychopharmacology*, **8**, 576–97.

Hayward, J., McMurran, M. and Sellen, J. (2007) Social problem solving in vulnerable adult prisoners: profile and intervention. *Journal of Forensic Psychiatry and Psychology*, **19**, 243–48.

Herrick, S.M. and Elliott, T.R. (2001) Social problem, solving abilities and personality disorder characteristics among dual-diagnosed persons in substance abuse treatment. *Journal of Clinical Psychology*, **57**, 75–92.

Hoaken, P.N.S., Shaughnessy, V.K. and Pihl, R.O. (2003) Executive cognitive function and aggression: is it an issue of impulsivity? *Aggressive Behavior*, **29**, 15–30.

Hollin, C.R., Palmer, E., McGuire, J. *et al.* (2003) *An Evaluation of Pathfinder Programmes in the Probation Service*, Home Office, London.

Howard, R.C., Huband, N., Duggan, C. and Mannion, A. (2008) Exploring the link between personality disorder and criminality in a community sample. *Journal of Personality Disorders*, **22**, 589–603.

Huband, N., McMurran, M., Evans, C. and Duggan, C. (2007) Social problem solving plus psychoeducation for adults with personality disorder: a pragmatic randomised controlled trial. *British Journal of Psychiatry*, **190**, 307–13.

Jaffee, W.B. and D'Zurilla, T.J. (2003) Adolescent problem solving, parent problem solving, and externalizing behaviour in adolescents. *Behavior Therapy*, **34**, 295–311.

Lieb, K., Zanarini, M.C., Schmahl, C. *et al.* (2004) Borderline personality disorder. *The Lancet*, **364**, 453–61.

Linehan, M.M. (1993) *Cognitive Behavioral Treatment of Borderline Personality Disorder*, Guilford, London.

Loranger, A.W. (1999) *International Personality Disorder Examination (IPDE)*, Psychological Assessment Resources, Odessa, FL.

Lösel, F. and Beelmann, A. (2005) Social problem-solving programs for preventing antisocial behaviour in children and youth, in *Social Problem Solving and Offending: Evidence, Evaluation, and Evolution* (eds M. McMurran and J. McGuire), John Wiley & Sons, Ltd, Chichester, pp. 127–43.

Lösel, F., Bliesener, T. and Bender, D. (2007) Social information processing, experiences of aggression in social contexts, and aggressive behavior in adolescents. *Criminal Justice and Behavior*, **34**, 330–47.

Lynam, D., Moffitt, T. and Stouthamer-Loeber, M. (1993) Explaining the relation between IQ and delinquency: class, race, test motivation, school failure, or self-control? *Journal of Abnormal Psychology*, **102**, 187–95.

Malouff, J.M., Thorsteinsson, E.B. and Schutte, N.S. (2007) The efficacy of problem solving therapy in reducing mental and physical health problems: a meta-analysis. *Clinical Psychology Review*, **27**, 46–57.

Matthys, W. and Lochman, J.E. (2005) Social problem solving in aggressive children, in *Social Problem Solving and Offending: Evidence, Evaluation, and Evolution* (eds M. McMurran and J. McGuire), John Wiley & Sons, Ltd, Chichester, pp. 51–66.

McCrae, R.R. and Costa, P.T., Jr. (2003) *Personality in Adulthood: A Five-Factor Theory Perspective*, 2nd edn, Guilford, New York.

McGuire, J. (2000) *Think First*, Home Office, London.

McGuire, J. (2002) Integrating findings from research reviews, in *Offender Rehabilitation and Treatment* (ed. J. McGuire), John Wiley & Sons, Ltd, Chichester, pp. 3–38.

McMurran, M. (2008) Alcohol and aggressive cognition, in *Aggressive Offenders' Cognition: Theory, Research and Practice* (eds T.A. Gannon, T. Ward, A.R. Beech and D. Fisher), John Wiley & Sons, Ltd, Chichester.

McMurran, M., Blair, M. and Egan, V. (2002) An investigation of the correlations between aggressiveness, impulsiveness, social problem-solving, and alcohol use. *Aggressive Behavior*, **28**, 439–45.

McMurran, M., Duggan, C., Christopher, G. and Huband, N. (2007) The relationships between personality disorders and social problem solving in adults. *Personality and Individual Differences*, **42**, 145–55.

McMurran, M., Egan, V., Blair, M. and Richardson, C. (2001a) The relationship between social problem-solving and personality in mentally disordered offenders. *Personality and Individual Differences*, **30**, 517–24.

McMurran, M., Egan, V. and Duggan, C. (2005) Stop & Think! Social problem-solving therapy with personality disordered offenders, in *Social Problem Solving and Offending: Evidence, Evaluation, and Evolution* (eds M. McMurran and J. McGuire), John Wiley & Sons, Ltd, Chichester.

McMurran, M., Egan, V., Richardson, C. and Ahmadi, S. (1999) Social problem-solving in mentally disordered offenders: a brief report. *Criminal Behaviour and Mental Health*, **9**, 315–22.

McMurran, M., Fyffe, S., McCarthy, L. *et al.* (2001b) 'Stop & Think!' Social problem solving therapy with personality disordered offenders. *Criminal Behaviour and Mental Health*, **11**, 273–85.

McMurran, M., Huband, N. and Duggan, C. (2008) The role of social problem solving in improving social functioning in therapy for adults with personality disorder. *Personality and Mental Health*, **2**, 1–6.

McMurran, M. and Wilmington, R. (2007) A Delphi survey of the views of adult male patients with personality disorders on psychoeducation and social problem solving therapy. *Criminal Behaviour and Mental Health*, **17**, 293–99.

Moeller, F.G., Barratt, E.S., Dougherty, D.M. *et al.* (2001) Psychiatric aspects of impulsivity. *American Journal of Psychiatry*, **158**, 1783–93.

Moffitt, T.E., Caspi, A., Harrington, H. and Milne, B.J. (2002) Males on the life-course persistent and adolescent-limited antisocial pathways: follow-up at 26 years. *Development and Psychopathology*, **14**, 179–207.

Nur, U., Tyrer, P., Merson, S. and Johnson, T. (2004) Relationship between clinical symptoms, personality disturbance, and social function: a statistical enquiry. *Irish Journal of Psychological Medicine*, **21**, 19–22.

Patton, J.H., Stanford, M.S. and Barratt, E.S. (1995) Factor structure of the Barratt Impulsiveness Scale. *Journal of Clinical Psychology*, **51**, 768–74.

Platt, J.J. and Spivack, G. (1975) *Manual for the Means-End Problem-Solving (MEPS): A measure of Interpersonal Problem Solving Skill*, Hahnemann Medical College and Hospital, Philadelphia.

Ramadan, R. and McMurran, M. (2005) Alcohol and aggression: gender differences in their relationships with impulsiveness, sensation-seeking, and social problem-solving. *Journal of Substance Use*, **4**, 215–24.

Ross, R.R., Fabiano, E.A. and Ross, R.D. (1986) *Reasoning and Rehabilitation: A Handbook for Teaching Cognitive Skills*, Centre for Cognitive Development, Ottawa.

Seivewright, H., Tyrer, P. and Johnson, T. (2004) Persistent social dysfunction in anxious and depressed patients with personality disorder. *Acta Psychiatrica Scandinavica*, **109**, 104–9.

Skodol, A.E., Pagano, M.E., Bender, D.S. *et al.* (2005) Stability of functional impairment in patients with schizotypal, borderline, avoidant, or obsessive-compulsive personality disorder over two years. *Psychological Medicine*, **35**, 443–51.

Spielberger, C.D. (1999) *STAXI-2: State-Trait Anger Expression Inventory-2*, Psychological Assessment Resources, Odessa, FL.

Sukhodolsky, D.G., Kassinove, H. and Gorman, B.S. (2004) Cognitive-behavioral therapy for anger in children and adolescents: a meta-analysis. *Aggression and Violent Behavior*, **9**, 247–69.

Tong, L.S.J. and Farrington, D.P. (2008) Effectiveness of "Reasoning and Rehabilitation" in reducing reoffending. *Psicothema*, **20**, 20–8.

Tyrer, P., Nur, U., Crawford, M. *et al.* (2005) The social functioning questionnaire: a rapid and robust measure of perceived functioning. *International Journal of Social Psychiatry*, **51**, 265–75.

Waschbusch, D.A., Walsh, T.M., Andrade, B.F. *et al.* (2007) Social problem solving, conduct problems, and callous-unemotional traits in children. *Child Psychiatry and Human Development*, **37**, 293–305.

Wong, W.-K. and Cornell, D.G. (1999) PIQ>VIQ discrepancy as a correlate of social problem solving and aggression in delinquent adolescent males. *Journal of Psychoeducational Assessment*, **17**, 104–12.

Zadeh, Z.Y., Im-Boulter, N. and Cohen, N.J. (2007) Social cognition and externalizing psychopathology: an investigation of the mediating role of language. *Journal of Abnormal Child Psychology*, **35**, 141–52.

Zelazo, P.D., Carter, A., Reznick, J.S. and Frye, D. (1997) Early development of executive function: a problem-solving framework. *Review of General Psychology*, **1**, 198–226.

Chapter 15

CRIMINAL THINKING

GLENN D. WALTERS

Federal Correctional Institution-Schuylkill, USA

Whenever a high profile violent crime is committed, one of the first things people ask is what was the perpetrator thinking when he or she committed the criminal act in question. In searching for an answer to this conundrum, we might be tempted to be flippant and simply reply that the individual was probably not thinking when he or she committed the violent crime in question and that this is precisely why he or she engaged in this seemingly mindless act of aggression in the first place. However, what those who have worked with offenders on a regular basis will probably tell you is that no matter how poorly organized or impulsive a behavior may seem, cognition nearly always precedes behavior in the commission of a violent criminal act. What we as researchers and clinicians need to understand is the nature of criminal cognition and the degree to which it deviates from non-criminal thinking and decision making. In this chapter, the reader will be introduced to the concept of criminal thinking as a means of describing, understanding, assessing and changing criminal behavior.

DEFINING CRIMINAL THINKING

Criminal thinking will be defined in this chapter as cognition designed to initiate and/or maintain the habitual violation of rules, codes and laws previously established by a legitimate governing body. In using the term legitimate governing body, I am referring to the controlling interest of a society, whether or not that controlling interest has formed an implicit social contract with the populace. Cesare Beccaria (1764), the Italian aristocrat and social reformer, invented the social contract concept to describe the process by which individual citizens surrender a portion of their individuality in order for the government to enact and enforce laws for the common good of the people and at the same time protect the natural rights of individual citizens to the extent possible. Obviously, this is an ideal that

Personality, Personality Disorder and Violence   Edited by Mary McMurran and Richard C. Howard
© 2009 John Wiley & Sons, Ltd

is never fully realized in any society. Hence, criminal thinking is relative to the society in which it takes place. Like cultural relativity, cognitive relativity holds that we cannot judge criminal thinking without taking into account the context in which it occurs. There is, nonetheless, at least one universal criterion against which criminal thinking can be judged, the criterion of adaptability, a subject to which we return later in this chapter.

Cognitive relativity and its role in promoting or frustrating the putative universal criterion of adaptability are discussed later in this chapter. For the time being, criminal thinking will be defined by both its content and process. In fact, the two go hand-in-hand. Some individuals entertain criminal thoughts without ever acting on them; others demonstrate a pattern of thinking that follows some of the same rules and conventions as criminal thinking yet are not chronic offenders. It is not until criminal thought content and criminal thought process come together in time and space that we have criminal thinking and it is not until the decision to act on a criminal thought is made that we have a criminal act. Criminal thinking, according to the perspective adopted in this chapter, is a necessary but not sufficient condition for criminal behavior. Consequently, while criminal thinking may have its foundation in everyday thought content and process, it is not until it fuels outward expressions of criminal behavior that we consider it sufficiently dangerous to warrant study.

DESCRIBING CRIMINAL THINKING

The lifestyle theory of crime (Walters, 1990, 2002), upon which much of the present chapter is based, attempts to avoid the tautology trap that has ensnared many other theories of crime by keeping description and explanation separate. The present section therefore describes criminal thinking while the next section attempts to explain it. Criminal thinking, according to the lifestyle perspective, is hierarchically organized. Schemes, a concept borrowed from the developmental psychologist Jean Piaget (1977), fall at the lowest level of the hierarchy. There are many definitions of scheme but the one that will be employed in this chapter considers a scheme a basic unit of meaning. A scheme develops through the human organism's ongoing interactions with the physical and social environment and the complex interplay of assimilation, whereby new information is incorporated into an existing scheme, and accommodation, whereby a new scheme is created in order to conceptualize information for which there is currently no scheme. The thought of getting even with someone for a perceived injustice or of taking a toy another child is currently playing with would be examples of crime-related schemes. Criminal schemes can be classified as content and process: content schemes encompass the specific aspects of a crime (the act itself, the target of the act, deterrents to the act) while process schemes involve the steps taken to enact the crime (motive, opportunity, priority).

Schemes alone do not generally lead to crime; they must be guided and reinforced by higher order cognition. The next major level of the hierarchy of criminal thinking proposed by lifestyle theory is comprised of schematic subnetworks, groups of interrelated schemes that help promote criminal behavior. Like schemes, schematic subnetworks can be classified as content schematic subnetworks and process schematic subnetworks. Content schematic subnetworks are cognitive templates that take as their focus a central or common theme like crime and justice. Process schematic subnetworks, on the other hand, are groups of schemes devoid of specific criminal content but which center on the means by which a crime is planned, enacted and later justified. Examples of process schematic subnetworks are criminal thinking styles such as entitlement and discontinuity (see Table 15.1), criminal attributions (e.g. blaming others), self-efficacy for crime (e.g. belief that one is good at crime), outcome expectancies for crime (e.g. crime will bring power, respect and financial gain), criminal goals (e.g. short-term objectives selected over long-term objectives) and criminal values (e.g. self-centered and hedonistic). It is the juxtaposition of these two elements, content schematic subnetworks for crime and process schematic subnetworks for crime, that sets the stage for actual criminal behavior.

Belief systems are found at the highest level of the criminal thinking hierarchy. Defined as collections of content and process schematic subnetworks, belief systems are global impressions the individual forms of himself or herself (self-view), the external environment (world-view), the past (past-view), the present (present-view) and the future (future-view). Each belief system is organized differently. The self-view is organized into five components (reflected appraisals, social comparisons, self-representations, role identity and possible selves), the world-view into four dimensions (mechanism–organicism, agenticism–fatalism, justice–inequity, malevolence–benevolence), the present-view into two functions (perceptual and executive), the past-view into recollections of the past, and the future-view into anticipations of the future. There is virtually no empirical research on the belief systems of violent criminal offenders but it is possible to speculate that many habitually violent criminals possess negative and antisocial self-views, world-views that highlight the mechanistic, fatalistic and malevolent sides of life, present-views beset by processing and decision-making deficits, past-views dominated by past criminal exploits, and future-views that anticipate the benefits and minimize the costs of future crime.

The hierarchical nature of criminal thought as exemplified by the three levels of criminal thinking just described is depicted in Figure 15.1. Several points need to be made about this system. First, movement within the system can go in either direction, from general to specific or from specific to general. In other words, the general aspects of criminal thinking (belief systems) influence the specific aspects (schematic subnetworks, schemes) as much as the specific aspects of criminal thinking (schemes) influence the general aspects (schematic subnetworks, belief systems), the former through deduction and the latter through induction. Specific criminal schemes therefore help shape belief systems and belief system, in turn, color specific criminal schemes. A second point that needs to be made about the criminal thinking hierarchy is that there are many sublevels within each of the three main levels and that general and specific are relative terms. For example, the thinking style of entitlement is specific to the more general notion of proactive criminal thinking but general to the more specific subelements of necessity, ownership and uniqueness, all within the schematic subnetwork level of the hierarchical system (see Figure 15.1). The notion that criminal thinking must be understood within a context is explored further in the next section of this chapter.

Table 15.1 Descriptions of the eight thinking styles

Thinking style	Sign	α	Description
Mollification	Mo	0.64	Externalizing blame for the negative consequences of a criminal act onto the environment, other people or society in general. Example: 'If government is the teacher, then violence is an appropriate way to express one's dissatisfaction with the government.'
Cutoff	Co	0.78	The rapid elimination of common deterrents to crime through use of an image, phrase (e.g. 'fuck it'), or alcohol and drugs. Example: 'I don't care, he disrespected me and now he's going to get what's coming to him.'
Entitlement	En	0.59	Belief that one is entitled to violate the rights of others and the rules of society for personal gain, often by misidentifying wants as needs. Example: 'I deserve a descent life and if the only way I am going to get a descent life is by taking from others then so be it.'
Power Orientation	Po	0.65	Desire for personal power and control over others. Example: 'There is nothing more exhilarating than ordering people to the floor of the bank during the course of a robbery.'
Sentimentality	Sn	0.55	Sense that a good deed (e.g. buying turkeys for the neighborhood during Thanksgiving) counteracts or negates the destructive impact of a criminal lifestyle. Example: 'I'm not a bad guy, I'm more like Robin Hood; take from the rich and give to the poor.'
Superoptimism	So	0.63	Unrealistic belief that one can escape the natural negative consequences of a criminal lifestyle (e.g. family problems, imprisonment, death) indefinitely. Example: 'It was like I was protected by a bulletproof vest, nobody could touch me.'
Cognitive Indolence	Ci	0.76	Lack of critical reasoning leading to ineffective and impulsive decision making and the tendency to take shortcuts. Example: 'Once the idea of burglarizing a home comes to mind I run with it, even if there are obvious problems with the plan.'
Discontinuity	Ds	0.79	Distractibility in the face of environmental events to the point where the individual has trouble following through on good initial intentions. Example: 'Every time I leave prison I do so with the best of intentions, but something I hadn't anticipated always seems to get in the way, throwing me off track in the process.'

Note. Thinking style: name of criminal thinking style; Sign: sign or symbol of the criminal thinking style used on the PICTS; α: Cronbach alpha coefficient of internal consistency from the original Walters (1995) normative sample ($N = 450$); Description: brief description of the thinking style along with an example.

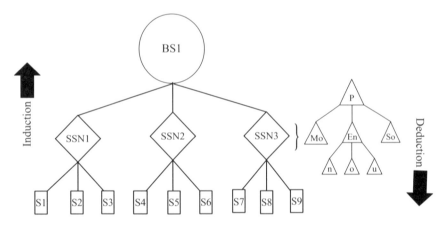

Figure 15.1 Graphic representation of the hierarchical organization of criminal thinking (BS, belief system; SSN, schematic subnetwork; S, scheme; P, Proactive Criminal Thinking; Mo, Mollification, En, Entitlement, So, Superoptimism; n, Necessity; o, Ownership; u, Uniqueness).

EXPLAINING CRIMINAL THINKING

Criminal thinking must be understood within its proper cultural, developmental and temporal context. Although there are a number of contexts that help shape a criminal lifestyle and the thinking that underpins this lifestyle, three are viewed to be particularly crucial in explaining and elucidating the nature of criminal thought content and process. These three contexts – cultural, developmental and temporal – will serve as the focus of attention in this section.

Cultural Context

Criminal thinking exists in a cultural context. We therefore cannot define, describe or explain criminal thinking without taking into account the culture in which it occurs. This is because a culture defines what is criminal, and while there are many acts that are considered criminal in most cultures, there are many other acts that are only criminal in certain cultures and subcultures. The degree to which a nation's governing structure honors its side of the social contract will determine the degree to which the laws of society reflect the will of the people. There is no guarantee, however, that these laws will be moral from a postconventional point of view (Kohlberg, 1984). Hitler's National Socialism was popular with many German citizens, at least up until Germany started losing the war, but it was an immoral government from the start. Citizens who harbored Jews and other 'undesirables' were considered criminals in the eyes of this culture and the thinking that led them to engage in this behavior could be considered criminal thinking because it violated the laws of that particular culture. To reiterate, there is nothing universal about criminal thinking because it must be understood within a cultural context. The cultural context within which criminal thinking will be understood in this chapter is represented by democratic societies in North American and western Europe, and there is no assumption that this information generalizes to non-democratic societies in Asia, Africa, South America or the Middle East.

The cognitive relativity espoused by lifestyle theory parallels the cultural relativity still popular in the field of anthropology. Cultural relativity is the holistic belief that knowledge must be considered within the context of the culture from which it originates and that there are no universal moral or ethical standards against which the value of a particular culture can be judged (Benedict, 1934; Diamond, 1974). Cognitive relativity, on the other hand, is the holistic notion that people should be understood within the context of their own belief systems and that there is no universal standard for objective reality (Walters, 2002). The cognitive relativity to which the lifestyle model subscribes, however, is qualified by a single universal criterion, the criterion of adaptability. According to lifestyle theory, adaptability or balance is the key to survival and the more balanced a person's cognitive system is the greater that person's chances are of survival. Balance at the schematic level is achieved through regular use of both poles of a scheme rather than rigid adherence to a single pole (Kelly, 1955). Balance at the schematic subnetwork level is achieved by avoiding the extreme thinking that gives rise to criminal thinking styles. Balance at the belief system level is realized through a synthesis of opposites and dynamic movement up and down the dimensions of a belief system rather than rigid adherence to any one aspect of that belief system. Criminal thinking, it is reasoned, involves a lack of balance and therefore poor adaptability.

Another facet of the cultural context of criminal thinking is that criminal thinking can be viewed as a manifestation of a collective belief system. Collective belief systems are beliefs held by a group of people that determine the group's actions by establishing rules, roles, rituals and relationships for everyday conduct. Religion, politics and even culture can be viewed, in part or in whole, as collective belief systems, so can lifestyles, such as the criminal lifestyle and the thinking that supports a criminal lifestyle. A collective belief system encounters problems when its principal field of construction is mythical in nature. In constructing perceptions of reality, individuals and groups make use of mythical (general, untested beliefs handed down by others), empirical (beliefs based on personal experience), teleological (organized groups of beliefs designed to achieve an end goal), and epistemological (beliefs that acknowledge the relatively and limitations of all constructions). Criminal thinking and the criminal lifestyle to which it gives birth are based nearly exclusively on mythical constructions, ideas passed down by others which the individual simply accepts on faith. The notion that one must be tough or violent to gain respect and the belief that the strong have a right to take from the weak are mythical constructions that lie at the core of a criminal lifestyle. However, once arrested, the primary mythical construction of 'me first,' takes precedence and the individual sees nothing wrong in informing on his or her cohorts.

Developmental Context

Just as surely as criminal thinking has a cultural context, it also has a developmental context. The Piagetian concepts of assimilation and accommodation (Piaget,

1977) are central to the formation of the criminal thinking hierarchy described in the previous section, from individual schemes to major belief systems. The developmental context that I would like to focus on here, however, derives from the work of Kenneth Dodge (1991) who has proposed the existence of two general classes of aggression in children: proactive or instrumental aggression and reactive or hostile aggression. Whereas proactive aggression is calculated, cold-blooded and goal-directed, reactive aggression is affective, hot-blooded and impulsive (Dodge and Coie, 1987). Research indicates that while proactive aggression is associated with positive outcome expectancies for aggression in children (Perry, Perry and Rasmussen, 1986) and delinquency in adolescents (Smithmyer, Hubbard and Simons, 2000), reactive aggression is associated with hostile attribution biases in both children (Crick and Dodge, 1996) and juvenile delinquents (Dodge *et al.*, 1990). Despite the differences, proactive and reactive aggression are correlated dimensions and it is not uncommon to find both operating in the same individual or even in the same aggressive incident (Poulin and Boivin, 2000). What remains to be seen is whether childhood proactive and reactive aggression relate in a meaningful way to adult aggression.

Walters (2005c) maintains that childhood aggression and adult aggression are linked by commonalities in thinking. Creating composite scales from selected thinking style, factor and content scales on the Psychological Inventory of Criminal Thinking Styles (PICTS), Walters (2007b) determined that the Proactive Criminal Thinking (P) composite scale predicted positive outcome expectancies for crime but not hostile attribution biases while the Reactive Criminal Thinking (R) composite scale predicted hostile attribution biases but not positive outcome expectancies for crime, paralleling research on proactive and reactive aggression in children and their countervailing relationships with positive outcome expectancies for aggression and hostile attribution biases (Crick and Dodge, 1996; Perry, Perry and Rasmussen, 1986). In a second study, scores on the P scale postdicted prior arrests for proactive or instrumental crime (robbery, burglary) but not reactive or hostile crime (assault, domestic violence), whereas the R scale did just the opposite, despite the presence of a moderately high correlation between the two scales (Walters, Frederick and Schlauch, 2007). It is speculated that proactive aggressive/ criminal thinking is responsible for the connection between instrumental aggression in children and proactive criminality in adults while reactive aggressive/ criminal thinking is responsible for hostile aggression in children and reactive criminality in adults. Unfortunately, the specific mechanism or mechanisms responsible for proactive and reactive criminal thinking are currently unknown, although peer- and parental-directed observational learning is likely involved to some extent.

Temporal Context

In addition to its cultural and developmental contexts, violent criminal behavior also has a temporal context. What I mean by a temporal context is that criminal thinking varies as a function of the point at which it occurs in the criminal event or career. Whether we are talking about a pattern of violence or a single violent episode, the sequence can be divided into at least two phases: an initiation phase and a maintenance phase. The initiation phase of violence explains how violence begins while the maintenance phase explains how violence continues. Different factors are held to be responsible for crime initiation and maintenance (Walters, 2002). Criminal thinking may play a role in both the initiation and maintenance of violence but the role likely varies as a function of the temporal context the thinking is designed to support. Situational cues and perceptual distortions are instrumental in initiating a violent criminal episode, while reinforcement and feedback are instrumental in maintaining a violent criminal episode. Criminal thought content, such as target selection, criminal technique and various ideas the individual may have about specific criminal acts would appear to be more involved in initiating a pattern of criminal violence than in maintaining a pattern of criminal violence. Violent crime maintenance, on the other hand, would appear to be a function of criminal thought process, from labeling, to outcome expectancies for crime, to the thinking styles assessed by the PICTS.

Some theories of crime do a good job of explaining crime initiation, other theories do a good job of explaining crime maintenance, but few theories do a good job of both. The social control (Gottfredson and Hirschi, 1990) and differential association (Sutherland and Cressey, 1978) theories of crime do a better job of explaining crime initiation than of explaining crime maintenance, while labeling (Lemert, 1951) and neutralization (Sykes and Matza, 1957) do a good job of explaining crime maintenance but a poor job of explaining crime initiation. Walters (2002) offers an integrated-interactive model of crime within the larger framework of lifestyle theory that explains both crime initiation and crime maintenance. It is therefore possible that this model does a better job of explaining the differential role of criminal thinking in initiating and maintaining violent criminal behavior than most traditional criminological theories. Models designed to explain the initiation and maintenance of specific violent criminal acts like sex offenses have also been devised. Ward *et al.* (1997), for instance, presented a theoretical overview of cognitive distortions in sex offenders and illustrated how attributional biases and perceptual distortions such as misinterpreting cues from a woman could initiate sexual offending, whereas information processing styles are used to maintain the attitudes, stereotypes and sex offending behavior of many sex offenders. The key to understanding the temporal context of criminal thinking is clarifying the differential role of a construct like criminal thinking in initiating and maintaining violent criminal behavior.

ASSESSING CRIMINAL THINKING

In order to properly assess criminal thinking, one must evaluate both criminal thought content and criminal thought process. There are two measures that seem particularly well suited to the task of assessing criminal thought content: the Criminal Sentiments Scale and the Measures of Criminal Attitudes and Associates. The Criminal Sentiments Scale (CSS: Gendreau *et al.*, 1979; Simourd, 1997) is a 41-item self-report inventory organized into three subscales: Attitudes Toward the Law, Court, and Police (LCP), Tolerance for Law Violations (TLV) and Identification with Criminal Others (ICO). Whereas the TLV appraises Sykes and Matza's (1957) techniques of neutralization, a feature of criminal thought process, the LCP and ICO are classic measures of criminal thought content. The CSS possesses construct validity (Simourd and Olver, 2002) and is effective in predicting violent recidivism (Simourd and van de Ven, 1999). The Measures of Criminal Attitudes and Associates (MCAA: Mills, Kroner and Forth, 2002) is comprised of two sections. The first section asks respondents to list the four adults with whom they spend the most free time along with a rating of each adult's level of criminal involvement. The second section is a 46-item self-report inventory organized into four scales: Violence, Entitlement, Antisocial Intent and Associates. Entitlement would appear to measure criminal thought process but the other three scales measure aspects of criminal thought content. A study by Mills, Kroner and Hemmati (2004) confirmed that the MCAA possesses incremental validity in predicting both general and violent recidivism beyond the contributions made by an actuarial risk assessment procedure.

Criminal thought process is perhaps best measured by the PICTS (Walters, 1995). The PICTS is an 80-item self-report measure that yields scores on two validity scales – Confusion-Revised (Cf-r) and Defensiveness-Revised (Df-r) – eight non-overlapping thinking style scales – Mollification (Mo), Cutoff (Co), Entitlement (En), Power Orientation (Po), Sentimentality (Sn), Superoptimism (So), Cognitive Indolence (Ci) and Discontinuity (Ds) – four factor scales – Problem Avoidance (PRB), Infrequency (INF), Self-Assertion/Deception (AST), and Denial of Harm (DNH) – two content scales – Current Criminal Thinking (CUR) and Historical Criminal Thinking (HIS) – two composite scales – Proactive Criminal Thinking (P) and Reactive Criminal Thinking (R) – and a global measure of criminal thinking – General Criminal Thinking (GCT). The construct validity of the PICTS has been corroborated by factor analytic research (Walters, 2005a), convergent–discriminant correlations with other personality measures (Walters and Geyer, 2005) and cross-national investigations (Palmer and Hollin, 2003; Healy and O'Donnell, 2006). After the GCT score, the PICTS composite scales are the most reliable predictors of future behavior available on the PICTS. Not only are they capable of predicting violent institutional infractions (Walters, 2006; Walters and Mandell, 2007), but they are also capable of predicting violent recidivism as measured by arrests for such aggressive crimes as robbery and assault (Walters, in press). The hierarchical nature of criminal thinking is illustrated by the GCT score which breaks down into the P and R scales, the P and R scales breaking down into the eight thinking style scales, the eight thinking style scales breaking down even further into thinking style subscales (see Figure 15.1).

CHANGING CRIMINAL THINKING

There are three questions that need to be answered before we can accept the premise, central to lifestyle theory that a change in criminal thinking leads to a change in criminal behavior. The first question is whether a relationship exists between criminal thinking and criminal behavior. Antisocial and pro-delinquent attitudes, two prominent features of criminal thought content, have been found to predict adult criminal behavior (Gendreau *et al.*, 1992), juvenile delinquency (Zhang, Loeber and Stouthamer-Loeber, 1997), adult recidivism (Gendreau, Little and Goggin, 1996), juvenile recidivism (Simourd and Andrews, 1994), adolescent aggression (Slaby and Guerra, 1988) and adult prison misconduct (Gendreau, Goggin and Law, 1997). The PICTS thinking style scales and GCT score, all manifestations of criminal thought process, are capable of predicting institutional adjustment in incarcerated male offenders (Walters and Mandell, 2007), recidivism in released male offenders (Walters, 2005b, in press), institutional adjustment in incarcerated female offenders (Walters and Elliott, 1999) and recidivism in released female offenders (Walters and Elliott, 1999). We can therefore answer the first question, whether criminal thought content and criminal thinking process correlate with criminal behavior, in the affirmative.

The second question for which we need an answer is whether criminal thinking can be altered through intervention. Just as important as determining whether criminal thinking can be modified through intervention is determining the types of interventions that are most likely to be effective in reducing criminal thought content and process. Criminal thought content as measured by the CSS dropped in offenders with a strong criminal self-concept following their participation in an intervention that directly addressed criminal attitudes and associates (Simourd, 2001). Scores on all three subscales of the CSS and scores on the Violence, Entitlement and Antisocial Intent subscales of the MCAA fell significantly in a large group of Canadian offenders exposed to a 40-hour community-based skills training program (Yessine and Kroner, 2004). Criminal thought process also appears to respond favorably to intervention. Cognitive–behavioral programs administered in the United States and Canada have led to significant reductions in participants' scores on the PICTS, particularly the Co, Ci and Ds thinking style scales and CUR content scale (Walters *et al.*, 2002). A cognitive program administered in England and Wales also produced significant reductions on many of PICTS scales, with the largest reductions being registered on the Ci thinking style scale (Blud *et al.*, 2003). In response to the second question, whether criminal thinking can be reduced and if so what techniques are most efficacious in accomplishing this task, it would appear that not only do criminal thought content and criminal thought process respond to intervention but cognitive and cognitive–behavioral interventions (see also Ross and Fabiano, 1985) also yield the best results.

The third and final question that needs to be answered before the role of criminal thinking in intervention can be fully elucidated is whether intervention ultimately influences criminal behavior by way of the intermediary or intervening action of criminal thinking. Berman (2004) examined the short- and long-term effects of a cognitive skills training program on criminal thinking and criminal behavior in a group of 372 Swedish male prisoners. Among the short-term effects noted by Berman were a rise in conventional attitudes toward the law and a reduction in identification with and tolerance for violations of the law as measured by the CSS. The long-term effect observed by Berman was a 25% reduction in recidivism relative to a group of matched controls over a 3-year period of follow-up. Although the results of this study suggest that intervention had an effect on both criminal thinking and criminal behavior, there is no way to tell whether the effect on criminal behavior was mediated by the program's effect on criminal thinking. The only way to know for sure whether intervention reduces criminal behavior by altering criminal thinking would be to conduct a randomized control longitudinal panel study in which the cross-lag correlations are analyzed with statistical procedures such as path analysis. Consequently, we have no answer to the third question, that is, whether cognitive and cognitive–behavioral interventions reduce recidivism by modifying criminal thinking, at the present time.

CONCLUSION

The present chapter outlines a model of criminal thinking comprised of two interlocking parts, criminal thought content and criminal thought process. In fact, criminal thinking was defined in this chapter as the juxtaposition of criminal thought content and criminal thought process in ways that bring the individual into conflict with the criminal codes of society. The implications the present chapter holds for research and practice in forensic and correctional psychology can be organized into four themes relating to the final four sections of this chapter: description, explanation, assessment and change. With respect to description, we need to form a clearer understanding of how people move up and down the criminal thinking hierarchy. Does information flow just as easily up the hierarchy (induction) as it does down the hierarchy (deduction)? This is an empirical question that could be addressed by an information processing approach to research on human cognition. In the meantime, we can gain an appreciation for the complexity of the hierarchy by using measures such as the PICTS to create even finer gradations between and within levels. This is because the PICTS is also hierarchically organized, with a global GCT score at the top, composite scales at the next level, thinking style scales below the composite scales and thinking style subscales at the bottom (see Figure 15.1).

In explaining the cultural, developmental and temporal context of criminal thinking, it is imperative that one appreciates the nature and structure of criminal thought. One of the principal issues involved in comprehending the nature of a theoretical construct like criminal thinking is whether the construct's latent structure is continuous (dimensional) or categorical (taxonic) (Ruscio, Haslam and Ruscio, 2006). Walters (2007a) recently subjected the PICTS and Lifestyle Criminality Screening Form (LCSF: Walters, White and Denney, 1991) to taxometric analysis using procedures such as mean above minus below a cut (MAMBAC), maximum eigenvalue (MAXEIG) and latent mode factor analysis (L-Mode). The results revealed moderate support for dimensional structure on the PICTS, modest support for dimensional structure on the LCSF and strong support for dimensional structure when the PICTS and LCSF were combined. A subsequent study by Walters and McCoy (2007) showed that the use of extreme groups (in terms of scores on the PICTS; namely, male and female college students and incarcerated offenders) did not alter the basic dimensional structure of the PICTS. One implication of these findings is that by virtue of its continuous nature, the theoretical construct of criminal thinking, at least as measured by the PICTS, is to some extent universal and that people differ in degree rather than in kind on this construct.

Two different classes of assessment procedure were proposed in this chapter, one designed to measure criminal thought content (CSS, MCAA) and the other designed to measure criminal thought process (PICTS), although it should be noted that these measures are not exclusive to their respective domains and that the CSS and MCAA measure aspects of criminal thought process just as the PICTS measures aspects of criminal thought content. It remains to be seen whether combining these two classes of assessment procedure generates results that are superior to what these two classes of procedure are capable of producing separately. It is also vital that we be able to demonstrate that an assessment procedure continues to predict prison infractions and recidivism even after variables such as age, criminal history (i.e. prior infractions or arrests) and popular non-self-report risk assessment procedures such as the Psychopathy Checklist or LCSF have been controlled. In this regard, Mills, Kroner and Hemmati (2004) found that the MCAA predicted general and violent recidivism after scores on the actuarial General Statistical Information on Recidivism (GSIR: Nuffield, 1982) had been controlled, and Walters and Mandell (2007) determined that the PICTS GCT score predicted general and aggressive disciplinary infractions after age, prior disciplinary infractions and scores on the Psychopathy Checklist: Screening Version (PCL:SV: Hart, Cox and Hare, 1995) had been controlled. What needs to be determined is whether the MCAA and PICTS possess incremental validity relative to age, criminal history, actuarial or risk assessment procedures such as the GSIR or PCL:SV, and each other.

Future research on change requires that we not only demonstrate that criminal thinking and criminal behavior are connected and that criminal thinking responds to cognitive and cognitive–behavioral intervention but we must also demonstrate that intervention-based alterations in criminal thinking are directly and causally linked to changes in criminal behavior. As was previously noted, path analysis and structured equation modeling (SEM) are well adapted to the task of addressing this particular research question. Using a longitudinal panel research design, one might initially assess whether selected criminological needs and risk factors play an interactive role in treatment response since research indicates that higher risk individuals with greater criminological needs tend to respond better to intervention than lower risk individuals with fewer criminological needs (Andrews et al., 1990). Participants could be randomly assigned to either an intervention or waiting list control group and at the end of the intervention both groups could be administered measures of criminal thought content (CSS, MCAA) and criminal thought process (PICTS), after which they could be followed for evidence of disciplinary infractions or recidivism. Using cross-lag correlations, the researchers could then determine whether changes in criminal thinking mediated the effect of intervention on subsequent disciplinary infractions or recidivism.

In closing, I would like to reiterate that criminal thinking is a construct comprised of two parts (content and process), that it is hierarchically organized, that it is dimensional and contextual in nature, that it can be assessed using various self-report measures, and that it is amenable to change. Future research and clinical application with respect to this construct are required to more fully comprehend the structure, function and nature of criminal thinking. The possibilities and hypotheses pertaining to criminal thinking far outnumber the studies that have been carried out on this construct and so there is still much work remaining to be done. There are so many possibilities and hypotheses, in fact, that many could not be included in this chapter. For instance, the proactive–reactive breakdown of criminal thought process may need to be taken into account when conducting interventions with criminal offenders because it is hypothesized that while traditional skill-based programs like anger management, stress management and problem solving training may be effective with reactive criminal thinking, such programs are likely to be ineffective with proactive criminal thinking. The present chapter has sought to organize current knowledge on criminal thinking and offer recommendations for both research and clinical practice. It will be up to the reader, however, as clinician and researcher to advance the field beyond its current rudimentary state.

REFERENCES

Andrews, D.A., Zinger, I., Hoge, R.D. *et al.* (1990) Does correctional treatment work? A clinically relevant and psychologically informed meta-analysis. *Criminology*, **28**, 369–404.

Benedict, R. (1934) *Patterns of Culture*, Houghton Mifflin, Boston.

Berman, A.H. (2004) The reasoning and rehabilitation program: assessing short- and long-term outcomes among Swedish prisoners. *Journal of Offender Rehabilitation*, **40**, 85–103.

Blud, L., Travers, R., Nugent, F. and Thornton, D. (2003) Accreditation of offending behaviour programmes in HM Prison Service: 'What Works' in practice. *Legal and Criminological Psychology*, **5**, 69–81.

Crick, N.R. and Dodge, K.A. (1996) Social information-processing mechanisms in reactive and proactive aggression. *Child Development*, **67**, 993–1002.

Diamond, S. (1974) *In Search of the Primitive: A Critique of Civilization*, Transaction Books, New Brunswick, NJ.

Dodge, K.A. (1991) The structure and function of reactive and proactive aggression, in *The Development and Treatment of Childhood Aggression* (eds D. Pepler and K. Rubin), Erlbaum, Hillsdale, NJ, pp. 201–18.

Dodge, K.A. and Coie, J.D. (1987) Social-information processing factors in reactive and proactive aggression in children's peer groups. *Journal of Personality and Social Psychology*, **53**, 1146–58.

Dodge, K.A., Price, J.M., Bachorowski, J.-A. and Newman, J.P. (1990) Hostile attributional biases in severely aggressive adolescents. *Journal of Abnormal Psychology*, **99**, 385–92.

Gendreau, P., Andrews, D.A., Goggin, C. and Chanteloupe, F. (1992) *The Development of Clinical and Policy Guidelines for the Prediction of Criminal Behaviour in Criminal Justice Settings* (Programs Branch user report), Ministry of the Solicitor General of Canada, Ottawa, Ontario, Canada.

Gendreau, P., Goggin, C.E. and Law, M.E. (1997) Predicting prison misconducts. *Criminal Justice and Behavior*, **24**, 414–31.

Gendreau, P., Little, T. and Goggin, C. (1996) A meta-analysis of predictors of adult recidivism: what works! *Criminology*, **34**, 401–33.

Gendreau, P., Grant, B.A., Leipciger, M. and Collins, C. (1979) Norms and recidivism rates for the MMPI and selected experimental scales on a Canadian delinquent sample. *Canadian Journal of Behavioral Science*, **11**, 21–31.

Gottfredson, M.R. and Hirschi, T. (1990) *A General Theory of Crime*, Stanford University Press, Stanford, CA.

Hart, S.D., Cox, D.N. and Hare, R.D. (1995) *Manual for the Psychopathy Checklist: Screening Version (PCL:SV)*, Multi-Health Systems, Toronto, Canada.

Healy, D. and O'Donnell, I. (2006) Criminal thinking on probation: a perspective from Ireland. *Criminal Justice and Behavior*, **33**, 782–802.

Kelly, G.A. (1955) *The Psychology of Personal Constructs*, Vols. **1 and 2**, Norton, New York.

Kohlberg, L. (1984) *Essays on Moral Development, Volume II. The Psychology of Moral Development: The Nature and Validity of Moral Stages*, Harper & Row, San Francisco.

Lemert, E.M. (1951) *Social Pathology*, McGraw-Hill, New York.

Mills, J.F., Kroner, D.G. and Forth, A.E. (2002) Measures of Criminal Attitudes and Associates (MCAA): development, factor structure, reliability, and validity. *Assessment*, **9**, 240–53.

Mills, J.F., Kroner, D.G. and Hemmati, T. (2004) The Measures of Criminal Attitudes and Associates (MCAA): the prediction of general and violent recidivism. *Criminal Justice and Behavior*, **31**, 717–33.

Nuffield, J. (1982) *Parole Decision-Making in Canada: Research Towards Decision Guidelines*, Solicitor General of Canada, Ottawa, Ontario, Canada.

Palmer, E.J. and Hollin, C.R. (2003) Using the psychological inventory of criminal thinking styles with English prisoners. *Legal and Criminological Psychology*, **8**, 175–87.

Perry, D.G., Perry, L.C. and Rasmussen, P. (1986) Cognitive social learning mediators of aggression. *Child Development*, **52**, 700–11.

Piaget, J. (1977) *The Development of Thought*, Viking, New York.

Poulin, F. and Boivin, M. (2000) Reactive and proactive aggression: evidence of a two-factor model. *Psychological Assessment*, **12**, 115–22.

Ross, R.R. and Fabiano, E. (1985) *Time to Think: A Cognitive Model of Delinquency Prevention and Offender Rehabilitation*, Institute of Social Sciences and Arts, Johnson City, TN.

Ruscio, J., Haslam, N. and Ruscio, A.M. (2006) *Introduction to the Taxometric Method: A Practical Guide*, Lawrence Erlbaum, Mahwah, NJ.

Simourd, D.J. (2001, March) *Criminal Attitudes: A Background of Theory, Assessment, and Intervention*, Workshop presented at Diversion Services, Tulsa, OK.

Simourd, D.J. (1997) The Criminal Sentiments Scale-Modified and Pride in Delinquency Scale: psychometric properties and construct validity of two measures of criminal attitudes. *Criminal Justice and Behavior*, **24**, 52–70.

Simourd, L. and Andrews, D.A. (1994) Correlates of delinquency: a look at gender differences. *Forum on Correctional Research*, **6**, 26–31.

Simourd, D.J. and Olver, M.E. (2002) The future of criminal attitude research and practice. *Criminal Justice and Behavior*, **29**, 427–46.

Simourd, D.J. and van de Ven, J. (1999) Assessment of criminal attitudes: criterion-related validity of the Criminal Sentiments Scale-Modified and Pride in Delinquency Scale. *Criminal Justice and Behavior*, **26**, 90–106.

Slaby, R.G. and Guerra, N.G. (1988) Cognitive mediators of aggression in adolescent offenders. I. Assessment. *Developmental Psychology*, **24**, 580–8.

Smithmyer, C.M., Hubbard, J.A. and Simons, R.F. (2000) Proactive and reactive aggression in delinquent adolescents: relations to aggression outcome expectancies. *Journal of Clinical Child Psychology*, **29**, 86–93.

Sutherland, E.H. and Cressey, D.R. (1978) *Principles of Criminology*, 10th edn, Lippincott, Philadelphia.

Sykes, G.M. and Matza, D. (1957) Techniques of neutralization: a theory of delinquency. *American Sociological Review*, **22**, 664–70.

Walters, G.D. (1990) *The Criminal Lifestyle: Patterns of Serious Criminal Conduct*, Sage, Newbury Park, CA.

Walters, G.D. (1995) The Psychological Inventory of Criminal Thinking Styles: Part I. Reliability and preliminary validity. *Criminal Justice and Behavior*, **22**, 437–55.

Walters, G.D. (2002) *Criminal Belief Systems: An Integrated-Interactive Theory of Lifestyles*, Praeger, Westport, CT.

Walters, G.D. (2005a) How many factors are there on the PICTS? *Criminal Behaviour and Mental Health*, **15**, 227–37.

Walters, G.D. (2005b) Incremental validity of the Psychological Inventory of Criminal Thinking Styles as a predictor of continuous and dichotomous measures of recidivism. *Assessment*, **12**, 19–27.

Walters, G.D. (2005c) Proactive and reactive aggression: a lifestyle view, in *Psychology of Aggression* (ed. J.P. Morgan), Nova Sciences, New York, pp. 29–43.

Walters, G.D. (2006) Proactive and reactive composite scales for the Psychological Inventory of Criminal Thinking Styles. *Journal of Offender Rehabilitation*, **42** (4), 23–36.

Walters, G.D. (2007a) *The Latent Structure of the Criminal Lifestyle: A Taxometric Analysis of the Lifestyle Criminality Screening Form and Psychological Inventory of Criminal Thinking Styles, Criminal Justice and Behavior*, **34**, 1623–37.

Walters, G.D. (2007b) Measuring proactive and reactive criminal thinking with the PICTS: correlations with outcome expectancies and hostile attribution biases. *Journal of Interpersonal Violence*, **22**, 371–85.

Walters, G.D. (in press) The Psychological Inventory of Criminal Thinking Styles and Psychopathy Checklist: Screening Version as incrementally valid predictors of recidivism. *Law and Human Behavior*.

Walters, G.D. and Elliott, W.N. (1999) Predicting release and disciplinary outcome with the Psychological Inventory of Criminal Thinking Styles: female data. *Legal and Criminological Psychology*, **4**, 15–21.

Walters, G.D., Frederick, A.A. and Schlauch, C. (2007) Postdicting arrests for proactive and reactive aggression with the PICTS proactive and reactive composite scales. *Journal of Interpersonal Violence*, **22**, 1415–30.

Walters, G.D. and Geyer, M.D. (2005) Construct validity of the Psychological Inventory of Criminal Thinking Styles in relationship to the PAI, disciplinary adjustment, and program completion. *Journal of Personality Assessment*, **84**, 252–60.

Walters, G.D. and Mandell, W. (2007) Incremental validity of the Psychological Inventory of Criminal Thinking Styles and Psychopathy Checklist: Screening Version in predicting disciplinary adjustment. *Law and Human Behavior*, **31**, 141–57.

Walters, G.D. and McCoy, K. (2007) Taxometric analysis of the Psychological Inventory of Criminal Thinking Styles in male and female incarcerated offenders and college students. *Criminal Justice and Behavior*, **34**, 781–93.

Walters, G.D., Trgovac, M., Rychlec, M. *et al.* (2002) Assessing change with the Psychological Inventory of Criminal Thinking Styles: a controlled analysis and multisite cross-validation. *Criminal Justice and Behavior*, **29**, 308–31.

Walters, G.D., White, T.W. and Denney, D. (1991) The Lifestyle Criminality Screening Form: preliminary data. *Criminal Justice and Behavior*, **75**, 406–18.

Ward, T.W., Hudson, S.M., Johnston, L. and Marshall, W.L. (1997) Cognitive distortions in sex offenders: an integrative review. *Clinical Psychology Review*, **17**, 479–507.

Yessine, A.K. and Kroner, D.G. (2004, June) *Altering Antisocial Attitudes Among Federal Male Offenders on Release: A Preliminary Analysis of the Counter-Point Community Program* (Research Report). Correctional Service of Canada, Ottawa, Ontario, Canada.

Zhang, Q., Loeber, R. and Stouthamer-Loeber, M. (1997) Developmental trends of delinquent attitudes and behavior: replication and synthesis across domains, times and samples. *Journal of Quantitative Criminology*, **13**, 181–216.

CONCLUSION

Chapter 16

PERSONALITY, PERSONALITY DISORDER AND VIOLENCE: IMPLICATIONS FOR FUTURE RESEARCH AND PRACTICE

MARY MCMURRAN AND RICHARD HOWARD
University of Nottingham, UK

INTRODUCTION

This volume has brought together researchers from a variety of disciplines within the behavioural sciences in an attempt to address some key issues concerning personality, personality disorder and violence. We have focused on those traits and disorders that are thought to be linked to an increased likelihood of violence, since the latter is clearly not an inevitable consequence of the former. Contributors have focused on impulsiveness, the Big Five personality dimensions, narcissism, psychopathy and antisocial personality disorder. Of special interest here is the question of *how* these traits and disorders increase the likelihood that violence will occur. Contributors have described the developmental route through which early antecedents translate across the lifespan into adult personality disorders with an associated elevated risk of violence. Some of the specific mechanisms that might elevate risk of violence have also been proposed and their empirical investigation described. These neurophysiological, cognitive, affective and social mechanisms are surely the foundation on which effective treatments can be developed. In this concluding chapter, we will identify some key themes that have emerged in this book. Our aims are twofold: first, to identify potentially fruitful new areas of research, and second to draw out implications for up-to-date evidence-based clinical practice.

Personality, Personality Disorder and Violence   Edited by Mary McMurran and Richard C. Howard
© 2009 John Wiley & Sons, Ltd

VARIANTS OF PSYCHOPATHY

Having a personality disorder is not a necessary condition for violence to occur; given the relevant predispositions and adverse circumstances, any one of us might behave violently. However, certain personality characteristics are evidently associated with an increased likelihood of chronic antisocial and violent behaviour. The dimensions discussed by authors in this text include anxiety, neuroticism, anger, disagreeableness, impulsivity, fear, emotion recognition ability and empathy. Clearly, we all possess these attributes to a greater or lesser degree, and their ability to explain violence likely depends upon the extent to which the individual is extreme on the adverse pole of these dimensions and the combination of extreme and adverse characteristics. Notwithstanding this, we must acknowledge Livesley's (2007a) point that an extreme score on a trait or dimension does not equate with disorder – high or low levels on a given trait such as agreeableness or conscientiousness are neither necessary nor sufficient to indicate disordered functioning. In other words, personality disorder is more than just a set of dysfunctional traits.

Some of the dysfunctional traits associated with violence may have a heritable basis but, nonetheless, their development and expression are influenced by social factors throughout the lifespan. These influences include parenting styles, school experiences, peer influences, neighbourhood atmosphere and broader social mores including the cultural context. These influences may also include criminal justice sanctions and psychological or other treatments. These social experiences likely explain why some antisocial and even highly psychopathic individuals are able to refrain from violence; some do learn emotional and behavioural control, perhaps learning to express their dysfunctional traits in a less maladaptive way. It is important to examine how some at-risk individuals learn to do this since it indicates possible directions for effective prevention and treatment.

While recent evidence suggests a modest association between the affective and antisocial facets of psychopathy, as measured by the psychopathy checklist, and violence (Vitacco, Neumann and Jackson, 2005), this picture is complicated by growing evidence for a range of sub-types of the 'psychopathic personality'. Skeem *et al.* (2003) have suggested that each psychopathy variant may have a distinct aetiology, different affective capacities and its own characteristic type of aggression, and that these different sub-types may be more or less amenable to change. Therefore, identifying different sub-types has important implications for violence risk assessment, management and treatment. In Chapter 6, Blackburn takes this a stage further by examining the relationship of his Antisocial Personality Questionnaire-based typology to psychopathy, as measured by the psychopathy checklist. The picture that emerges is one of multiple variants of psychopathy, each associated with a complex pattern of comorbidity, both with DSM personality disorders and Axis I disorders. He points out that each psychopathy variant might have a distinctive pattern or type of violence associated with it, and future research will need to address this possibility.

De Brito and Hodgins (Chapter 7) propose three antisocial personality disorder sub-types: (1) an anxious, emotionally under-controlled/reactive sub-type;

(2) a non-anxious non-psychopathic sub-type; and (3) a non-anxious, psychopathic sub-type. The second and third sub-types are distinguished by the absence (in the case of the non-psychopathic sub-type) or presence (in the case of the psychopathic sub-type) of callous-unemotional traits in childhood. De Brito and Hodgins suggest that these three sub-types correspond to genetic types. They also highlight the importance of recognising aetiological pathways, and particularly they draw attention to the heterogeneity of conduct disorder. There is no doubt that this is a useful attempt to map different trajectories from childhood conduct disorder to adult antisocial behaviour.

The views of De Brito and Hodgins are supported by the findings of others. For example, in studies of personality disorders in an adult forensic sample, Blackburn (2007) found that conduct disorder disaggregated into non-aggressive (stealing, housebreaking, staying out late, conning others) and interpersonally harmful (cruelty to others, aggression, bullying) behaviours. While these might appear to relate to De Brito and Hodgins' anxious and non-anxious types, respectively, Blackburn (2007) found that the interpersonal harm aspect of conduct disorder correlated not just with the affective facet of psychopath but with all facets, including interpersonal, behavioural and antisocial aspects. De Brito and Hodgins' focus on the affective deficiency facet of psychopathy contrasts with the stance of Hare and colleagues, who warn against a selective focus on any one facet (Neumann, Hare and Newman, 2007). They argue that, while the affective domain reflects a critical component of psychopathy, it should not be considered *a priori* more central to the disorder than the other three dimensions, namely the interpersonal, lifestyle and antisocial domains.

In explaining violence and other criminal behaviours, it is important to keep these behaviours separate from the putative explanatory construct. Skeem and Cooke (in press) have pointed to the need for theoretically-driven conceptualisations of psychopathy sub-types that distinguish between dispositions or traits (e.g. impulsiveness, callousness) and socially sanctioned behaviours (e.g. crime, antisocial behaviours). Having done so, researchers and practitioners must separate the process of understanding the psychopathic personalities from the enterprise of predicting violence. Nevertheless, we must acknowledge, in accord with Blackburn (2007), that violations of social rules can be manifestations of a personality trait. Blackburn's analysis of the relationship between DSM personality disorders and psychopathy facets in a forensic sample led him to conclude that antisocial behaviour, broadly conceived, is a characteristic feature of psychopathy, although the underlying trait, an aggressive interpersonal style, need not necessarily manifest itself in criminal behaviour. The same conclusion can be drawn from a recent study of personality disorders in a community sample, where measures of criminal behaviour, including violence, loaded on a higher order psychopathy factor (Howard *et al.*, 2008). One must also be wary of assuming a one-way relationship between personality disorder (and psychopathy in particular) and violence, when a bidirectional relationship may very well obtain. That is to say, not only may psychopathic traits lead to a greater risk of violence, but also engaging in violent acts may itself lead to the development of psychopathic traits such as callousness (Neumann *et al.*, 2005).

MECHANISMS FOR UNDERSTANDING THE LINKS BETWEEN PERSONALITY, PERSONALITY DISORDER AND VIOLENCE

If there are different psychopathic disorders, then, as Skeem *et al.* (2003) suggest, these are likely to relate differently to violence. Relevant to this is Howard's typology of violence (see Chapter 8), which may help direct research, and this area of investigation will be assisted by a greater understanding of issues such as impulsiveness, neuroticism, anger, attachment difficulties, low empathy, difficulties with processing emotional information, poor problem solving and criminal thinking styles.

The Psychopathy Paradox

Perhaps the central paradox of psychopathy is that lack of emotional responsiveness, expressed in the psychopath's coldness and callousness, can go hand-in-hand with emotional dyscontrol and reactive violence. In the violence typology presented by Howard in Chapter 8, impulsive violence can be associated with either positive or negative affect. When associated with negative affect, it is accompanied by explosive or reactive anger and by subjective distress; behaviourally, it manifests as violent acting-out driven by negative affect. This may be more associated with the emotional dysregulation seen in borderline personality disorder and secondary psychopathy. When associated with positive affect, impulsive violence is accompanied by subjective exhilaration and excitement, and the emotion of anger is experienced as affectively positive. The behavioural manifestation is driven by thrill seeking and a need for increasingly higher levels of stimulation. This, it is argued, may be more associated with antisocial personality disorder, particularly when this co-occurs with sexual sadism (Berner, Berger and Hill, 2003). Kirsch and Becker (2007) point out that, while capable of recognising emotional distress in others, sexual sadists may respond to this by experiencing pleasure rather than feelings of sympathy or personal distress. During the violent act, empathy for their victim is necessarily suspended – an example of the sort of victim-specific empathy discussed by Marshall, Marshall and Serin in Chapter 12, and of the modulation of empathy achieved by antisocial individuals to facilitate their criminal acts mentioned by Logan in her discussion of narcissism in Chapter 5. Narcissists are said to show a more pervasive emotional inability to identify with and feel for other people. Secondary psychopaths, who show aspects of both borderline and antisocial personality disorders, will putatively show both types of impulsive violence and will often switch between alternate types of impulsive violence depending on internal state (e.g. high vs. low anxiety) and context (e.g. whether the environment is experienced as threatening or exciting).

Another attempt to get to grips with this paradox is the model of psychopathy developed by Blair, an aspect of which is presented in Chapter 9. Blair's solution to this paradox is to relate the affective deficiency facet of psychopathy (cold, callous, unemotional traits) to deficits in fear and empathy, which give rise, he argues, to poor socialisation. Underlying the deficits in fear and empathy are deficits in stimulus–reinforcement association, underpinned by an amygdala dysfunction.

The emotional dyscontrol aspect he relates upstream to reactive aggression and to the antisocial behaviour aspect of psychopathy; downstream to risk for frustration, a deficit in altering stimulus–response associations; and ultimately to a prefrontal cortex dysfunction. Thus an affective deficiency characterised by cold and callous traits could in principle, according to Blair's formulation, co-exist in the same psychopathic individual with emotional dyscontrol. In light of Logan's discussion of narcissism in Chapter 5, this affective deficiency might be said to characterise the antisocial individual with strong pathological narcissism – the 'psychopathic narcissist', in whom a lack of empathic capacity is a salient feature.

Neuropsychological Mechanisms

There are striking parallels between the response modulation deficit model of psychopathy outlined by Vitale and Newman (Chapter 13) and the neuropsychological model of affective dyscontrol outlined by Howard (Chapter 8). According to the former, the essential deficit manifested by psychopathic individuals is that '. . . the "call for processing" emerging from the existence of a discrepancy between the outcome of a behaviour and a set of goals or standards is not answered by top-down attention processes' (p. 256). This corresponds closely to Howard's suggestion, originally formulated in the context of a neuropsychological model of goal-directed behaviour (Howard, 1981; Howard, Fenton and Fenwick, 1982), that affectively impulsive individuals show weak activation of the neural action acceptor that detects a discrepancy between an expected and an obtained outcome (e.g. actual non-reward or punishment in the context of expected reward/non-punishment). In the event that there is sustained 'mismatch' in the action acceptor (i.e. the expectancy for reward or non-punishment continues to be disconfirmed), the top-down 'mismatch' signal would normally be of sufficient strength to activate an opposing aversive motivational system, resulting in a shift of the attentional spotlight to cues signalling punishment or non-reward. Following this, the cues that originally were linked to the 'Go' system would normally, by associative learning, become linked to the 'No Go' system. As in the response modulation deficit model of psychopathy, the essential deficit lies in a failure of the action acceptor to detect 'mismatch', which would normally initiate a switch from 'Go' (approach) to 'No Go' (withdrawal). In the Vitale and Newman formulation, disinhibition, said by to be shown by psychopathic individuals, lies in the intensification of the dominant response set. This corresponds, in the Howard model, to continued excitation by the mismatch signal of the reward motivational system and its allied attentional mechanism (called 'active attention' in Howard, Fenton and Fenwick, 1982). This results, as in Vitale and Newman, in sustained approach to cues that in others would elicit withdrawal. Vitale and Newman give an elegant account of how this failure to register a discrepancy between expected and obtained outcomes, triggering a failure of the response modulation process, can account for a failure to self-regulate in the context of an instigation to aggression.

Despite their striking similarities, the two accounts diverge at some points. First, Vitale and Newman attribute this deficit to psychopaths, and sometimes to primary (low anxious) psychopaths. At times they seem to imply that psychopaths fail to resist emotional impulses such as 'strong aggressive urges' (p. 259). Summarising the response modulation deficit hypothesis, Vitale and Newman suggest that psychopaths '. . . are predisposed to act on *urges* once they become prepotent . . .' (p. 258; italics added). By contrast, Howard attributes this deficit to affectively impulsive individuals who are prone to what he calls impulsive violence, either offensive or defensive, in his violence typology. While affective impulsivity is a common feature in psychopaths, it is a more salient feature of secondary than of primary psychopaths, as Blackburn points out in Chapter 6. Secondary psychopaths are said by Blackburn to be more prone to the emotional dysregulation of borderline personality disorder. It is of interest to note here that borderline personality disorder patients have been reported to show the passive avoidance deficit that is a behavioural marker of the response modulation deficit (Hochhausen, Lorenz and Newman, 2002). It remains, therefore, for further research to determine whether the deficit common to the accounts of both Vitale and Newman (Chapter 13) and Howard (Chapter 8) is a feature particularly of the affective dyscontrol aspect of psychopathy, or of some other aspects, or indeed whether the deficit characterises psychopathy as a higher order construct.

A second point of divergence between the two accounts lies in the importance assigned to an affective deficit in psychopaths. While Vitale and Newman highlight the affective poverty shown by psychopaths in the classic Cleckleyan account, their response modulation deficit model emphasises attention, rather than affect, as the core deficit. On the face of it, it is difficult to see how such an attentional deficit could account for the affective deficit shown by psychopaths – their quotation from Cleckley emphasises that it is a global deficit involving positive as well as negative affect. Howard's account, in contrast, suggests that positive and negative affect arise out of the operation of appetitive and aversive motivational systems, respectively. If these systems are not adequately excited by input from the action acceptors that encode expectancies for reward/non-punishment and punishment/non-reward, an inevitable consequence will be a lack of positive and negative affect, respectively. As a result, psychopaths will appear as lacking both desire and fear. However, consistent with Vitale and Newman's account, psychopaths' affective poverty is said to arise out of a more basic neurocognitive deficit.

Blair's formulation (Chapter 9), by contrast, suggests specific, rather than global, affective deficits and that these are associated with different facets of psychopathy. Deficits in fear and empathy are associated with the affective deficiency facet, while a high risk for frustration is said to underlie reactive aggression and the antisocial/behavioural facet. This is at odds with the original Cleckleyan concept of a global affective deficit in psychopathy, including deficiencies in both positive and negative affect.

An important plank in Blair's formulation, as presented in Chapter 9, is the supposed deficit in the recognition of facial affect, specifically in the recognition of fearful and sad expressions, in psychopathic individuals. Blair acknowledges that the literature on recognition of facial affect has yielded rather mixed results, with at least one study reporting a lack of recognition impairment in psychopaths (Glass and Newman, 2006). Even one negative result must cast some doubt on the generality of the deficit in psychopaths. It is possible, for example, that the various samples of PCL-defined psychopaths that yielded different results may have differed in terms of the presence of comorbid disorders. Of particular relevance is the co-occurrence of alcohol dependence. The literature on recognition of facial affect in alcoholics consistently indicates a deficit, even when they have been abstinent for months or years (for a review, see Philippot, Kornreich and Blairy, 2001). Brain imaging studies of facial affect recognition in alcoholics are rare, but one recent event-related fMRI study reported decreased brain activation in alcoholics relative to non-alcoholic controls when they decoded facial expressions of fear, disgust and sadness, but not when they decoded facial expressions of anger (Salloum et al., 2007). As Blair points out in Chapter 9, it is perhaps significant that deficits in the recognition of fear, disgust and sadness have been reported in the psychopathy literature. Blair argues, on the basis of a meta-analysis conducted by Marsh and Blair (2008), that the impairment of facial affect recognition shown by psychopaths is limited to fear and sadness. However, one is left wondering what the result of this meta-analysis would have been had the individual studies controlled for a history of alcohol abuse, and particularly of early-onset alcohol abuse. In short, it is arguable that the deficit in processing facial affect claimed for psychopaths is attributable to comorbid alcohol abuse and dependence.

The strength of this argument would, however, be somewhat diminished if the selective impairment of the processing of sad and fearful expressions in children with psychopathic tendencies reported by Blair et al. (2001) were confirmed in pre-pubertal children, who would be unlikely to use alcohol and other substances. It is notable in this regard that some of the psychopathic 'children' in Blair et al.'s (2001) study were adolescents – the upper end of the age range was 17 years – so that a proportion of them was likely abusing alcohol and other substances (no data pertaining to this were reported). Given the high comorbidity between core features of psychopathy and substance use disorders (Walsh, Allen and Kosson, 2007), it would be difficult to disentangle, in adolescent or adult psychopaths, the effect of psychopathy from that of substance use on facial affect recognition. Studies of facial affect recognition in pre-pubertal children with psychopathic traits are rare, but one recent study examined recognition of facial expressions of emotion in children aged 7–12 who scored high or low on callous and unemotional traits, the hallmark of childhood psychopathy (Woodworth and Waschbusch, 2008). Children who scored high on callous and unemotional traits were, in comparison with those scoring low, less accurate in identifying sad facial expressions but, contra Blair, more accurate in interpreting fearful expressions. Clearly, more research is needed to clarify this issue.

Affective and Cognitive Processes in a Developmental Context

Personality disorder is a diagnosis reserved for adults on the basis that personality is forming during childhood and adolescence and cannot be definitively said to be disordered until it has finally formed. This implies that personality (disordered or otherwise) is fixed in adulthood. There is, however, evidence of change over time, particularly with regard to improvement in emotional dysregulation (Lenzenweger and Willett, 2007). Recent studies, reviewed by Tyrer et al. (2007), demonstrate change in personality status in both clinical and population samples.

A consistent finding from all the studies reviewed is that those patients who present for treatment, particularly (but not exclusively) those with borderline personality disorder, show a steady improvement in both the short and longer term. As Tyrer *et al.* state: 'We can no longer ... refuse to accept that spontaneous change in personality features can take place independent of any treatment effects' (p. s54). All across the lifespan, the individual's dispositions and basic characteristics are in a reciprocal interaction with the social environment to produce the complex pattern of thoughts, feelings and behaviour that is personality. This reciprocal interaction does not cease in adulthood, thus giving some hope that change is possible even though entrenched patterns of experiencing, thinking and behaving are difficult to alter.

In infants and children, individual differences are evident in temperament, including sociability, emotionality, activity, attention and impulsivity. These domains of temperament may have biological bases, linked to neural systems governing functions such as behavioural activation, behavioural inhibition, affect regulation and attention. Even at an early age, there is an interaction between the individual and his or her environment, such that individual differences can never be explained by genetics or neuroscience alone (Paris, 2005). It is the interaction between traits and experiences over the lifespan that helps us understand personality, whether disordered or not.

Longitudinal studies have examined the developmental trajectory of antisocial personality disorder, identifying factors associated with the emergence, escalation, persistence and desistance from antisocial behaviour. In his review of the childhood origins of antisocial behaviour, Farrington (2005) summarises the most important risk factors as early impulsivity, low intelligence, poor parental supervision, harsh and erratic discipline, maltreatment by parents, parental conflict, lone mother, disrupted families, antisocial parents, large families, low socioeconomic status, low commitment to school, poor educational attainment and delinquent peers. Of interest here are the processes by which these risk factors increase the likelihood of antisocial personality disorder in adulthood. Farrington (2005) conceptualises these in his Integrated Cognitive Antisocial Potential (ICAP) theory, in which the individual's antisocial potential is a function of traits (e.g. impulsivity), interacting with social factors (e.g. family management, peer associations) and opportunities for prosocial and antisocial activities (e.g. employment, neighbourhood), via mechanisms such as attachment, self-regulation, cognitive development, skills acquisition and labelling. These processes are addressed in this text by looking at attachment difficulties (Chapter 11), anger (Chapter 10), problem solving (Chapter 14) and criminal thinking styles (Chapter 15).

The challenge is to dismantle the 'fuzzy' construct of personality disorder into clearer, theoretically based sets of constructs that may be empirically investigated to clarify the processes that underpin personality disorder. In this way, we will further our understanding of the differences (in type or degree) between disordered and non-disordered individuals, and hence will identify what should be targeted in prevention and treatment efforts. Taking a developmental approach is one way to understand the complexity of personality. Livesley (2007a, 2007b) draws an important distinction between disturbances in the *contents* of personality, which includes dysfunctional traits, regulatory problems, maladaptive behaviours and cognitions, and disturbances in the *structure*, or organisation, of personality, characterised by a failure to establish coherent representations of self and others, and chronic interpersonal dysfunction. He suggests two levels of construct, in addition to the trait level, that need to be addressed in evaluating individual differences in personality disorder: first, personal concerns, including motives, roles, goals and coping strategies; and second, the life narrative which provides an integrated account of past, present and future. Assessment and treatment need to be targeted at all three levels.

While there is currently little empirical research addressing the structural aspects of personality in personality-disordered individuals, levels other than the trait level are beginning to be addressed in offender treatments. Reflections on offenders' life goals and the need for developing coherent, satisfying and prosocial life plans have been presented by Ward (2002) in his 'Good Lives Model' of offender rehabilitation. Specifying these life goals as personal concerns that may be assessed and changed in therapy has been addressed by McMurran and colleagues (McMurran *et al.*, 2008; McMurran and Ward, 2004). Finally, the role of life narratives in promoting and sustaining desistance from offending has been investigated by Maruna (2001). These approaches have potential value in application with personality-disordered offenders.

CO-OCCURRENCE OF DISORDERS

An important theme to emerge in this volume is the very high degree to which personality disorders co-occur, both among themselves and with other mental disorders, in personality-disordered people at risk of violence. This raises the question of whether the co-occurrence is an artefact of overlapping diagnostic criteria (consanguinity rather than true comorbidity; Tyrer *et al.*, 2007), rather than the clinical conditions in question being distinct disorders. Overlapping diagnostic criteria may, for example, in part explain the common co-occurrence of antisocial and borderline personality disorders, both of which contain criteria relating to poor anger control and aggression (Widiger and Trull, 1994). The co-occurrence of antisocial personality disorder and psychopathy may be due to a combination of including criminality in the criteria and an emphasis on the study of criminal populations. The inclusion of criminality ensures that a high proportion of offenders meet the criteria for antisocial personality disorder (around 50% of prisoners, according to Fazel and Danesh, 2002). Of these, only a proportion will meet the additional affective and interpersonal deficit criteria required for a diagnosis of psychopathy (among UK prisoners, 4.5% have a PCL-R score of 30 or more, and 13% have a score of 25 or more; Hare *et al.*, 2000). This leads to the situation where more or less all criminal psychopaths have antisocial personality disorder, although not all of those with antisocial personality disorder are psychopaths.

Clearly, these possible artefacts need to be addressed, first by revising diagnostic criteria to reduce overlap, and second by conducting research on non-offender populations as well as offenders. Meanwhile, the current situation has implications in relation to interpreting research on specific personality disorders when 'pure' cases of any personality disorder are a rarity. This applies particularly to studies of psychopathy where 'psychopaths' are defined by a cut-off score on the psychopathy checklist. Samples defined in this way may vary considerably in terms of co-occurring personality disorders, making interpretation of results across studies difficult.

The co-occurrence of personality disorders with DSM Axis I disorders further complicates the picture. Co-occurring mood disorders are not uncommon in people with high psychopathy traits and antisocial personality disorder (Widiger, 2006). Antisocial personality disorder commonly occurs with a range of anxiety disorders (see Chapter 7). Personality disorders, and psychopathy in particular, commonly co-occur with substance use disorders (Walsh, Allen and Kosson, 2007). Analysis of data from a UK general population sample estimated a prevalence of personality disorder of 4% (Coid *et al.*, 2006). The odds of alcohol dependence were much greater for those with a Cluster B disorder (compared with those with no Cluster B disorder), as were the odds of a criminal conviction. Those in Cluster A were somewhat more likely to be alcohol dependent, but those in Cluster C were less likely to be alcohol dependent. The risks presented by co-occurring problems are illustrated in a study of 90 mentally ill men (78% were schizophrenic) who had either committed one or more homicides (72%) or had attempted to kill someone (28%) (Putkonen *et al.*, 2004). Having an additional diagnosis of antisocial personality disorder conferred a substantially increased risk of violence on those (three-quarters of the total sample) who received dual diagnoses of mental illness and substance use disorder.

Clinically, this high degree of 'comorbidity' is important. First, forensic mental health clinicians may be well advised to screen personality-disordered patients for other (e.g. Axis I) disorders, and vice versa. Second, treatment plans should take into account multiple diagnoses so that appropriate treatment for personality disorders and other mental disorders can be offered.

ASSESSMENT AND TREATMENT OF VIOLENCE RELATED TO PERSONALITY AND PERSONALITY DISORDERS

Assessment

It is clear that there is much work to be done in clarifying definitions and refining methods of measurement, and this applies to both personality disorders and personality traits. Diagnostic overlap, focusing research only on clinical or offender populations, and confounding explanatory variables with the construct under study are all sources of confusion. Clarity will be achieved partly by better empirical identification of sub-types of psychopathic disorders and the design of new assessments that can differentiate among these. These assessments will likely identify higher order constructs, such as Livesley's (2007a) secondary domains of emotional dysregulation, dissocial behaviour, inhibitedness and compulsivity, and underpinning lower order traits, such as Livesley's (2007a) domain of primary traits. For example, underpinning the dissocial behaviour domain are primary traits of impulsiveness, sensation seeking, narcissism, exploitativeness, sadism, conduct problems, hostile-dominance, suspiciousness and egocentrism.

Theoretically-driven longitudinal research, good quality cross-sectional studies and experimental studies all have the potential to contribute to developments in this area.

Meanwhile, researchers and clinicians should consider in-depth assessment of the core features of psychopathic and antisocial personality disorders. For the former, these include deficits in affective experience, deficits in processing emotional information, cognitive-attention deficits that impair behaviour control and narcissism. For the latter, impulsivity, anxiety, antisocial thinking styles and poor interpersonal problem solving apply. Assessments may be conducted via clinical interview and self-report checklists, but, in a quest to augment the 'softer' measures, there is much scope for the development of laboratory methods into clinically useful formats that are likely to be more widely used. These may include reaction time tasks, psychophysiological measures and examination of cognitive processes using methods that make internal processes more transparent.

Treatment

One certainty is that there is little evidence for effective treatments for people with high psychopathic traits or for people with antisocial personality disorder (D'Silva, Duggan and McCarthy, 2004; Duggan et al., 2007). However, an absence of evidence for effective treatment is not evidence that effective treatment is impossible. Much further work is needed to develop and evaluate treatments for people with personality problems who are violent. If there are different sub-types of personality-driven violence, then clearly different treatments will be required. Traditional interventions will have their place, including increasing self-control and emotion regulation, teaching problem solving skills, improving perspective-taking and cognitive empathy, and challenging antisocial thinking and values. These will have greater effect if there is also attention to controlling drinking and drug use and improving social inclusion, that is assisting people to find stable accommodation, jobs and supportive social networks.

In developing the effectiveness of these traditional interventions for both psychopathic and antisocial individuals, attention needs to be paid to implicit cognitive processes, as suggested by a number of contributors to this book. These processes include, for example, specific attentional functioning idiosyncrasies, poor recognition of emotional cues or problem solving under conditions of high physiological arousal induced by threat. They may not be most amenable to change through interventions that teach people new ways of thinking and operating in the world. Rather, interventions may need to include attentional retraining, sensitisation to emotional cues and skills practice under conditions of high arousal. These interventions would be based more upon classical and operant conditioning techniques than upon cognitive interventions. However, perhaps the greatest challenge to those involved in the treatment of personality-disordered offenders will be to move beyond interventions aimed solely at producing change in what Livesley (2007a) refers to as the contents of personality, to interventions aimed at changing its structure, such as promoting more cohesive personality functioning.

CONCLUSION

We conclude this book in the hope that it will contribute to an expansion of research interest and activity, and in the realisation that many of the ideas contained in it will fall by the wayside as new findings emerge. We will be happy if this book serves only to highlight our current state of relative ignorance concerning the relationship between personality disorder and violence. We will console ourselves with the thought that wisdom is the growing appreciation (or awareness) of our ignorance, and look forward to the need for a revised edition of this work in a few years' time.

REFERENCES

Berner, W., Berger, P. and Hill, A. (2003) Sexual sadism. *International Journal of Offender Therapy and Comparative Criminology*, **47**, 383–95.

Blackburn, R. (2007) Personality disorder and antisocial deviance: comments on the debate on the structure of the psychopathy checklist – revised. *Journal of Personality Disorders*, **21**, 142–59.

Blair, R.J., Colledge, E., Murray, L. and Mitchell, D.G. (2001) A selective impairment in the processing of sad and fearful expressions in children with psychopathic tendencies. *Journal of Abnormal Child Psychology*, **29**, 491–8.

Coid, J., Yang, M., Tyrer, P. *et al.* (2006) Prevalence and correlates of personality disorder in Great Britain. *British Journal of Psychiatry*, **188**, 423–31.

D'Silva, K., Duggan, C. and McCarthy, L. (2004) Does treatment really make psychopaths worse? A review of the evidence. *Journal of Personality Disorders*, **18**, 163–77.

Duggan, C., Huband, N., Smailagic, N. *et al.* (2007) The use of psychological treatments for people with personality disorder: a systematic review of randomized controlled trails. *Personality and Mental Health*, **1**, 95–125.

Farrington, D.P. (2005) Childhood origins of antisocial behaviour. *Clinical Psychology and Psychotherapy*, **12**, 177–90.

Fazel, S. and Danesh, J. (2002) Serious mental disorder in 23 000 prisoners: a systematic review of 62 surveys. *The Lancet*, **359**, 545–50.

Glass, S.J. and Newman, J.P. (2006) Recognition of facial affect in psychopathic offenders. *Journal of Abnormal Psychology*, **115**, 815–20.

Hare, R.D., Clark, D., Grann, M. and Thornton, D. (2000) Psychopathy and the predictive validity of the PCL-R: an international perspective. *Behavioral Sciences and the Law*, **18**, 623–45.

Hochhausen, N.M., Lorenz, A.R. and Newman, J.P. (2002) Specifying the impulsivity of female inmates with borderline personality disorder. *Journal of Abnormal Psychology*, **111**, 495–501.

Howard, R.C. (1981) *Slow Cerebral Event-Related Potentials, Conditioning and Personality*, Unpublished PhD Thesis. Faculty of Medicine, The Queen's University of Belfast, Belfast.

Howard, R.C., Fenton, G.W.F. and Fenwick, P.B.C. (1982) *Event-Related Brain Potentials in Personality and Psychopathology: A Pavlovian Approach*, Research Studies Press, Wiley, Letchworth.

Howard, R.C., Huband, N., Mannion, A. and Duggan, C. (2008) Exploring the link between personality disorder and criminality in a community sample. *Journal of Personality Disorders*, **22**, 589–603.

Kirsch, L.G. and Becker, J.V. (2007) Emotional deficits in psychopathy and sexual sadism: implications for violent and sadistic behavior. *Clinical Psychology Review*, **27**, 904–22.

Lenzenweger, M.F. and Willett, J.B. (2007) Predicting individual change in personality disorder features by simultaneous individual change in personality dimensions linked to neurobehavioral systems: the longitudinal study of personality disorders. *Journal of Abnormal Psychology*, **116**, 684–700.

Livesley, W.J. (2007a) A framework for integrating dimensional and categorical classifications of personality disorder. *Journal of Personality Disorders*, **21**, 199–224.

Livesley, W.J. (2007b) The relevance of an integrated approach to the treatment of personality disordered offenders. *Psychology, Crime and Law*, **13**, 27–46.

Marsh, A.A. and Blair, R.J. (2008) Deficits in facial affect recognition among antisocial populations: a meta-analysis. *Neuroscience and Biobehavioral Reviews*, **32**, 454–65.

Maruna, S. (2001) *Making good: How Ex-Convicts Reform and Rebuild Their Lives*, American Psychological Association, Washington DC.

McMurran, M., Theodosi, E., Sweeney, A. and Sellen, J. (2008) What do prisoners want? Current concerns of adult male prisoners. *Psychology, Crime and Law*, **14**, 267–74.

McMurran, M. and Ward, T. (2004) Motivating offenders to change in therapy: an organising framework. *Legal and Criminological Psychology*, **9**, 295–311.

Neumann, C.S., Hare, R.D. and Newman, J.P. (2007) The nature of the psychopathy checklist – revised. *Journal of Personality Disorders*, **21**, 102–17.

Neumann, C.S., Vitacco, M.J., Hare, R.D. and Wupperman, P. (2005) Reconstruing the "reconstruction" of psychopathy: a comment on Cooke, Michie, Hart, and Clark. *Journal of Personality Disorders*, **19**, 624–40.

Paris, J. (2005) Neurobiological dimensional models of personality: a review of the models of Cloninger, Depue, and Siever. *Journal of Personality Disorders*, **19**, 156–70.

Philippot, P., Kornreich, C. and Blairy, S. (2001) Nonverbal deficits and interpersonal regulation in alcoholics, in *Nonverbal Behavior in Clinical Context* (eds P. Philippot, E.J. Coats and R.S. Feldman), Oxford University Press, New York.

Putkonen, A., Kotilainen, I., Joyal, C.C. and Tühonen, J. (2004) Comorbid personality disorders and substance use disorders of mentally ill homicide offenders: a structured clinical study on dual and triple diagnoses. *Schizophrenia Bulletin*, **30**, 59–72.

Salloum, J.B., Ramchandani, V.A., Bodurka, J. *et al.* (2007) Blunted rostral anterior cingulated response during a simplified decoding task of negative emotional facial expressions in alcoholic patients. *Alcoholism: Clinical and Experimental Research*, **31**, 1490–1504.

Skeem, J. and Cooke, D.J. (in press) Is criminal behaviour a central component of psychopathy? Conceptual directions for resolving the debate. *Psychological Assessment*.

Skeem, J.L., Poythress, N., Edens, J.F. *et al.* (2003) Psychopathic personality or personalities? Exploring potential variants of psychopathy and their implications for risk assessment. *Aggression and Violent Behavior*, **8**, 513–46.

Tyrer, P., Coombs, N., Ibrahimi, F. *et al.* (2007) Critical developments in the assessment of personality disorder. *British Journal of Psychiatry*, **190** (Suppl. 49), s51–9.

Vitacco, M.J., Neumann, C.S. and Jackson, R.L. (2005) Testing a four-factor model of psychopathy and its association with ethnicity, gender, intelligence, and violence. *Journal of Consulting and Clinical Psychology*, **73**, 466–76.

Walsh, Z., Allen, L.C. and Kosson, D. (2007) Beyond social deviance: substance use disorders and the dimensions of psychopathy. *Journal of Personality Disorders*, **21**, 273–88.

Ward, T. (2002) Good lives and the rehabilitation of offenders: promises and problems. *Aggression and Violent Behaviour*, **7**, 513–28.

Widiger, T.A. (2006) Psychopathy and DSM-IV psychopathology, in *Handbook of Psychopathy* (ed. C.J. Patrick), Guilfordm, New York.

Widiger, T.A. and Trull, T.J. (1994) Personality disorders and violence, in *Violence and Mental Disorder: Developments in Risk Assessment* (eds J. Monahan and H.J. Steadman), University of Chicago Press, Chicago.

Woodworth, M. and Waschbusch, D. (2008) Emotional processing in children with conduct problems and callous/unemotional traits. *Child: Care, Health and Development*, **34**, 234–44.

INDEX

abandonment 216
absence of nervousness 118
abuse 9, 214, 216–17, 219, 224, 235–7, 273
action acceptor mechanism 168, 303
Activity Preference Questionnaire 250
ADHD *see* attention deficit hyperactivity
    disorder
ADS *see* Anger Disorders Scale
aetiological conceptions 114–15
affect 155–244
   affective dyscontrol 157–74
   angry affect 191–211
   attachment difficulties 213–28, 302
   empathy and offending behaviour 229–44
   processing of emotional expression
     information 175–90
   regulation of 6, 30
affectionlessness 216
affective dyscontrol 136, 146, 157–74
affective poverty 304
affective processes in developmental
    context 305–7
age-limited personality disorder 23
aggression and violence 63–83, 126–7,
    191–211
   as learned behaviours 69–70
   in psychopaths 126–7
   and psychoticism 70–1
   social problem solving 267–8
aggressive psychopaths 121
aggressive–predatory anethopaths 114
agreeableness 63–83
alcoholism 26, 158, 165–6, 251, 305
amenability to treatment 247
amygdala function 13, 145, 147, 166, 179–81,
    184–6, 213, 220–1, 224, 259, 302–3
   in attachment problems 220
anankastic factors 74–5
anger 191–211, 300
   and personality 201–2
   in personality disordered people 198–9

and theories of aggression 196–7
   see also angry affect and aggression
Anger Disorders Scale 199
anger links to personality disorder 204–5
anger management 128, 196, 205–6, 293
angry affect and aggression 191–211
   anger links to personality disorder 204–5
   anger and personality 201–2
   anger in personality disordered people
     198–9
   anger and theories of aggression 196–7
   definitions 192–3
   DSM and anger 199–201
   psychopathy and anger 202–4
   self-regulation 197–8
   sexual aggression 195–6
   treatment of anger in personality
     disorders 205–6
   see also aggression and violence
antagonism 118, 122
antisocial behaviours 72, 76–7
antisocial personality disorder 5–14, 26–7,
    34, 100, 123–5, 133–53, 158–9, 166,
    199–202, 218, 271–2
   correlates of 138
   criminality and 141–2
   criteria for 133–4
   diagnosis of 134–5
   differential diagnosis of 135–7
   disorders co-morbid with 139–41
   disorders co-morbid with CD 139
   prevalence of 137–8
   prevalence of CD 137
   and violence 142–7
Antisocial Personality Questionnaire (APQ)
    121, 300
Antisocial Process Screening Device 73, 255
antisociality and attachment 217–19
anxiety and personality 117–19
   see also psychopathy
APQ typology and PCL-R 123–7

arrogant variant of pathological
   narcissism 91
arson 25, 28
assessment 100–3, 125, 166–7, 288–9, 308–9
   of criminal thinking 288–9
   of PD-related violence 308–9
   of risk of violence 166–7
   of risks of narcissistic client 100–3
associations between FFM and antisocial
   behaviours 76
at-risk children 143, 170
attachment 94–5, 100, 213–28
   ambivalent 214–15, 219
   autonomous 214
   avoidant 215
   depressed-hypo-arousing 95
   difficulties with 213–28, 302
   dismissive 215, 217, 219, 221–3
   disorganized 215–16, 218
   evolutionary change 213–14
   insecure-resistant 95, 215–17, 222
   particular types of offence 223–4
   preoccupied 214–15, 219, 222
   problematic 219, 223
   secure 214, 217, 222
   styles of 214–19
   towards neurobiological model of
      attachment-related problems 219–22
   treatment for attachment-related
      problems 222–3
   unresolved 215
attachment problems and violence
   214–19
   general antisociality 217–19
   problem attachment and child sexual
      abuse 219
attachment-related problems in offenders
   219–22
attention deficit hyperactivity disorder
   43–4, 48, 57–8, 163, 167, 267
autonomic arousal 126, 192, 200
avoidance of punishment 251
avoidant personality disorder 159

Barratt Impulsiveness Scale 269
BAS see behavioural activation system
basic cognitive abilities 266
behavioural activation system 115, 168
behavioural deficits 11
behavioural inhibition system 115, 168
'Big Five' 63–83, 160, 299
   aggression and violence as learned
      behaviours 69–70
   associations between FFM and specific
      antisocial behaviours 76
   developmental issues 72–3

dimensional model of personality
   disorders 73–6
Eysenck's PEN model 68–9
five dimensions of personality 64–8
'jangle fallacies' 63–4
neuroticism 71–2
personality traits and antisocial
   behaviour 68
problems with Eysenck's theory 71
psychoticism and violence and
   aggression 70–1
sexual offending 77–8
violent crime and general offending 76–7
biofeedback training 167
bipolar spectrum disorder 102, 106, 198
BIS see behavioural inhibition system
blood oxygen level dependent responses
   177, 180–4
BOLD responses see blood oxygen level
   dependent responses
borderline personality disorder 10, 14, 25–9,
   34, 77, 88, 93, 101, 120–4, 158–9, 162,
   166, 199–202, 204, 218, 223, 272–3
   sex differences 169–70
Bowlby, John 213–14, 216
BPD see borderline personality disorder
brain measures of affective impulsivity
   162–6
Buss–Perry Aggression Questionnaire 269

callous–unemotional traits 72, 76, 113, 135,
   144, 146, 269–70, 301
Cambridge Study in Delinquent
   Development 46, 52
card-playing task 252–3, 260
Cattell's 16 Personality Factors (16PF) 64
causal models 29–32
   incompatibility between causal models
      29–31
   presumption of unidirectionality 31–2
causality 19–37
   see also 'functional link' between PD and
      violence
CBT see cognitive–behavioural therapy
CD see conduct disorder
changing criminal thinking 289–91
Chart of Interpersonal Reactions in Closed
   Environments 102, 157
child sexual abuse 123, 202, 216–17, 219,
   224, 235–7
   see also sexual offending
childhood impulsiveness and relationship
   to later violence 41–61
CIRCLE see Chart of Interpersonal
   Reactions in Closed Environments
classification of entities 113–14

Cleckley's construct of the psychopath 113, 116–19, 121, 125, 203–4, 249–50, 259–60, 304
Cloninger's tridimensional model of personality 64–5, 68
clusters of personality disorders 5
co-occurrence of disorders 27–8, 93–4, 169, 307–8
cognition 245–95
  criminal thinking 281–95
  psychopathic violence 247–63
  social problem solving 265–79
cognitive deficits 11
cognitive processes in developmental context 305–7
cognitive–attention perspective on psychopathic violence 247–63
cognitive–behavioural therapy 14, 30, 59, 105, 127–8, 196, 205, 222–3
cold-blooded aggression 76, 287
comorbidity 25–7, 34, 74, 133, 139–44, 146, 305, 308
Compassionate Mind Training 223
Comprehensive System for the Rorschach 102
conditioning 181, 185
conduct disorder 133–53, 163
conscientiousness 63–83
coping skills 237, 265
Criminal Sentiments Scale 288–92
criminal thinking 281–95, 302
  assessment of 288–9
  change in 289–91
  composition of 291–3
  definition of 281–2
  description of 282–5
  explanation of 285–8
criminality 27, 141–2, 217
critical appraisal of personality disorder and violence 1–37
  defining violence 3–18
CSS see Criminal Sentiments Scale
culpability 10, 70

dACC see dorsal anterior cingulate cortex
Dangerous and Severe Personality Disorder 157–74
dangerousness 21–2
dark triad of personality 75–6
DBT see dialectical behaviour therapy
deceitfulness 134–6, 200
defensive aggression 160–2
delinquency 43, 72, 76, 267, 287, 290
dementia 9
depressive disorder 26, 87, 106, 139–40, 198
diagnosis of ASPD 134–5

diagnostic overlap 308
Diagnostic and Statistical Manual of Mental Disorders IV 5, 8–10, 19, 22–3, 27, 74–5, 85, 90, 101–4, 120, 124, 133–8, 142, 157, 205, 215–18, 300–2
dialectical behaviour therapy 167
differential association theory of crime 288
Dimensional Assessment of Personality Pathology 75, 101
disinhibition 215, 253, 260, 303
disinhibitory psychopathology 163–5
dismissive attachment 215, 217, 219, 221–3
disorganized attachment 215–16, 218
dissocial behaviour 75, 135
dissocial personality disorder 75, 134, 218
dissociation 78, 177–8
distress reduction 229–30, 232, 238
dominance 65, 124, 308
dopamine 65
dorsal anterior cingulate cortex 178
drinking 41, 169–70
  see also alcoholism; substance abuse
drinking trajectories 169–70
drug monitoring 8, 14
DSM 199–201
  and anger 199–201
DSM-IV see Diagnostic and Statistical Manual of Mental Disorders IV
Dunedin Multidisciplinary Health and Development Study 29, 46, 48
dysphoria 91, 200

early temperament 266
early-onset alcohol abuse 305
ECF see executive cognitive functioning
effect sizes 52
egocentrism 69, 308
electric shock 179, 251, 269
emotional dysregulation 11–12, 25–7, 75, 93, 128, 164, 305
emotional empathy 175–81
  see also empathy
emotional expression information 175–90, 300–2, 305
emotional responding 179–81
emotional response position 178–9
emotional stimuli 179
emotional susceptibility 72
emotionally stable psychopaths 121
empathic accuracy 231
empathy 175–81, 229–44
  as deficits in offenders 13, 69, 233–6, 239
  emotional responding 179–81
  emotional response position 178–9
  mirror neuron analogy position 177–8

empathy (*continued*)
  mirror neuron position 176–7
  and offending behaviour 229–44
empirical classifications 119–25
  APQ typology and PCL-R 123–5
  questionnaire typology of mentally
    disordered offenders 121–2
  variants within PCL-R 119–21
empirical evidence linking PA to violence
    25–9
empty depression 93
engaging narcissistic clients 107
ES psychopaths *see* emotionally stable
    psychopaths
establishing causality 20–5
  covariation between the variables 21–2
  establishing logical connection between
    variables 25
  exclusion of alternative explanation for
    relationship 23–5
  temporal precedence of causal variable
    22–3
European Convention on Human Rights
    33
executive cognitive functioning 266–7, 269,
    272
exhibitionism 91
externalization 73–4, 100, 143, 165–6, 218,
    267
externalizing syndrome 143
extraversion 63–83, 115
Eysenck Impulsivity Scale 45
Eysenck's 'Gigantic Three' 64
Eysenck's PEN model 65, 68–9, 75
  problems with 71
Eysenck's theory of criminality 115

factor-analytic approach to personality
    64–5, 289
factors predisposing violence in PD 30
failure of socialization 197
fear-based conditioning 181, 300
FFM 63–8, 118, 122, 202
five dimensions of personality 64–8
Five-Factor Model *see* FFM
flight or fight 196
formal education 42
Fowles–Gray theory of psychopathy 116
Freud, Sigmund 87–8, 99
frontal cortex function 13, 158, 163, 166,
    170–1, 259, 303
frustration tolerance 94
'functional link' between PD and violence
    19–37
  clinical and political considerations 33–4
  consequences of limited causal models
    29–32

contention in medico-legal practice 19–20
  difficulties in applying causality criteria
    34–5
  empirical evidence linking PD to
    violence 25–9
  establishing causality 20–5
'fuzzy' constructs 306

gender differences in personality disorders
    169–70, 267–8
General Aggression model 196–7
general antisociality 217–19
general offending 76–7
General Statistical Information of
    Recidivism (GSIR) 292
General Theory of Crime 42
genetic polymorphism 145
genetics 11–12, 30, 117, 143, 146, 270
Go/No Go paradigm 163–9, 252, 260, 303
Good Lives Model 307
Gough's Socialization (*So*) scale 119–21,
    165
grandiosity 91, 95–6, 102, 105–7, 127
Grasmick self-control scale 43

heritability 94, 146, 300
histrionic personality disorder 26–7, 34, 74,
    94, 120, 124, 127, 199, 218
  sex differences 169–70
Hitler, Adolf 285
Hogan's Empathy Scale 234
hostility 69, 120–1, 124, 128, 192–4, 197,
    202–4, 308
Hume, David 229
hyperactivity 41–4, 48, 251
hyperresponsiveness 200
hypervigilance 90, 94–5, 146
hypochondria 87
hysteria 251

ICD-10 *see* International Classification of
    Diseases 10
identifying treatment targets 10–13
  antisocial personality disorder 11–12
  psychopathy 12–13
impulse control 6, 30
impulsive/careless problem solving 270,
    272–4
impulsivity 25, 41–61, 69, 115–16, 122–4,
    133, 135, 144, 159–66, 194–5, 200, 218,
    268–71, 300–2
  brain measures of 162–6
  and personality disorders 159–62
inhibition 75, 215, 252, 259
insecure-resistant attachment 95, 215–17,
    222
institutional misconduct 117

instrumental psychopathic violence 126, 142, 145, 162, 166, 194, 259
Integrated Cognitive Antisocial Potential (ICAP) theory 306
intellectual disability 9
intermittent explosive disorder 10
International Classification of Diseases (ICD-10) 5, 10, 19, 22, 27, 134–5, 157, 205, 218
International Personality Disorder Examination 102, 124, 137, 160, 271
Interpersonal Adjective Scales 73
Interpersonal Measure of Psychopathy (IM-P) 120
interpersonal therapy 30, 105
interpersonal violence as major social problem 3–4
Iowa Gambling Task 168
IPT *see* interpersonal therapy
IQ 267
irritability 72, 121, 133, 135, 199–200

'jangle fallacies' 63–4, 71–2
jealousy 201

lack of fear 13, 73, 117, 250–4
LCSF *see* Lifestyle Criminality Screening Form
learned behaviours 69–70
learnt helplessness 23
left hemisphere maturation 267–8
lexical studies of personality 64
Lifestyle Criminality Screening Form 291–2
lifestyle theory of crime 282, 285–6, 288–9, 291
limbic system theory 179
locus of control 71
low self-control 42–3

Machiavellianism 75
maladaptive traits 157
malignant narcissism 72, 92
malnutrition 143
maltreatment 306
management of risk with narcissistic client 100–4
  options 103–4
MAOA *see* monoamine oxidase A
Mask of Sanity 248–50
Maudsley Obsessive–Compulsive Inventory 78
MCAA *see* Measures of Criminal Attitudes and Associates
means–end action plan 269
Means–End Problem-Solving test 273
Measures of Criminal Attitudes and Associates 288–92

mechanisms for understanding links between PD and violence 302–7
mentally disordered offenders 121–2
MEPS test *see* Means–End Problem-Solving test
milieu therapy 222
Millon Clinical Multiaxial Inventory-III (MCMI-III) 101, 122, 159
mindfulness 206, 223
Minnesota Multiphasic Personality Inventory–2 101, 121, 126, 160
mirror neuron analogy position 177–8
mirror neuron position 176–7
mitigation 9–10, 13
MMPI *see* Minnesota Multiphasic Personality Inventory–2
MOCI *see* Maudsley Obsessive–Compulsive Inventory
model of attachment-related problems 219–22
  differences in amygdala function 220
  differences in neuropeptide function 220–2
model of response modulation 250–6
Models of Causality in Psychopathy 20
models of empathy 230–3
monoamine oxidase A 11–12, 145–7
moral codes 8, 33, 300
moral reasoning 175, 185
moral socialization 184–5
motor restlessness 48, 52
MPQ *see* Multidimensional Personality Questionnaire
Multidimensional Personality Questionnaire 64, 115–16, 118, 121

narcissism 6, 25–7, 30, 34, 73–5, 85–112, 195, 302
  definition 85–96
  engaging narcissistic clients 107
  future directions 106–7
  risk assessment and management 100–4
  treatment 104–5
  and violence 96–100
narcissistic personality disorder 90–107, 120–2, 199–202
  sex differences 169–70
Narcissistic Personality Inventory (NPI) 101
narcissistic rage 97
narcissistic reactance theory of rape 99–100
Narcissus 86–8
National Comorbidity Survey 140
National Household Survey of Great Britain 144
National Socialism 285
negative affect 192–3, 196, 200–4, 206

negative cognitive evaluation 192
negative emotionality 115–16, 203
negative problem orientation 268, 270,
    273–5
neglect 215, 224, 273
NEO-Five Factor Inventory (NEO-FFI)
    63–5, 74–5, 78, 123–4, 270
NEO-Personality Inventory (NEO-PI) 63–5
neurobiological model of
    attachment-related problems 219–22
neurobiological substrates of affective
    self-regulation 168–9
neurobiology of affective dyscontrol
    157–74
  affective impulsivity and PDs 159–62
  assessing risk of violence 166–7
  brain measures of affective impulsivity
    162–6
  combination of antisocial and borderline
    traits 170–1
  levels of personality disorder 157–8
  neurobiological substrates of affective
    self-regulation 168–9
  relationship between PD and violent
    offending 158–9
  sex differences and clues about aetiology
    169–70
neuropeptide function in attachment
    problems 220–2
neurotic introversion 115
neuroticism 63–83, 115, 123, 202, 270,
    300–2
  'jangle fallacies' 63–4, 71–2
New York State Longitudinal Study 46
nonsexual offending 233–4
  see also empathy
  noradrenaline 65
Novaco Anger Scale 126
novelty seeking 65
NPD see narcissistic personality disorder
NPO see negative problem orientation

obsessive–compulsive personality disorder
    74, 78, 94, 124, 144, 159, 199
oddball task 165
offence paralleling behaviour 23
offending and attachment-related problems
    219–22
offending behaviour 41, 229–44
  see also empathy
offensive aggression 160–2
openness 63–83
options for risk management with
    narcissistic client 103–4
Orebro Project (Sweden) 46
orienting responses 266

paedophilia 219–24, 232
panic disorder 30, 144, 202
paradox of psychopathy 302–3
paranoia 25, 32
paranoid cognitive personality style 6
paranoid personality disorders 25–6, 30, 34,
    74, 77, 94, 100, 120, 199–202, 218
  sex differences 169–70
paranoid schizophrenia 102
parental modelling 12
passive-aggressive disorder 159
passive–parasitic anethopaths 114
pathological lying 125
pathological narcissism 85–96, 99–103
  development of 94–6
  treatment of 104–5
  variants 91–4
PCL-R 7, 19, 92–3, 102–3, 113–32, 133, 136,
    162, 202–3, 239, 248–50, 259–60, 292
  APQ typology and 123–5
  variants within 119–21
PCL:SV 74, 217–18, 292
PEN model 68–9
perfectionism 74, 94
persistent offending 28–9
personality 201–2, 268–70, 299–311
  aggression and social problem solving
    268–70
  and anger 201–2
  callous–unemotional traits 269–70
  impulsivity 268–9
Personality Assessment Inventory (PAI) 101
personality disorder:
  and angry affect 191–211
  antisocial personality disorder 271–2
  borderline personality disorder 272–3
  and social problem solving 265–79
  and violence 5–8, 265–79
personality problems as mitigation 9–10
personality traits and antisocial behaviour
    68
pessimism 91, 127
pharmacological intervention 128, 186, 223
Piaget, Jean 286–7
PICTS see Psychological Inventory of
    Criminal Thinking Styles
Pittsburgh Youth Study 46, 48
political considerations 33–4
  see also clinical and political
    considerations
political ideology 63
poor concentration 41, 46, 48, 52
poor parenting 42, 134, 146–7, 215, 306
pornography 77–8
positive emotionality 115–16
positive problem orientation 270, 274

post-traumatic stress disorder 25, 115, 198
PPO *see* positive problem orientation
pre-potent response intensification 160, 304
precipitants of violence 30–1
prediction of later violence 21–2, 43, 58–9
predictive power 186
predisposing factors in PD violence 30
prefrontal cortex function 31
premature responses 268–9
premeditation 268–9
preoccupied attachment 214–15, 219, 222
prevalence of ASP 137–8
prevalence of CD 137
primary psychopathy 72, 114–22, 127–8
  in personality theories 115–16
  problem with distinction from secondary 116–17
Prisoner's Dilemma 177–9
problem-solving skills 266
problematic attachment 219, 223
problems with Eysenck's theory 71
problems with socialization 184–5
processing of emotional expression information 137, 143, 175–90
  difficulties in socialization 184–5
  empathy 175–81
  future clinical implications 185–6
  responding to emotional expressions 181–4
  selective impairment 175
prolonged anger arousal 197
prosocial behaviour 229
prototypical psychopathy 119
provocation 193–6, 200–2, 204, 269
pseudo-psychopathic psychopathy 119–20
pseudopsychopathy 218
psychiatric morbidity 76, 198
psychodynamic psychotherapy 105, 127–8
psychological intervention in psychopathy 128–9
Psychological Inventory of Criminal Thinking Styles 76, 287–92
psychopathic narcissism 91–2
psychopathic self-regulation 256–60
psychopathic violence 126, 247–63
  clinical evidence 248–50
  conceptualizing aetiological processes 260–1
  evolution of response modulation model 250–6
  response modulation and psychopathic self-regulation 256–60

psychopathy 12–13, 75–6, 100, 113–32, 175–90, 202–4, 248–50
  and anger 202–4
  anxiety and personality 117–19
  clinical evidence for 248–50
  processing emotional expression information 175–90
Psychopathy Checklist – Revised *see* PCL-R
psychoticism 64, 70–1, 115
  and violence and aggression 70–1
PTSD *see* post-traumatic stress disorder
punishment vs. treatment 8–10
  personality problems as mitigation 9–10
  see also treatment

Questionnaire Measure of Emotional Empathy 234

Rampton Hospital 199
range of sexual offending behaviours 77
rape 79, 86, 99–100, 195–6, 219
reactive psychopathic violence 126, 142, 145, 162, 166, 259
recidivism 10, 15, 247–8, 273–4, 289–92
recklessness 134–5
reconviction rates 8
rehabilitation 59, 239, 307
reinforcement 42, 179–81, 185, 302
relationship between childhood impulsiveness and later violence 41–61
  current investigation 44–57
  prediction of later violence 58–9
  previous reviews of relationship 42–4
  results of review 57–8
relationship between personality disorder and violent offending 158–9
religion 286
remediable brain dysfunction 32
remorselessness 133, 135, 249
re-offending 102, 195, 239
reparative response 229
responding to emotional expressions in psychopathy 181–4
  generalized impairment 182–3
  indications of impairment 181–2
  nature of impairment seen 183–4
response modulation 250–60, 303–5
  and psychopathic self-regulation 256–60
  responsivity 239
restlessness 44, 46, 48
restorative justice 98
reversal theory 161
review of relationship between childhood impulsiveness and later violence 41–61

risk assessment with narcissistic client
100–4
  assessing risks of narcissistic client
  100–3
  options for risk management 103–4
risk management with narcissistic client
103–4
Risk for Sexual Violence Protocol 102–3
risk of violence 166–7
risk-taking 44, 48, 56–7, 89, 102, 116

sadism 92, 99, 199, 233, 238, 302
sado-masochism 3
schizophrenia 218–19, 308
Seattle Social Development Study 46, 58
secondary psychopathy 72, 114–22,
127–8
  in personality theories 115–16
  problem with distinction from primary
  116–17
secure attachment 214, 217, 222
selective attention 255
selective impairment 175–90
self-defeating traits 199
self-directedness 64
self-dramatising 74
self-efficacy 283
self-enhancement 91
self-esteem 25, 71–2, 94–5, 127, 236–7
self-harming 273
self-love 86–7, 93
self-regulation 15, 31–2, 157–74, 197–8, 236,
256–60, 271
  in psychopaths 256–60
self-righteousness 97–8
self-soothing 206, 213, 223
self-transcendence 64
sensation seeking 69, 76, 160–2, 166, 308
septal syndrome 251, 253
serious violence 7–8
serotonin 65, 145–6
severe personality disorder see Dangerous
and Severe Personality Disorder
severity criteria 22
sex differences in personality disorders
169–70
Sex Offenders Assessment Package 78
sex-specific drinking patterns 170
sexual aggression 99–100, 195–6
  and angry affect 195–6
  and narcissism 99–100
sexual offending 27–8, 77–8, 234–6
  see also empathy
sexual perversion 99
sexuality 99
shallow affect 118

shame 97–8, 122, 236, 249
SHAPS see Special Hospital Assessment of
Personality and Socialization
short sharp shock 8
shy variant of pathological narcissism 91
skills training 59, 273, 290
skin conductance responses 182–3
Smith, Adam 229
smoking 41, 143
SOAP see Sex Offenders Assessment
Package
sociability 306
social contract 281
social control theory of crime 288
social functioning 266
Social Functioning Questionnaire 275
social problem solving 265–79
  aggression and violence 267–8
  personality and aggression 268–70
  personality disorder and aggression
  270–3
  and social functioning 266
  targeting deficits 275–6
  treatment 273–5
Social Problem Solving Inventory – Revised
268–75
socialization 13, 115, 118–20, 175, 184–6,
197
socialization problems 175, 184–5
societal norms 8, 33
socio-economic status 58, 72, 138, 234
sociopathy 114–15
somatic markers 71
somatosensory cortex 178
Special Hospital Assessment of Personality
and Socialization 121
SPSI-R see Social Problem Solving
Inventory – Revised
State–Trait Anger Expression Inventory
275
states of intoxication 191
stereotyping 288
Stop & Think! 274–5
straightforwardness 77
stress management 293
Stroop paradigm 254–5
structural phenomenology 157
Structured Clinical Interview for DSM-IV
Axis II Disorders (SCID-II) 102, 138,
142
styles of attachment 214–19
subclinical psychopathic tendencies 182
substance abuse 15, 23–4, 26–9, 100, 106,
120, 139–40, 145, 147, 158–9, 163–6,
169–70, 217–18, 271, 305, 308
substrates of affective self-regulation 168–9

subtypes of psychopath 113–32
   attempting intervention with
      psychopaths 128–9
   classification of entities 113–14
   clinical implications 125–8
   concepts of primary and secondary
      psychopathy 114–17
   empirical classifications 119–25
   psychopathy, anxiety and personality
      117–19
suicidal ideation 140, 272–3
supertraits of personality 68–9, 165
   see also Eysenck's PEN model
   supervision 103–5, 107
surveillance 8
suspiciousness 94, 102, 201, 308
sympathy 230
   see also empathy

Taylor Manifest Anxiety Scale 117
Tellegen's three MPQ trait dimensions 64,
      68, 115–16, 118, 121
temporal context of criminal thinking
      287–8
temporal precedence of causal variable 22–3
Thematic Apperception Test 102
theories of aggression 196–7
Theory of Mind 175–6
Trail Making Test 45
trait response 230
traits 39–153
   antisocial personality disorder 133–53
   'Big Five' 63–83
   childhood impulsiveness and later
      violence 41–61
   narcissism 85–112
   subtypes of psychopath 113–32
traumatising history 123
treatment
   of aggressive behaviour 273–5
   of anger in personality disorders 205–6
   for attachment problems 222–3
   of empathy deficits 236–9
   of narcissism 104–5
   for offenders with personality disorders
      13–14

   for offenders without personality
      disorders 14–15
   of PD-related violence 309
   of psychopathy 127–8
treatment of narcissism 104–5
   evidence for treatment of pathological
      narcissism 104–5
   options for treatment of pathological
      narcissism 104–5
truancy 12

UK Prisoner Cohort Study 169
unemotional traits 269–70
unresolved attachment 215
unrestrained behaviour 70

vandalism 28, 76
variants of psychopathy 113–32, 300–1
variants within PCL-R 119–21
vasopressin 221, 223
ventromedial prefrontal cortex 184–6, 218
verbal ability 267–8
verbal abuse 192–3
victim safety planning 104
victimization 218
violence and aggression as learned
   behaviours 69–70
violence and attachment problems 214–19
Violence Inhibition Mechanism Model 259
violence and narcissism 96–100
   link between narcissism and violence
      96–9
   narcissism and sexual aggression 99–100
violent crime 76–7, 158–9
   and general offending 76–7
   relationship to personality disorder
      158–9
vmPFC see ventromedial prefrontal cortex
vulnerability 77, 91, 99, 105, 116, 127, 143–5

Welsh Anxiety Scale (WAS) 116
WHO see World Health Organization
World Health Organization 3–4, 10, 134–5

Zuckerman's Alternative Five Factor model
      115